ROCK ISLAND REQUIEM

ROCK ISLAND REQUIEM

The Collapse of a Mighty Fine Line

Gregory L. Schneider

University Press of Kansas

© 2013 by the University Press of Kansas
All rights reserved

Published by the University Press of Kansas (Lawrence, Kansas 66045), which was organized by the Kansas Board of Regents and is operated and funded by Emporia State University, Fort Hays State University, Kansas State University, Pittsburg State University, the University of Kansas, and Wichita State University

Library of Congress Cataloging-in-Publication Data

Schneider, Gregory L., 1965–
Rock Island requiem : the collapse of a mighty fine line / Gregory L. Schneider.
pages cm
Includes bibliographical references and index.
ISBN 978-0-7006-1918-4 (cloth : alk. paper)
ISBN 978-0-7006-2962-6 (paperback)
  1. Chicago, Rock Island, and Pacific Railroad Company (1948–) 2. Railroads—United States—History—20th century. 3. Railroads—United States—Finance—History—20th century. 4. Business failures—United States—History—20th century. I. Title.
HE2791.C674153S36 2013
385.06'577—dc23
2013009247

British Library Cataloguing-in-Publication Data is available.

Printed in the United States of America

10 9 8 7 6 5 4 3 2 1

FOR MY CHILDREN, BAILEY AND BALIN

CONTENTS

Acknowledgments   ix
List of Illustrations   xv
List of Acronyms and Abbreviations   xvii

Introduction   1

ACT ONE: MERGER

CHAPTER ONE
A Mighty Fine Line   13

CHAPTER TWO
Merge or Die   37

CHAPTER THREE
Bleak House   59

CHAPTER FOUR
The Waiting Is the Hardest Part   83

CHAPTER FIVE
Too Big to Fail   101

ACT TWO: BANKRUPTCY

CHAPTER SIX
Bankruptcy Blue(s)   125

CHAPTER SEVEN
Stayin' Alive   153

CHAPTER EIGHT
The Omen   175

CHAPTER NINE
Walking Dead Men   201

CHAPTER TEN
The Rock Is Dead   225

ACT THREE: LIQUIDATION

CHAPTER ELEVEN
Too Late the Hero 253

CHAPTER TWELVE
Long Live the Rock 277

Conclusion 297

Notes 303

Selected Bibliography 353

Index 361

ACKNOWLEDGMENTS

For most of my life I have lived in the shadow of the Rock Island Railroad. I grew up in Brookfield, Illinois, in west suburban Chicago, nestled along the Burlington Northern Railroad's triple-track, high-speed, high-density freight and passenger mainline. For as long as I can remember, I was captivated by trains. My father worked for a time at Electro-Motive Division in LaGrange before leaving to teach high school mathematics, and my grandfather worked at EMD for close to 40 years. I used to watch Burlington Northern trains go by Bob's Barber Shop in downtown Brookfield and then watched while playing Little League baseball at Kiwanis Park—part of the reason (I tell myself) I never made it to the Major Leagues. I also lived close to the crossing of the BN with the Indiana Harbor Belt Railroad at Congress Park, which led me trackside, camera in hand, hoping to catch the odd locomotive and the different railroads that traversed the tracks near my childhood home. I captured many on film, but much to my heart's discontent, I never captured a Rock Island locomotive. My railfan days began as the Rock was at its endgame, and, as I didn't yet drive, the Rock was too far away from my cloistered little world. I did see Rock Island commuter trains several times as a boy in the 1970s while sitting on Comiskey Park's leftfield upper deck and staring out of the Comiskey arches to watch trains across the Dan Ryan Expressway (watching the White Sox in the 1970s, apart from South Side hit men of 1977, was painful, so watching trains while at the game was a relief).

As a student at Quigley North High School (it, too, now gone, but its building now occupied by the Archdiocese of Chicago), I commuted into the city, witnessing the decline of the railroads, the many changes in store between 1979 and 1983. And the one line I fell in love with more than any other was the Rock Island. As a commuter into Union Station in Chicago, I could glance (read: "stare") out of my bilevel coach window and see the crimson and yellow bilevel commuter cars bearing the Rock Island letters coming into nearby LaSalle Street Station. Once in a while, I could even see the Rock Island Electro-Motive Division SW-1, moving cars to and fro on the Regional Transportation Authority track (it is still in service as a Metra switcher today). Being a bit romantic, and idealistic, I could imagine seeing the *Rocket* pulling into the station, the train I had read about in articles about the Rock Island in *Trains* magazine, which I devoured more eagerly than other boys my age devoured *Playboy*.

Two events that happened in high school influenced my later decision to write on the Rock Island. I wrote a history paper on the Rock Island. The second was writing a short opinion piece for the *Chicago Tribune*, which was published in 1982 as "A Requiem for the Railroads." I could have neither envisioned then, nor assumed later, that I would write a book with a similar title. I assumed I would have been running a locomotive, not writing about them.

But here I am, living in Topeka, Kansas (a Rock Island town), where the writing of this book was completed, after having attended college at Drake University in Des Moines, Iowa (a Rock Island town), and returning to the University of Illinois at Chicago for a Ph.D. (clearly, a Rock Island town). The only years of my life not centered on the Rock Island were spent working on an M.A. in diplomatic history at Ohio University in Athens (hey, it had the Baltimore & Ohio, so that wasn't too shabby either). I am writing about the railroad I fell in love with as a young man, and hopefully I have done the story of its long and rather sad collapse historical justice.

This is my first railroad history book after having spent my career writing on the history of American conservatism. I owe thanks to many of the fine railroad scholars whose work I have drawn on and who have helped me, sometimes inadvertently, along the way. H. Roger Grant provided a great sounding board for ideas and was gracious with his loan of photographs for the book, and for pointing out some silly errors before it went to press. Don Hofsommer's work on Iowa railroads, and the SP, is first-rate. Maury Klein's encyclopedic knowledge of the Union Pacific Railroad is unsurpassed, and I drew heavily on his trilogy of the UP in the book. Rush Loving Jr., Don Phillips, and Fred Frailey, knowledgeable railroad journalists, also informed and inspired this work. I have never met any of these gentlemen, but their work on railroads has been an inspiration. My good friend Don Critchlow of Arizona State University always provided a sounding board for my ideas and listened patiently to me going on about the Rock Island. He even arranged for me to give a talk to a discussion group on railroad history and public history, where the Phoenicians heard a lot about a former Midwestern railroad—but then everyone who lives in Arizona is from Chicago, so they already probably knew about it. Of course, I alone am responsible for any errors that remain.

I had the great privilege of speaking about the themes of the book in October 2011 to the Sandhouse Gang at Northwestern University's Transportation Center and was treated to a wonderful audience of knowledgeable railroad officials, historians, attorneys, and engineers. It was a bit intimidating, but the Sandhouse Gang was a lovely experience, one I hope to repeat. John Barriger IV was in attendance, as was then–Union Pacific Vice President for Strategic Planning John Rebensdorf (who I was told came into town just for the talk; thanks, John). All the individuals in attendance that day gave me fruitful points to consider as I finished the book, and I am very grateful for their expertise and interest in the project. I also thank them for providing an excellent lunch focused on the Rock Island. I thank Norman Carlson, Diana Marek, William Sippel, Paul Schuch, David Burns, Edward Burkhardt, Daniel Behr, Mike Arizzi, and all the others who attended. To others who I inadvertently left out, thank you for a wonderful event.

I would also like to thank the innumerable archivists and librarians who helped me in the various archives I visited to complete this work. These individuals are indispensible to a historian doing primary research. I would especially like to thank Albert Nason of the Carter Presidential Library; the staff of the Hagley Museum and Library; Hank Zalitel of the Iowa Department of Transportation; the Hoover Institution; the Gerald Ford, Harry Truman, and Dwight Eisenhower Presidential Libraries; and all of the other libraries and archival staffs who helped with the book. I am especially grateful to Brice Oakley for arranging, and Robert Ray for allowing me the permission to use the Governor Robert Ray papers at the Iowa State Historical Society. Ray was a former president of Drake University (more important than being governor of Iowa?), and he probably didn't know I was a Drake Bulldog through and through.

I am especially grateful to Daniel Murray of the law firm Jenner & Block, who took time out of his busy schedule to talk to me about the bankruptcy case and arranged for me to meet with Lester Crown. Dan's expertise proved especially important as I waded into railroad bankruptcy law, and he has always been available to me for my mundane questions about the law. He is a gentleman and a fine attorney.

My research was supported by several institutions. I owe immeasurable thanks to the Earhart Foundation, which supplied me with a generous research grant that allowed me to complete almost all the research in one long summer of travel in 2009. Earhart has supported my work consistently, and I owe Ingrid Gregg and Montgomery Brown a tremendous debt of gratitude. I was awarded a research grant to complete an article on the Rock Island and the state of Iowa's efforts to save it, and I thank the Iowa Historical Society for their munificence. Finally, I thank Emporia State University for its support of the manuscript, both for a research grant that allowed me to complete research in the summer of 2012, as well as for a sabbatical leave in the fall of 2012 that allowed me to complete the writing of the manuscript.

I chose specifically not to do many interviews with former Rock Island employees. Everyone has their own opinion on why the Rock failed, and I did not want to get too bogged down in separating the wheat from the chaff. I wanted the book to reflect my own work and opinions on why the Rock Island collapsed. I could have learned much about the Rock from the thousands of people who worked for it, and I hope to do so now that the book is done. You can certainly feel free to tell me where I went wrong. However, I did conduct a few interviews and thank Ted Desch, the last surviving CEO of the Rock Island, as well as Dr. Paul Banner, Paul Victor, and Dennis Opferman for their insights on the Rock Island and successor lines. Alas, all of the principal figures in the bankruptcy case are now deceased, most recently Judge Frank McGarr (in 2012), Nicholas Manos (in 2011), Albert Jenner (1988), John Ingram (2008), and William Gibbons (1988). I would have relished meeting them all.

Many individuals allowed me the use of photographs for the book. I thank Tom Kline, Joe Pierson of the Chicago and North Western Historical Society, Jenner & Block, Mark Llanuza, William McGarr, and all the others who sent me photos for consideration to use in the book. The Rock Island Technical Society listserv was a valuable sounding board for me, and I appreciate all of the Rock's fans who responded to my request for photos.

I also want to thank the extraordinary staff at the University Press of Kansas. I have known Fred Woodward for about ten years now, and I am very happy to be able to have this book published by UPK. I want to thank Sara Henderson White for her help with the photographs, Larisa Martin for her assistance getting the manuscript into shape for publication, Susan Schott for her marketing expertise, and the entire staff of this wonderful press. I hope this is the beginning of a long and fruitful partnership. I also want to thank Edward Brunner, one of the reviewers of the manuscript for the press, who worked for the Rock Island from 1973 to 1980 while a graduate student in English at the University of Iowa and was a huge supporter of the proposal and the book. What Ed doesn't know is that his articles on the Rock Island published by *Trains*, especially "Tales from the Peoria Rocket" (1983), were the main reasons I fell in love with this charming Midwestern line. I thank him for his contributions to my love affair with the Rock Island and for helping me see it to realization with the publication of this book.

Finally, I have no bigger supporters of my work than my family. My wife, Petra, has put up with constant travel, separate vacations to do research (while the family goes to the beach), and the constant irritability of a grumpy author. She has done this now through five books, and I suspect there will be five more (I hope) before it's all said and done. Poor Petra! While other newly married thirty-somethings went to the Caribbean on vacation, she was driven along U.S. Highway 6 to take pictures of old Rock Island depots in western Illinois and eastern Iowa. Words cannot express how much that means to me.

The dedication goes to my two children, Bailey Noelle and Balin Gerhart. They are both growing up too fast and now find themselves in high school and middle school. I hope that they will one day read this book to better understand their father's passions (and quirks) and come to understand how history can enlighten and inspire. They mean the world to me and, with Petra, are the rocks in my life.

ILLUSTRATIONS

Maps

Map 1.1 Map of the Chicago, Rock Island and Pacific Railroad as it looked in 1975   xx

Map 3.1 Map of the proposed merger, showing Rock Island lines to be transferred to the Union Pacific and the Southern Pacific   63

Photographs

Photo 1.1 The first board of directors meeting of the new Chicago, Rock Island and Pacific Railroad Company, January 5, 1948   14

Photo 2.1 The industrialist and investor Henry Crown, Chicago, 1965   41

Photo 2.2 Rock Island Executive Vice President Eaton Adams conferring with R. E. Johnson, Rock Island's president, at the November 15, 1963, shareholders meeting to vote on the proposed Union Pacific–Rock Island merger   53

Photo 2.3 Jervis Langdon, the doctor of sick railroads—and Rock Island's new president—in Chicago, 1965   55

Photo 3.1 Why Is This Man Smiling? Ben Heineman, chairman of the Chicago and North Western Railway in 1966   77

Photo 5.1 Sponsors of the Regional Rail Reorganization Act (the 3R Act): Representative Brock Adams (D–Wash.), seated left, and Representative Richard Shoup (R–Mont.), seated right, at a 1973 dinner   120

Photo 6.1 John W. Ingram, former head of the Federal Railroad Administration and controversial last president of the Rock Island, 1974   141

Photo 6.2 Larry Provo, president of the Chicago & North Western   149

Photo 7.1 President Gerald Ford discussing the fate of the Rock Island aid bills in Congress, April 17, 1975   156

Photo 7.2 Judge Frank McGarr, in a picture from the 1960s   158

Photo 7.3 Rock Island bankruptcy Trustee William Gibbons with attorney Nicholas Manos in front of a newly painted ROCK diesel locomotive in Des Moines, Iowa, August 7, 1975   160

Photo 7.4 Two photos show a Rock Island commuter train in Mokena, Illinois, in 1977, and a new RTA locomotive waiting for the evening rush at LaSalle Street Station   172–173

Photo 8.1 Albert Jenner, Henry Crown's attorney in the bankruptcy case   180

Photo 8.2 From the cab window of a Rock Island locomotive, one can see the deterioration of the track conditions in Dallas, as the end of the railroad approaches   186

Photo 8.3 Two passengers on board Train No. 12: Joe Pierson (taking the picture) and George Strombeck   192

Photo 8.4 The *Peoria Rocket* had seen better days by 1978, shown rounding the curve at Morris, Illinois   195

Photo 9.1 President Gerald R. Ford signing the Regional Railroad Revitalization and Reform Act (the 4R Act) in February 1976   208

Photo 9.2 Officials discussing airline deregulation   223

Photo 10.1 Joliet, Illinois: A seemingly healthy Rock Island freight consist moving company property to staging yards to prepare for shutdown in March 1980   247

Photo 11.1 LaSalle Street Station in Chicago   266

Photo 11.2 The Katy's OKT subsidiary operating over former Rock Island track in Kingfisher, Oklahoma, 1982   274

Photo 12.1 Daniel Murray, who would argue the winning case for the Rock Island Trustee in *Railway Labor Executives' Association v. Gibbons*   279

Photo 12.2 Two Iowa Interstate diesel locomotives await their westbound train to Council Bluffs in the Rock Island's former Burr Oak Yard in Blue Island, Illinois, 1997   290

ACRONYMS AND ABBREVIATIONS

"A-OK"	Arkansas-Oklahoma Railroad
AAR	Association of American Railroads
ADM	Archer Daniels Midland
ASTRO	America's Sound Transportation Review Organization
ATSF	Atchison, Topeka and Santa Fe
B&O	Baltimore and Ohio Railroad
BLE	Illinois Brotherhood of Locomotive Engineers
BN	Burlington Northern
BNSF	Burlington Northern Santa Fe Railway
BRAC	Brotherhood of Railway and Airline Clerks
C&O	Chesapeake and Ohio Railway
CAB	Civil Aeronautics Board
CB&Q	Chicago, Burlington and Quincy Railroad
CDOs	collateralized debt obligations
CEA	Council of Economic Advisors
CGW	Chicago Great Western Railway
CNJ	Central Railroad of New Jersey
C&NW	Chicago and North Western Railway
ConFac	Consolidated Facilities
Conrail	Consolidated Rail Corporation
CPI	Consumer Price Index
DOT	U.S. Department of Transportation
DRGW	Denver and Rio Grande Western
DSO	Directed Service Order
EL	Erie Lackawanna
ERSA	Emergency Rail Services Assistance Act
FEC	Florida East Coast Railway
FRA	Federal Railroad Administration
FSP	final system plan
GM&O	Gulf, Mobile and Ohio Railroad
IC	Illinois Central Railroad
ICC	Interstate Commerce Commission
Iowa DOT	Iowa Department of Transportation

Katy	Missouri–Kansas–Texas Railroad
KCT	Kansas City Terminal Railroad
M&StL	Minneapolis and St. Louis Railway
Monon	Chicago, Indianapolis, and Louisville Railroad
MP ("MoPac")	Missouri Pacific Railroad
MRRA	Milwaukee Road Restructuring Act
N&W	Norfolk and Western Railway
NHL	National Hockey League
NWI	Northwest Industries
OKT	Oklahoma, Kansas, Texas
OMB	Office of Management and Budget
OPEC	Organization of the Oil Exporting Countries
PC	Penn Central Railroad
PRR	Pennsylvania Railroad
RFC	Reconstruction Finance Corporation
RI or CRIP	Chicago, Rock Island and Pacific Railroad
RLEA	Railway Labor Executives' Association
RTA	Regional Transportation Authority
SP	Southern Pacific Railroad
TARP	Troubled Assets Relief Program
TOFC	trailer on a flat car
TP&W	Toledo, Peoria and Western Railway
UP	Union Pacific Railroad
UPC	Union Pacific Corporation
USRA	United States Railway Association (1970s); to be distinguished from the United States Railroad Administration (1917–1920)
UTU	United Transportation Union

ROCK ISLAND REQUIEM

Map 1.1 Map of the Chicago, Rock Island and Pacific Railroad as it looked in 1975. Author's collection.

INTRODUCTION

The story received news coverage worthy of the financial deals of Gilded Age railroad baron Jay Gould. In November 2009, Warren Buffett, the veteran investment capitalist known as the "Sage of Omaha," announced he was buying a railroad; to be exact, the rest of a railroad. His Berkshire Hathaway Corporation was purchasing 77 percent of the remaining stock of the Burlington Northern Santa Fe Railway (BNSF) to acquire total ownership of the mammoth 32,000-mile system. Buffett paid $26 billion for BNSF, offering stockholders $100 per share to buy out the company, a huge inflation of the stock's trade that day of $67 per share; stockholders approved the deal in February 2010. "This is all happening because my father didn't buy me a train set as a kid," Buffett joked to the *New York Times*.[1]

More serious, it was happening because railroads had not only rebounded to prove their worth as investments; they were also energy efficient transportation companies certain to benefit as "green" corporations in the future. During one of the worst economic recessions in modern American history, and one in which President Barack Obama touted green energy and fuel-efficient transportation alternatives, Buffett was making a statement not only about his faith in the American economy but also in an old smokestack–style industry reborn for the twenty-first century.

Buffett's decision to buy BNSF focused attention on the quiet revolution in American transportation that had been at work for the previous thirty years. If you weren't stopping, looking, and listening, you easily would have missed the revival of the railroads. Since the early 1980s, the railroad industry had reemerged as a major force in the American economy. A major reason for this revitalization was the Staggers Rail Act, signed into law by President Jimmy Carter on October 14, 1980. Staggers *partially* deregulated the railroads. It kept the railroads under the regulatory control of the Interstate Commerce Commission (ICC) while allowing them greater flexibility over ratemaking. Effectively, Staggers ended the maximum and minimum ratemaking power of the ICC, which for much of the twentieth century constrained railroad competition with other modes of government-subsidized transportation.²

This partial deregulation helped revolutionize the industry. Railroads could speed up abandonment procedures on unprofitable branches and mainlines that in the past had taken as long as a year due to lengthy and expensive public hearings. Often railroads had simply postponed abandonment procedures due to litigation costs and kept operating unprofitable lines.³ They could negotiate long-term contracts with major shippers who benefited by seeing their transport costs go down by as much 49 percent, which allowed them to ship twice as much freight compared to prices being paid in the 1970s.⁴ Railroads were able to reinvest profits back into plant and equipment with astounding regularity. By 2006, railroads ranked just below the median Fortune 500 index of return on equity, at 15 percent, a far cry from the 2.6 percent investment return of the industry in 1970, a figure that remained static the entire decade.⁵

By the end of the twentieth century railroads had pared their mileage from a high of 254,000 miles in 1915 to less than half that number, around 120,000 miles.⁶ Railroad workers have declined from 480,000 in 1980 to 164,000 by 2008; however, they are much better compensated, with the average wages rising from $24,659 to $72,836 during that same period.⁷ To tap lucrative traffic in Wyoming's Powder River coal basin, railroads considered expanded lines—the Dakota, Minnesota and Eastern (now a subsidiary of Canadian Pacific Railway) proposed construction of a 250-mile extension of its route into the coal fields of eastern Wyoming before postponing the project.⁸ The Union Pacific Railroad (UP) was so busy with traffic in the late twentieth century that it triple-tracked part of its original mainline through Nebraska. The overall reduction in railroad mileage and the profitability of the industry reflected many things—a changing economy, the deindustrialization of America, more intense competition in specific corridors with trucks and barges, and the globalization of the world economy. Consolidations, mergers, and liquidations led to fewer and fewer railroads running trains through fewer parts of the continental United States, a rationalization of the railroad system long sought by executives, politicians, and regulators.⁹ By the mid-1990s the number of Class I railroads (defined by the ICC's successor, the Surface Transportation Board, as a railroad with more than $250 million in operating revenue) in the United States had declined to six.¹⁰ But the six remaining Class I systems were powerful and profitable.

It was not always that way. The transformation of the American economy during the 1970s and 1980s, from an industrial and manufacturing economy to a service-oriented economy that imported much of its manufactured goods, impacted railroads drastically, especially lines in the industrialized Northeast and Midwest. By 1976, the bankrupt Penn Central Railroad (PC), Erie Lackawanna (EL), Reading, Lehigh Valley, Central Railroad of New Jersey (CNJ), Ann Arbor, and Lehigh and Hudson River companies were joined into the federally owned Consolidated Rail Corporation (Conrail). In the Midwest, the Chicago, Rock Island and Pacific Railroad (RI or CRIP) declared bankruptcy in 1975, followed in 1977 by the Chicago, Milwaukee, St. Paul and Pacific (the Milwaukee Road). Teetering on the brink of bankruptcy in this era were the Missouri–Kansas–Texas Railroad (Katy) and the Illinois Central Gulf as well. Politicians and railroad managers feared outright nationalization of all remaining railroads if the industry could not improve its performance.

Railroads depended on strong industrial production and a vital agricultural sector. By the mid-1970s, however, American industry was staggering under the weight of increased foreign competition, aging plants, environmental regulations, and high labor costs. Many steel mills were operating at 50 percent of capacity, and foreign steel was undercutting the market for American-produced products. Beginning in 1977, steel companies began the long process of shutting down mills throughout the Midwest. Youngstown Sheet and Tube Company of Ohio would abruptly close its Campbell Works in its namesake city on September 17, 1977, furloughing 5,000 workers in the process. Such a shutdown was shocking enough, but it paled compared to what was yet to come. By 1983 more than half of the operating steel mills in the country had been shutdown, with more than 250,000 steel workers thrown out of their jobs. The economic and social devastation to cities like Youngstown, South Chicago, and Homestead and Braddock in Pennsylvania was not seen since the Great Depression; unlike the 1930s, however, these mills closed for good.[11]

Other industries were in dire straits as well. Chrysler Corporation would require a federal bailout. General Motors and Ford Motor Company shut down plants and sold fewer automobiles than at any other point in postwar history as American consumers turned to fuel-efficient Japanese cars. Heavy industry, anthracite coal mining, and manufacturing all took downward turns in Northeast and Midwest industrial states. America's industrial economy was in ruins as workers and corporations adjusted to the grim realities of the new globalized international capitalism.

Although the industrial sector lagged, agriculture boomed for much of the 1970s before surpluses, inflation, and debt triggered a farm crisis in the 1980s. Farmers were increasingly more efficient producers, blending new technology, equipment, better fertilizers, and insecticides to produce more food. As new export markets opened in Europe and Asia, especially brought about by the export of wheat to the Soviet Union (a consequence of Richard Nixon's détente policy), American farm income grew during the 1970s. Low interest rates allowed farmers to return capital to their operations, purchasing more land and equipment. Farm income soared. But at the same time, inflation led to additional costs of farming—especially fuel and transport—which increased drastically, eventually outpacing returns on crop prices. Diesel fuel shortages in the Midwest in 1979, owed to the OPEC oil embargo, as well as historically harsh winters each year from 1977 to 1979, compounded the problem. To stem the inflationary spiral in the wider economy, the chairman of the Federal Reserve Board, Paul Volcker, supported driving up interest rates, effectively cutting off credit and borrowing for small farmers and businesses. Interest rates reached 18 percent by 1981. Soon thereafter, farm foreclosures and personal bankruptcies reached levels in rural America unseen since the Great Depression. The perfect storm of agricultural depression reached its crescendo when Jimmy Carter placed a grain embargo on the Soviet Union following the Soviet invasion of Afghanistan in December 1979.[12]

By any appreciable measure the state of the nation's economy in the late 1970s was dire. Inflation was the main culprit, but the declining dollar, trade deficits, a tumbling bond market, and a bearish Wall Street also contributed to the malaise. (The Dow Jones average had topped 1,000 in 1973 during the Arab oil embargo, would retrench to half that number in the recession of 1974–1975, and would not attain the 1,000 figure again until 1986.) The postwar economic boom seemed at an end. Economic growth weakened substantially in the 1970s, averaging 1.8 percent from 1973 to 1982, after having attained consistent growth of 3.3 percent from 1945 to 1968, and the same level from 1983 to 2007.[13]

"Stagflation," first used by *Washington Post* columnist Joseph Craft in 1971, became the term employed to describe the stagnant economy: a combination of high unemployment and inflation. Economists had no ready explanation for why it was occurring. If one accepted the Keynesian formula that government could fine-tune the economy through fiscal policy, there was supposed to be a tradeoff between unemployment and inflation and not a twin rise in both. However, both were increasing simultaneously, challenging the Keynesian consensus and allowing economists dubious of Keynes, such as Milton Friedman, Robert Mundell, and Arthur Laffer, an opening to tout their proposals for monetary discipline, cuts in government spending, and lower taxes. The supply-side economists proposed cuts in marginal income tax rates as a solution to the economic doldrums. Combined with controls and cuts in government spending, supply-side economists argued that economic growth would return.[14] Inflation proved a more intractable problem. To deal with inflationary pressures, the Federal Reserve would have to raise interest rates. Doing that, however, worked against economic growth, a real dilemma for the administrations of Carter and his successor, Ronald Reagan, as the Federal Reserve Board increased interest rates to end inflation. There was no easy solution to the economic problems of the 1970s.

Economic and business conditions were so poor during the 1970s that corporations clamored for relief from corporate tax burdens and government regulations. It was natural that businesses sought to restore competitiveness, cut labor costs, promote efficiencies, and restore profitability in the face of declining revenues, high costs of production, and slackening demand for American manufactured goods.

Historians of the 1970s economy have been nearly unanimous in their verdict concerning the role of business activism in the making of the Reagan revolution. Many have argued that deregulation was brought about by a cabal of free-market economists, business elites, think-tanks, and conservative politicians to end government regulation of the private sector, restore the power and profitability of business, and reduce the power of the New Deal electoral coalition and organized labor. In this reading, deregulation was not a necessity for business but rather a sordid effort to roll back the progressive agenda of governmental support for workers' rights. When examined in that context, the deregulation movement was simply a political process engineered by business elites and their allies within the developing conservative movement.[15] Beginning with Democrat Jimmy Carter, the deregulation of industry, transportation, banking, finances, communications, energy, and health and safety, some historians conclude, has had deleterious consequences for the country and the public interest. Political scientist Philip Cooper has concluded: "The war against regulation has indeed been the wrong war with the wrong enemy at the wrong time in the wrong place."[16]

The collapse of energy firms such as Enron, accounting firms like Arthur Anderson, insurance giants like AIG, and investment banks such as Bear Stearns and Lehman Brothers seems to support the thesis that in a war between regulators and deregulation advocates victory has come to the latter, with staggering consequences for the economy and for taxpayers who have had to bail out firms "too big to fail." Add to this the environmental catastrophe of the BP Oil spill in the Gulf of Mexico in the spring and summer of 2010—the largest of many environmental failures in the previous two decades—and is there any wonder why the historical literature is replete with the failures of deregulation?

In the "Great Recession" of 2008–2010, the focus of pundits, politicians, and the public at large has been on how an unregulated marketplace brought about the collapse of the banking system through an inflated housing bubble created by deregulation of the financial system. In the 1970s, however, regulation proved the culprit in helping to weaken the railroad industry. Government responses to the crisis, such as the formation of Conrail and Amtrak, proved ineffective in solving the railroad problem. Only deregulation and the removal of impediments to competition could return railroads to profitability.

For the railroad industry, deregulation came at exactly the right time and has been a staggering success. But a price was paid before the policy success embodied by the Staggers legislation. For railroads like the Rock Island, deregulation came too late. And it was the failure of entire railroads like the Rock Island that made possible the restructuring of the regulatory regime governing the railroad industry. The Rock Island's story presents in microcosm the story of the railroad industry's larger problems in postwar America and, in relief, the story of American economic failures during the 1960s and 1970s.

On March 17, 1975, the Chicago, Rock Island and Pacific Railroad Company filed for bankruptcy protection for the third and final time. The storied railroad once boasted 70-mile-per-hour freights and streamlined *Rocket* passenger trains but now was in its death throes. It was hurt by a failed merger with the Union Pacific, unnecessarily prolonged in duration by bureaucratic malfeasance on the part of the Interstate Commerce Commission as well as by rival railroads who wished to prevent any merger of the two lines. Left to languish without significant investment capital, running in marginal territory with ample branches but few long-haul routes conducive for moving large quantities of freight, and with little online industry, Rock Island management could do little but wait for a lifeline that would never come. Meanwhile the railroad hemorrhaged cash, running staggering deficits amounting to $100 million between 1964 and its bankruptcy filing in March 1975. (See Map 1.1 above, depicting the Rock Island network in 1975.)

No one expected the Rock Island story to continue long after that fateful St. Patrick's Day. Major bondholders and shareholders in the company sought a quick liquidation. The administration of Gerald Ford offered no federal bailout, preoccupied with the Northeast's railroad problems and the creation of Conrail. Instead, Judge Frank McGarr of the United States District Court for the Northern District of Illinois–Eastern Division, appointed a bankruptcy Trustee, his former law partner William Gibbons, who decided to save the railroad, placing it on a path toward reorganization. For five more years "The Rock," as it was renamed, was kept alive; during those years investors, led by Chicago billionaire businessman Henry Crown, fought the Trustee in federal court while making the case for reorganization. The failure to submit a plan for reorganization, long delayed by the Trustee and his attorney, a series of catastrophic economic conditions, historically bad winter weather through much of the railroad's territory, the collapsing bond market, high inflation, and a strike against the railroad in August 1979—necessitating the operation of the railroad through ICC-directed service orders—prevented the company's reorganization. Judge McGarr ordered the Rock Island's liquidation in January 1980, and on March 31, 1980, the railroad ceased operations, embargoing service on 7,300 miles of track serving twelve states. It was the largest railroad liquidation in American history and one of the largest liquidations of any corporation to that time.

The story may have ended there, but what followed was one of the most successful reorganizations in the history of American business. The Rock Island retired its debt, with interest, paid back bondholders and major creditors, and gave shareholders options in a new investment company, entirely out of the railroad business, named Chicago Pacific Corporation. The Rock's balance sheet went from a deficit of $400 million when liquidated in 1980 to a capitalization of $300 million for the new corporation, most of it cash assets, by 1984. In 1989, after acquiring the Hoover Corporation, Chicago Pacific was sold to Maytag Corporation, and the long history of the Rock Island Railroad finally receded into history.

In *Rock Island Requiem* the history of a railroad's ill-fated demise will be revealed in a three-act requiem: 1: Merger, 2: Bankruptcy, and 3: Liquidation. The story of the Rock Island's ill-fated merger agreement with the Union Pacific will be told in detail, focusing on the reasons both railroads sought a merger, as well as how the climate of railroad regulation made mergers one of the few practical ways for marginal railroads to survive. The merger story consumed 48,000 pages of testimony and financial dockets, plus some 200,000 pages of evidence in hearings conducted by the Interstate Commerce Commission. The ICC took eleven years to adjudicate the case, and during that period the Rock Island's financial fortunes collapsed. With no federal assistance available, the Rock Island declared bankruptcy.

In Act 1: Merger, the complete story of the merger proceedings, the role of rival railroads in opposition to the merger, the bureaucratic malfeasance of the ICC, and the role of both the Rock Island and the Union Pacific Railroad management in their internal discussions of the merger will be presented for the first time. The wider context of the railroad problem in the administrations of Richard Nixon and Gerald Ford, and the deliberations in Congress—especially regarding the bailout of the Penn Central Transportation Company and discussions ranging from complete nationalization to deregulation of the railroads—will be highlighted as well.

Act 2: Bankruptcy will focus on the bankruptcy of the Rock Island and the court battle between the bankruptcy Trustee and the intervenors in the case, primarily the interests of Henry Crown, over the reorganization of the property. It will also focus on the railroad's efforts to secure help from the federal government to rehabilitate lines, the agreements it reached with states to do so, and how, in the face of increasingly difficult odds, it kept running for five years before the inevitable shutdown was ordered in 1980. By the winter of 1979, the Rock Island's fortunes were severely tested by miserable weather, a stagnant economy, high inflation, and shortages of diesel fuel in its operating territory. The strike by members of the Brotherhood of Railway and Airline Clerks (BRAC) in August 1979 proved to be the last straw; five months after that strike began Judge McGarr ordered the railroad's liquidation.

In the wider political and economic arenas the fight to deregulate the railroads gained momentum under the Carter administration. The failures of both the Rock Island and the Milwaukee Road, which also declared bankruptcy, in 1977, magnified the crisis. The cost of Conrail and the refusal to create a Midwest variation on that railroad also led to stronger considerations for deregulation. Debates within the Carter administration between the president and his advisers will be highlighted, as will the congressional discussions leading to the passage of the Staggers legislation in October 1980.

Act 3: Liquidation will focus on the efforts of the bankruptcy Trustee, now working in close coordination with former adversaries such as Henry Crown, to liquidate the railroad and to ensure the viability of a reorganized corporation. The potentially destructive issue of employee compensation for back pay and vacations remained an obstacle, but Judge McGarr and attorneys for the Chicago law firm Jenner & Block (who had represented Crown's interests in the bankruptcy) won a major case in the U.S. Supreme Court vacating $75 million in claims by labor unions against the property. With that achieved, the reorganization of the railroad was ensured, and in 1983 the plan for reorganization was approved by the court; a year later the new corporation was created and in 1989 sold to Maytag, ending the corporate history of what blues singer Leadbelly (in his famous "Rock Island Line") referred to as a "mighty fine line."

Rock Island Requiem is a policy history of the Rock Island Railroad's final quarter-century, a deposition on what forces killed an enterprise and what lessons the collapse of this specific railroad can teach us about what economist Joseph Schumpeter once labeled the "mixed economy," including its benefits and its limitations. The story of the Rock Island's collapse is a marked departure in the annals of railroad history. It showcases not only the failures of the industry—focusing on the depressing amalgam of decaying infrastructure, failed public policy, and the void of leadership—but also how the seeds for rebirth rose out of the ashes of failure. Was the Rock Island a sacrificial lamb? Was the complete failure of this specific railroad necessary in order to revitalize the industry and end regulation of the industry? While no smoking gun points in any single direction, this requiem for the Rock Island shows clearly the failures of regulation and the limits to government intervention in the industry. The Rock Island's collapse can be seen as a transition between the old order of regulation, with its concomitant failures, and the new order of deregulation and the success it has held for the railroad industry. The Rock's collapse was not necessary for the new regime to arrive, but on the heels of its failure a new world did indeed arise.

ACT ONE

MERGER

ONE

A MIGHTY FINE LINE

We're in excellent shape, financially and physically. Unless we do something silly, we should get along all right.

—Rock Island president John Dow Farrington, January 19, 1948, *Time* magazine

The Chicago, Rock Island and Pacific Railroad Company emerged from its second corporate bankruptcy on January 1, 1948. The board of directors was all smiles in a publicity photograph at the first board meeting of the newly reorganized company, led by redoubtable John Dow Farrington, a Franklin D. Roosevelt look-alike whose chiseled visage and piercing gaze looked forward to a bright future on the railroad. Farrington had been with the Rock Island since 1936, recruited from the Fort Worth and Denver Railroad, a subsidiary of the Chicago, Burlington and Quincy (CB&Q), which he had rebuilt substantially while general manager of the line. When he arrived on the Rock Island as Chief Operating Officer, the railroad, like many others during the Great Depression, was in receivership, its losses magnified by an agricultural depression in the 1920s and 1930s that weakened Midwestern railroads like the Rock Island. Management had compounded the problem, paying dividends on stock instead of returning profits into maintenance and rebuilding. Farrington told the Rock Island's trustees that it would take $30 million to get the railroad back into shape.[1] See Photo 1.1.

Farrington swept onto the property like a dust storm through the western plains. He inspected the property, finding it in disrepair. To raise capital to rebuild the line, Farrington scrapped old locomotives and pulled up worn-out rail in order to acquire heavier rail for mainlines. He salvaged whatever could be salvaged and used the money to purchase additional 4–8–4 steam locomotives to haul heavier and longer trains through Rock Island territory, giving the Rock Island the largest fleet of these engines.[2] At the same time Farrington began to acquire diesel-electric locomotives and yard switchers from Electro-Motive Corporation (a Cleveland company that was bought by General Motors in 1930 and became known as the Electro-Motive Division

Photo 1.1 The first board of directors meeting of the new Chicago, Rock Island and Pacific Railroad Company, January 5, 1948. Pictured bottom row, L to R: Edward F. Brown, chairman of the Board; John Dow Farrington, president of the Rock Island; and Harry Darby, president of the Darby Corporation, Kansas City, Kansas. Back row, L to R: Frederick M. Mayer, president of the Continental Supply Company, Dallas; Robert McKinney, rancher and investor, Tucumcari, New Mexico; L. B. Neumiller, president of Caterpillar Tractor, Peoria, Illinois; and Herbert L. Horton, president of the Iowa–Des Moines National Bank and Trust Company. Author's collection.

[EMD] a decade later). Farrington used trustee certificates to purchase diesel locomotives and streamlined passenger cars for use on the railroad's dilapidated passenger trains.[3] Christened the *Rocket*, the first streamliner on the system ran between Chicago and Peoria; soon he would add the *Golden State Limited* and the *Rocky Mountain Rocket*, among other *Rocket* trains. By the 1948–1949 Chicago Railroad Fair, a national exposition of railroad technology and history, Farrington could brag of twenty-two *Rocket* passenger trains.[4] Modeled on the Chicago, Burlington, and Quincy Railroad's *Pioneer Zephyr*, the *Rockets* brought excitement and glamour back to the line, and passenger revenues rose appreciably.[5] His efforts increased morale among dispirited Rock Island workers who respected and liked their new operating officer.[6]

Farrington called his reforms "planned progress" and used the slogan to market the railroad. Among his great achievements rebuilding the railroad was the construction of a mammoth railroad bridge in southwestern Kansas over the Cimarron River. The bridge, nicknamed Samson of the Cimarron, replaced a low bridge crossing that was subject to washouts during floods and proved an operational headache for the Rock Island. The new bridge was an engineering marvel, constructed in just under a year and measuring 1,269 feet in length standing 112 feet above the riverbed below.[7] The Golden State Route stretching from Topeka, Kansas, to Santa Rosa, New Mexico, and a connection with the Southern Pacific Railroad (SP) was rebuilt entirely. Grades, curvature, and bridges were reduced throughout the property, with 12 miles of line chopped off along the route between Chicago and Kansas City.[8]

Railroading was in Farrington's blood. He was born in St. Paul, Minnesota, in 1891, his father a financial officer and close friend of James J. Hill, the legendary founder and builder of the Great Northern Railway. He spent several summers working with Great Northern surveying crews before leaving home at age nineteen to join the Burlington. He advanced quickly, starting at the bottom with a track gang and later serving as a trainmaster when the United States entered World War I. He entered the U.S. Army as a lieutenant and in France served as an engineer, leaving the military in 1919 with the rank of major. During the 1920s he returned to the Burlington and served as divisional superintendent in Omaha; St. Joseph, Missouri; and Kansas City. He was efficient and capable and promoted accordingly, moving to the Fort Worth and Denver as general manager and from there to the Rock Island.[9]

The challenges he faced rehabilitating the Rock Island's physical property were nothing compared to the problems he encountered with the railroad's emergence from bankruptcy. Judge James Wilkerson of the United States District Court for the Northern District of Illinois appointed three trustees to oversee the reorganization of the Rock Island in 1933: James Gorman, the president of the railroad; Chicago attorney Joseph Fleming; and a former Illinois governor, Frank Lowden, a Republican presidential hopeful in 1920. Eight committees of bondholders and the Reconstruction Finance Corporation (RFC), holding more than $250 million in Rock Island bonds, petitioned the federal court to appoint "impartial trustees" to supervise the reorganization of the railroad. New York attorney Elihu Root Jr., the son of President William Howard Taft's secretary of state (1909–1913), representing a committee of bondholders with assets of $150 million in first mortgage bonds, told the court that Rock Island management favored stockholders over creditors. "We want somebody who does not owe primary allegiance to the debtor company," Root stated, arguing that the management had continued to pay dividends on stock even when they "knew the company was in trouble."[10]

The railroad industry was in crisis during the early years of the Great Depression. More than 70,000 miles of rail line was in receivership as late as 1936, with major railroads facing the prospect of lengthy reorganizations under the guidance of new laws and government organizations to promote corporate reorganization. Government provided huge sums to bail out railroad corporations with the creation of the Reconstruction Finance Corporation in January 1932, part of Herbert Hoover's plan to restore business investment. By 1933, the RFC had loaned $1.8 billion to businesses and banks and took a proprietary interest in the spate of railroad bankruptcies during the first years of the Depression. The RFC had loaned $300 million to railroads by 1933, with an additional $100 million under consideration by the agency.[11] Its total loans to railroads by 1937 would be $600 million.

Franklin Roosevelt's New Deal programs emphasized the destructiveness of unfettered competition as one of the main causes of the Depression. Seeking a way to control the "wasteful practices" of the railroad industry, Roosevelt appointed Interstate Commerce Commission member Joseph Eastman as federal coordinator of transportation, a position designed to promote efficiency and reduce cutthroat competition. Eastman achieved little. Fond of surveys and questionnaires, Eastman's role as an ICC commissioner, and his desire to keep the office he ran outside of the effective control of FDR and the executive branch, reduced his influence measurably. Railroads did not heed his suggestions, and by 1936 his office was eliminated when the legislation creating it expired.[12]

The new federal bankruptcy law, Hoover's last proposed measure, passed Congress in March 1933 and provided a sounder vehicle for reorganizing the nation's bankrupt railroads. Section 77 of the Bankruptcy Act of 1933 dealt with railroad bankruptcies. Under the law, a railroad could file for bankruptcy protection with a federal district court when it became insolvent. At that point the assigned judge could appoint a trustee who would take title to the assets of the corporation and continue to operate the railroad. The Interstate Commerce Commission continued to have authority in approving the court-designated trustee. It also continued in its traditional regulatory role regarding finance and operations of the railroad. Within six months of filing, with extensions granted by the court (without a designated time limit), the Trustee would file a plan of reorganization needing both ICC and court approval before taking effect.[13] Under Section 77 the Trustee and federal judge had effective control over the property and the act protected bondholders and creditors in the railroad superseding the interests of stockholders and shippers. A railroad in bankruptcy continued to operate in the public interest, and it was required to operate its common carrier obligations as governed by the regulations of the ICC and statute. If a railroad could not be reorganized, the presiding judge could order its liquidation. If so ordered, with ICC approval, the Trustee would sell the assets of the railroad, which would no longer exist as a corporation and would no longer be required to operate under its common carrier obligations.

The new law was thought to be a marked improvement over the old bankruptcy statute, which granted power to the corporation itself to nominate a trustee and shepherd a railroad through bankruptcy. The new law was designed to accelerate the process of railroad bankruptcy, allowing for the reorganization of lines both financially and physically. However, due to the sheer number of railroad bankruptcies during the Depression, some roads took longer to reorganize than others. The Rock Island was one, entering bankruptcy on June 7, 1933, and reemerging fifteen years later. The Missouri Pacific Railroad (MP, or "MoPac") was another, with its bankruptcy process lasting a staggering twenty-four years.

The Rock Island bankruptcy proved prolonged owing to the complex issues of mortgage debt, the debt and rights of subsidiary companies, and the rights of senior and junior bondholders in the company. A workable plan was delayed, and several competing plans were placed before the ICC. The ICC rejected one plan arguing for the railroad's inclusion in a merger between the St. Louis–San Francisco (Frisco) Railroad and the Chicago and Eastern Illinois Railroad as "impracticable" in December 1935.[14] Another plan, favored by Gorman, the company president, would have unified the entire system with all the Rock Island subsidiary companies under one management with the property capitalized at $450 million and new mortgage bonds issued at 4.5 percent interest. This is the plan that would eventually be accepted by the court. However, the ICC ruled that the Rock Island would have to take control of a weak and indebted line, the Wichita Northwestern Railway, which had lost money for ten years and owed the federal government $600,000 in loans, as well as unpaid taxes to the State of Kansas totaling $100,000. This unification scheme went nowhere.[15]

Another complication for speedy reorganization was Texas lawyer Jesse Jones, head of the Reconstruction Finance Corporation. Jones demanded that the Rock Island seek new management. Although the $13.5 million the Rock Island owed to the RFC was not large in comparison to other roads, it still gave Jones added power to influence reorganization, which he was willing to do if he believed the trustees and the court were hindering reorganization. When the Rock Island trustees wanted to hire attorney Otis Glenn to help with the development of a reorganization plan, the RFC filed an injunction against his hiring because it violated terms of the agreement reached between the railroad and the RFC on the hiring of officials making more than $4,000 per year. Judge Evan Evans reminded the RFC that counsel was within the right of trustees under Section 77 and that the reorganization plan needed to be filed quickly.[16] In response to the hiring of Glenn, the RFC raised its interest rate charged on loans to 6 percent, arguing that the railroad had failed to uphold its end of the agreement when it came to government supervision of hiring.

Jones also had tried to sell $54 million in Rock Island securities, used as collateral for loans entered into by the RFC and five Chicago banks, but he was prevented from doing so by Wilkerson. The U.S. Supreme Court determined that Jones had overstepped his bounds as a creditor, ruling in favor of Wilkerson's injunction, which would "seriously embarrass and probably prevent the formulation and consummation of a plan of reorganization."[17] For the next year the RFC fought Wilkerson for the right to do so, insisting, finally, that at the least the railroad secure new management and force Gorman into retirement as Rock Island president.[18] Only then did the RFC let up on the Rock Island, reverting back to 4 percent interest, which the railroad was having a tough enough time paying anyway.[19]

The trustees hired Edward M. "Ned" Durham Jr., a senior vice-president with the Missouri Pacific Railroad, as the new CEO. It was Durham who brought Farrington aboard. Both men sought to improve the system, and soon the Rock Island began to turn around its finances.[20] In 1941, and during the war years, the railroad increased both its share of profits and decreased its debt as the nation's economy boomed. But the reorganization remained in limbo. Judge Wilkerson retired in 1941 and a new judge, Michael Igoe, was reassigned the case. Igoe was a Democrat, a member of the Illinois House of Representatives for close to twenty years before winning a congressional race in 1934. After only six months in Congress, Igoe resigned to take a position as U.S. attorney for the northern district of Illinois. In 1939 Franklin Roosevelt named him as judge for the U.S. district court in that district.

Further personnel changes came about when Gorman, the company president, died in March 1942. A career railroader, Gorman started as a car checker at age fourteen, rising through the ranks to attain the Rock Island presidency shortly before World War I; he held the position until 1935.[21] Durham retired in July 1942, and Frank Lowden died in March 1943. Farrington assumed Durham's position as chief executive officer of the railroad, and while he had to contend with wartime edicts from the War Production Board concerning essential materials, Farrington continued to rebuild the railroad. All he needed was a chance to run it outside of receivership.[22]

That chance would not come for another five years. On April 19, 1943, Igoe replaced Lowden with a new trustee, Aaron Colnon, a Chicago realtor and president of Fort Dearborn Mortgage Company. Colnon quickly dominated the longer-serving Fleming. He used his power to influence the judge in the case, to massage the Rock Island board of directors, and to harass Farrington. Fleming supported Farrington and backed his plans to rebuild the railroad, which continued as much as possible through the war years. But the reorganization continued to be delayed. A reorganization plan submitted to Igoe was turned down by the court in March 1943 and returned to the ICC. Two years later, Igoe approved an amended plan with a smaller capitalization (from $368 million to $356 million) and the appointment of a reorganization committee, which became a source of contention for the court.[23]

Junior creditors—those who owned bonds in subsidiary companies and those who owned their debt in the company over a shorter period of time—immediately filed suit in federal court charging that the reduced valuation of the railroad put their interests at risk, but the court ruled it did not. On appeal to the United States Court of Appeals for the Seventh Circuit, the junior creditors lost again, with the court holding that valuation of property was not subject to judicial review.[24] Still, Igoe hesitated to confirm the railroad's reorganization, giving rival attorneys from bondholder committees' additional time to make their case as to the harm that would befall their interests. On June 29, 1946, fearing that pending federal legislation would make a quick decision moot, Igoe returned the case to the ICC for a new study. In doing so, Igoe argued that "the plan does not make adequate provisions for fair and equitable treatment for the holders of convertible bonds." Echoing a bill that had just passed the Senate, Igoe commented that "we have a plan that except for slight modifications was prepared by the commission in 1940 and rests on studies of earnings going back to 1937 and beyond."[25]

Igoe was referring to a bill drafted by Senator Burton Wheeler (D–Mont.), who feared that the reorganization of railroads that had been in receivership since before World War II would harm "widows and orphans" and that the nation's bankruptcy laws governing railroad reorganization favored bondholders and investment holding companies at the expense of small investors. Wheeler proposed a new law designed to return bankrupt railroads to their debtor companies for 18 months to complete their own reorganization under the direction of the court. The essence of what became known as the Wheeler Bill (S. 1253) was to allow stockholders—the widows and orphans, it was thought—some control over their investments and to speed up long-delayed court reorganizations.[26] But it turned out that one of the largest widows and orphans was Wall Street financier Robert R. Young, whose Alleghany Corporation controlled the majority of common stock in the Missouri Pacific as well as stock in other bankrupt railroads.[27] The bill passed Congress, but President Harry Truman pocket-vetoed it, convinced it favored certain railroads over others, and proposed a reworked bill in the next Congress.[28]

In October 1946, Colnon proposed his own plan to speed up reorganization. Colnon favored paying off bondholders in Rock Island subsidiary companies and cutting the interest on remaining first mortgage bonds from 4.5 percent to 3 percent. A new issue of mortgage bonds stamped with the changed interest rate would result in a substantial reduction in the railroad's debt and eliminate the claims of subsidiary bondholders.[29] Other bondholders objected to the prices being offered subsidiary companies, which were double the face value of the bonds outstanding; they also objected to the cost of the proposal, which was said to be $57 million, leaving the Rock Island $15 million in working capital after reorganization. Accusations of impropriety flew at the hearing on the proposal. Colnon accused bondholder committees represented by New York attorney Edward Bourne that his clients—New York insurance companies—were trying to manipulate the case to assume control of the railroad. Bourne replied that Colnon seemed to be evading bankruptcy law and that their clients were worried that Colnon was seeking control of the railroad. In the end, Igoe sided with Colnon's plan, calling it "just and reasonable." Appeals were immediately filed in federal circuit court by bondholder committees.[30]

The appellate hearing before the circuit court on January 30, 1947, was equally contentious. In his remarks Bourne referred to the proposal as the Colnon-Igoe plan, to which Colnon objected. Bourne also argued that the reorganization plan at the ICC was being unnecessarily delayed by Colnon and Igoe, wasting the railroad's assets. Colnon replied that "I did the best I could without the legal draftsmanship ability enjoyed by the cream of the crop attorneys from New York City." The court—headed by Judges Otto Kerner (a future Illinois governor); Sherman Minton, a future Supreme Court justice; and J. Paul Major—took the appeal under advisement.[31]

Further adding to the controversy in the case was the entry of a "friend of the court" *amicus curiae* brief by lawyers for the Alleghany Corporation. In their entry into the case as an intervenor, Alleghany's attorneys pointed to its recent acquisition of $17 million in Rock Island stocks and bonds, $2 million of it purchased in the three months since the Colnon proposal was submitted to Igoe for consideration. By the end of the year, in fact, Alleghany had doubled the holdings of the next nearest Rock Island investor. Young's interest in the Rock Island was driven by a desire to create a truly transcontinental ownership in rail. Young was attempting to secure control of the New York Central System (NYC); a link with the Rock Island at Chicago and the purchase of an additional railroad in the West would give him control over a nationwide railroad empire.[32] Alleghany attorneys supported the Colnon proposal, leading to rumors of collusion between Colnon, Young, and Judge Igoe.

The Seventh Circuit delivered its ruling on February 21, 1947, reversing Judge Igoe's decision, remanding the case to the ICC, and affirming the reorganization plan submitted to Igoe's court in 1943. All three judges described Igoe's decision to reverse his stance on the reorganization as "an error of law" and stated that "changes in economic conditions cannot be used as a wedge to have the commission reexamine its former evaluation figures. When changes occur as they are bound to do, a court may not set aside a plan previously determined to be fair and equitable when the changes are such that they have been foreseen and considered in formulating the plan." The judges reaffirmed that the claims of senior creditors be satisfied before any other claims could be dealt with by the court.[33] There seemed little doubt the railroad would finally be reorganized after the Seventh Circuit ruling.

The plan confirmed the wiping-out of stockholders in the old company who would get nothing from the reorganization. The so-called Reed bill (a rewrite of the vetoed Wheeler bill of the previous year) was still in the pipeline, and stockholders at the meeting demanded the appointment of three Texas stockholders to the new board, revealing they had the votes of 250,000 Rock Island stockholders to do so. The Texans were elected to seats on the board after two of the management candidates, including diplomat Paul H. Nitze, withdrew from consideration. Judge Igoe scheduled a hearing to confirm the reorganization managers, and it was expected as well that the senior bondholders would file a motion to confirm the plan of reorganization. But John Gerdes, a vice president and general counsel for the Rock Island, told the *Chicago Tribune* that the debtor, junior creditors, and preferred stockholders would file a writ of certiorari (request for review) with the U.S. Supreme Court asking for a delay in the reorganization.[34]

At a hearing on May 6 Igoe blasted "New York attorneys who try to come in here and run things in their own manner." The judge treated Bourne with particular venom, attacking him for failing to "serve notice on adversaries when you go into court." When Bourne said that due to an illness of the judge he had waited until now to make his motion to confirm the reorganization plan, Igoe stated "that is the first time they [New York lawyers] have shown such . . . concern for the Court."[35] Igoe continued the case until May 22.

On that day all of the bad blood spilled out in what was one of the more remarkable hearings in the case's tortured history. The Rock Island had proposed a slate of reorganization managers consisting of Edward A. Brown of the First National Bank of Chicago; Mark Brown, president of Harris Bank and Trust; James Norris of Norris Grain Company; and Roy Ingersoll of Ingersoll Steel and Disc Company (later sold to BorgWarner). The court was given the right to name one member. Norris withdrew in favor of Charles Deere Wiman of John Deere & Company when Igoe made it clear that he wanted the managers to be men who had invested in the company before the war. Norris had accumulated his holdings over the course of the previous year. The court should have easily confirmed such men; all were Chicagoans, and all fit the predisposition of the judge to find "Midwestern men to run a Midwestern railroad." Igoe announced that he would be confirming the Rock Island's plan but wanted to appoint three of the managers, stating that Mark Brown and Wiman were nominees of security committees that no longer existed. The real reason was due to the fact that the men were nominated by Harry Hagerty, chairman of the New York–based Metropolitan Life Insurance Company. Bourne exploded and accused Igoe of taking a direct interest in controlling the reorganization. After a warning from the bench that his language was "unfit for this court," Bourne stated that "your honor is directly interested in control of the reorganized road." "For that statement," Igoe said, "I fine you $100 for contempt of court." Bourne took out the money from his wallet and then continued, charging Colnon with "making false statements" in support of the Reed legislation making its way through congressional hearings. "Mr. Colnon recently told a House subcommittee in Washington that the Metropolitan Life Insurance Company controls the majority of Rock Island bondholders committees. His statements were recklessly untrue—false, stupid and silly. He also tried to get a group of New York brokers to support the [Reed] reorganization bill." Colnon then appeared to defend his statements and defended the stockholders' rights, which would be protected in the Reed bill.[36]

On May 27, Bourne appeared before the Seventh Circuit Court of Appeals asking for a writ of mandamus against Igoe to deny the appointment of the three managers. He also asked that Igoe be removed from the case and that Trustee Colnon also be removed. "The District Court disobeyed your mandate of April 27 that the reorganization plans be confirmed forthwith. He [Igoe] did not confirm the plan you ordered, but another plan created by his alterations. He took it upon himself the power to appoint a majority of the reorganization managers. He took that power away from the creditors." Igoe's attorney defended his actions and argued that the case was not one bearing the providence of a mandamus writ but rather of a regular appeal.[37]

The appellate court delivered its opinion and ruling on June 9. The three judges reversed Igoe's ruling on the managers, stating "the court had no right to substitute a means of execution [of the 1943 plan of reorganization] of its own, contrary to and in derogation of the plan." The judges also ruled that the writ of mandamus was legal in this case. "The courts have uniformly held that, where a lower court has failed to comply with the mandate of the reviewing court, compliance with the mandate may be compelled by a writ of mandamus."[38] It was the second reversal for Igoe in less than a year, and the Rock Island's reorganization seemed assured.

Two days later the second appeal, on the removal of Igoe from the case, was heard by Judge Evan A. Evans, a senior member of the circuit court. Bourne argued that "Judge Igoe has repeatedly delayed any action in furtherance of the reorganization plan and has repeatedly taken actions intended to defeat the plan." He charged Colnon with making "grotesquely untrue" statements to the congressional committee and argued there was "open hostility" between the two trustees of the railroad. Evans doubted he had the power to remove Igoe and concluded that "this is past history. The plan has been confirmed. I want to get this thing out of the courts."[39] On June 21, 1947, Evans ruled that Igoe had not intentionally delayed the plan and that he (Evans) had no authority to act on the request to remove Igoe. He chided all parties in the case, saying, "Statements of Colnon which appear in the record . . . indicate he has misconceived his duties and entertained magnified ideas about the part he is to play in the reorganization." But he also criticized attorneys for the creditors and stockholders: "I received the impression that these creditors and stockholders are not seeking to carry out the plan or reorganization, but that they applaud the Trustee [Colnon] because he is blocking it and doing all he can to prevents its execution. I do not respect their action or their motives." Evans concluded, "I state emphatically that I think 14 years is longer than necessary to reorganize any debtor."[40] Whether or not the challenge to Igoe's authority was intended to pressure him into making a final decision, he finally confirmed the plan and ordered the reorganization of the railroad on June 26, 1947. The long saga appeared to be over.[41]

However, nothing in the Rock Island's reorganization was ever that easy. Congress was still debating the Reed reorganization bill—the reworked

Wheeler law of the previous year—proposed by Representative Chauncey Reed (R–Ill.) in the House and Senator Clyde Reed (R–Kan.) in the Senate. Both Young and Colnon supported the bill, which would have helped in their plan to control the Rock Island. But opposition to Young's machinations and to the bill itself was strong, and after congressional hearings in which Colnon, Young, and Igoe were singled out for their inappropriate conduct in actively supporting a bill that would have defeated a plan of reorganization approved in Igoe's court, the House Rules Committee failed to move the bill to the floor and it unceremoniously died in committee in July 1947. Meanwhile the U.S. Supreme Court heard a writ of certiorari filed by junior creditors a year earlier. The Interstate Commerce Commission made the decision to join with the junior creditors, writing Chief Justice Fred Vinson that if the writ were granted the ICC would reopen the Rock Island case. It was an amazing about-face. The Supreme Court, however, denied the petition for a writ and the old corporation was ended.[42] On October 29, the new managers presented to the ICC for approval an application, which included a new corporate charter, mortgages, and a slate for the board of directors. Yet Judge Igoe allowed the third-party motion for intervention in the form of an appeal by the Texas state attorney general over the question of the road's incorporation in Delaware.[43] Texas had never before been a party to the case, and this maneuver delayed the proceedings yet again. After Judge Igoe ruled on December 30 that Texas had no standing as an intervenor, the Texas attorney general went to the court of appeals, where finally, on December 31, 1947, the appellate court rejected the Texas intervention. Igoe signed the order creating the new corporation "with protest." "I have tried to bring this matter to the attention of the higher courts without success," he stated. "I know I must comply with orders of the Circuit Court of Appeals."[44] The Rock Island finally was freed from the clutches of bankruptcy, and the new corporation came into existence on January 1, 1948.[45]

While the reorganization proceeded in court and in Congress, president Farrington had not been idle. He had continued his campaign of "planned progress." By the time the railroad had emerged from bankruptcy, he had improved the property drastically, constructing two large classification yards, at Kansas City (Armourdale) and at Silvis, Illinois (still the biggest such yard in railroading a decade later). With the Milwaukee Road, he split costs for a new bridge over the Missouri River that sped passenger trains to Kansas City Union Station. The bridge was named after Harry Truman. He constructed a new coach shop and yard in 1946 at 47th Street in Chicago and purchased the Pullman Railroad, a major switching and industrial railroad, along with 365 acres of property, on the far South Side of Chicago.[46] The

Rock Island added automatic block signals to more than 3,200 miles of line and centralized traffic control to 592 miles. The total amount spent to turn the railroad into a first-class property was $130.8 million, far above the estimate of $30 million Farrington made to the company in 1936. But the results were impressive; by the end of 1948 the railroad had gross revenues of $197 million, with a net operating income of $21.8 million.[47]

The new board of directors continued to authorize spending on improvements to the property, including more diesel locomotives, passenger equipment, and freight cars.[48] Nearly every board member was from territory and businesses served by the Rock Island. The significant board members were Edward Brown of the First National Bank of Chicago; Roy Ingersoll of Borg-Warner; Charles Deere Wiman, president of John Deere & Company; Mark Brown, the executive vice president of Chicago's Harris Bank and Trust; Harry Darby, a steel manufacturer from Kansas City; L. B. Neumiller of Caterpillar Tractor; James Norris of the Norris Grain Company; and Henry Crown, a Chicago investor and chairman of Material Service Corporation. Within a decade the Crown and Norris interests would hold more than 250,000 shares of Rock Island stock and Henry Crown would be the largest bondholder in the railroad.[49]

Of all the board members, James E. Norris probably had the most interesting pedigree. Born in Quebec in 1879, Norris entered his family's grain business, which moved its interests to Chicago in 1909. He had developed a passionate interest in hockey and attempted to secure control of the Chicago Blackhawks in the newly formed National Hockey League (NHL) but did not win the approval of the league commissioner. He tried to bring another club to Chicago, without success, before securing ownership of the indebted Detroit franchise, which he renamed the Detroit Red Wings in 1933 and helped lead to five Stanley Cup championships before his death in 1952. Norris helped finance Chicago Stadium, later becoming owner of the facility, bought a controlling interest in the Blackhawks, and possessed a share of Madison Square Garden in New York, the landlord of the New York Rangers.[50] Today the Norris Trophy is awarded to the best defenseman in the NHL; one of the leagues conferences is also named in his honor. His son, James D. Norris, who owned the Blackhawks, remained connected to the Rock Island until his death from a heart attack in 1966. Grandson Bruce Norris also was a member of the Rock Island board for many years. The Norris family remained the second-largest holders of Rock Island stock through the mid-1970s.

Henry Crown would prove to be the most crucial investor in the new company. Crown (née Krinsky) was born in Chicago in 1896, the third son of the Russian-Jewish immigrants Arie and Ida Crown. Arie Crown emigrated from Russia to New York in the 1880s, joining thousands of other Jews leaving the Pale of Settlement after pogroms against Jews who were blamed for the assassination of Tsar Alexander II in 1881. Arie found odd jobs in New York and traveled until he secured a factory job in Chicago making suspenders, allowing him to save enough to marry. The Crowns lived on the city's northwest side surrounded by the population of immigrants who provided the city its polyglot character. There was opportunity there for immigrants willing to work, and Arie soon became a peddler, securing enough money to purchase a house and to support seven children.[51]

The oldest brothers, Sol (1893–1921), Irving (1894–1987), and Henry (1896–1990), all began working at an early age. Sol would attend high school and take night classes at John Marshall Law School before realizing he had to work to help the family. At age eighteen he became a sales manager with the Chicago Fire Brick Company. Henry dropped out of school at fourteen and secured a variety of jobs, from newspaper delivery boy to messenger, before showing remarkable perseverance in getting a job as a salesman for the Union Drop Forge Company, writing dozens of letters to company presidents on purchased stationery before hearing back from the forge company. The boys were ambitious, like many sons of immigrants, and soon began investing in and selling steel and building materials themselves, starting the Sol R. Crown Company, the forerunner of Material Service Corporation, a building supply company incorporated in 1919 with a capitalization of $20,000 divided between the three brothers.[52]

During the 1920s Material Service Corporation boomed, and after the tragic death of Sol from tuberculosis in 1921 Henry soon became the leading figure in the company, making deals and securing investments in new quarries and equipment for the booming company. "Throughout the 1920s," Crown recalled, "our business showed substantial improvement each year over the previous one." Crown worked to make political connections with the Republican mayor, William Thompson, as well as Democrat pols, securing contracts to supply materials for the city's growth. The brothers expanded operations, buying barges to ship limestone and other material from Michigan and Wisconsin to the Calumet River ports on the city's South Side. As more and more investment went into the company the Crowns became rich and, in 1928, decided to take it public, issuing stocks in Material Service Corporation. With sales of $10 million in 1928, all seemed well and the Crowns had made it, redeeming their father's faith in America.[53]

The Great Depression hit their interests hard. Company sales sunk to a decade-low $3 million. Crown was worried, as he owed First National Bank of Chicago $1 million in outstanding loans. Bank vice president Hugo Anderson met with Crown and told him the value of the corporation was not worth the bank's outstanding paper; Crown offered every asset, including his home, to back up the loans and Anderson took a second look at the books, discovering that Crown had underrated the company's worth substantially. Anderson stuck with Crown and helped him reorganize the company's debt. The two men developed a close and cordial relationship for the remainder of their working lives. Material Service, through astute management, hung on through the grimmest years of the Depression, even helping customers do the same by extending credit. By the end of the decade, the company was again profitable, and in 1939 it posted sales of $11 million.[54]

When World War II started, Crown's oldest son joined the U.S. Navy, and Henry wished to serve his country as well. He secured a job in the U.S. Army Corps of Engineers, using his industry connections to aid wartime procurement. He was awarded the rank of colonel—a sobriquet many still referred to him by decades later—and helped procure more than $1 billion of resources for the war effort. When the war ended, Crown returned to the helm of Material Service and began to seek new investment opportunities. He met and befriended Conrad Hilton and was an original investor in his hotel corporation. He looked for opportunities to enhance the portfolio of Material Service as well as his own family's investments, and in 1946, while recovering from a horseback-riding accident, Crown started investing in the low-priced bonds of the Rock Island Railroad.[55]

Crown began to purchase the bonds when he received a prospectus showing that the bankrupt railroad had assets far exceeding liabilities and that its defaulted bonds were selling for as little as 30 cents on the dollar. By the end of 1947 Crown had bond holdings worth more than $4 million, which he exchanged for 100,000 shares of Rock Island common and preferred stock on the day the railroad reorganized. Banker Robert Young had purchased 250,000 shares, but he was interested in selling to focus his attention on an effort to purchase the New York Central, so Crown, James Norris, and Charles Deere Wiman bought out Young in 1949. Young would make the deal only if Crown took shares of the Seaboard Air Line Railroad off his hands. Crown did so and the price of Seaboard stock later soared, doubling his investment. *Time* magazine later reported: "In addition, the $4 million he put into the Rock Island bonds has nearly tripled." Crown also owned substantial stock in Rock Island rival St. Louis–San Francisco (Frisco) and the Baltimore & Ohio as well. Yet Crown's purchase of Rock Island paper at such low prices made him the most important single investor in the railroad from the reorganization until its final bankruptcy in 1975.[56]

Throughout the early 1950s Henry Crown's investment seemed a wise one. The railroad prospered, continuing investments in passenger service, dieselization (which it achieved completely by 1954), and track and equipment. For the first half of the decade the entire railroad industry seemed profitable, with traffic increasing due to the Korean War. But there were troubles on the horizon. Korean War–induced inflation was pressing on railroad profitability. Subsidized competition from trucks and airlines dented railroad passenger traffic, which continued to decline. President Dwight Eisenhower's focus on constructing the Interstate system of highways, as well as the St. Lawrence Seaway, proved costly to railroads due to the diversion of traffic to barges and trucks. Soon, private airlines were ferrying more passengers to their destinations than were railroads. The growing competition with rival forms of transportation quickly took a toll on the industry. Trucks rolled on subsidized highways; airliners parked at municipal-owned and -funded airports. Railroads had to pay taxes on land, stations, maintenance buildings, and other property to municipalities, states, and the federal government. In the Rock Island's first year of operations after bankruptcy in 1948, the company's net operating revenue before taxes was $55 million. After taxes, it was around $32 million. Eleven percent of every dollar it spent went toward taxes.[57] Almost a decade later, the Rock Island paid 8 percent of every dollar on taxes.[58] Trucks and airlines did not have to pay any taxes on the subsidized roads, bridges, and airports they used. Barges along the Mississippi River and oceangoing vessels on the St. Lawrence Seaway did not have to pay taxes either.

Railroads began to suffer from declining returns on investment, which made it increasingly difficult to raise private capital to fund improvements and made railroads a less than attractive investment for commercial banks. Indications of both problems were put forth in testimony by Rock Island's vice president of finance, Paul Major, at ICC hearings on the Rock Island and Union Pacific merger in 1965. Major showed the marked decline in net income after taxes between 1948 and 1963. The first six years after reorganization were good years, with average net income of around $24 million. "In 1952 and 1953, it enjoyed pre-tax income as high as $37.3 million and $38.1 million, respectively." The Korean War was the main reason for providing such increases to income. But once the war ended, net income declined precipitously. Major told a disheartening tale:

> The shrinkage of Rock Island's income since 1948 is illustrated by the fact that the Rock Island's income before taxes in 1948 of $32.1 million was eleven times more than the Rock Island's income in 1962,

and nine times its income in 1964.... Thus, Rock Island's income before taxes in 1962, 1963 and 1964 averages approximately $3.5 million. This means that Rock Island's income before taxes has declined approximately 89 percent, whether compared with 1948 or the average of the first six post-reorganization years, 1948–1953.[59]

More problematic was the erosion of the property's return on investment. "In 1948 the Rock Island earned a return on investment of 6.69 percent and reached a subsequent high of 6.67 percent in 1953," Major said. "Since that date there has been a steady erosion, and return on investment declined to a low of 1.70 percent in 1964." While the railroad continued to invest in plant and equipment in that sixteen-year period, "Rock Island has not been able to improve its rate of return, despite these continuing investments." Without a good rate of return the railroad had trouble securing private capital from banks; the railroad's working capital continued to decline (by 83 percent from $52.9 million in 1948 to $9.2 million in 1964).[60]

The Rock Island was hardly alone in its struggle to secure capital. During the decade after World War II, the railroad industry had a dismal return on investment of less than 4 percent.[61] Railroads were struggling with increased costs and inflation in the economy. Labor costs increasingly took up more of the share of spending. Almost half of the Rock Island's expenses were for wages and benefits by the end of the 1950s. After dieselization of operations, featherbedding by labor unions representing firemen—the jobs of stoking the fire on *steam* locomotives were protected until the late 1960s—contributed to the problems of increased labor costs. Deficits from passenger service—both from commuter operations in major urban areas as well as intercity service—cost railroads significant amounts of money. Railroads like the New York Central and the Pennsylvania Railroad (PRR) experienced passenger deficits of *$500 million* throughout the first postwar decade. The Pennsylvania Railroad had a $54.7 million deficit for passenger service in 1956 alone.[62] No railroad made money from passenger trains and increasingly sought to cut service on unprofitable routes.

The deteriorating condition of the railroads worried President Dwight Eisenhower, who saw transportation as a vital link in a strong national economy. Eisenhower sought modified deregulation, worried about consumer prices and rising inflation. He established the Presidential Advisory Committee on Transport Policy and Organization, headed by his good friend, Secretary of Commerce Sinclair Weeks. The so-called Weeks Report, released in April 1955, called for limited deregulation of the trucking and railroad industries, allowing both the right to establish their own maximum and minimum rates without interference from the ICC.[63] Weeks told a House committee that "we conceive that the proper role of rate regulatory policy is to establish reasonable bounds within which common carrier management is free to compete on a price as well as a service basis without governmental interference, provided no customer or area is discriminated against or unduly preferred or prejudiced."[64] While the report was heralded by Eisenhower as "a brilliant piece of work," foreshadowing later efforts to achieve deregulation, the Weeks Report fell on deaf ears in Congress.[65] The American Truckers Association aligned with the ICC to prevent deregulation, the former fearful of losing business to railroads, and the latter of losing its institutional authority to control rates.[66] Weeks failed to convinced Congress that his report did not "propos[e] any change in the general pattern of regulation by the ICC." Neither was it proposed to help railroads secure rates that "would drive truckers off the roads."[67] But Weeks failed to convince either Congress or truckers that his modified deregulation would work. Meanwhile, the "railroad problem," as it was becoming known, continued to fester, unresolved by government.

Railroads searched for new ways to innovate and to develop greater market share and attract investment capital. In 1954 the Chicago and North Western Railway (C&NW) secured permission from the ICC to deliver door-to-door service from Chicago to Green Bay, Wisconsin, via a trailer on a flat car (TOFC) owned completely by the railroad. Within five years fifty-seven railroads offered "piggyback" service of their own. Piggyback service dated to the 1930s but became truly innovative during the postwar decade. To take advantage of this service, railroads had been allowed to form subsidiary trucking companies; the Rock Island had established Rock Island Motor Transit in the 1940s. The piggyback revolution allowed railroads to handle shipments on their own lines via their own subsidiary trucking companies. The ICC endorsed the concept and determined that further study was needed.[68] Despite such potential, by the mid-1960s piggyback service and TOFC was more common on the head end of passenger trains, carrying mail and other priority items, than on dedicated freight service. It represented only about 5 percent of all freight shipped by American railroads in 1966.

The Rock Island's management remained innovative throughout the 1950s, embracing the new piggyback technology, completing dieselization, and continuing to invest large sums in rebuilding property. In 1955 John Farrington stepped down as president to become chairman of the board. He had been grooming the young and talented Downing Bland Jenks, an Ivy League graduate whose father had been general manager of the Spokane, Portland and Seattle Railroad; his grandfather Cyrus Jenks was a superintendent on the Great Northern Railway. Downing Jenks, much like Farrington, had railroading in his blood and proved an inspiring choice as president.[69]

Jenks was born in Portland, Oregon, in 1915. He received an engineering degree from Yale University in 1937 and worked for several railroads, including the Pennsylvania and the Great Northern. During World War II he operated military railroads in North Africa, Italy, and Germany. After the war he was appointed to be general manager of the Chicago and Eastern Illinois Railroad, where he came to the attention of Farrington, who brought him to the Rock Island in 1950 as vice president and general manager. He rose quickly through the ranks with diligence and organization: vice president for operations in 1951, executive vice president in 1953, and president in 1956 (at age forty).[70]

Jenks faced a series of problems that had been mounting through the decade. First was the increasing cost of railroad operations, particularly wages. Labor unions were a powerful force on the nation's railroads. Backed by Democrats in Congress, labor used its muscle to secure significant wage increases throughout the decade after the Rock Island's reorganization. In 1957 Jenks told the stockholders that a new three-year contract with railroad brotherhoods resulted in wage increases of 12–13 percent along with a cost-of-living escalator clause. By 1957 the wage and benefits paid to employees had risen 59 percent above the average of 1948—a stunning trend.

Inflationary pressures were mounting across the board during the period 1948–1957. Prices for material, including ties, ballast rock, and steel rails, increased by about 40 percent during the postwar decade. This was in spite of significant rate increases granted by the ICC in that time frame of 50 percent higher than in the first year out of bankruptcy. As Jenks reported, "An emergency increase of 5 percent towards the close of 1956 had been put into effect, and after protracted hearings early in 1957, the ICC granted in August 1957, another 7 percent rate rise. The lines in the West thus received in a period covering almost a year, a total increase of 12 percent—far from enough to reach a break-even point on costs."[71] More alarming—Jenks called it "a matter of serious concern"—was the $6 million decrease in net income from 1956, with the Rock Island posting a net income of $9.7 million in 1957.

The pressures of operating a granger railroad were becoming apparent. The Rock Island had little online industry, and while the railroad waged an aggressive program to attract industry, the territory it served was primarily agricultural and subject to the vagaries of weather, crop failure, and price fluctuations. Increasingly, unregulated rural truckers were poaching grain shipments that Midwestern roads otherwise relied upon for income. Barge traffic along the Mississippi River impacted shipments of grain to Gulf ports as well.

These were hardly the only problems facing railroads. The national economy went into a tailspin in the last quarter of 1957, a contraction lasting eight months; gross domestic product dropped 3.7 percent, far worse than any recession in the period after World War II to that time. Hard times hit the auto industry as well; 1957 sales plummeted 37 percent. When General Motors sneezed, the rest of the economy caught a cold as demand for steel, mining products, and transportation all slumped. Agricultural production also declined, worsening conditions for the Rock Island and other Midwestern roads. The only thing that did not fall, confounding Eisenhower's economic advisers, was inflation. Consumer prices all rose during the downturn, which produced an unemployment rate of 8 percent by the spring of 1958.

Jenks reacted to the downturn by cutting back on tie replacement and new rail on Rock Island track. In fact, one can see the long decline of the railroad beginning with the recession of 1958. That year, the railroad replaced only 5,656 tons of rail, a precipitous drop from its postbankruptcy average of about 20,000 tons per year. Crossties on mainline track also declined precipitously, from 460,861 in 1957 to 246,485 a year later. The result was permanent, in that the Rock Island never recovered in maintenance of its track. Such a short-run cut in maintenance suggested problems that were ahead for the railroad as the 1958 recession took its toll on industry profitability.[72]

To address the situation and to investigate the deeper problems of the railroads, Senator George Smathers (D–Fla.) called for hearings on the deteriorating railroad situation. More than twenty railroad executives gathered in Washington, D.C., on January 17, 1958, before the Senate Subcommittee for Surface Transportation. In late December, railroad carloads in one week dropped to their lowest point since December 1932, with 410,022 cars loaded. Railroad net income had sunk 39 percent from 1955 to 1957, coming in at the end of the latter year at $46 million. Working capital had also declined precipitously since 1955, from $880 million to $576 million. While the economy was in recession, the railroads seemed to be troubled for other reasons. "There is little question that today our railroads are in serious condition," Senator Smathers stated at the hearings. "A mighty industry has come upon sick and precarious times."[73]

James Symes, president of the dominant Pennsylvania Railroad, set the tone for the hearings: "The railroads stand at this moment at the crossroads of decision—Government decision—as to whether they follow the free enterprise system with their illnesses corrected by proven American methods, or the socialistic road with alien remedies and exceedingly dangerous implications."[74] Symes called for greater freedom to set rates, less control by the ICC, and the ability to abandon unprofitable passenger service. Other railroad executives recommended changing the tax system for railroads, which, as owners of large amounts of property, paid taxes to local, state, and federal governments while their competition in trucking, barges, and airlines did not. Alfred Perlman of the New York Central System sought an end to cumbersome regulation of passenger service. Others wanted to do away with wartime federal excise taxes on railroads (a charge of 3 percent on freight and 10 percent on passengers) and to improve the efficiency of the ICC while reducing its ratemaking power.

Aside from concerns over the ICC's power to set rates, Rock Island president Downing Jenks spoke out against ICC decisions that prevented railroads from having ownership stakes in trucking companies or other transportation modes, a concern of antitrust advocates. Declining traffic on the Rock Island, Jenks suggested, was due to competition with trucks as well as to "narrow interpretations of national transportation policy by the ICC." Jenks asked for legislation allowing railroads to diversify by owning competitive trucking companies, thereby creating a truly seamless transportation network.[75] Railroad executives also discussed speeding up possibilities for mergers to allow for reduction of operating costs and the end of redundancy within the railroad network.[76] But there was not a unified position on any one issue. The lack of unity impeded any reforms from being adopted that could have produced a stabilized industry.[77]

Two months later, the Commerce Department's Transportation Study Group released proposals to address the railroad problem. The members of the group blamed both management and governmental policies. Managers were faulted for lacking imagination in working within the confines of regulation. "There has been a substantial reluctance to adopt new methods of promotion, accounting, equipment utilization, and research, to mention a few." The group recommended establishing a separate Department of Transportation (DOT) to coordinate industry options. It also recommended, like the railroad executives, changes in the ratemaking power of the ICC, helping to develop better depreciation schedules for railroads so that they could maximize capital, and the elimination of excise taxes dating back to World War II.[78]

Railroads had only one way out of the predicament of subsidized competition, increased operating costs, and government regulation. That was through consolidation and merger. Discussions between the Pennsylvania Railroad and New York Central System to merge had already been under way at the time of the hearings in 1958. Executives of the Great Northern, the Northern Pacific, and the Chicago, Burlington and Quincy began talks in 1955, which stalled but would resume again in 1960, leading to the creation of the Burlington Northern Railroad in 1970. Smaller railroads were absorbed into larger systems, such as the Minneapolis and St. Louis Railway's (M&StL) acquisition by the Chicago and North Western Railway and the Norfolk and Western Railway's (N&W) acquisition of the Virginian, a coal hauler. For railroads, it was either merge or die.

The Rock Island seemed a likely prospect for merger. It was a granger line with the majority of its 7,300-mile system serving agricultural states like Iowa, Kansas, Illinois, Oklahoma, and Texas. As of 1959 it was still a profitable railroad, ranking twenty-second in *Fortune* magazine's Top Fifty Transportation Companies, with gross revenues of $219.5 million (but only a net income of $8.3 million). Its rate of return on equity was a dismal 2.9 percent in 1959, far above top-tier railroads like the Pennsylvania and the New York Central but below those of railroads in the Midwest and West.[79] It was a railroad with attractive prospects for merger, with an eastern terminus in Chicago and serving cities such as Omaha, Denver, Dallas, Houston, Des Moines, Kansas City, Minneapolis, and Little Rock. It had the longest north-south run of any railroad in the country, from Minneapolis to Houston, and its access to Gulf ports made that line a significant asset.

The Rock Island board of directors felt that the time to merge was now while the railroad possessed significant assets. Henry Crown, the largest investor, arranged a meeting between Farrington, Jenks, and Ben Heineman, the young chairman of the Chicago & North Western. But the talks collapsed after four days with "too large a difference between what we thought the Northwestern would be worth and what they thought it was worth."[80] For Crown, Heineman was a bold executive, a young man who he respected and personally liked, someone who might even run the Rock Island some day. Crown and Jenks did not get along personally, and the brash Heineman—who had turned around the C&NW since taking the helm in 1954—was more to Crown's taste.

In November 1959, Farrington proposed a merger with the Chicago, Milwaukee, St. Paul and Pacific Railroad, a 10,000-mile granger line with a Pacific Coast extension.[81] The Rock Island and Milwaukee Road boards agreed to a merger study. Crown "concurred in what is now the unanimous view of the Executive Committee that the proposed study as to the desirability of merger with the Milwaukee Railroad should be undertaken with as little delay as possible."[82] In October 1960, with discussions between the two sides going well, and with the preliminary report prepared by the firm

Coverdale & Colpitts showing "an annual savings of $25 million to be realized from the merger.... Farrington and Jenks were authorized to commence negotiations with the Milwaukee Road looking toward the merger of the two properties."[83]

At the November 19 board meeting, Crown pulled the plug on the merger, for reasons that remain murky. In a *Fortune* magazine article published in 1966, Crown later said that "the study made a case against any Rock Island–Milwaukee merger; both needed a crutch and neither was able to support the other." Jenks disagreed, saying that "Crown seemed to be in favor of all the merger proposals except the one we were working on." Crown then retorted that "there were no other merger proposals before the board and add[ed], 'we never authorized Jenks to negotiate with the Milwaukee. He was doing that on his own.'"[84] The evidence from the February 1960 board meeting authorizing the merger discussions would undermine Crown's view.

Historian Craig Miner argued that Jenks and William Quinn, president of the Milwaukee Road, "were within one-tenth of a share of an understanding on exchange terms [when] the deal was scotched by objections from Henry Crown who was interested in a Milwaukee–North Western merger. Crown suggested that the Rock Island seek a merger with the Missouri Pacific (MoPac)... as an alternative."[85] Jenks dutifully visited the St. Louis headquarters of MoPac and found the executives interested more in him than in the Rock Island. But Jenks still thought he would prevail on the Rock Island board; when Crown scratched the merger on November 19, 1960, Jenks called the Missouri Pacific and told them he was available. MoPac's interest in Jenks was reported in the press on December 14, 1960.[86] He left the Rock Island on February 1, 1961, and became legendary for turning around MoPac and making it a valuable property.

There may have been another reason for the merger's failure other than the battle between Crown and Jenks. Farrington, who resumed the presidency of the railroad after Jenks's departure, revealed that

> a meeting was being held in New York between representatives of the Metropolitan and Equitable Life Insurance companies and representatives of the Milwaukee Road and the Chicago and Northwestern Railway. I felt that if the two insurance companies—very large holders of securities in our railroad—plus the [C&NW] management, were to oppose the merger vigorously, considering the fact that we were not assured the support of some of our own large stockholders, there was little chance of accomplishment. As it turned

out, that is precisely the situation. I saw Mr. [James J.] Oates (president of the Equitable) yesterday and he informed me that he would have to oppose any merger that excluded the [C&NW] and that they had been definitely informed that any merger that left the [C&NW] out, in view of its present weak financial condition, would be politically impossible of accomplishment, and seriously urged us to give consideration to a three-way merger.

Farrington opposed a three-way combination.[87]

The rationale was not hard to fathom. The advantages, as Farrington laid out, were "great traffic strength, improved volume for our long haul lines to the West and Southwest and the Milwaukee extension to the [Pacific] Coast, and elimination of much duplication of mileage, both main line and branch line." But the disadvantages outweighed any such advantages. The downside included "the multiplication of suburban operations [in Chicago]," which became a drain on operating costs, "large number of freight yards and passenger depots in Chicago, few of which could be eliminated, large numbers of light branch lines even after elimination of duplication of lines, very high debt structure which would result in heavy sinking funds" (more for the C&NW and the Milwaukee than the Rock Island), and "the obvious lack of earning power for the carriers involved." Farrington: "I told [Oates] my opposition to that was largely because of the financial weaknesses of the properties involved."[88]

It was an astute analysis and one that, in the example of a proposed merger between weak northeastern railroads like the New York Central and the Pennsylvania, should have been heeded. Combination for the sake of combination, particularly of weakened properties, would have assured the bankruptcy of all three once the merger was finalized. With Heineman interested for the time being in exploring a merger with the Milwaukee Road without the Rock Island, the prospects for a three-way merger—favored by Crown—went nowhere.[89] The Rock Island still had no suitor and no prospects for merger as the new decade began.

Farrington's second go-round as Rock Island president was cut short by his death from a heart attack in October 1961.[90] Farrington was a legend in the company and in railroading, but his age and the stress had taken a toll. He had rebuilt the railroad entirely during his tenure and had secured the faith and respect of board members and employees. He had transformed the Rock Island into a mighty fine line during his twenty-five-year tenure. Now it would be up to his successors if the Rock Island was to continue on its successful pathway.

TWO

MERGE OR DIE

Rock Island's problems cannot be postponed. They are here and now and must be dealt with.

—Rock Island board chairman Jervis Langdon Jr., 1964

John Farrington spent his last year as Rock Island president exploring the possibilities of a merger with the Union Pacific Railroad. Following the unexpected and sudden collapse of talks with the Milwaukee Road and the departure of Downing Jenks to the Missouri Pacific, Farrington continued to fulfill the Rock Island board's mandate to find a suitable partner. On January 10, 1961, Farrington wrote A. E. Stoddard, the Union Pacific president, concerning a Standard & Poor's report "regarding the feasibility of a merger." Stoddard replied,

> We have, of course, been aware for some time of the potential which might be derived from UP joining with one or more of several different roads, of which the Rock Island is one, we would desire to consider. However, up to the present we have not thought the timing was right, even if we should eventually decide to proceed in this direction. Our thinking has not progressed to the point where we would want any other road to proceed or fail to proceed with its own plans, based on any assumption as to what we might do in the future.[1]

The Union Pacific had reacted to the postwar merger movement with caution, generally having little interest in crossing its historic eastern terminus at the Missouri River in Omaha, Nebraska. There, the UP exchanged traffic with no fewer than five railroads, including the Rock Island. Its main partner remained the Chicago & North Western (they exchanged traffic at Fremont, Nebraska), and if relations were better between the two, the C&NW seemed the natural fit for a merger to provide UP a gateway into Chicago. But the relationship had soured throughout the 1950s; matters got so bad that in 1955 the UP dropped the C&NW from serving its passenger trains into Chicago and opted instead for the Milwaukee Road as the partner to run its famed *City* streamliners into the Windy City.[2]

In 1960 Robert Lovett, chairman of UP's board of directors, proposed a study to find a suitable merger partner. UP president Stoddard hired the respected firm Wyer, Dick to study the advantages of merger, and in January 1961—around when Farrington contacted the UP about a merger—the report "suggested the Rock Island as the best candidate." William Wyer, however, favored the Chicago, Burlington and Quincy, and meetings were held to that end between executives of the UP and the CB&Q. But the latter was already engaged in merger talks with the Northern Pacific and the Great Northern and postponed any future decision with UP until ICC action on any other merger was completed.[3]

Farrington pressed Stoddard for a decision on a Rock Island–UP merger throughout that spring, but it appeared a lost cause as the UP dallied. Yet the Rock Island continued to pursue the idea, preparing traffic studies and an outline of savings from a hypothetical merger.[4] The UP proposed a separate study of its traffic partners, especially the thirteen railroads that interchanged traffic with the UP at all its eastern connections. That study, by UP vice president of traffic, J. R. MacAnally, revealed that the UP originated more traffic than its connecting lines, allowing the UP board to realize that "other roads needed the Union Pacific far more than the Union Pacific needed them." It also revealed that if the UP reached Chicago and St. Louis, it could exchange traffic with twenty railroads without dependence on the bridgelines between Chicago and Omaha. But only one railroad had lines from connections with the Union Pacific to both cities: the Rock Island.[5]

UP management still hesitated. Its own study of the Rock Island revealed a railroad in need of significant capital, estimated at $147 million for track and other improvements and $118 million for equipment. UP chairman Lovett and general counsel Frank Barnett held a meeting in New York in September 1961 stipulating how the railroad needed access to Chicago and St. Louis and "that the Rock Island best fit these needs." But UP still delayed. UP president Stoddard continued to pursue a merger with another line, favoring the Illinois Central Railroad (IC), which would need far less reconstruction; the UP also controlled 23 percent of that company's stock.[6] Railroad operations officers concurred, with UP's VP of operations Edd Bailey arguing against the acquisition of the Rock Island, with which the UP exchanged only 6 percent of its traffic.[7]

In January 1962, the firm Wyer, Dick released its analysis of MacAnally's traffic study, concurring that the Rock Island was the best line for merger. "It would appear essential," the firm concluded, "that the Rock Island be prevented from falling into other hands and that this road at the same time offers the best opportunity of offsetting the losses which appear likely as a result of mergers with other lines." This sealed it for the UP board, and in March 1962 it authorized meetings with the Rock Island about a merger.[8]

However, the UP sought this merger to remain competitive and to reach new cities like Chicago and St. Louis, whereas the Rock Island desperately needed it to survive. In spite of the improvements that the Rock Island made during the 1950s, by 1960, according to a report prepared for the directors by board member Robert Ingersoll, net operating income had plunged "from $8.9 million (average of years from 1954–1956) to $876,000 in 1960." The Rock Island was experiencing freight-car shortages and was also paying heavily for increased worker compensation, even though employment declined from 22,243 personnel in 1951 to 16,491 in 1960.[9] Working capital was diminishing as well, and the railroad was beginning to defer important maintenance on track and equipment. Yet it still paid dividends on stock—a huge error in judgment: In 1962, it paid $3.7 million in dividends out of dwindling working capital.[10]

In June 1962, Rock Island's board reauthorized discussions relating to mergers with other lines. Henry Crown stated outright: "The Southern Pacific Railroad appears to be interested in the possibility of a merger with this company." The board approved contact and a study if the Southern Pacific was interested. The SP already had its own study under way. The two railroads were already close partners, on the Golden State Route and their historic connection at Santa Rosa, New Mexico. The *Golden State Limited*—the Rock Island's marquee passenger train—ran in cooperation with the SP from Chicago to Los Angeles and fostered a large interchange of freight traffic on the same route. The SP eyed its own route into Kansas City via the Rock Island, as well as access to St. Louis and Chicago. The SP study was completed on August 1, 1962, and revealed that although the physical condition of the Rock Island's line remained in good shape its equipment and cars were not. "The primary objective in acquiring the Rock Island," the report noted, "would be to place the Southern Pacific in a more fully competitive position with the Santa Fe which presently has a one-line control of service and rate adjustments between Chicago and Arizona-California." It was imperative for the SP to secure its own transcontinental line into Chicago—and the Rock Island was the vehicle to achieve this.[11]

SP executives knew that the Union Pacific was interested in the Rock Island, and SP president Donald Russell had informed UP chairman Lovett about SP's interest. UP president Stoddard went ballistic: "Those SOBs are going all over the Rock Island with the idea of buying it!" But UP chairman

Lovett knew that its competitor's interests were in the Golden State Route and the connections at Kansas City with faster service to Chicago; UP's interests were in the northern half and direct entry into Chicago and St. Louis. There was room for compromise, however, and so the rivals began to work out a deal to merge the Rock Island and split its property in half.[12]

Henry Crown took the lead in negotiating on behalf of the Rock Island. After Farrington's death in October 1961, Crown had been trying to bring in someone from the outside as chairman, but the board selected R. Ellis Johnson, a former operations man and current executive vice president, someone with limited experience and knowledge of the financial side.[13] Described alternatively as a "pleasant, soft-spoken executive" or as "a caretaker president, an old-time railroader who liked to cuss a lot," Johnson possessed neither the vision nor the managerial skills to supervise a merger of the size proposed by the UP and SP.[14] Yet Johnson had been groomed for the job by Farrington himself and took the presidency after his death.[15] By default—with holdings in the railroad and business expertise—Crown led the negotiations, with board members Bruce Norris and Robert Ingersoll also playing active roles. Robert Lovett later said, in a compliment to his adversary, "No one can accuse Colonel Crown of not being a good trader. If you check, nobody has taken anything from him without paying for it."[16]

Meetings between representatives of the three railroads began on September 13, 1962, with Crown (Rock Island), Russell (Southern Pacific), and Lovett (Union Pacific) releasing a joint statement to the press.[17] On September 24, 1962, a meeting between UP general counsel Frank Barnett, SP's Ben Biaggini, and Rock Island's vice president for law, Eaton Adams, discussed the SP–UP proposal to split the Rock Island in half, with SP acquiring the southern half of the railroad (about 3,300 miles) and UP acquiring the northern lines (4,000 miles). Coverdale & Colpitts was retained to make an engineering study of the Rock Island property. In November the Rock Island board retained the brokerage firm Glore Forgan to head up negotiations for the exchange ratio of Rock Island stock.[18]

On February 6, 1963, Crown and Bruce Norris met with Russell, Lovett, and E. R. (Roland) Harriman in New York to discuss the merger. Crown reported:

> During the conversation it was brought out that: a) the merger study naturally affects morale of our personnel and such study should not be prolonged; b) it is not the intention of the UP to buy stock control in the Rock Island; c) UP is to be the merging company with the RI; d) UP will conduct separate negotiations between themselves and the SP;

Photo 2.1 The industrialist and investor Henry Crown, Chicago, 1965. Crown was one of the largest stockholders and the largest bondholder of the Rock Island from the late 1940s until the 1975 bankruptcy. Photo courtesy of the collection of H. Roger Grant.

and e) negotiating teams have been selected for the UP and the SP and will be calling on the Rock Island to complete negotiations.[19]

At a meeting between the negotiators on February 25 and 26, 1963, the UP and SP made their presentation. Frank Barnett "assured that no senior officer of the RI would be hurt very badly, financially (in the event of a merger). They started with an offer of 2/3 UP for 1 RI share. Then concluded with 7/10 to 1. This was out of the question." Crown, who did not attend the meeting but was briefed by R. E. Johnson about the specific proposals discussed, stated, "[It's] interesting that they [UP and SP] come up with 7/10 to 1 maximum and we come up with 1 [and] 5/10 minimum." (See Photo 2.1.) Johnson replied, "Think they understand that none of our interests have been buying our stock, particularly in view of our dividend cut, which was a necessity, and done knowing that merger negotiations were pending." On February 26, after discussing the specific details of the Glore Forgan report, including the Rock Island pensions, personnel, and salvage basis of track and equipment—standard discussions in any railroad merger—Johnson asked whether the 7/10–1 stock transfer "was a firm figure and Mr. Barnett said 'pretty firm'—a halfway answer. I told them that I wasn't being pessimistic, but that I was sure 7/10 wouldn't 'get it.'"[20]

Crown was the main problem in the discussions over the stock-exchange ratio. Norris and Ingersoll favored a deal, fearing that UP would walk away if Rock Island didn't accept the terms offered. Crown "had an inflated notion of the value of his railroad" and clung to a figure of 1.5–1.8 for each share of Rock Island common stock.[21] In March, as negotiations intensified, Crown would not budge and insisted that UP finally accept the exchange ratio of 1.5 UP stock for each share of Rock Island stock. Finally, pressured by other directors, he relented, and on May 13 management informed shareholders at the annual Rock Island meeting that the three railroads' managements had come to an agreement concerning a merger:

> Under the plan, Union Pacific and Rock Island will merge through the exchange of .718 of an authorized but unissued common share of Union Pacific for each share of Rock Island. The UP now has 22,429,235 common shares outstanding and Rock Island has 2,916,711 common shares outstanding. . . . Under an agreement between UP and the Southern Pacific, it is contemplated that Rock Island south and southwest of Kansas City will be transferred to the Southern Pacific shortly after consummation of the merger.[22]

None of the railroads speculated about how long it would take to secure ICC approval of the merger; a special stockholder meeting would be held in November 1963 to approve the UP-RI exchange.

Before the ink could dry on the press release, Ben Heineman, CEO of the Chicago & North Western, entered the fray. Heineman was born in 1914 in Wausau, Wisconsin. His father ran a profitable lumber business established by Heineman's German-Jewish grandfather in the 1860s, but the Great Depression hit the father's interests hard and he committed suicide in 1930. Heineman attended the University of Michigan and after his third year persuaded Northwestern University School of Law to admit him without a bachelor's degree. He graduated from Northwestern in 1936 and entered private practice in corporate law in Chicago.

During World War II Heineman, who was blind in one eye, served as assistant general counsel with the Office of Price Administration from 1941 to 1943 and then spent a year abroad working for the State Department. He returned to Chicago, where he opened his own firm with partner Max Swiren and made a name for himself by negotiating an out-of-court settlement with shareholders of the Chicago Great Western Railway (CGW) in a dividend claim against it in 1950. In 1953 he secured appointment to the board of directors of the Minneapolis and St. Louis Railway. In 1954 he became the chairman of the executive committee of that line and attempted to rebuild the property and to merge the M&StL with the Toledo, Peoria and Western Railway (TP&W) and the Chicago, Indianapolis, and Louisville Railroad (Monon) but was opposed by the Santa Fe and the Pennsylvania Railroad, who jointly owned the TP&W. In 1955 Heineman led a group of investors in a fight to control the stock of the Chicago & North Western. Interested in avoiding a proxy fight, Heineman was elected chairman of the board and CEO of the C&NW in February 1956.[23]

The Chicago & North Western system was a 9,400-mile Midwestern railroad stretching from Chicago northwest to Wisconsin and Minnesota as well as directly west of Chicago into Iowa, Nebraska, and South Dakota. With a heavy concentration of branchlines serving small towns and grain elevators in the Midwest, large commuter operations on three separate lines in the Chicago area, and deficits from passenger service as well, the C&NW was teetering on the brink of bankruptcy when Heineman assumed control. But Heineman cut costs, securing the abandonment of unprofitable passenger service and branchlines. He used the cost savings to improve the property, purchasing bilevel passenger cars and developing a new push-pull configuration to more efficiently move commuters in Chicago. Heineman bragged about making money on commuter service, unlike other Chicago railroads. He also built a new car-repair shop at Clinton, Iowa, to centralize all repairs at one facility.[24]

Heineman was interested in mergers as well. In 1960 the ICC approved the C&NW's acquisition of the 1,400-mile Minneapolis & St. Louis, which gave the C&NW access to Peoria, Illinois, and other industrial centers. But employees of the M&StL were not pleased by the acquisition. Many workers on the merged railroad resented the manner in which their railroad was dismantled by the C&NW. For some workers, it felt like a personal assault by Heineman. "There were those who hated [Heineman] so badly that if he had tried to become friendly with the M&StL employees, he might have been dragged out in the weeds and when he returned he would be singing soprano."[25]

Heineman's failure to secure a tripartite merger between the Rock Island–C&NW–Milwaukee Road in 1961 left the C&NW vulnerable when Union Pacific and Rock Island announced their merger in May 1963. The Chicago & North Western exchanged 175,000 cars per year at its Fremont, Nebraska, connection with the UP—by far its largest partner in the Omaha area. If the merger went through, the C&NW would lose this traffic and be harmed beyond repair. Heineman decided on a course of action that came to define merger proceedings for the next decade: He threatened a hostile takeover of the Rock Island.

On June 24, 1963, Heineman made his offer to the Rock Island board "for the purpose of acquiring control of the Rock Island Railroad, through stock ownership, with the intent of effecting promptly thereafter unification through merger or consolidation." The C&NW board had approved Heineman's offer, which consisted of an exchange, for each share of Rock Island common stock, "(1) one 6% Collateral Trust Income Bond in the principal amount of $30, all such bonds to be secured both as to principal and interest by any and all shares of common stock of the Rock Island received in exchange; (2) 0.2778 shares of the common stock of the Northwestern; (3) $5.00 in cash." Heineman argued, "In addition to $14,583,555 in cash, the Rock Island security holders would receive $87,501,330 principle amount of the 6% Collateral Income Bonds and 810,320 shares of Northwestern common stock." The deadline placed by the C&NW for action by the Rock Island board was October 31, 1963.[26]

The C&NW proposal also contained a rationale for the takeover not supportable by any evidence. Perhaps citing the Coverdale & Colpitts report on cost savings emanating from the Rock Island–Milwaukee combination released to the Rock Island board in 1960, Heineman stated "studies we have made over the past year, and again recently, have satisfied us that included among the many public and other benefits resulting from the control and ultimate merger or consolidation of the two railroads, will be direct annual monetary benefits of at least $25 million a year." He then admitted that the C&NW board "has also instructed us to initiate negotiations promptly with representatives of the Milwaukee Railroad, looking toward the inclusion of such railroad in the ultimate unification of the Rock Island and Northwestern." The Rock Island had been down this road already and rejected such a merger possibility. Heineman's conclusion about cost savings were not demonstrated by any evidence or studies released to the Rock Island Board.[27]

An analysis of the C&NW exchange offer was made by Rock Island attorneys, who asked some pertinent questions about the offer:

> Would the Rock Island stockholders be better off with the Bonds secured by their Rock Island stock than by retaining the stock? What would the Common Stock be worth? It would be subordinate to the Northwestern Preferred stock. . . . Through possible dilution, Rock Island stockholders would be reduced to 22% minority position if all stock were exchanged. Isn't Northwestern Common overpriced in the

market due to speculation? No dividends have been paid for 9 years. Profits from land sales and income tax refunds must have some limit. What advantage would Rock Island stockholders derive from Northwestern control? Can the Exchange Offer by a marginal railroad be better than merger with one of the prime railroads of the country?

At the time, C&NW's stock was selling at 25 7/8 compared to UP's 40 7/8 close. Comparing the offer, the attorneys concluded that the tax advantages of the UP offer were far better than the C&NW offer, "which probably accounts for the $5 cash item." Under the C&NW offer the Rock Island stockholders would be taxed on their exchange of C&NW stock whereas the UP offer was nontaxable.[28]

Heineman followed up his proposal with the filing of an application for control of the Rock Island with the ICC on July 6, 1963. The Rock Island board was holding a special meeting on July 11 to consider the C&NW offer. The UP was nervous, especially after comments attributed to Crown appeared in the *Wall Street Journal* stating that "we have every intention of making the Union Pacific and North Western offers available to our shareholders."[29] Robert Lovett wrote the Rock Island board regarding its position on the C&NW offer, telling the board that "the Union Pacific will oppose the Northwestern application with every resource at its command and will file within a few days a petition to intervene in the Northwestern proceeding for that purpose. . . . The Union Pacific will expect the Rock Island to oppose the Northwestern application." Lovett discussed the "misleading nature" of the C&NW offer reiterating the same comments made by Rock Island lawyers on June 26. He focused attention on Moody's ratings of C&NW bonds, which for 1962 rated as Ba and Caa—"bonds of poor standing." Rock Island bonds were rated Baa and its stock was also rated higher by Moody's than comparable issues by the C&NW.[30]

Lovett also fired a warning shot across the bow at Rock Island management:

> It would appear inconceivable, not only to the railroad industry but to general business circles, that the Rock Island Board of Directors could enter into a merger agreement on June 27, 1963, and two weeks thereafter take action which could be regarded as an endorsement of a conflicting proposal or an indication of "neutrality." . . . You have before you a serious question of policy which has far-reaching implications. I am sure that the common efforts and the current relationships between the Union Pacific and the Rock Island will

continue to be based on mutual respect and confidence—whatever the reaction of your Board of Directors may be to what seems to us clearly to be a transparent attempt to obstruct and to confuse the real issues soon to be placed before your shareholders.[31]

The implied threat to the Rock Island board, owing to its obligations to the signed merger agreement, contained the seeds of future tensions between the two railroads and revealed all too clearly who was in charge of the merger.

Lovett need not have worried. "The Rock Island board had been so enthusiastic about a merger with the Union Pacific that they couldn't wait to approve it," as Jervis Langdon, who came to the Rock Island in 1964, said later.[32] Heineman had requested a current list of Rock Island stockholders in a July 1 letter to the Rock Island board in order to send them the North Western offer and allow for due consideration of both proposals. This was summarily rejected by Johnson, who told Heineman, "We do not conceive this to be either a legal obligation or a sound policy for the Rock Island or any other corporation to follow. You make this request not as a stockholder of the Rock Island but as an outside interest purporting to present a question of policy as to whether Rock Island stockholders are to be denied the 'freest and fullest opportunity to determine which of the two merger offers they wish to accept.'"[33]

What followed was a proxy fight organized by Rock Island shareholders led by Chicago attorney Samuel Young. Young was said to represent several hundred Rock Island shareholders who wrote the Rock Island board on July 24 making a request for the transmittal of both the UP and C&NW offers. Johnson replied:

> The Rock Island and a majority of its directors entered into a Plan and Agreement of Merger with the Union Pacific. . . . The North Western's proposed exchange offer is solely between that railroad and the Rock Island's stockholders. The fact that Mr. Heineman purported to make the offer to the directors as well as the stockholders is of no more significance than an offer to buy any other property which the Rock Island doesn't own. If your clients do not wish to await full information, and are already committed to the Northwestern exchange offer, there is, of course, nothing to prevent them from tendering their stock to the Northwestern, if it will accept it.[34]

Johnson consulted the Chicago law firm of Sidley, Austin, Burgess & Smith, which reviewed the Young and Heineman correspondence at the request of Rock Island's general counsel, Eaton Adams. Neither Young nor Heineman had legal standing to request stockholder names or for the separate tender of an offer by the C&NW to the Rock Island's stockholders. "In our opinion North Western has no legal right to inspect the books or obtain a list of Rock Island stockholders if it is not a stockholder of Rock Island, which we understand is a fact." Under Delaware law, which applied in this instance, Young's request to be provided a list of stockholders "for the purpose of communicating with stockholders regarding the proposed merger proposal with the UP and/or a proposal for an exchange of stock by the [C&NW]" was disallowed. Young could inspect the stock ledger, but he could not be provided a list of stockholders under the law.[35]

Young prevailed. Under the less than ideal letterhead name "Chicago, Rock Island and Pacific Railroad Company Stockholders' Committee for North Western's Exchange Offer and Against Rock Island–UP Merger," Young filed a writ of mandamus against the Rock Island in Cook County, Illinois, superior court; it was resolved by allowing the stockholders the right to mail the C&NW exchange offer to stockholders from a list provided by the Rock Island. Eight stockholders formed the committee that followed up their mailing with a letter urging stockholders to reject the UP exchange offer. The C&NW also sent separate letters to stockholders after the solicitation of proxy votes was allowed between October 1 and November 15, 1963.[36]

The Union Pacific took two actions to detour North Western's efforts: It filed a motion to dismiss the C&NW application with the ICC, and it placed a full-page advertisement in Chicago newspapers arguing that the UP merger with the Rock Island "is better for growth, service and the national economy." Heineman immediately charged that the advertisement "contains many false and misleading statements of material fact." "We are informed," Heineman continued, "that this advertisement had not been filed or cleared with the Securities and Exchange Commission [SEC] as the law requires of material for such a purpose, and we intend to make the strongest possible protest to the SEC."[37] On July 29, the SEC ruled in favor of the C&NW.

On July 30, 1963, the Young Committee filed suit in federal district court to secure an injunction against the Rock Island and UP solicitation of proxies through newspaper advertisements. The SEC was rumored to be in support of Young's injunction, even going so far to consider filing an amicus curiae brief in the district court.[38] But the SEC never took that step. On September 13, 1963, Judge Michael Igoe—who probably assumed his days of ruling on the Rock Island were long behind him—ruled that the UP advertisement was not a proxy solicitation and reversed the SEC's order.[39]

The Rock Island solicitation offer, twenty pages in length with the

Coverdale & Colpitts report on savings from a UP merger, went out to the stockholders in early October. R. Ellis Johnson told the proxy voters that "failure to vote will have the same effect as a vote 'against' [merger]."[40] In mid-October the Young Committee sent out its proxy solicitation, calling the proposed merger unfair. Rumors circulated that Heineman and the C&NW were helping the committee and that Young had once been retained by Heineman in C&NW business, adding a conflict of interest to the drama. This pressure worked to slow the responses from Rock Island stockholders. Fearing they would not get close to the required two-thirds approval, Rock Island and UP officers and Henry Crown held a press conference to reassure stockholders that the merger was sound. Part of the concern was a letter from Glore, Forgan (the investment firm hired by Rock Island to help with the stock exchange ratio) reporting that a fairer exchange between stockholders would be 0.9 shares of UP–Rock Island, rather than the 0.718 negotiated in the deal. UP president Stoddard told the reporters that its own engineering studies necessitated an investment of $200 million to bring the track up to UP's standards and an additional $100 million for cars, locomotives, and yards.[41]

Heineman took his fight to brokerage houses on Wall Street, hoping to convince enough brokers—estimated to hold one-third of all Rock Island stock—not to vote for the UP merger on November 15, 1963.[42] He had a weapon: the "progress report" of Hayden, Stone research associate Pierre Bretey concerning the offer to acquire the Rock Island by the C&NW. Bretey argued that the C&NW offer was "far more attractive" than the UP offer. He said that the ICC "is not likely" to approve a Rock Island–UP merger because of the harm such a merger would bring to railroads like the North Western and the Milwaukee Road. Sounding like he received much of his information from C&NW, which he would later be accused of, Bretey argued that the best possible combination would be a three-way merger between Rock Island, the Milwaukee Road, and C&NW. "It is this leverage inherent in either a two-way merger between North Western and Rock Island," he concluded, "or a three-way merger which would include the Milwaukee which lends far greater attraction to the North Western offer as compared to the Union Pacific."[43]

Quickly, the C&NW printed 7,500 copies of the report to distribute to brokerage houses and to stockholders.[44] The Securities and Exchange Commission was prompted to investigate the distribution of the letter after the UP complained it would unfairly influence stockholders. After meeting with Bretey and other Hayden, Stone officials, the SEC recalled the letter, and even though the majority of the reports were never returned the SEC rebuked the firm for failing to secure permission before it was distributed.

Heineman and Crown took their roadshow to Wall Street. On October 24, Crown told a press conference that the C&NW offer was not really an offer at all and it "diverted stockholders' attention from the one and only real issue before the stockholders—merger with the Union Pacific." That same day the ICC allowed public hearings on the C&NW offer. Yet it was Heineman who arguably made the bigger news that week. On October 30, he told the Transportation Securities Club in a Chicago luncheon address that the Rock Island–UP merger would produce the "greatest alliance of railroads ever seen" to prevent it—what turned out to be a remarkably accurate prediction. He also reiterated how the C&NW offer was not only more financially sweet for shareholders but also better for Chicago.[45]

Through the fall, the Rock Island was not idle. Directors were contacting blocks of stockholders to secure support for merger. The most important stockholders remained the Crown and Norris interests, who controlled 15 percent of the stock, with Crown's family and interests holding 138,000 shares and Norris controlling 223,677 shares.[46] The directors were after smaller fish, making calls to individuals with 500 shares or more of stock who had not yet returned voting cards. Many of the stockholders were concerned about Heineman and the C&NW offer. One called Heineman an "in-and-outer who took over the company not to make money by developing the company as such, but by manipulation." Some were stubborn, refusing to sign the offer and holding out. One stockholder who owned 1,000 shares refused entreaties to sign as he was "unhappy because the stock had not gone up as he had expected." Many others were unimpressed by the UP stock-exchange offer and were equally unimpressed that the two major stockholders had helped negotiate the deal. One stockholder contacted by Rock Island attorney Martin Cassell "was a close friend of Ben Heineman's, so the call was short."[47]

The UP worried about the Bretey report and the damage it could do. On the eve of the stockholder meeting, UP went to federal district court in Chicago to secure an injunction preventing it, charging that the C&NW had violated SEC regulations and that the meeting would irreparably harm the UP.[48] Judge Julius Hoffman—who would gain national fame as the judge in the Chicago Seven conspiracy trial resulting from protests at the 1968 Democratic National Convention—granted a temporary restraining order (injunctive relief that was less severe than a full-blown permanent injunction) to block the counting of votes at the stockholder meeting. UP attorneys charged that the Bretey letter did irreparable harm to the effort to secure two-thirds support.[49] Stockholders met the next day but adjourned without any business conducted. The *Chicago Tribune* reported "there were more lawyers at the meeting than stockholders" when Johnson read the restraining order to those in attendance.⁵⁰

The hearings began on November 19 with thirteen lawyers crowding the courtroom, representing the interests of the Rock Island, UP, C&NW, and the Young Committee. UP attorneys requested a court-ordered injunction against the stockholder meeting, citing the Bretey letter. The UP called C&NW vice president Larry Provo to testify as an adverse witness, and Samuel Young was called in the same capacity. On November 22, William Wyer testified against the C&NW utilizing merger studies between the Rock Island and Milwaukee Road as the basis of its acquisition, saying that it "would not form the basis of a reliable estimate" for merger between the two companies.⁵¹

The assassination of President John F. Kennedy delayed the hearings for several days. When they resumed, Frank Barnett, a vice president and general counsel for Union Pacific and summoned as an adverse witness by C&NW, revealed that in the week before the Rock Island shareholder meeting in November the UP had attempted to purchase 300,000 shares of stock at $3 per share from groups of investment banks and New York insurance companies who had not yet committed to the solicitation request for the proxy vote.⁵² Barnett's admission was a crippling one in that the UP believed—as he admitted—that it feared it lacked the votes for a merger. Ben Heineman testified two weeks later that six investment funds, holding more than 200,000 shares of Rock Island stock, had sent their proxies to the Young Committee. Heineman also stated that he had not solicited Bretey for the Hayden, Stone letter and had no personal relationship with Bretey. In the fifteenth and last day of the hearing, it seemed unclear how Judge Hoffman would proceed. In early January the judge heard supplemental oral arguments, essentially encapsulating the arguments made in the hearings the previous year.

On February 18, 1964, Judge Hoffman ruled in favor of UP's request for the permanent injunction, and the stockholder meeting was rescheduled to vote on the merger offer but not on the C&NW exchange. Hoffman's order rested squarely on the SEC's determination that Bretey's "Progress Report" was "misleading, in the circumstances of its use. Whatever its value for other purposes," the court concluded, "it was inappropriate for use in proxy solicitation under the demanding standards of conduct established in the public interest for all sides in such a contest." The court found particularly egregious Bretey's use of data submitted by C&NW. His report was hardly "disinterested," the court stated, and "whether the prediction is the product of an intention to mislead or of innocent over-enthusiasm, the misleading effect upon the public is the same."⁵³

The court order approving UP's request for injunction was a hollow victory. Heineman had won the first round, as the public relations and press the C&NW received was far more positive, especially in the Chicago media. It also forced UP back to the bargaining table with Rock Island. Their offer was not sweet enough, but as UP officials realized, it would cost an estimated $200 million to rebuild the property and both UP and Southern Pacific officials were beginning to wonder about whether the property was worth it. Ben Biaggini of Southern Pacific said it best: The Rock Island and C&NW were "two broken-down properties trying to whipsaw us into paying more than the property was worth."[54] Biaggini stated that SP would pay no more than $95 million for its half of the system, with UP countering with $130 million. No final decision was made about the cost to SP.

A meeting in Chicago between Crown, Frank Barnett, and the railroads' attorneys on the same day as Hoffman's decision led to a commitment by Barnett to raise the Union Pacific's stock offer. But at a meeting on February 25 at Brown Brothers Harriman & Co. in New York, Robert Lovett unequivocally refused to increase the offer, telling Crown that "if Rock Island was dissatisfied with the present merger agreement, UP would gladly agree to its termination by Rock Island." The merger appeared dead, with Barnett telling Rock Island's management and attorneys on April 1 that UP could not raise its offer. On April 24, Leslie Hodson, a partner for the Chicago law firm Kirkland, Ellis, Hodson, Chaffetz & Masters, who the Rock Island had retained the previous year, telephoned Barnett and informed him there would be a special meeting of the Rock Island board of directors on April 28, "at which time Mr. Hodson would recommend that the Rock Island accept Mr. Lovett's offer to Col. Crown that the Plan and Agreement of Merger be terminated. Barnett replied that Mr. Lovett had no authority to make such an offer; it could be made only by UP's Executive Committee."[55]

Whether or not Hodson's phone call was a bluff, it worked. On Monday, April 27, Hodson received a phone call from Barnett inviting him to meet in New York. The next day, Barnett informed Hodson that the exchange offer would be increased. Before that occurred, however, Ben Heineman contacted the Rock Island to discuss a possible Rock Island–North Western merger with a meeting held on May 11 between Heineman, Larry Provo, and Rock Island directors and executives. "Mr. Heineman was informed that any North Western offer would be carefully considered," but no proposal ever arrived. Within a week the Rock Island received a new stock-exchange offer from UP.

Rock Island shareholders were offered the right to deposit their shares with UP, for which they would receive deposit certificates. Upon approval of the merger, shareholders would exchange deposit certificates for one share of new preferred voting stock, valued at a $1.80 dividend, which would then be convertible at UP's option at 0.85 per share. When one-third of all shares were exchanged, UP would gain effective control over the Rock Island; when two-thirds were exchanged, the merger could go forward. Henry Crown expected stockholders to accept the deal. It was complicated, but the Rock Island Board approved the new offer on May 26, which one spokesman called "much better" than the previous arrangement.[56] Probably the most astute comment came from an unattributed source, who said that "Rock Island shareholders owe Ben Heineman a vote of thanks. If the North Western had not made its offer for the Rock Island, the original exchange offer probably would have been approved."[57]

Yet a huge question remained on the table: Would Heineman go away? The C&NW was negotiating to merge with the Chicago Great Western Railway and had reopened talks with the Milwaukee Road. But Heineman still had eyes for the Rock Island, particularly as the battle switched from the federal courthouse to the ICC. "The North Western is very much in the running in the battle for the Rock Island, and we cannot see anything but ultimate success," Heineman told the *Chicago Tribune*. "Eight months or a year can change a lot of conditions. I don't believe this fight over the Rock Island will be resolved in less than five years, and who can tell where we will be five years from now?"[58] Heineman again showed remarkable prescience in describing the coming fight over the Rock Island merger. At the end of June the C&NW sold 214,000 shares of Rock Island common, earning $6.2 million from the sale, which was added to the railroad's working capital, necessary to complete the merger with the Chicago Great Western. But it still planned to push for victory over the Union Pacific at the ICC.

After several other adjustments—including the reimbursement to Rock Island of all associated expenses "excluding officers' compensation and attorney fees"—UP executed the merger agreement and transmitted it to Rock Island's stockholders. Then on September 1, 1964, UP submitted the agreement to the ICC.[59] Unlike the previous year, Rock Island's stockholders gave the proposed merger majority support. In response, C&NW's gambit was to solicit RI stockholders with a brochure showing the problems inherent in any UP–Rock Island merger. Additionally five railroads submitted statements in opposition to the merger, which would transform traffic and operations throughout the western United States. The C&NW brochure also detailed price uncertainty over the sale of lines to Southern Pacific.[60] This time, however, C&NW's entreaties fell on deaf ears. Rock Island shareholders voted

Photo 2.2 Rock Island Executive Vice President Eaton Adams, left, conferring with R. E. Johnson, Rock Island's president, at the November 15, 1963, shareholders meeting to vote on the proposed Union Pacific–Rock Island merger. UPI Telephoto. Used with permission of UPI.

on January 7, 1965, and after three days counting votes more than 90 percent approved the new terms.[61] (See Photo 2.2.)

As lawyers and judges increasingly determined the fate of the Rock Island, the company continued the struggle to remain competitive. A memorandum from the operating department to president R. E. Johnson in October 1963 offered numerous suggestions for improvement, including an emphasis on "profitable traffic" and greater cooperation among three important departments of the railroad: Traffic, Accounting, and Operations. But at the same time, the memo outlined some of the crucial problems. As of December 31, 1962, Rock Island owned 26,319 cars, a decline of 6,500 from a decade earlier. The number of cars with bad orders and in need of heavy repairs tallied 2,763. Rock Island depended heavily on railcar leases, especially the more expensive covered hopper cars (for moving grain), refrigerated cars, and flatcars (all more expensive than boxcars). Whenever the cars ventured off Rock Island tracks in exchange with other outside cars, the per-diem costs to the

Rock Island were not recouped. "In most instances we do not own cars of these types to offset mileage paid out on cars of other ownerships."[62]

During the early 1960s the Rock Island aggressively courted and advertised industrial development along its lines, including the distribution of full-page advertisements in magazines discussing the advantages of developing businesses along the railroad's lines. "Through use of dramatic simulated aerial photographs of particular cities and surrounding countryside, the advertisements have . . . attracted an impressive number of inquiries from industry executives."[63] Although this helped in establishing the location of hundreds of new industries, and the expansion of hundreds more, in Rock Island territory throughout the 1960s, the railroad never published details concerning the number of carloads hauled as a result.

The Rock Island board had determined that the company needed new leadership to steer the merger through the next phase: ICC approval. For two years Henry Crown had been attempting to secure an experienced railroad executive to lead the railroad. As he stated at the board meeting on October 8, 1964, "As the members knew, for two years they had been seeking someone to head the Company, and about two weeks ago he learned that Jervis Langdon, Jr. . . . might be available for that position."[64] Crown never liked Johnson and thought Langdon would be the type of leader the railroad needed. As Crown stated, "We brought Langdon in because Rock Island had been managed badly."[65] Johnson would remain as president until 1965, when Jervis Langdon Jr. assumed that role and Johnson became vice president.

Langdon was a "visionary railroader," as biographer H. Roger Grant described him. Born in Elmira, New York, in 1905, Jervis was the product of a well-respected, upper-middle-class family who had achieved success due to the hard work and ambition of his namesake great-grandfather. His ancestor had developed several coalfields in the anthracite regions of northwestern Pennsylvania, forming J. Langdon & Company in the 1870s in partnership with his sons. The company did well and the Langdons lived in a comfortable home in Elmira, also purchasing a nearby property named Quarry Farm. (One of Jervis's daughters married writer Samuel Clemens, who wrote *Huckleberry Finn*, *The Adventures of Tom Sawyer*, and other works while ensconced in a writing shed near the home at Quarry Farm.)

The Langdons prospered and possessed a civic-mindedness representative of protestant Yankee capitalists. They were abolitionist and Republican, and famous guests—including Henry Beecher, Ulysses Grant, and Roscoe Conkling—frequented their home. Jervis Sr. worked for J. Langdon & Company, branching out to secure coal for the Lackawanna Railroad and vari-

Photo 2.3 Jervis Langdon, the doctor of sick railroads—and Rock Island's new president—in Chicago, 1965. Langdon was brought over to the Rock Island from the Baltimore & Ohio. Photo courtesy of the collection of H. Roger Grant.

ous companies created by his father, including the Chemung Coal Company. At Cornell University he trained in engineering and continued the civic-mindedness of his ancestors. His son, Jervis Langdon Jr., was born in 1905.

Langdon Jr. was formally educated, prepping at the Hill School in Pottstown, Pennsylvania, before Cornell, where he studied engineering. After graduating he secured a clerk's position on the Lehigh Valley Railroad, then pursued a law degree at Cornell after his marriage to Jean Gordon Bancroft in 1931. In 1934 he joined the New York Central's law department and specialized in rate cases and regulatory issues. From there he joined the Chesapeake and Ohio Railroad (C&O) as an attorney. During this time Langdon learned to fly airplanes, a skill he never relinquished, and during World War II he enlisted in the U.S. Army Air Corps and was sent to the China–Burma–India theater, where he flew dangerous missions over the Himalayan Mountains (the Hump) to provide aid to Chiang Kai-shek at Chonqqing and helped with logistics at American bases in India. He was promoted to colonel, eventually returning to railroad work at the C&O in 1946.

From there he rose quickly. He was appointed special counsel for the Association of Southeastern Railroads and became its chairman in 1953. In 1956 he became general counsel of the Baltimore and Ohio (B&O), was named vice president in 1958, and then president in 1961. He helped secure the integration of the B&O into the C&O system, which occurred in 1962. Much of the same expectations drove Crown to seek Langdon to head up the Rock Island, and the board believed that Langdon and Johnson would work effectively to reform the Rock Island and to secure the UP merger.[66]

The merger was a necessity for the Rock Island's very survival as an operating railroad. A memorandum to this effect was prepared by its Law Department in May 1964 by Martin Cassell. Cassell argued that "the Rock Island finds itself in competition with major lines of greater wealth who either presently or prospectively favor other connections." In the Southwest the key competition was the Santa Fe, which had its own single route from Chicago to Los Angeles. In the central region, Cassell argued, "if all matters were to be left in status quo, the Rock Island, while not in a favored position, would not be at a substantial disadvantage." In the north region, the pending merger of the Burlington Route, Great Northern, and Northern Pacific "posed an insurmountable, competitive disadvantage for the Rock Island." "Not only is the Rock Island feeling the competitive pinch of these lines with greater geographic advantage, but this geographic advantage is expressed in many instances in the form of a diversion of traffic heretofore enjoyed by the Rock Island." "The accumulative effect of these reorganizations is such that the Rock Island must react defensively by a realignment of its own."[67]

Cassell was developing the strategy for the next requirement for the merger: ICC approval. He was laying out Rock Island's defensive strategy (i.e., other mergers were ongoing, all of them threatening Rock Island's traffic numbers). In fulfillment of the objectives laid out in the Transportation Act of 1920, which gave the ICC power to complete a rationalization of railroad lines, the Rock Island was moving to assure its own future in the western territory. But other railroads were on the move as well; while the C&NW proved to be the Rock Island's nemesis in battling against the merger with its own stockholders, four other railroads (the Frisco, the Denver and Rio Grande Western, the Milwaukee Road, and MoPac) were poised to file intervenor petitions with the ICC against the merger. "The merger of the Union Pacific and the Rock Island could result in a diversion of important revenue producing traffic away from the Frisco," Frisco president Louis Menk told the ICC.[68]

Much was at stake in the Rock Island–UP merger. It included geographic and traffic advantages, as Cassell importantly noted and Menk reaffirmed. It also touched on the competitive landscape of the western railroad system. Nobody knew it then—least of all the new chairman of the Rock Island, Jervis Langdon Jr., who sought, and expected, a quick merger from the ICC—but the Rock Island–Union Pacific merger was about to enter a long delay. This helped to destroy the Rock Island as a corporate entity. But it also helped reconstruct the relationship between the railroad industry and the federal government.

THREE

BLEAK HOUSE

> Jarndyce and Jarndyce drones on. This scarecrow of a suit has, in time, become so complicated, that no man alive knows what it means.
> —Charles Dickens, *Bleak House* (1853)

In September 1968, Daniel Hardin, a member of the Interstate Commerce Commission, wrote Senator Everett Dirksen of Illinois about the prolonged Rock Island hearings. Dirksen, prompted to write after receiving a letter from Jervis Langdon, was concerned that the Rock Island might not survive lengthy delays. Hardin told the senator that "the hearings were closed on August 22, 1968." With some pride, he explained that "the record consists of some 48,000 pages of testimony and about 1,375 exhibits, the latter in the aggregate number of pages being several times that of the testimony." "The great scope and importance of transportation services have placed before the Commission the most complex and largest rail unification ever to have been presented for its consideration," Hardin argued. "With but several exceptions, every class I rail carrier operating west of the Mississippi River is an active participant in the proceedings." He could offer Dirksen and the Rock Island nothing further about when a decision would be reached in the case, shifting blame to the rail carriers and their inability to come to a consensus on the merger.[1]

The institutional and statutory role of the ICC to protect the public interest placed the agency at odds with railroads throughout its history.[2] When the ICC was created in 1887, the railroad industry had a monopoly on transportation. There was a need to have a body to help organize the chaotic rate structure existing at the time even as the commission did not see its role "as a creator of rates but as a controller of rates."[3] The ICC replaced the self-created and self-regulated pool arrangements in which private railroads secured the rates in a given territory in order to control competition. Pools were often anarchic, and railroads willingly shed them in favor of some system of regulation.[4] The ICC also replaced a system of state regulations, dubbed granger laws, passed in Midwestern state legislatures by antimonopolist politicians lobbied by the National Grange movement. However, the U.S. Supreme Court declared the state laws unconstitutional in *Wabash Railroad v. Illinois* (1886). The "battle between antimonopolists . . . and railroad managers," historian Richard White wrote, "resulted in a fragile truce whose fruit was the Interstate Commerce Commission."[5]

The new law was vague about some of the ICC's powers, a result of the act being a melding between quite different House and Senate bills. It created the Interstate Commerce Commission with five members appointed by the president to six-year terms; the two political parties had equal representation, and the commissioners received a substantial salary for the time, at $7,500 per year. Its most important impact was the model for later regulatory agencies in Washington.[6] It banned pooling and allowed the commission to end discrimination in rates between short and long hauls, and it also empowered the ICC to decide on rates that were "fair and reasonable." Yet most of the regulatory authority remained vested in the railroads, and they continued to implement their own rules on rates.[7] Railroads used their political leverage to challenge any reforms that would strengthen the power of regulation. Part of the problem was that the ICC was unsure whether its function was legislative, judicial, or executive; when it acted as a judge, the railroads took the commission to court, and judges in the late nineteenth century saw their role to preserve and to protect the rights of property and laissez-faire capitalism.[8]

The reform impulse and the demand for strengthened railroad regulation grew out of major corporate consolidations at the end of the century, a movement that seemed to necessitate, in the progressive reform impulse growing within the Republican Party at the time, a strengthened ICC. The Elkins Act (1903) ended rebates to large shippers by mandating published tariff rates and holding executives accountable to those tariff schedules. The Hepburn Act (1906) went further, giving the ICC power to set maximum rates, expanding the commission's sole authority in rate decisions governing railroads.[9] The Mann-Elkins Act (1910) added a short-lived Commerce Court and took the Hepburn Act a step further by placing the burden of proof on railroads to show the ICC why they needed a rate increase. The latter two acts greatly expanded the regulatory functions of the commission and its power to adjudicate "fair and reasonable rates."[10]

The growing regulatory intrusion of the ICC during this era set in motion the long decline of the nation's railroads. Railroads were not allowed to innovate, did not control their own price system, and, through federalization of railroads during World War I, were operated by a government agency under private managerial control. In the Transportation Act of 1920, railroads were freed from government control, but the ICC now established the power to set minimum rates. Given the task of valuating the worth of railroad securities and investments and reorganizing the nation's railroads into a coherent and rational structure, with stronger roads redistributing profits to weaker roads (or absorbing them), the ICC was granted too much bureaucratic power and failed to do its job properly. "The Commission lacked economic wisdom," historian Albro Martin wrote. Commissioners were often incapable of grasping the wider economic significance of their statutory authority. "The ICC insisted on seeing itself as a tribunal for adjudicating individual rates in respect to their reasonableness." But they were never able to define what "reasonable" meant, and as long as they did not, their authority was cumbersome and a hindrance to profitability and competitiveness within the railroad industry.[11]

This was never more true than during the post–World War II era when railroad profits sagged and competition with airplanes and highways removed passengers and freight from the rails. Interstate trucking was regulated by the ICC through the Motor Carrier Act of 1935, and water transportation was added to the ICC's authority in the Transportation Act of 1940, but the majority of trucks remained outside regulation and the highways on which trucks traveled and the waterways on which barges operated were subsidized entirely by the government.[12] The railroad industry after the peak traffic years of World War II no longer possessed a monopoly on freight and passenger traffic; in fact the continuing decline of both rail freight and passenger traffic should have yielded some consensus on moving away from the heavy hand of government regulation.[13] Yet the commission clung to outdated regulatory authority, stymieing railroad management from dealing constructively with new competitive forces and new agents of government-subsidized transportation such as airlines, trucks, and automobiles. Railroad management consistently complained that the ICC favored shippers' interests and prolonged decisions having to do with track abandonments, ending passenger train service, and rate increases. The ICC responded that it was serving many diverse transportation interests and did not favor one type over another.[14]

ICC Commissioner Robert Murphy was one of many of the commissioners who argued the agency's position in the postwar era. "[Regulation] does not mean control of the carriers by the Commission, just as it does not signify that the Commission may generally and without limitation restrict the carriers under its jurisdiction. . . . Such [statutory] authority as [the ICC] has is not only limited in nature but from the beginning has been directed primarily toward protecting the public from unlawful discriminatory practices by the carriers."[15] "There are those who have asserted that all of the problems of the railroad industry can be traced to the doorstep of that building at 12th and Constitution Avenue in Washington," ICC Commissioner Paul Tierney told a trade group in October 1964. "As you know, the Internal Revenue Service is also located at [the same building]," he joked. Tierney called for a balance between "our regulatory scheme, what degree of control can be imposed which at the same time will leave carriers sufficiently unencumbered to exercise the initiative, vision and imagination so necessary for a progressive transportation system."[16]

The ICC had taken a very proactive and forthright approach on mergers, allowing for the consolidation of redundant rail lines and seeking to rationalize the railroad system as the agency was given the task to do so under the Transportation Act of 1920.[17] "The Commission is not unaware of what have been the principal deterrents to economic rail operations—excess capacity and duplication," Tierney said. "I do not think that it would be apt to describe the Commission's policy respecting mergers as one which is unduly hampering management's attempt to alleviate this problem."[18]

The ICC certainly did not *seem* an impediment to railroad mergers. Of the major mergers proposed in the 1960s, only the Rock Island–Union Pacific merger faltered, and it was eventually approved (albeit with massive conditions). However, its approval after eleven years came too late to help the Rock Island survive as a corporation. Megamergers like the combination of the New York Central System and the Pennsylvania Railroad into the Penn Central Transportation Company in 1968, and the merger of the Northern Pacific Railroad, the Great Northern Railway, and the Chicago, Burlington and Quincy Railroad into Burlington Northern Railroad in 1970, never caused the consternation and uproar as the Rock Island–UP merger. This was the case even though such mergers proved detrimental to traffic on several railroads and, in the case of the Penn Central, involved complicated and, in the end, deleterious financial questions resulting in the new line's bankruptcy two years after the merger was effected.[19] Dozens of other mergers also proceeded through the ICC during the years in which the Rock Island case was under consideration. Why did the Rock Island case stall? What made it such a controversial decision?

It was difficult for the ICC to find consensus in the Rock Island–Union Pacific merger proceedings. And it proved especially difficult as well for the ICC to effectuate a neutral position in a merger fraught with possibilities for remaking the western railroad map. The rationale for the merger was crystal-clear to the merging railroads. The Rock Island needed the merger in order to survive as an operating railroad. The Union Pacific needed single-

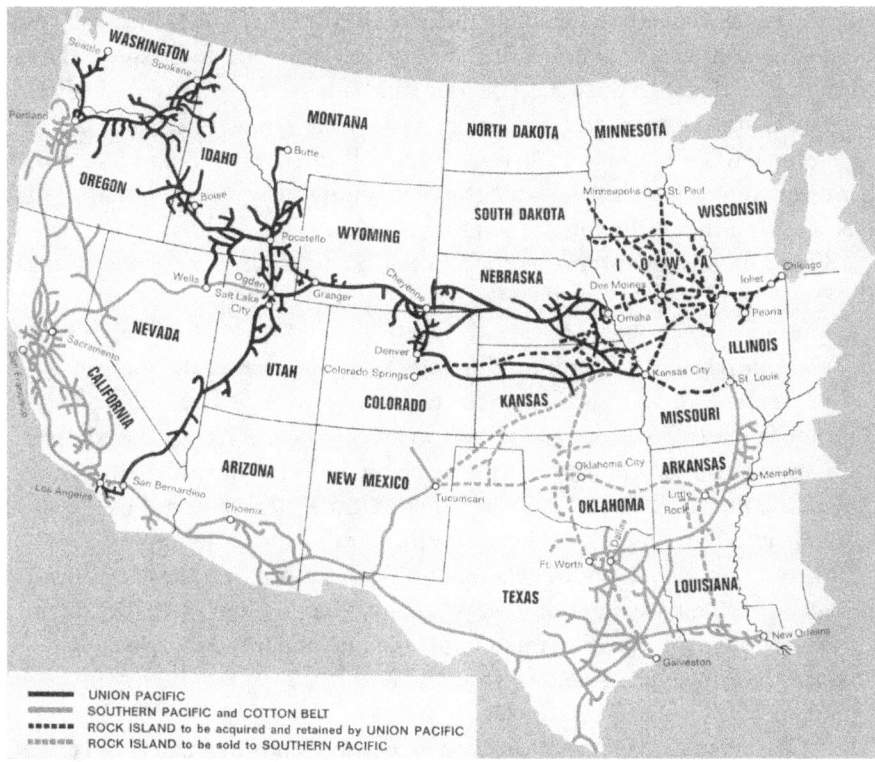

Map 3.1 Map of the proposed merger, showing Rock Island lines to be transferred to the Union Pacific and the Southern Pacific. Photo in author's collection.

line service from its eastern terminus at the Missouri River to Chicago. Pending mergers in the West, including the Burlington Northern, Chicago & North Western, Chicago Great Western, and Milwaukee Road, and Missouri Pacific and Chicago and Eastern Illinois, would provide single-line service to three new large railroads. If the UP merger with Rock Island did not occur, the UP would be in a dire competitive situation.[20]

The ICC faced a huge problem. Five railroads immediately filed interventions in the merger as soon as the Rock Island and UP filed for merger with the ICC on September 1, 1964 (see Map 3.1, depicting the proposed merger; eventually eleven railroads would intervene in the case). The C&NW was already an intervenor in the case, filing its intention to take over the Rock Island in August 1963. That financial docket remained open, known as the C&NW control application (Finance Docket 23286). In February 1966, the Rock Island and UP submitted exhibits and testimony to the ICC, and the hearings were to begin in Chicago on March 7, 1966. But they were delayed as four other railroads filed motions to intervene and requested time to submit evidence to the ICC. The four railroads were the Milwaukee Road, the Atchison, Topeka and Santa Fe (ATSF), the Denver and Rio Grande Western (DRGW), and the Missouri Pacific Railroad. Each had its reasons for opposing the merger and for the new competitive balance that would emerge from the reshaping of the railroad map.

One unnamed western railroad executive told the *Wall Street Journal* that

> since nearly every US railroad is somehow involved in the merger movement, most of us, unfortunately, find ourselves in a dual role before the ICC—as an advocate and an opponent. We're all asking the commission to bless our merger as being good for the railroad and the public interest but to damn the other fellow's plans because we'd get hurt and the public would suffer. I think this kind of scrapping hurts the merger movement in general and what's more I think we all know it. But I don't see any other way out. Just imagine me going before my shareholders and telling them I approve of something that would obviously cost us some business.[21]

The Milwaukee Road entered the case as an intervenor in August 1965. Milwaukee President William J. Quinn told the press that "it is impossible to imagine any combination of railroads that would be destructive of fundamental transportation service. The merger would impair the Milwaukee's ability to render service anywhere." Instead, Quinn called for a three-way merger between the Rock Island, C&NW, and Milwaukee Road.[22] Langdon "was sorry to see the Milwaukee Road take this action, since the Rock Island certainly supports the principle—that of sound railroad mergers—that led the Milwaukee to conclude its own merger agreement with the Chicago and North Western Railway. And we would hope that other lines could proceed with their own merger plans and we with ours without a long and bitter fight."[23]

In October Ben Heineman again proposed a stock buyout of the UP certificates of deposit (CDs) that Rock Island shareholders had subscribed to the previous year. Edd Bailey, UP's president, said that the offer "is a last ditch effort to confuse the Rock Island stockholders, the public and the market." But it appeared intriguing to analysts who understood Heineman's motivation was to get the ICC to think about the rival C&NW proposal when hearings began.[24] The Santa Fe also took preemptive action against the merger, with Santa Fe president William Marsh joining Heineman to announce a sale of the southern lines of the Rock Island to the Santa Fe for $100 million should the C&NW win control of the Rock Island. "We are convinced that North Western control of Rock Island, coupled with sale to Santa Fe of certain Rock Island lines . . . would be the best assurance to the public that adequate, efficient, and competitive rail transportation would be preserved," Marsh told the press.[25]

The railroads distributed lengthy pamphlets both defending and attacking the proposed merger. The C&NW released a thirty-page fact book and other pamphlets in January 1966 arguing against the merger, foreshadowing arguments North Western executives would make in hearings before the ICC. It referred to the UP acquisition of the Rock Island as a "menace" and reminded stockholders that mergers would have to be judged on their merits as to whether they were in the public interest. The UP would be allowed to enter Midwestern territory, resulting in a "potential diversion of almost a quarter billion dollars annually in revenues from railroads with which Union Pacific and Rock Island are at present interchanging freight."[26]

The Missouri Pacific Railroad pamphlet focused on how its lines had been substantially rebuilt following its lengthy reorganization and how the merger posed a serious threat to its continued operations. Downing Jenks argued that "the merger would amount to a sharp cut in competition, and the building of a monopoly position by railroad giants already dominating much of the economy and traffic to and from the west." Hyperbolically, Jenks concluded that "soundly conceived mergers that will strengthen the nation's transportation system are necessary. But one such as this, which would weaken other railroads and diminish their ability to maintain present services, reduce or eliminate competition, seriously harm communities, reduce railroad employment, and bring possible abandonments, would have the opposite effect."[27]

The opposition to the merger was the last thing the Rock Island needed. By the end of 1965 there were reports in the press that several Rock Island boardmembers wondered if the merger would ever occur. One stated "if the ICC approves the issuance of certificates of deposit by the North Western for Union Pacific certificates, I wouldn't be a bit surprised if a majority of Rock Island holders accepted the North Western offer. . . . Our principal positive answer to the ICC is that 92 percent of the Rock Island stockholders favor the merger."[28] The Rock Island, UP, and SP were also forced to sell the merger to the public, releasing their own glossy booklet focusing on three propositions behind the merger: improved rail service for the nation; new capital to fund major improvements in Rock Island facilities; and the strengthening of the economy through healthy competition. The railroads made the case for a strengthened competitive rail system, showing data on how trucks, barges, and airlines had taken over markets from weaker railroads. "A Union Pacific–Rock Island merger would help to strengthen both roads against these growing rivals."[29] The two railroads said nothing about opposition to their merger, focusing instead on soliciting assistance from shippers, and Rock Island communities, as part of their strategy.

Railroad mergers are acts of corporate diplomacy comparable to the relations between nations. When a nation acts aggressively, neighboring nations have two choices: to jump on the bandwagon with the aggressor, or to seek alliances to balance against the aggressive nation. In the case of the Rock Island merger, the rival railroads allied against the UP in order to squelch the merger, seeing the merger as a threat to their own interests and operating territory.[30] The UP failed to reach any consensus between the rival roads—it was the merger as proposed or nothing. The Rock Island was more amenable to a settlement among the roads. Jervis Langdon was the Neville Chamberlain of the merger proceedings, willing to appease the opposition in order to prevent his railroad's destruction. During his five-year tenure as chairman and president of the Rock Island, Langdon proved willing to engage in diplomacy with rivals whereas the UP did not.

The Rock Island was in critical financial trouble by the time the merger was finally approved by UP stockholders in early 1965. That year, the railroad suffered its first loss—$1.4 million—since the reorganization in 1948. Its operating revenues for 1965 were $210 million against expenses of $174 million, producing a high expense-to-revenue ratio of 82.94 for the year.[31] Working capital had sunk to $6 million and would continue to decline. While Langdon was optimistic about the prospects for the following year, he told stockholders that two factors would hurt the railroad if it continued to operate independent of a more powerful system like the UP: its deferred maintenance and equipment needs, which Langdon attributed to be around $237 million; and its operating territory, which was crowded with competing carriers who served 23 percent to 27 percent of the national economy.

Langdon began to take action to address the losses. He brought on board a new senior vice president of operations, G. W. Kelly, from the Southern Pacific, where he had been general manager of that road's Texas and Louisiana lines. A bulldog of a man who would be dead from a massive heart attack within three years, the cigar-chomping Kelly sought to reorient the Rock Island's antiquated operating practices and was responsible for maintenance and operations over the entire system.[32] He added fast freights, improving speeds of freight trains on vital routes and bypassing congested yards en route. The railroad invested in data processing and computer equipment to more efficiently track cars and equipment, and there was a consolidation of heavy-equipment repair shops in Kansas City, Kansas, in El Reno, Oklahoma, and in Little Rock.[33]

In order to build markets and to ensure seamless operations, the Rock Island needed to acquire more freight cars and modern locomotive power. Langdon told UP president Edd Bailey that "we are presently at the lowest point in regard to serviceable freight cars that we have been since the reorganization of the Company in 1948. . . . During the last three months at least, we have been losing literally hundreds of car [loads] a day because of shortage of equipment." Langdon also told Bailey "we are seriously short of power, and during March [1965] when there was some restoration of a normal traffic level following the reopening of the ports of Houston and Galveston [following a dock strike], we were forced to rent power from other railroads. . . . In this connection, the Union Pacific gave us some valuable help."[34]

But he worried what the UP's reaction would be if the Rock Island was forced by financial circumstances to take action outside the "ordinary course of business." In the merger agreement, the Rock Island had agreed to what Langdon called a "nebulous concept, impossible of precise definition" that the railroad could take action on transactions "outside the ordinary course of business" without approval of the UP. He wrote UP general counsel Frank Barnett in May 1965 about this very idea, explaining "our problem is to make ends meet and do the best we possibly can until the merger with the Union Pacific is consummated." Langdon sought UP's understanding of "ordinary" in this context, as well as what the UP would do to help the Rock Island be in the "best possible shape" when the merger finally was approved by the ICC.[35]

The concern was well justified, as the financial situation of the railroad, and therefore its operational capacity, continued to decay. Vice president for finance Paul Major, who testified before the ICC hearings in August 1966, had prepared much of his testimony with the assistance of Langdon the previous year, basing its long-term analysis on data from 1948–1964. The most precarious problem was the decline of the railroad's working capital, from $56 million in 1948 to $9 million in 1964 (84 percent). Much of the shrinkage came in 1948 when the Rock Island retired $37 million in long-term debt, but it was eroding steadily without the onetime write off. Working capital is current assets, including accounts receivable and liabilities. Its decline leaves businesses with less cash on hand to pay bills, payroll, and current liabilities. Shortages of working capital, as Major explained, makes financing new purchases of equipment very difficult, leaving the Rock Island little choice but to raise more working capital through the issuance of long-term mortgage bonds. One such issue in 1958 of first mortgage Series "C" bonds raised $16 million in working capital, but this was spent, and by 1964 working capital "was less than one-third of its working capital at the end of 1958."[36]

The situation was a classic catch-22. The decline in railroad income led to a decline in working capital, necessitating more borrowing to pay for improvements in the property and in equipment. However, improvements funded by long-term debt obligations led to an increase in income being used for debt payments. If income was stagnant, then interest on debt increasingly took more of the income from working capital. Major continued: "With the deterioration of Rock Island's earnings the Moody rating of these bonds dropped in March 1965 from Baa to Ba, which means they are judged to 'have speculative elements; their future cannot be considered as well assured.'" "The basic problem confronting the Rock Island," Major stated, "is the intensifying squeeze being exerted by relatively static revenues and mounting expenses. The result of these adverse trends has been declining net income and a precarious working capital position."[37]

How and why did the Rock Island fall so far and so fast? Langdon explained it well in his testimony before the ICC hearings in 1966 and 1967. There were too many railroads operating in the Midwestern states where the Rock Island operated; it was too dependent on the vagaries of agricultural commodities; and it competed intensively for interline business at key points with substantially better and higher-revenue railroads. In only one of the thirteen states where the Rock Island ran (Kansas), Langdon testified, did the line lead in revenue. In every other state it was near the bottom. If revenues continued to lag behind competitors' roads, there was little the Rock Island could do to improve and rebuild the property. "Rock Island's ability to go it alone is thus subject to serious question."[38]

The merger was also subject to an interminable delay on the part of government officials. On January 20, 1966, the Justice Department called for the ICC to "make special traffic studies of the entire western railroad picture before the commission hears testimony in the merger and control applications." Worried "that many of the railroads involved . . . are engaged in a desperate scramble for merger positions which take little or no account of the public interest," Justice lawyers asked the ICC for a delay.[39] The ICC did not allow a full traffic study of all western railroads, but it did allow a delay for opposition railroads to prepare testimony and evidence in the case. The two-month delay—the hearings opened on May 4—was not costly, but it was a sign of things to come. Langdon began to despair and predicted a lengthy case and years before a decision was reached.

The ICC also rejected a UP proposal to force the C&NW not to offer certificates of deposit to stockholders who had already accepted the UP's offer. The ICC had decided this in December 1965, but the UP appealed, and on March 7, 1966, the ICC noted that any Rock Island shareholder "should be free to avail himself of the benefit of either or both offers . . . and to obligate himself accordingly." The certificates were mailed to shareholders two weeks later. The offer was contingent on 51 percent of shareholders accepting by May 18, at which time the C&NW "becomes irrevocably committed to the terms of its offer." If shareholders subscribed, the UP certificates would be listed on the New York Stock Exchange as Series A and Rock Island common stock as Series B. The C&NW offer was taxable, whereas the UP's offer was not.[40]

The railroads continued to position themselves to the public in the eight weeks before the merger. UP officials Edd Bailey, Frank Barnett, and Robert Lovett gave an interview to *Chicago Tribune* reporter Louis Dombrowski describing their intentions for the merger and countering claims made by Heineman that the diversion of traffic from the C&NW would effectively destroy competition in the western territory. Heineman claimed that the loss of traffic to other railroads in the UP–Rock Island merger would be $229 million, which Lovett called "a fantastic assumption," and that the loss to all railroads would be no greater than $20 million, with C&NW's portion being about $1.6 million. Frank Barnett said "the North Western wants a series of regional railroad monopolies—isolated fiefdoms. If the North Western is permitted to acquire the Rock Island as well as the Chicago Great Western and the Milwaukee Road, it will control four of the six lines between Chicago and Omaha." Stating that service would be markedly improved by single-line, end-to-end service from a UP–Rock Island combination, the executives said only the UP had the financial strength to rescue the Rock Island and to improve competition. A merger of the C&NW and Rock Island would create two weak properties, not one strong one, the UP executives concluded.[41]

The hearings finally opened on May 4, 1966, at the Conrad Hilton Hotel in downtown Chicago. ICC examiner Paul Albus presided. UP executives testified first, followed by Rock Island and SP officials. After that testimony concluded, the C&NW witnesses would present their case for control of the Rock Island, with the Santa Fe also testifying in support of the C&NW control application. After that came rebuttals from earlier witnesses. The hearings were expected to last nine months, but Langdon worried about how long the ICC would take to come to a decision, believing it would be years before the merger was decided.

A week before the hearings on the Rock Island opened, the ICC released three major decisions. On April 27, 1966, the ICC approved the mammoth Penn Central merger, disapproved the Burlington Northern (BN) merger, and allowed the New Haven Railroad to discontinue dozens of passenger trains. Eventually, as a further condition of merging, the Penn Central Railroad would be forced to take control of the weak and bankrupt New Haven, a mainly passenger route running between New York and Boston and serving all of the major cities in the New England states. The Burlington decision was decided by a 6–5 vote of ICC commissioners, which seemed to give the railroads some hope if they were willing to work out their differences.[42] Within a few years the railroads did just that, and the BN merger was consummated in 1970.

The rulings were a mixed bag for the Rock Island and UP. The Chicago, Burlington and Quincy Railroad decided soon after the ICC decision that it needed to intervene in opposition to both the UP–Rock Island merger and to the C&NW control application. CB&Q President Louis Menk told the press that had the BN merger gone through the railroad would have been strong enough "to withstand Union Pacific–Rock Island competition."[43] Langdon was disheartened and quoted in a wire-service report saying "there is no question that this can be viewed as a discouraging development." "But our case has two basic and important distinctions which are most significant. First, our merger is essentially end-to-end. . . . Second, this merger would involve one strong road—the Union Pacific—and what is at best a marginal road, the Rock Island." UP's Frank Barnett was quoted stating that there were "essential differences" between the UP–Rock Island merger and the Northern Lines merger and was "confident that the UP–Rock Island merger would be approved."[44]

The Penn Central decision had less immediate impact on the Rock Island proceedings. But it was a merger equally fraught with worry for the industry. The Pennsylvania Railroad and New York Central System had agreed to merge in 1962 after talks extending back to the mid-1950s. Both railroads needed a merger in order to remain competitive in the eastern territory where rival passenger competition from airlines and highway travel were costing the two railroads millions of dollars each year to fund intercity and commuter passenger operations. Both railroads had high terminal costs associated with their location in congested metropolitan areas and labor costs were diminishing profitability as well. When Al Perlman came on board as president of the New York Central in 1954 the railroad was "an operational bankrupt" with most of its lines delivering little online traffic, with trucks taking away the short-haul traffic (too expensive to operate anyway due to high labor costs), and with passenger train deficits totaling a half-billion dollars through the 1950s.[45]

The two railroads shared common problems. Built to deliver coal and manufactured products to ports or to factories in the East, they lacked the long hauls that made the western railroads far healthier in the post–World War II period. There were too many parallel lines linking New York with Chicago, including both railroads, the recently merged Erie Lackawanna Railroad, and the Baltimore and Ohio Railroad. Like other railroads through the 1950s the two lines had "cannibalized" their systems for savings in terms of line abandonments, cutbacks on service, and passenger train embargoes. Pennsylvania chairman James Symes said that this process could not continue. "The bottom of the barrel is being reached. . . . A merger of the two companies will substantially benefit this situation."[46] A merger would reduce terminals, lead to consolidation of facilities, and improve service. It would also make the lines more financially viable than without a merger.

The Penn Central merger was opposed by shippers, by communities, and by railroads like the New Haven, which was eventually included as part of the conditions for merger. But the mammoth merger of these two eastern lines, considered necessary for the survival of freight and passenger service in the eastern territory, never received the type of opposition the Rock Island–UP merger received. The executives of both the Rock Island and the UP must have taken the approval of the Penn Central merger as a good sign; if a railroad that large could be merged together, what could stop their merger from being approved?

The UP testimony took two months, beginning on May 4, 1966, and concluding in mid-July. UP officials testified about the need for the railroad to have a line into Chicago and St. Louis in order to compete effectively in its own territory, or else the railroad would be at a "competitive disadvantage" with other railroads, Robert Lovett said at the first day of hearings. Lovett, who spent four days on the stand, was questioned by MoPac lawyer Leon Leighton about whether the access would give the railroad a greater advantage than other lines, to which Lovett answered, "No, they already have access to such gateways." As reported in the press the clear strategy of the opposition railroads was to show how the diversion of traffic—estimated by one UP study to be $220 million—would harm the competition and cause railroads like the C&NW, Milwaukee Road, MoPac, and ATSF enormous harm.[47]

Some of the key nuggets in the UP testimony and cross-examinations included an exchange between C&NW attorney William McGovern and Edd Bailey of the UP, who was asked whether the UP intended to invest, as Bailey had claimed, $154 million into new equipment on the Rock Island. McGovern cited Rock Island management saying that the railroad "had budgeted 135 million dollars for the purchase of 7,873 new freight cars and 125 locomotives. If, by completion of the program, the Rock Island adds 7,873 cars, how much is left for the UP?" "A program is one thing," Bailey retorted, "getting it accomplished is another. Under present [Rock Island] circumstances, it is hardly possible."[48] Another bombshell came from UP vice president and controller Reginald Sutton, who revealed in testimony that the original stock offer for the Rock Island, later increased after a C&NW–led proxy fight, was worth $81 million. The amount of money the SP was going to pay the UP to buy the Rock Island's southern lines was also questioned, as that figure had been set at $120 million (the Santa Fe was offering $100 million in its support of the C&NW control application).[49]

The most controversial witness for the UP was William Wyer, the consultant who had originally pushed for the Rock Island–UP merger in 1962. Wyer presented more than 500 pages of testimony and evidence on the merger, much of it consisting of traffic studies provided by the UP and Rock Island. Wyer contended that the merger would save $27 million over five years and estimated that the C&NW and CB&Q would be the biggest losers, with the North Western losing an estimated $2.5 million in revenues and the Burlington $2.1 million. The UP's own MacAnally report, released in 1962 as well but questioned by Wyer's data, showed a potential loss to all connections of $229 million, a figure C&NW lawyers continually used to justify rejecting the merger. If Wyer's lesser figures were to prevail with ICC rail examiner Albus, then the merger would not be as detrimental as the opposing railroads claimed. The strategy shifted to discredit Wyer's expertise altogether, with Leon Leighton questioning whether he was truly a rail "expert" even though he had been in business as a consultant since 1920. Lawyers for C&NW and MoPac also focused on errors in the data, pointing out inconsistencies that they brought to Albus's attention.[50] Wyer would spend sixteen days on the stand, "a personal record," he later said, defending not only the data in the merger books but also his own professional integrity.

Through the summer of 1966 other mergers were proposed, including several involving intervenors in this case. In June, the Missouri Pacific and its parent Mississippi River Corporation announced the intention to file for control of the Santa Fe. MoPac had been acquiring Santa Fe stock since January 1966 and announced its intention after Santa Fe President E. S. Marsh had informed the company it was not interested in a merger. Part of the problem was that the offer was not sweet enough for the Santa Fe, but in part the railroad did not want to be controlled by the Missouri Pacific. Plus, to control it would require $340 million, and that was simply to secure 50 percent of Santa Fe's voting stock. MoPac did not possess the means to secure control of the Santa Fe. As Craig Miner described, it was an audacious move. Every railroad involved in the Rock Island merger case opposed it and opposed the proposal from being made part of the Rock Island docket, including the Santa Fe. The MoPac had other merger applications pending, including its merger with the Chicago and Eastern Illinois Railroad and its control application of the Texas and Pacific. Both were awaiting decision by the ICC at the time.[51] The ICC let the MoPac control application proceed and left open the inclusion of the matter into the Rock Island case.

The C&NW and Milwaukee Road filed merger proceedings with the ICC in June 1966 as well, a case that was decided two years later and that produced 19,000 pages of testimony and evidence. The proposal would have created a large northwestern system to rival the Burlington Northern, but the Milwaukee Road was weak, mainly a granger line with a Pacific Coast extension—and with declining traffic compared to its rivals, the Great Northern and Northern Pacific. While both Ben Heineman and William Quinn of the Milwaukee saw the merger as a natural and "ideal merger" that would lead to an estimated savings of $50 million, the two sides could never effectuate the merger. After delays owing to a C&NW proposal to include the Rock Island in a four-way merger with the Milwaukee and the Chicago Great Western, which the C&NW took over in February 1968, the ideal merger between the two roads collapsed.[52]

All of the merger discussions left UP officials confident of victory in their acquisition of the Rock Island. Robert Lovett told the *Chicago Tribune* that the MoPac filing, and the C&NW–Milwaukee Road filing, all made him "confident that the commission will make an affirmative decision involving western railroads, beginning with our case."[53] A few days after this interview, lawyers for the UP and SP filed a petition to join the UP–Rock Island and C&NW–Milwaukee merger cases together, which Ben Heineman saw "as a public concession of weakness" concerning UP's strategy. "It seems apparent that the Union Pacific recognizes it has a hopeless cause under present conditions. I think the UP is in trouble," Heineman concluded. UP general counsel Frank Barnett argued that it made perfect sense to consolidate the cases to prevent duplication of evidence and to shorten the hearings.[54] But after UP lawyers made their day-long presentation, Albus stated dryly, "Petition denied. Next?"[55]

The UP testimony proved underwhelming to many observers at the hearings, including Langdon, who singled out Bailey in particular as "a disaster as a witness." A Denver and Rio Grande Western official stated: "The total absence of surprise in the testimony of its star witnesses has amazed many big and powerful railroad's strategists with uncommon brilliance."⁵⁶ Much more was expected, and UP officials failed to deliver.

Rock Island testimony began with Jervis Langdon on August 15, 1966. Langdon's strategy was to show how marginal the Rock Island was and how it desperately needed a merger with the stronger Union Pacific in order to survive. Langdon and Rock Island officials, including vice president for operations G. W. Kelly, VP of finance Paul Major, and others, concentrated on two key components: the declining traffic on an independent Rock Island; and the need for a financial infusion from the stronger UP. Langdon set out to demonstrate how Rock Island operating territory was oversupplied with rail service, that the largely agricultural area served by the railroad consisted of 41 percent of the nation's rail miles but only 26 percent of the nation's population. Worse, it was a territory that relied on farm products for 45 percent of its cash receipts, whereas industry and manufacturing were just 21 percent. "Rock Island is particularly affected because 27 percent of its total freight revenues come from the movement of agricultural commodities," Langdon said.⁵⁷

"The heavy dependence on the products of agriculture is evidence of weakness," Langdon continued. "When moving by truck, or barge, agricultural commodities are completely exempt from any economic regulations, and for this reason the competitive position of railroads which are as fully regulated in transporting agricultural commodities as any other traffic is highly vulnerable."⁵⁸ The growth of nonunion truckers in rural America delivering meat, dairy, and other agricultural commodities existed outside ICC regulation, and it was this growing competition that stifled railroads like the Rock Island in moving nonbulk commodities on branchlines through Iowa and other Midwestern states.⁵⁹

The railroad also had problems competing for traffic with other railroads in its own territory, producing enough online traffic, and handling enough interline shipments from other carriers. Langdon concluded,

> Here, in short, is Rock Island's basic weakness: a relatively lower revenue level, largely incurable, makes that property almost wholly dependent upon (1) an uninterrupted growth in the national economy, (2) the maintenance of the railroad's relative position in that growing economy, (3) the sharpest possible management in the providing of good service at the lowest cost, and (4) a great many more "good breaks" than "bad breaks." If any of these conditions is not fulfilled in the days ahead, even for a relatively short period, Rock Island may not be able to serve its territory adequately.⁶⁰

...

> From the standpoint of Rock Island and of those who rely upon it for service . . . its merger with Union Pacific is of crucial importance.[61]

The Rock Island strategy to rely on documenting its weakness as an independent rail operation may have seemed like a good strategy to ensure the merger. But it made its merger partner somewhat leery of just what they were getting into with the Rock Island. Operations VP Kelly told the hearings that the railroads would need $87 million over five years, but that figure "could easily exceed 100 million dollars."[62] Finance VP Paul Major echoed Langdon, stating that adequate service to the public "will require financial resources exceeding those available" to the company.[63] UP officials were well aware of the Rock Island's problems and willing to pay (at that moment) for the "rehabilitation and improvement programs" to allow the railroad to maintain its competitive position.[64] But if the merger languished and the Rock Island continued to disintegrate physically, would the UP still be interested in investing the money necessary to rehabilitate the property? That remained an open question.

Langdon had been well prepared for his testimony and for potential questions by Rock Island's VP and general counsel, Eaton Adams, and Kirkland attorney E. Houston Harsha. The strategy was followed to the letter. Harsha made reference to an interview with Langdon in the *Chicago Tribune* about a 10 percent rate increase, to which Langdon responded, "JL defines viable as dividends during good times, no bankruptcy during poor times, successful=dividends at all times." "In that sense, then, is the Rock Island a viable property? JL—Yes, but not in a position to take a recession." In reference to a Rock Island press release describing the acquisition of $19 million in new freight cars in 1966, allowing the railroad to improve and increase train schedules, Harsha advised Langdon "to attribute this to overenthusiastic public relations." Rock Island executives were well prepared to make the case for the weakness of their railroad.[65]

The Southern Pacific testified about its interest in securing the southern half of the Rock Island. The SP and UP had agreed on a final price of $120 million for the line, which still hosted the Rock Island's premier passenger train, the *Golden State Limited*, and was rebuilt substantially during the 1940s and 1950s. Ben Biaggini, who had replaced Donald Russell as president of the SP in 1964, and in 1968 added the title of CEO, was a respected railroad man who testified that the acquisition would provide "direct and immediate benefits" to shippers on the Rock Island. The SP was also a financially viable and powerful railroad, and Biaggini testified that the SP would improve the Rock Island's car fleet and produce greater efficiencies and economic savings if the sale was approved.[66] The SP was especially concerned about the Santa Fe positioning itself as an ally to the C&NW in the merger; its goal in acquiring the southern half of the Rock Island was to allow the SP to become a true transcontinental road and to gain access to Kansas City and St. Louis.[67]

The star witness in the proceeding turned out to be Ben Heineman, who made his first appearance on November 14, 1966, followed by a string of C&NW executives, including executive VP Larry Provo. Heineman had two jobs. The first was to convince the ICC why the C&NW would be a better merger partner for the Rock Island than the UP. The second job was to show how the public interest was threatened by the Rock Island–UP merger proposal. He performed both of these jobs admirably. His task was primarily guided by obfuscation—to keep the UP from gaining entry into Chicago and preventing a combination with the Rock Island, which would have dealt the C&NW a death blow. (See Photo 3.1.) In the end, this killed the Rock Island, but if some corporation was going to be victimized by the remaking of the western railroad map, Heineman was clear it would not be the C&NW.[68]

Heineman described how the C&NW had improved as a property since he took over as chairman in 1956. By reorganizing the company, pursuing dieselization, abandoning costly passenger service, investing in new car shops, improving service on Chicago commuter operations, and modernizing plant and equipment, "the efforts of the last ten years have resulted in substantial increases in net income. From a loss of $5,529,000 in 1956, we reached a net income of $11,030,000 in 1965 from transportation operations."[69] Heineman discussed a remarkable financial turnaround, but like other Midwestern railroads, the C&NW had failed to increase its freight revenues and its costs were rising, particularly labor costs.

> At the present time, we have nearly exhausted the potential opportunities for further savings within the framework of our present operations. . . . With our increasingly heavy program of capital improvements, I hope that the North Western will be able to reclaim a portion of the freight traffic which it has lost to trucks and the barges and which economically belongs on the railroads. . . . However, we must face the fact that the public facilities used by our intermodal competitors will not remain static. Public expenditures continue for an expanding highway system and the extension and improvement of inland waterways.[70]

Photo 3.1 Why Is This Man Smiling? Ben Heineman, chairman of the Chicago and North Western Railway in 1966. His railway system survived the tumult of the proposed Rock Island–Union Pacific merger. Photo courtesy of the Chicago and Northwestern Railway Historical Society. Used with permission of Railway Age *magazine.*

Much of Heineman's argument about the state of Midwestern railroading was an exact duplication of what Langdon had testified to in August: too much rail competition chasing too few passengers and too little freight, leading to declining revenues and high-cost service. "The diffusion of traffic among an excessive number of carriers means low levels of freight revenues and with the burdens of high individual costs, that has meant a generally distressed Midwestern railroad industry," Heineman argued in his effort to demonstrate operational savings from a union of the Rock Island and C&NW. Most of the Midwestern railroads suffered from too many branchlines and too few long-haul operations. The average length of a haul in the Western territory was 363 miles; the UP average was the highest, at 588 miles per haul, and the SP averaged 488 miles. The Milwaukee Road was just below the average at 361, and the Rock Island was surprisingly high at 351 miles. The C&NW was at the bottom with a 256-mile average.[71]

Heineman kept his focus on how a regional network of Midwestern railroads "will eliminate the delays and inefficiencies which are the inevitable result of the present fragmented rail service." Yet he did not demonstrate how the creation of a network of four weak railroads would improve service and be profitable. Heineman noted that the "North Western's rate of return on net investment in transportation property was only 2.6% in 1965, the Rock Island's was only 0.6%, the Milwaukee's was 2.5%, and the Great Western's was 1.3%.... The public interest in a continually improving rail plant in the Middle West dictates that these rates of return be improved." No doubt, but how? Heineman never addressed where capital was to come from, whereas Langdon and the UP executives had demonstrated the millions of dollars the UP would expend on the Rock Island to improve its efficiency and its service.[72]

Perhaps the strangest part of Heineman's testimony was his short history of the C&NW–Rock Island merger negotiations preceding the UP entry into the matter in 1963. Heineman described meetings over three months in early 1962 "with respect to a North Western–Rock Island merger. *This was before there had been any communications on this subject between the Rock Island and the Union Pacific.*" Heineman then discussed a telephone call with Crown concerning the general terms outlined in the control application. "Colonel Crown indicated that in general these terms were acceptable to him and to the Rock Island Board, but that he believed that the Rock Island stockholders should receive a guarantee of their then current Rock Island dividend. *In view of our inability at that time to place our own common stock on a dividend-paying basis, we were unable to agree to this type of arrangement.*"[73]

If the Rock Island board decided against a merger with C&NW, or did not take action at all in facilitating such a merger, a C&NW discussion to merge did not take precedence over an actual agreement between the UP and Rock Island. It was an amazing argument, devoid of practical logic and legal authority. Discussions about merging were not the same as binding legal agreements. Clearly, Heineman hoped to confuse the issue by insisting that a merger was being consummated when it was not *by his own testimony*. Another problem in his testimony had to do with the exchange offer. As Rock Island officials had been arguing, if the C&NW could not pay (and had not paid) a dividend on its common stock, how could it get the finances to offer stockholders control of the Rock Island? There were some glaring inconsistencies in his testimony.

However, Heineman had made a strong case for a regional rail network of Midwestern lines. He had accomplished what he intended: to show how the Rock Island would be better served as part of a network of Midwestern lines rather than as part of a transcontinental system. He had shown how the public interest would be served in such a merger; the C&NW proposed no sale of lines, and the integrity of the Rock Island would be left intact. The means by which this could be done was less important than planting seeds of doubts about the merger among the public and the ICC. As Langdon later said to UP's Frank Barnett, "whether we like it or not, the [C&NW] has made the plight of the Midwestern roads the central public issue in the case."[74] This proved especially important as the hearings finished their first phase.

The mundane matter of running a railroad seemed to pale in comparison with the merger hearings. The Rock Island continued to run in the red, posting deficits of $2.6 million in 1966 and a disastrous $16.1 million in 1967. The loss was "principally by a drop of almost 44,000 in car loadings of grain and a $5 million decrease in passenger service revenue from 1966, as well as a continuing and rapid escalation in wage and material costs."[75] The drop in grain traffic was especially worrisome, as Langdon pointed out how much of that traffic was lost to unregulated trucks taking wheat from Oklahoma to ports in Houston and Galveston, Texas.

To stop this drain of traffic the Rock Island cut rates for moving grain from Oklahoma and Kansas and corn from Iowa in order to compete with trucks. Unit trains of wheat and corn began moving from Rock Island Midwestern destinations to Gulf ports. In some cases the unit trains stretched 2 miles, combining over a hundred hopper cars—many newly purchased—and as many as ten diesel locomotives. A Rock Island brochure promoting the new market for export grain shipments claimed that wheat hauled to Gulf ports "zoomed upward from 8,596,000 bushels in 1967 to 41,600,000 bushels in 1968." Newspapers in Iowa, Oklahoma, Texas, and Kansas praised the new service. The railroad touted the more efficient use of freight cars, as well as the ability to take grain directly from farm to market, utilizing cooperative elevators and keeping costs down in the process.[76] The improvement allowed the Rock Island to cut its deficit to $4 million in 1968.

Passenger train deficits were another problem for the Rock Island. Fewer Americans were taking the train by the late 1960s, yet the Rock Island continued to operate several intercity passenger trains, including marquee trains like the *Rocky Mountain Rocket* and the *Golden State* (which alone of all Rock Island trains by 1966 had sleeping cars). Langdon wanted to end passenger service as delicately as possible. Several trains were discontinued in 1967, including the *Rocky Mountain Rocket*, which at one time operated in two sections, splitting at Limon, Colorado, with one locomotive taking one section to Colorado Springs and the other to Denver. The westbound *Imperial* was discontinued in 1966 between Kansas City and Tucumcari, New Mexico, and the *Twin Star Rocket*, the longest north-south passenger route in the nation, run in conjunction with the CB&Q between the Twin Cities and Houston, was ended as well.

Rock Island management was cognizant of the public relations impact of passenger service. "Although passenger revenues continued to decline in 1966 and are expected to drop further in 1967," according to the author of the annual report, "the Company has nevertheless taken steps to give service on the remaining trains that is as good as circumstances permit."[77] As late as February 1968, in its last published schedule, the joint Rock Island–SP *Golden State* still boasted Pullman bedroom cars and roomettes as well as a club diner. The train advertised a 46-hour schedule on its daily runs to and from Chicago and Los Angeles.[78] It may have been a far cry from the train operating twenty years earlier, combining observation cars, several sets of sleepers, full service dining, and even a barber and valet, but for late-1960s railroading the *Golden State* delivered as much style as it could on a railroad increasingly shorn of resources to support marquee trains. The *Golden State* would make its last run on February 20, 1968, ending a service to Los Angeles that began operating in 1902.[79]

None of this belt-tightening could make the Rock Island a profitable stand-alone operation in the climate of railroading in the 1960s. Millions of dollars in capital expenditures were necessary just to keep up with current operations. Langdon wrote: "On the Rock Island there is much deferred maintenance. Each year there should be at least 100 miles of new rail laid, 600,000 new ties inserted, and 600,000 cubic yards of ballast applied, but even under the accelerated program of last year, new rail was limited to 50 miles, new ties to 430,000 and ballast to 450,000 cubic yards. . . . If Rock Island has $100 million to spend, it could improve its plant and make it much easier to operate efficiently." But the merger had to occur first, and as Langdon reminded stockholders in early 1967, the ICC had heard 23,000 pages of testimony, and "when the record is closed, the argument stage will begin—first before the ICC and later (unless there is acceptance of the action taken by the ICC), before the courts."[80]

It was a sober warning of dark days ahead, of a case suspended. Like prizefighters stumbling around a ring in Round 15, unwilling to quit, railroads were uninterested in settling the dispute over the merger. The second round of hearings and the ultimate decision by the ICC was yet to come as Langdon put the finishing touches on a stockholder report focusing on a bad couple of years for the Rock Island. Regardless of every effort made by management during these days, Langdon reminded shareholders that "if every aspect of the proposed merger has to be litigated to the end, and every remedy exhausted, the Rock Island will have to wait a very long time, and this will be hard to do."[81] As the second year of hearings in the case was about to begin, with no outcome in the near future, the Rock Island case slogged on with no green light for the merger on the horizon.

FOUR

THE WAITING IS THE HARDEST PART

> I am a career civil servant, not in the sense that I'm servile, but I try to look realistically and sympathetically at the public need.
>
> —Nathan Klitenic, quoted in *Forbes*, October 15, 1972

Civil servants typically operate in the shadows, avoiding the limelight and public spectacle. They are, according to early-twentieth-century German social theorist Max Weber, the rational experts whose technical knowledge, lifelong dedication to their job, and efficiency allow for the operation of a centralized organization.[1] Whether in the service of the state, the labor union, the military, or the corporation, bureaucracy was a function of modernity and was, without question, a product of capitalist development. Historian Alfred Chandler argued that "modern business enterprise took the place of market mechanisms in coordinating the activities of the economy and for allocating its resources.... The visible hand of management replaced what Adam Smith referred to as the invisible hand of market forces."[2] The emergence of the firm and the corporation, with railroads playing the crucial role in the corporation's development, helped pioneer the modern bureaucratic role of social organization. It is no surprise that governmental bureaucracies developed from the same model.[3]

Social organization theory prized expert management in either business or government. While the theory had reached its crescendo among intellectuals with John Kenneth Galbraith's celebrated idea of countervailing powers between government, organized labor, and big business as the wellspring for a new American capitalism, by the time of the Rock Island–Union Pacific merger case, bureaucracy, bigness, and centralization all had become dirty words among intellectuals. Challenged by a congeries of New Left activists, environmentalists, economists, and even some businessmen concerned about the stifling impact of "corporate liberalism" on the nation and the world, the era of countervailing powers seemed at an end.[4]

Yet the railroad industry and the government body regulating it were both trapped in a time warp. Innovation was not the watchword within an industry controlled by a regulatory agency impervious to change. With high fixed costs and high levels of bonded indebtedness, and plagued by inflationary spirals in labor, material, and fuel costs, railroads by the late 1960s found the industry on the precipice. Like a line from Robert Frost's immortal poem "The Road Not Taken," the industry could take one of two paths—toward nationalization, which many executives feared; or toward deregulation, a prospect fraught with uncertainty. Technological innovation, such as dieselization, had not solved the industry's problems. Cost-cutting could be taken only so far if the regulatory apparatus remained indifferent to their plight as common carriers interested in protecting shippers over rail lines. Railroad executives wanted less regulation but had no coordinated strategy in mind to replace it. They worried about government nationalization of rail lines but saw this as a possible outcome if they did not get their own house in order.[5] Jervis Langdon gave voice to this concern in 1968: "If the individual railroad properties can do no better than to operate as they have in the past—an aggregate of quarreling entities with no real sense of national system responsibility—the continuance of private ownership and operation is open to serious question; in these circumstances, the government could be forced to take them over."[6]

If the railroad industry was hamstrung by an archaic organizational structure and feared breaking with tradition, the ICC was hindered by the same fears. While the commission had allowed many railroad mergers to go forward, it failed to see how its rulings on rates and innovation unfairly impacted railroads at the expense of other transportation alternatives outside of their regulatory reach. The Southern Railway developed a 100-ton hopper car, nicknamed Big John, to haul grain, replacing 40-foot boxcars, which hauled only 25 tons of grain and were cumbersome to load and unload. As a result of being able to haul more grain, the Southern cut its rates by 60 percent, leading to a marked shift in movement of grain by the railroad and by others that adopted the new technology. But the ICC ruled that the Southern Railway's rate was unfair to other railroads and ordered a rate increase. Southern president William Brosnan took the ICC to court, and eventually the U.S. Supreme Court ruled against the commission and allowed the Southern Railway's rate to remain in place.[7] Soon other railroads employed the new hoppers; by doing so, the Rock Island was able to slash rates on unit grain trains headed to Gulf ports from Iowa, Kansas, and Oklahoma.

The ICC was stuck in its historical role as a protector of competition among different forms of transport and as a regulator of railroads as a monopoly, which they no longer were. As a result, the ICC vacillated in its powers to determine its ratemaking functions, clinging to the minimum ratemaking powers granted to the commission in the 1906 Hepburn Act while also allowing for compensatory rates to bring balance to the rates between regulated and unregulated carriers. The ICC's "more formidable task . . . has been to see that competition does not get out of hand, to the injury of carriers, shippers and the public," Charles Morgan, the head of the ICC Bureau of Economics and Statistics, wrote in 1953.[8] But a fairer way to ensure such competition would be to do away with ICC authority on ratemaking altogether. The advocates of deregulation were also making their case during this period. They insisted that cost structures of transportation had to be understood before any rational competitive market could be developed, and once costs were understood a movement away from regulation was imperative for the industry to survive.[9]

This subject was not broached in the hearings on the Rock Island–UP merger, but the outcome of the merger led to the discussion of these issues in earnest during the 1970s. When hearings on the merger resumed in 1967, ICC rail examiner Nathan Klitenic, who joined Paul Albus at the hearings after the commissioner broke his ankle in late 1966, saw his task in the merger case as a restructuring of the western railroad map. Klitenic oversaw the vast and complex fight over the Rock Island, and it was he who was given the sole task by the commissioners of writing the report on the merger. "I am not trying to nationalize the railroads or reduce the railroads or reduce competition or anything like that. But no one should be surprised if our recommendations don't fit with tradition. What was true about the railroads 50 years ago is no longer true today," Klitenic told *Forbes* on the eve of the release of his third report on the Rock Island merger.[10]

How did the merger of two railroads become the basis for one civil servant to remake the western railroad map? Certainly, as *Forbes* noted, he wasn't acting alone and had the support of the commissioners, but how was his decision in the public interest? Why did the case come to rest on the power of one official in the ICC to decide the fate of an entire industry?

In part it devolved from the continued failure of the railroads in the hearings to come to any acceptable consensus on the merger. Hearings dragged on through 1967 and into the next year before concluding in August 1968. Opposition railroads testified early in 1967 with the Santa Fe witnesses arguing in favor of the C&NW control application and gaining access for that railroad into St. Louis and Memphis, which the Santa Fe would acquire should the C&NW be awarded the Rock Island. The Missouri–Kansas–Texas Railroad joined in opposition to the merger as well. John W. Barriger, a former Rock Island vice president who had assumed the presidency of the

Katy in 1963, testified in favor of C&NW control as the merger hearings moved to Dallas in the spring of 1967.[11]

In the midst of testimony on the Rock Island, hearings were begun in the merger proposal between the C&NW and Milwaukee Road in February. The UP and Southern Pacific both announced it would oppose the merger unless the C&NW dropped its control application for the Rock Island, but Ben Heineman saw the two proposals intertwined and had no intention of ending his effort to merge the Midwestern lines. Heineman put the merger savings at $29 million. If the ICC allowed the C&NW to acquire the Chicago Great Western, the savings with a three-way merger would be $38 million. Major opposition came from the Soo Line Railroad and from smaller regional lines in Wisconsin, and the merger was expected to go forward without serious delay.[12]

Heineman's plan to build a regional rail system, with or without the Rock Island, was coming to fruition, something that had worried Langdon, who felt the UP was not taking the matter seriously and neglecting to strike a deal to save it. Langdon sought to tie the merger proposals together when he testified in the C&NW–Milwaukee Road hearings on May 31. Langdon insisted that the Rock Island–UP merger be allowed first as a condition to the C&NW–Milwaukee Road merger. "I want to emphasize that the Rock Island is not opposed to the consolidation here proposed. But we do insist upon a condition that Rock Island's proposed merger with Union Pacific be allowed to go forward before or concurrently with the application under consideration."[13] ICC rail examiner Henry Darmstadter, officiating at the C&NW hearing, said that "he cannot rule on whether the UP-RI merger is in the public interest." But he left the matter open as to whether the two mergers could be dealt with together in the future.[14] The two proposals remained separate.

Langdon had spent the better part of the year pleading with the railroad industry to get its act together and find a solution to the impasse in the western territory. He saw clearer than most of his cohorts that unless they took action someone else would. He actually suggested that the newly created federal Department of Transportation could play a role breaking the logjam. The DOT could hold a dinner and invite the heads of all western railroads, Langdon told a Transportation Association of America audience, then give the railroads thirty days to come up with a solution. If that failed, DOT should host another dinner and use the influence of government to produce a compromise. When asked if the UP had been "guilty of a headstrong attitude" in the merger process, Langdon replied, "all of us have been guilty of this, including the Rock Island. . . . Everyone agrees that a merger would be a good thing for the Rock Island and for other railroads and probably for the country. I believe there has to be and is a solution, but the way we're going at it is ridiculous."[15]

The Department of Transportation was not interested in wading into the swamp. What is striking as the industry unraveled and its economic condition became more precarious was how willing the executive branch was to ignore the plight of the railroads. Dwight Eisenhower had suggested the creation of a federal department to oversee transportation policy in the mid-1950s, yet once it was created under Lyndon Johnson in 1966, the cabinet agency only reacted to crisis, as it would after the bankruptcy of the Penn Central in 1970. It left the merger mess to the ICC. Its chairman, William Tucker, warned the railroads that "unless some of the parties do an abrupt about-face from their present positions, they may be in for a rude awakening." "Many of the railroads appear to be merely maximizing their own special positions without any real regard for the public interest or the interest of other railroads and the vital services that such roads perform," Tucker said. Claiming that the ICC might shut down all merger hearings, Tucker argued that the ICC couldn't afford extensive staff time if railroads "continue to plunge blindly into a quagmire of self-interest manipulations and to indulge in an endless parade of unrealistic claims, counterclaims and recriminations, and to proceed toward the creation of an insoluble mess."[16]

Tucker had diagnosed the illness but offered no cure as the insoluble mess dragged on. At the end of the summer the Rock Island's interest in merging quickly, and with conditions, grew. Langdon predicted a $10 million loss for 1967 in his rebuttal testimony before the ICC hearings in September. Soon after, the railroad asked the ICC for permission to discontinue the *Golden State* passenger train and three other trains as a way to pare losses. But a merger was necessary as soon as possible, Langdon reiterated.

Heineman appeared for the second time, on rebuttal to Rock Island and UP testimony. UP's Reginald Sutton had testified about how the C&NW had exaggerated its economic problems, that it was not a marginal line, and that through a merger with the Milwaukee Road "it has the potential of vastly improving its position in the industry." Heineman showed how through selective data Sutton had arrived at this position and concluded that "in view of the reverses suffered during the past year by the independent Midwestern carriers, there can be little question that, as presently organized, these roads must be regarded as marginal."[17]

Heineman consistently argued for a regional Midwestern rail system capable of surviving economic downturns and rejuvenating the region's rail service. "The truth of the matter is that a combined North Western–Rock

Island (with or without the Great Western or the Milwaukee Road) will not be an immensely affluent system. We can expect our savings to be eaten away at least in part by rising costs. . . . But neither will such a combination of roads be poverty-stricken if spared diversion of traffic by the Union Pacific."[18] He labeled the UP an affluent transcontinental and challenged Langdon's characterization of the C&NW as too marginal an operation to infuse the Rock Island with needed cash for rebuilding. "I am confident that savings realizable under control will provide valuable financial support both to the North Western and to the Rock Island."[19] "I believe the Milwaukee–North Western–Great Western combination would be viable if the Rock Island was to stand alone," Heineman said under UP cross-examination, "but if the Rock Island were to come under the ownership of the Union Pacific, the Milwaukee–North Western–Great Western, separately or in combination, would be doomed to bankruptcy in a short period of time."[20]

A more intriguing proposal for reorganizing the western railroad map appeared a week after Heineman's testimony when the Illinois Central Railroad and the Gulf, Mobile and Ohio Railroad (GM&O) announced their intention to merge. The two roads were roughly parallel routes from Chicago to New Orleans (IC) and Mobile, Alabama (GM&O). The IC had a western route to Council Bluffs, Iowa, from Chicago, and the GM&O had a line from Springfield, Illinois, to Kansas City. It was the archetype of a perfect combination merger that would eliminate redundant lines and coordinate savings between the two roads.[21]

The UP now faced an intriguing prospect. Since the late nineteenth century, the UP had been a major stockholder in the Illinois Central, owning 24 percent of its common stock in 1967. With the Rock Island case bogged down, speculation in the press and among rail analysts was that the UP would jettison the Rock Island in favor of merger with the IC and GM&O. This speculation forced UP chairman Frank Barnett to issue a statement categorically denying the railroad's interest: "We have committed ourselves with the Rock Island and we intend to proceed with that merger."[22] Unknown to Rock Island executives, however, Ben Heineman understood that the UP might be more interested in merging with the IC than it let on. In October he met with UP officials (SP's Ben Biaggini also was involved) a few times to discuss a deal. If the UP would drop its opposition to the C&NW control of the Rock Island, then the C&NW would support a UP effort to control the IC and GM&O. Nothing came of the talks.[23]

It is an intriguing counterfactual to imagine what might have happened if such a deal was struck. The UP would have gained access to Chicago via the IC's Iowa line (a far lesser line in terms of traffic than the Rock Island).

It also would have gained control over a railroad with a southern extension to the Gulf ports. The C&NW would have secured control of the Rock Island and perhaps would have created the regional system envisioned by Heineman. Whether the SP or the Santa Fe would have still been interested in securing or splitting the Rock Island's southern routes would probably have caused the biggest fight. Biaggini's presence at the talks signifies some interest on the part of the SP in the deal.

But the status quo remained. Langdon had been pressing the UP to make a deal with the opposition railroads, but he would have been completely caught off guard by the duplicity involved in meeting without his knowledge or his presence to discuss the future of his railroad. Like the European powers discussing the fate of Czechoslovakia at the 1938 Munich Conference without the Czechs present, the Rock Island was uninvolved in the discussions on its corporate future. Langdon grew disenchanted with his merger partners, telling Barnett at one point, "Frank, you're never going to be able to win this case, if you yourself don't take the lead . . . in trying to work this out," to which Barnett replied, "Oh the hell with it! Leave it up to the lawyers." "Well, look," Langdon recalled, "they left it to the lawyers, and the lawyers of course loved it. Lawyers love to litigate." There would be no compromise, and the outlook for the merger grew even dimmer.[24]

Langdon actually believed the UP had already lost the case and that it was time to negotiate. But it was not too late to change the situation—if the UP was interested in doing so. He wrote SP president Ben Biaggini to make the case for "interim control of the Rock Island" by the UP. This was "essential if UP is to win the merger case." The financial situation was so desperate, Langdon wrote, that "unless Rock Island receives early help, reorganization in bankruptcy appears ultimately to be inevitable. The moment this happens, Rock Island comes under the jurisdiction of a federal court in Chicago, and no such court, under the influences and pressures that exist in this town, is ever going to approve unification of the debtor's property with the UP, based in Omaha." If the UP was to win the case,

> the UP must show its strength and actually *do* something to help Rock Island, even at some risk. The equipment leases represent no risk [the UP had leased cars and locomotive power for the Rock Island]. . . . An *actual demonstration* of UP help, coming at a time when help is needed, would take the place of thousands of pages of testimony and printed briefs in convincing the ICC of the sincerity of UP's case. Moreover, bold affirmative action of this kind is the only way to beat the [C&NW].[25]

Heineman testified for the third time in the proceedings in March 1968. Once again, he defended the idea of a Midwestern regional railroad, adding the Rock Island to the C&NW–Milwaukee Road–CGW combination. "I believe that the central issue in this case is whether the independent Midwestern rails are to be allowed to form themselves into a healthy regional system or whether that effort is to be hopelessly undermined in order to permit two of the strongest and wealthiest railroads in the country to enlarge their own 'spheres of influence.'"[26] Heineman went over the UP's testimony to challenge its view of how a merger would benefit an already affluent railroad. He also outlined how the UP's goal for single-line service into Chicago was not a strong rationale for merger.

> Neither the Union Pacific nor Southern Pacific is at a disadvantage against any railroad in the United States. . . . The Union Pacific has faced for many years the limited single-line competition which it cites, but this competition has not prevented it from becoming an extraordinary prosperous railroad. It has showed a steady profit for the last 70 years, and has not skipped a dividend since 1900. . . . In 1966, the Union Pacific's net income before taxes registered a 17.1 percent advance from the prior year to reach a total of $109.7. The UP now ranks as the most profitable railroad company in the United States, challenged only by the Southern Pacific, with 1966 earnings of $102.3.[27]

It was an important and in many ways devastating argument. If the UP was strong, what would protect the other railroads in the Midwest? The Missouri Pacific soon changed its stripes. Initially it opposed both the UP merger and the C&NW control application, but in February 1968 Downing Jenks now turned to support C&NW's bid for the Rock Island. "If it [Rock Island] is doing as badly as it is alleged to be doing now, it would appear that it should become part of another system. That system should be the North Western." The other merger proposal would "make the rich richer and the poor poorer."[28]

Heineman's testimony about a four-way merger between Midwestern lines worried Langdon, who sought Frank Barnett's advice about how to respond in his testimony scheduled for July 8. Langdon told Barnett that "Rock Island, in resisting this proposal, plans to argue that the consolidation of four marginal carriers in the Midwest cannot produce a strong system." He then described how the C&NW, "whether we like it or not . . . has made the plight of the Midwestern railroads the central public interest issue in the case. . . . My own view is that, as the record stands now, the ICC will lean in the direction of the solution offered by the [C&NW] as representing an affirmative step to alleviate the problem of all Midwest carriers."[29]

It was time to make a deal. "I thus come to the conclusion," Langdon wrote, "that to win the case the UP should consider an offer to include in the merger either the [C&NW] or the Milwaukee, or possibly both." He continued: "The Northern Lines might be persuaded to take one or the other, and thus relieve the UP in part. Then it would be the UP which would be moving affirmatively to solve the Midwestern railroad problem. . . . An offer to include these carriers may well spell the difference between victory and defeat."[30] Barnett offered instead to guarantee the C&NW loss from diversion of traffic for seven years, "perhaps longer." "The UP will make up to the North Western any revenues on lost traffic above the amount estimated by the UP." Heineman was unimpressed, stating in reply that "the monetary payments, inadequate as they would be, would cease at about the time we would be experiencing the full progressive effects of traffic diversion from the Union Pacific."[31]

Langdon had been making this argument to deaf ears. The Rock Island board refused to reconsider the merger—"I told the board I did not think this thing was going to fly." The ICC refused to force the issue, even though John Kramer had made a similar argument about railroads solving their own problems, Heineman was unmoved, and the UP remained stubborn. When Barnett finally approached Heineman about making a deal the following year, he was no longer interested in merger as a solution to the C&NW's long-term problems, focused on creating a new corporation, Northwest Industries (NWI), which would invest in real estate and other nonrailroad properties and would sell the railroad to its employees.[32]

On August 21, 1968, the Rock Island hearings finally ground to a halt. After 27 months and 274 days of hearings, there was still no consensus. Several thousand people, including executives from all the major western railroads as well as lawyers, operating officers, clerks, shippers, and other interest groups, had testified before the commission, producing an incredible amount of paperwork—48,000 pages of testimony and some 200,000 pages of evidence (much of it traffic diversion studies). One lawyer thought "we believe this has been the longest case in history for any administrative agency of the Government." The ICC said it was "easily the biggest case we ever handled," doubling the length and the paperwork of the recently concluded Penn Central merger. "Our recommended report," Paul Albus told the press, "may take as much as a year." But no one thought that the ICC staff would be able to make a recommendation in that short time.[33]

Meanwhile the Rock Island disintegrated further. Langdon attempted to get the board to consider other alternatives for merger, but it remained adamant that the UP was the right partner. He tried desperately to get the UP to help pay for maintenance of the railroad—UP had provided leases for locomotives and equipment—to no avail. The result, as Langdon revealed in ICC testimony, was that "the Rock Island has fallen far short of a normal maintenance program in respect of new rail, ties and ballast. . . . Rock Island, for lack of cash, has had to defer many capital expenditures [including] properly spaced and longer sidings; yard improvements; car repair; signal replacing; hotbox detectors; a better communication network; and mechanized work equipment and vehicles." It was a grim situation made worse by the railroad's inability to raise private capital sufficient to improve track and equipment.[34]

The UP, meanwhile, was flush with cash by the late 1960s. It invested heavily in computers, microwave communications, locomotives, and cars, and it put a premium on track maintenance and upgrading its mainlines. It was the richest railroad in the nation, and as part of a long-sought effort to split the railroad from its nonrail business ventures in oil, real estate, and minerals, Frank Barnett formed the Union Pacific Corporation (UPC) in 1969.[35]

Diversification and investment into nonrailroad and transportation business, especially real estate, was becoming a normal part of the railroad industry by the 1960s as railroads attempted to find additional capital to reinvest into particular companies. Robert Lovett had set the process of diversification in motion in 1959, persuading UP board chairman Roland Harriman that it was the right thing to do. "Our problem," Lovett said, "was to get out of the iron maiden we were in . . . the past construction of the law which prohibited a railroad from doing anything other than operating a railroad."[36] The law prevented railroads from owning other transportation companies, such as barge lines, airlines, and trucking companies. Laws also prevented railroads from developing mineral resources on their own land; railroads could not haul commodities developed on their own property, which meant that resources went undeveloped in many parts of the country.

Frank Barnett coordinated the reorganization of the railroad into three divisions—transportation, natural resources, and real estate. The UP had always been a two-headed corporation, with the board and chairman located in New York City and the operations in Omaha. Under Barnett's direction, all management responsibility for the corporation would be headquartered in New York, with all divisions reporting to Lovett as chairman of the board. In 1967 Lovett retired after the death of E. R. Harriman. Barnett became chairman and president of the railroad, chasing both the corporate reorganization and a merger with the Rock Island. Barnett recruited talented managers from each division and brought Penn Central president Al Perlman's protégé John Kenefick to the UP to succeed him as head of the railroad. By 1969 the reorganization was in place and, after exchanging stock in the new corporation, UPC was born.[37]

Heineman also recognized the limitations to corporate profits within the railroad industry. In 1965 the C&NW formed Northwest Industries, a wholly owned subsidiary of C&NW, and began acquiring nonrailroad properties such as the Velsicol Chemical Corporation, which controlled the Michigan Chemical Corporation, a manufacturer of herbicides, fungicides, paints, and industrial chemicals. During the first six months of ownership of the company the C&NW showed $5 million in net income, a substantial amount that could be invested into the railroad or used to pay off debt.[38]

By 1968, NWI had become a conglomerate, taking control of the Philadelphia and Reading Corporation, a holding company whose diversified portfolio included Fruit of the Loom (underwear), Lone Star Steel (pipelines), and a number of other manufacturing companies. Sales for NWI reached $330 million by 1966 with an after-tax profit of $24 million—far greater than the losses being experienced by the C&NW by the late 1960s.[39]

Other railroads, including the Illinois Central, formed holding companies that soon dwarfed the railroad's assets. Illinois Central Industries, which changed its name to IC Industries in 1975, acquired Abex, a manufacturer of brakes for the automobile and railroad industries. In the early 1970s it acquired Pepsi-Cola Company and Midas Brakes before selling its railroad interests entirely in the 1980s and reorganizing as the Whitman Corporation. Santa Fe Industries, Southern Pacific Corporation, and the Penn Central Transportation Company were other important railroad holding companies during the late 1960s and 1970s.

The Rock Island had no diversified corporate structure and, with its financial house in disarray, no way to achieve one. Without the ability to secure private investment capital to rebuild its lines and to purchase equipment, the railroad increasingly relied on trusts and leases of equipment supplied through the UP. Much of the money spent went to secondhand locomotives, including former UP passenger motive power placed into revenue freight service. Executive board minutes from the late 1950s to the 1970s reveal the sale of property throughout the system to divest itself of taxable real estate as well as a means to finance improvements. They reveal no nonrail acquisitions. Railroads like the Rock Island increasingly found themselves on the margins within an industry engaged in fundamental financial and corporate diversification.

It is important to note that diversification did not lead to improvements in railroad operations or even investments back into the railroad property.

Conditions had become so desperate within the industry by the late 1960s that few executives could have imagined the rapid transformation a decade or more in the future. Railroads continued to be poor investments. The C&NW hemorrhaged cash; the Penn Central declared bankruptcy in 1970; the Santa Fe and Southern Pacific took money out of railroad operations to secure its other investments; and IC Industries let the rail property decay, only to sell it off in the early 1980s. The UP blossomed as a railroad property through this period, investing heavily in computers, maintenance, new sources of traffic, and improved equipment and cars. This positioned the UP to advance as one of the major railroads in the era of railroad deregulation.

In January 1969 the U.S. Justice Department approved the merger of the UP and Rock Island, "under appropriate conditions," including the sale of the Rock Island's line between Denver and Kansas City and Denver and Council Bluffs, to the Denver and Rio Grande Western Railroad; the sale of the Memphis–Tucumcari line to the Santa Fe as well as half interest in the Kansas City–St. Louis route; and the sale of the remaining southern lines for which the railroad applied to the SP. If the C&NW–Milwaukee Road merger went through, the C&NW would not be authorized to acquire the Rock Island. Justice Department lawyers were convinced that the Rock Island–UP merger would help rehabilitate the Rock Island as a long-haul carrier without the reduction in facilities necessitated by the C&NW control application.[40]

Heineman was unappeased. Seeking to upset the applecart toward merger, Heineman filed a motion with the ICC in the Illinois Central–GM&O merger hearing to examine the records of the UP, Illinois Central Industries, the IC railroad, and the New York commercial bank Brown Brothers Harriman. Charging that Brown Brothers was pressuring the merger between the two roads, Heineman appealed that "North Western seeks further to develop what these interests intend to accomplish by these applications." The UP had long been a major holder of IC stock but had not controlled the railroad for more than fifty years; IC president William Johnson testified that the UP had no more than 16 percent of IC stock, and in 1968 the UP had placed 23 percent of its stock in IC Industries in voting trusts with three banks as a condition of merger with the Rock Island.[41]

The ICC aimed to reopen the hearings in November 1969, further delaying the expected report on the merger. The main issue was whether UPC was controlled by Brown Brothers Harriman; if it was, then the firm would have to be a party to the case. The ICC allowed the UPC to become a party to the case at that time. The hearings were further delayed when the C&NW petitioned the commission to investigate the harm that might befall the C&NW

if the new corporation took over the Rock Island. ICC examiners called for a conference on April 1, 1970, to hear motions about extending the hearings further.[42] In reaction to the news, Jervis Langdon said that "so far as we know, the new hearing involves only a technical matter relating to the Union Pacific holding company and does not deal with the merits of the proposed Rock Island–UP merger."[43]

In the meantime the C&NW, like most Midwestern railroads, was declining as a property. Deferred maintenance on mainlines and branchlines led to an operating deficit of $5.7 million in 1969, after good years through the mid-1960s. Larry Provo, a young protégé of Heineman, became the new president in 1967, allowing Heineman to dedicate more time to Northwest Industries (including an attempt to acquire tire manufacturer B.F. Goodrich, which cost NWI about $50 per share in 1969 and half its earnings). Provo instantly began to prepare a plan for selling the railroad to its employees, freeing NWI of $300 million in debt in the process. In 1970 the sale was consummated for $19 million, and in 1972 the Chicago and North Western Transportation Company was formed, with "employee owned" emblazoned on the heralds of its locomotives and cars.[44]

In 1968 the ICC ruled in a complex and not entirely satisfactory decision that the C&NW could merge with the Milwaukee Road. But no one was happy with the decision. The Soo Line Railroad wanted the case reopened. A group of dissident stockholders of the Milwaukee Road, believing its earnings greater than the C&NW, pleaded to renegotiate the exchange ratio of the stock. Heineman met with Milwaukee president William Quinn in 1969 to make an offer to purchase the Milwaukee Road with no cash but a new equity issue of Milwaukee shares in exchange for C&NW stock. The tax loss for the C&NW would be a boon for North West Industries. Quinn, who was given thirty days to think about the offer, turned it down. Richard Saunders called Quinn's rejection "the road's death warrant."[45]

The Rock Island was quick to petition the ICC to halt the C&NW bid for control of the railroad in light of the termination of the C&NW–Milwaukee Road merger. On March 9, 1970, Rock Island lawyers filed their motion: "Clearly, in light of present reality, North Western's application to control Rock Island is now devoid of substance, and the examiners need no longer engage in evaluating two competing applications," the petition said. The whole effort by the C&NW was a "monumental and shocking waste of time and money since the concocted virtues of a 'Midwest regional' empire, as spread of record in scores of North Western exhibits and thousands of pages of testimony, now lie obviously abandoned by North Western's management."[46]

The petition highlighted North Western's recent announcement that it was terminating its merger agreement with the Milwaukee and that "it was seeking to dispose of its unprofitable railroad business" *to the Milwaukee Road*. C&NW attorneys and executives had argued for years that the formation of a Midwestern regional rail system—which Rock Island lawyers called "mythical"—would be the basis for a strong system and provide benefits in the public interest. "The Midwest Regional System advocated by North Western has just committed *hari-kari*, and striking North Western's evidence presented on behalf of that 'System' will only be recognizing its demise."[47] The delays in postponing the decision on the merger "has been injurious to the Rock Island" and contributed to its deteriorating financial condition.

North Western responded that a regional system "is still believed by North Western to be a desirable goal," arguing that the Rock Island sought to strike the entire economic case from the merger. "The immediate consequences of Union Pacific's acquisition of Rock Island, fraught with danger before, now obviously cannot be countenanced in the light of the dismal 1969 results of the Midwest carriers." The key for the C&NW was to leave the evidence in the record and to gain a conclusion from the rail examiner designed to keep the Midwest regional system alive. That was the only way to prevent the UP from becoming the dominant carrier in the western territory.[48]

Rock Island finances continued to decline at an alarming rate. The railroad experienced a $9.3 million loss in 1969 in spite of ridding the system of all but one of its remaining passenger trains, also ending service on two nameless Chicago-Omaha trains (Trains 7 and 10), which lost $1.2 million and carried "a station wagon full of passengers (nine passengers) westbound and a motorcycle full (two) eastbound." The ICC allowed the Rock Island to abandon those trains on May 31, 1970, leaving only the *Peoria Rocket* as an intercity train on the Rock Island. The Chicago area commuter service was faring a little better under Langdon, who had secured leases for bilevel, push-pull, air-conditioned and heated cars and developed ticket-by-mail options and standardized fares. The service broke even by the end of the 1960s with these investments, but the days of privately operated commuter service were coming to an end.[49]

Langdon spent the last year of his tenure as president of the railroad lobbying for a quick settlement of the merger case before the Rock Island collapsed. He wrote ICC chairman George Stafford, explaining the difficulty he had attracting financing for equipment. When they had a deal worked out and news of Rock Island deferring on interest payments on income bonds became public (the railroad had deferred interest payments on such bonds for three years at that time), "our financing arrangement fell apart and the people with the $16 million walked away from us. In walking away from us, the financial people pointed to the absence of any proposed report in our merger as one reason why they could not take a chance in financing this badly needed equipment." That left the Rock Island no recourse but to go to the UP, and "if they say no, we shall have to do without."[50]

On July 8, 1970, the Rock Island finally received some measure of good news. Rail Examiner Nathan Klitenic released a five-page syllabus denying the C&NW control application and the Santa Fe's proposal to purchase the southern lines if C&NW won control. Klitenic's syllabus endorsed the merger of the UP with the Rock Island and sale to the Southern Pacific of the southern lines. "Hopefully," Jervis Langdon said, "the railroads involved in this litigation can now compose their differences and, before the case is submitted to the ICC for final decision, reach a general agreement, using the examiner's recommendations as a base." Larry Provo said, ominously, that he could not "conceive of the ICC approving anything like the examiner's recommendation. . . . The same factors that put us in that case still exist."[51] It appeared that any report to follow would bring about a court case and even lengthier delays. No one was interested in settling the case—with the exception of the Rock Island.

Langdon would not remain to oversee the death throes of the Rock Island. Reaching the mandatory retirement age of sixty-five in 1970, Langdon was frustrated by the failure of the railroads and the UP to negotiate a solution to the merger mess. He implored Henry Crown to sit down and talk with the UP, which both men did shortly before the Klitenic syllabus was released. Langdon and Crown suggested that UP offer to buy the C&NW, but they refused to budge. "We couldn't do that. Don't have enough money and so forth and all kinds of phony excuses," Langdon later said. That meeting proved to be the icing on the cake. He wanted out, and an opportunity came from the June 1970 bankruptcy of the mammoth Penn Central Transportation Company. On July 26, 1970, Jervis Langdon was named one of four trustees for the company, resigning from the Rock Island the same day.[52]

The Rock Island board deferred naming an immediate successor, anointing Langdon protégé William J. Dixon as the man in charge without promoting him from senior vice president. In September, the board split the duties, naming Dixon president and Peter Kiewit (a board member from Nebraska and head of the Peter Kiewit Sons' Corporation, one of the largest engineering and construction companies in the world) acting chairman. Rock Island general counsel Theodore "Ted" Desch was named vice chairman and CEO.[53]

Peter Kiewit was born in Omaha in 1900 and started working for his father's and uncle's firm in 1914. A construction firm doing the bulk of its work in Nebraska, including the state capital building, Omaha Union Station, and other prominent buildings during the Depression and World War II, the firm expanded to become a national operation, building highways and military and naval bases. Kiewit also moved the firm into coal mining and during the 1950s, and until his death in 1979 the firm constructed missile silos in addition to military bases and was a major contractor for the building and maintenance of the Interstate Highway system. Kiewit built the Eisenhower Tunnel on Interstate 70 west of Denver, as well as dams and other major engineering projects.

William Dixon was one of "Jerv's boys," the nickname for a number of prominent railroad executives who were Jervis Langdon's protégés. He came to the Rock Island in 1965 from the Baltimore and Ohio Railroad, where he had been general manager of the industrial engineering department. Dixon was a native of Pittsburgh and attended Carnegie Institute of Technology, graduating in 1940 with a degree in chemical engineering. During World War II he served in the Army Military Railroad Service constructing railroads in Louisiana as well as a vital link for transporting military supplies to the Soviet Union, the Trans-Iranian Railroad. After the war he advised the Korean government in reconstructing its railroad system before joining the B&O in 1948. Skilled and experienced, he was recognized for his talent by Langdon and followed him to the Rock Island, where he rose through the ranks to become senior vice president and heir apparent to Langdon.[54]

Ted Desch was a native to the Rock Island. Growing up in the Beverly neighborhood of Chicago on the Rock Island suburban branch, Desch graduated from the University of Illinois with a law degree in 1954 and, after serving in the U.S. Army, joined the law department of the Rock Island. He worked on a variety of mundane legal matters—including property deeds and real estate—and became one of the leading principals on the merger agreement with the UP. He was appointed vice president and general counsel in 1968 and CEO upon Langdon's departure in 1970.[55]

The triumvirate faced a grim future as heads of the corporation. The railroad lost $16 million in 1970, and Dixon projected a loss of $26 million for the following year in an ICC rate case (if the rates were raised 15 percent the Rock Island would experience $13 million deficit for 1971, Dixon told the commission).[56] In 1970 the Rock Island increased operating revenues to $286 million, up $15 million from 1969. However, expenses rose by $12 million over the previous year, mostly due to the nationwide labor agreements. More ominously, the railroad's working capital deficit expanded by $9 million, with the railroad reporting a deficit in working capital of $10.2 million. While the railroad was able to make improvements, adding a computerized car-location system pioneered by IBM, the capital improvements to repair track and buy new equipment were lacking. Sounding like the broken record it was, Rock Island pleaded for a quick settlement of the prolonged merger case.[57]

A quick settlement of the merger was in doubt. Soon after the publication of Klitenic's five-page syllabus, the rail examiner suffered a heart attack and faced a prolonged recovery. The expected report on the merger kept getting postponed for the remainder of the year. On January 6, 1971, the ICC announced that it would appoint a three-member panel in the finance division to write the report, but other railroads objected to the switch. Klitenic returned to work in the spring of 1971, and in three staggering volumes, totaling more than 1,500 pages, he recommended a merger of the two railroads with conditions so onerous that there was little chance it would go through.

The first volume of the report, released in September 1971, spent 717 pages rehashing the main evidence presented in the case, including the position of the fifteen railroads involved as applicants or intervening carriers. Klitenic recommended that the C&NW control application and the ATSF application for control of southern portions of the Rock Island be denied. He approved the merger of the UP and Rock Island "subject to conditions." The conditions remained a subject for further volumes of the report. Klitenic outlined the proceedings in detail, presented the competing evidence for and against merger, and supported his understanding accordingly in favor of the UP–Rock Island merger.[58] Most of his focus was on the traffic patterns of the railroads and how they would be impacted by a merger, though evidentiary material on traffic was submitted rather than analysis. That would have to await the second and third volumes of the report. Delay had become the watchword for the Rock Island merger. But the lengthy gap between reports was a form of "Chinese water torture," as historian Richard Saunders called it.[59]

Missed by many chronicles of the merger was the striking similarity between Klitenic's proposal and a January 1969 report, "Western Railroad Mergers," prepared by the DOT's office of the assistant secretary for policy development and the Federal Railroad Administration (FRA). The staff recommended a redrawing of the western map into four or five hypothetical systems. These systems would meet the criteria of strategic balance, cost considerations, competitiveness, and financial strength. These were not recommendations that the DOT agency was making to the ICC, but they did strike a remarkable consistency with Klitenic's redrawing of the western map.

Unlike the ICC, however, the DOT staff was not required to appeal to the requirements of the merging railroads. The paper proposed instead a new arrangement for the western railroads with or without a Rock Island–UP combination.[60]

The Rock Island's response to Klitenic's first report was marginally optimistic. Management told stockholders that "only the application of the C&NW for control of the Rock Island through stock ownership was disposed of on its merits in the first volume. . . . Disposition of the other applications, including the all important conditions to the merger with the Union Pacific, will be covered in another volume." Was this false hope? Management also revealed that when the report was finally issued there was the matter of the Milwaukee Road's petition for inclusion in the merger, which itself necessitated a hearing before the ICC, and the commission would need more time to rule on the report. Then there would be litigation.[61] It would be a long time until the merger was consummated. Would the Rock Island survive?

FIVE

TOO BIG TO FAIL

I did not come to the Penn Central to liquidate it.
—Stuart Saunders, CEO, Penn Central Transportation Company

On June 21, 1970, the Penn Central Transportation Company filed for federal bankruptcy protection under Section 77 of the Bankruptcy Act of 1933. The nation's largest transportation company, with assets of $7 billion and revenues near $2 billion, running one-third of all passenger service and delivering one-eighth of the nation's freight, now was under the protection of a federal judge, John P. Fullam, who hurriedly appointed four trustees to oversee reorganization of the company, assuring nervous Wall Street investment banks that the company would continue operating. The Penn Central was a 19,000-mile system, with more than 100,000 employees. Formed in a merger between the Pennsylvania Railroad and the New York Central in February 1968, the railroad had lost $446 million in the two and a half years it was in business. To that date it was the largest failure of a corporation in American history.

The standard account of why the Penn Central failed is due to problems with coordinating operations once the new company was merged in February 1968. The two rail systems were very different operations. New York Central president Alfred Perlman, a dynamic railroad manager, had been hired in 1954 to turn around the declining fortunes of the road by then-CEO Robert Young. Seeking to modernize operations, and to invest in and improve passenger and freight operations, Perlman faced huge obstacles, including the declining industrial economy of the northeastern territory the NYC served, as well as the opening of the Interstate Highway System and the St. Lawrence Seaway. In 1958, the NYC posted a first quarter loss of $17.5 million. "You can't keep going like that for very long," Perlman told a congressional committee.[1]

The Pennsylvania Railroad, once heralding itself as the "standard railroad of the world," found itself in similar circumstances by the late 1950s. While it was a stronger road in terms of revenue and traffic than the NYC, it suffered economic pressures just the same. To compensate, both railroads slashed payrolls, abandoned passenger trains, and deferred maintenance on track and equipment. Yet losses still piled up. James Symes told the same congressional committee in 1958 that the Pennsylvania would lose $9 million in two months in April and May of that year.[2] Without crucial aid coming from government, the two railroads sought merger as a solution to their problems. Initially, Perlman was interested in merging with the Chesapeake and Ohio and the Baltimore and Ohio Railroads, but Walter Touhy, the canny and shrewd president of the C&O, acquired full control of the Baltimore & Ohio, forcing the two eastern giants into each other's arms in the process. Perlman thought the Pennsylvania would have been better off taking full control of the Norfolk and Western Railroad, as a way of splitting up the eastern map, with the NYC joining the C&O/B&O combination. But it was not to be. Disliked by Symes, Perlman never accepted the idea of merger with the Pennsylvania, yet there was nowhere else to turn, and he was forced to work toward a combination of the two lines.[3]

In 1963, after divesting itself of stock control of the coal-hauling Norfolk and Western, which had acquired NYC rivals Nickel Plate and was to lease the Wabash Railroad in 1964, N&W president Stuart Saunders was brought on board as Pennsylvania president to effectuate the merger with the NYC.[4] Interstate Commerce Commission hearings on the merger began in March 1962, with 25,000 pages of testimony and more than 100,000 pages of evidence produced from 129 days of hearings. The two railroads sold the merger to the public and to skeptical shippers and railroads by focusing on improved service, greater efficiency, and more competition.[5] The claim was that no losses of jobs and an estimated $60 million in savings would result from a merger. Labor unions reached agreements with both Perlman and Saunders to protect union jobs, allowing the company to transfer workers to other positions and locations on the system, but not to cut jobs.[6]

The administration of Lyndon Johnson supported the merger after Saunders convinced the president that he could upgrade tracks on the Northeast Corridor route to run 120-mile-per-hour Metroliners and do so for only $10 million. Johnson saw the high-speed line as a crucial mechanism for transportation in the congested Northeast. The Metroliners looked good and customers were pleased, but the equipment suffered routine mechanical breakdowns and often had to be pulled by ancient electric GG-1 locomotives built in the 1930s, defusing the space-age salesmanship the railroad offered riders of the new trains. Saunders seriously underestimated the cost to upgrade the line, which wound up costing $40 million that was better used elsewhere. But LBJ was mollified, and the Justice Department approved the merger.[7]

The fact that the new railroad would be the largest in the country worried management of smaller northeastern roads such as the Erie Lackawanna, Boston and Maine and the bankrupt New York, New Haven and Hartford Railroad, a largely passenger operation that had fallen on hard times after World War II. The Erie Lackawanna, itself a newly merged line, ran from Hoboken, New Jersey, connecting by rail ferry to New York and then westward to Chicago along the southern tier in New York, hugging the Pennsylvania border to Buffalo and thence northwest toward Chicago. At just over 3,500 miles, the EL was opposed to the merger unless it could join the new system.[8] No one wanted the New Haven, but as a condition of the merger, the Penn Central was forced to take it, inheriting a $28 million deficit and what historian Richard Saunders described as a "cadaverous railroad."[9] The Erie Lackawanna ended its opposition to the merger when it was included instead in a new arrangement with the C&O and Norfolk and Western Railroad called Dereco, a holding company that assumed operations over the EL but not its debt.[10] That latter proposition left the EL vulnerable to economic recession and natural disaster. After a severe recession in 1973 and major damage incurred on its northern tier line from Hurricane Agnes, the EL joined with the Penn Central, Jersey Central, Reading, Lehigh Valley and Boston & Maine in federal bankruptcy court.

The combined Penn Central Transportation Company posted transportation revenues of $1.7 billion in 1967, with real-estate holdings and dividends producing a total income of $2 billion. The company's consolidated earnings for the year were $71 million, half the amount from the year before due to write-offs from the merger, which gave the PC a loss of $203 million in its first year of operations. As Saunders and Perlman noted in the annual report, "Penn Central's consolidated earnings . . . reflect a growing contribution to profits by non-railroad subsidiaries, but a sharp decline in railroad net income. It was a poor year for the entire railroad industry, and particularly for those in the East."[11]

There were huge problems on the horizon. Railroad operations were taking a backseat to the acquisition of subsidiary companies. In fact, since Saunders came on board, the acquisition of subsidiary firms such as Great Southwest, Executive Jet Aviation, and other companies had diverted millions of dollars away from the railroad, in spite of what Pennsylvania Railroad VP for finance David Bevan told the board and the public. Bevan claimed that the railroad received a $146 million return by investing in new companies, but a congressional investigation into the diversification program showed that the railroad received a net return of $19.9 million while spending $144 million. "The $144 million expended by the Pennsylvania Company (the holding company for the Pennsylvania Railroad) on diversification involved the use of funds that ultimately could have been made available to the Railroad," the congressional staff report concluded. "Accordingly, it is clear that the diversification program, in effect, represented a very substantial cash drain on the Railroad."[12] Stuart Saunders disagreed, telling a House committee in July 1970 that "the railroad industry and the Penn Central in particular have been hit very hard by the recession, inflation, tight money and high interest rates." Saunders blamed inflation as the primary culprit, contributing to increased operating costs, the recession in 1969, and regulation and inadequacy of freight rate changes.[13]

Other railroads had diversified in the 1960s and had not experienced such problems as the Penn Central. Certainly, other factors played a role in the collapse of the system. Operational problems were a far clearer indication of management culpability in contributing to the PC's bankruptcy. Managers allowed for the creation of two separate operational cultures—the red team (PRR) and the green team (NYC)—contributing to inferior service, lost trains, and declining revenues. The lack of premerger planning in the coordination of computer systems, billing, and a unified management structure also worsened the situation out on the line. Shippers quit the Penn Central in droves, switching to trucks or other railroads if possible. Slow orders and declining maintenance took their toll on service, as train speeds declined and derailments and accidents increased. Promises to labor unions not to cut jobs as a condition of the merger now came back to haunt management, which could not decrease the number of union employees or abandon service.[14]

Irregularities in the reporting of Pennsylvania Railroad income to the ICC in order not to show railroad losses before the merger, and accounting practices that defied credulity, contributed as well to the company's financial weakness. The borrowing of huge sums of commercial paper from investment banks to fund working capital and payroll—to the tune of $200 million by 1970—contributed to a wretched financial outlook, much of which was hidden from regulators, government officials, investors, and the public. The culprit for congressional investigators was Penn Central finance VP David Bevan, who was eventually tried, and acquitted, on conspiracy charges after $4 million went missing from the company.[15]

Congressional investigators looked to find a fall guy to explain the collapse of the company. While the congressional reports on the Penn Central failure found fault with management, corporate boards interlocked with major investment banking houses, and individual charges of malfeasance against Bevan and Saunders for their role in the PC's failure, the investigations fell far short of offering the public a true rationale for the *railroad's* failure. It wasn't diversification alone; other railroads had diversified and had not engaged in corrupt or unethical accounting practices to hide their problems from the public. While individual managers and corporate officers were held accountable for the failure of the Penn Central, the failure of the railroad lay at the hands of archaic government regulations and policies favoring air, barge, and truck transport over railroads. The merger problems and subsequent corporate scandal blamed for the Penn Central failure were only pieces of a bigger puzzle in the railroad industry as a whole. The cause of the Penn Central's failure was no different from the anguish the Rock Island was experiencing in the late 1960s and early 1970s—government regulatory policies were destroying the railroad industry.

The railroad industry has been innovative in many areas over the course of its long history. It has helped in the process of industrialization and centralization of manufacturing; it has been a leading innovator in new technologies such as airbrakes, steam engines, and diesel locomotives, lately embracing alternating current traction locomotives as a power source; it fueled the development of the West and helped in the economic transformation of much of the United States; it developed new forms of corporate organization and financing; and it also helped in the development of labor organization.[16] It even contributed to the rise of the hospitality industry in America with Fred Harvey's pioneering Harvey House restaurants located along the Santa Fe mainline.[17] While many of these innovations were products of railroads, associated companies such as Pullman Corporation, Electro-Motive Division of General Motors, Westinghouse, and Baldwin Locomotive Works all helped make the railroads innovative and in the front rank of industrial and economic progress throughout much of the nineteenth and twentieth centuries.

One innovation the industry would rather not be remembered for, however, was its reliance on government bailouts. The $700 billion bailout of prominent Wall Street firms through passage of the Troubled Assets Relief Program (TARP) in October 2008 focused renewed attention on the relatively recent history of the federal government bailing out private companies. Stretching back through the bailouts of the airline industry (2001), the savings and loan industry (1989), Continental Bank of Illinois (1984), Chrysler Corporation (1980), and Lockheed (1972), taxpayer money to save corporations from bankruptcy was enshrined in law with the passage of the Emergency Loan Guarantee Act (1971), which provided $250 million for Lockheed.[18] The root of all modern government bailouts was the collapse of the Penn Central Transportation Company and the $3.2 billion credit line supplied to the railroad by the Federal Reserve Board.[19]

If you don't count the Reconstruction Finance Corporation (RFC) in the 1930s providing emergency loans to bankrupt railroads and banks, the bailout culture began in earnest with the shocking bankruptcy of the Penn Central Transportation Company in 1970 only two years after the new company was formed. The Penn Central was the seventh-largest corporation in America at the time of its bankruptcy filing and the largest transportation firm, holding assets of $7 billion in 1969. But its losses, magnified by an accounting scandal similar in its mendacity to that engaged in by the firm of Arthur Anderson and its client, Enron Corporation, were hovering around $300 million the same year. Since the Penn Central was reporting false figures to the ICC, no one really knew how big the losses were.[20]

The Penn Central bankruptcy drew significant government interest. The railroad operated 19,000 miles of track in the heavily populated Northeast and Midwest and ran the most passenger trains (both commuter operations in the Northeast and intercity trains) of any railroad. If the railroad failed, many officials worried, there would be economic chaos. Something had to be done to prevent the railroad's collapse. But how could government bail out a private company? Richard Nixon's administration and Congress would work out the details to prevent the complete failure and liquidation of the line, a real possibility. By doing so, the government helped usher in the era of "too big to fail."

Too big to fail is a phrase generally attributed to describe government action in the financial crisis of 2008 when Secretary of the Treasury Hank Paulson created the TARP program to restructure the "toxic assets" of mortgages held on the books of Wall Street banks. As a result, too big to fail became a derisive phrase, signifying that some banks and businesses, as a result of their size and importance to the global economy, would not be allowed to fail, while others would not be saved. Critics rightly worried that moral hazard would go out the window; if the government would bail out a firm due to its size alone, then what was to stop such a firm from engaging in the same risks in the future knowing it would be bailed out again? The collusion between Wall Street and Washington seemed assured with the passage of TARP.[21]

Critics of the Wall Street bailout have blamed the problem on a deregulated financial market. But no marketplace has ever been entirely deregulated in modern America. At best there has been an impasse between those who favor privatization and those who see a role for a continued defense of the public interest. Much of this battle has reflected ideological divisions within American politics since the 1970s.[22] The failure of regulators to prevent the financial meltdown and the housing bubble is as much to blame for the economic recession of 2008–2010 as is any attempt by the financial service industry to escape federal regulations. In the specific case of the railroad industry in the 1960s and 1970s, regulation proved the culprit in bringing about a culture of too big to fail. Deregulation proved to be the industry's saving grace.

If deregulation was a cause for the financial crisis in 2008, then how, in the heavily regulated railroad industry, could a too-big-to-fail culture develop? While deregulation may have been one culprit in bringing down the financial system, it was not the only cause for its failure and for the bailout of Wall Street that followed. But too much regulation *was* the principal cause for the bailout of railroads and other industries that developed through the 1970s and 1980s. Without freedom to control their own pricing, without freedom to abandon unprofitable lines and passenger service, and hamstrung by archaic rules and regulations dating back to the turn of the previous century, railroads diversified their portfolios, forming holding companies that used the railroad as the basis for capital to fund other, more lucrative investments. Certain railroads, such as the Union Pacific, managed this deftly and put money back into the railroad, but others, like the Penn Central, allowed the railroad to decay past a point of no return. While government bailouts would provide a short-term answer for the railroad problem in the 1970s, deregulation proved to be the long-term solution. Both possibilities loomed large in the minds of railroad executives during the decade.

Railroads like the Rock Island and Milwaukee Road, both of which filed for bankruptcy during the 1970s, should have benefited from the bailout culture. But they were too small to succeed, not granted the access to government funds used to shore up bankrupt railroads in the Northeast. In the remaking of the railroad industry during the decade, railroads like the Rock Island, which had been victimized by the long-delayed report on the Union Pacific merger, was victimized once again by being refused sufficient money for track rehabilitation, which it desperately needed in order to survive as a railroad.

On June 30, 1970, America's Sound Transportation Review Organization (ASTRO), a group sponsored by the Association of American Railroads (AAR), released a report, "The American Railroad Industry: A Prospectus." Founded the previous year by a former senator, George Smathers (D–Fla.), and Robert Blanchette (appointed as one of the trustees of the Penn Central), the Astro Report, as it became known, was designed to show the importance of railroads to the economy as well as to make recommendations concerning how railroads could prosper in the coming decade. Rumors of imminent nationalization were fueled by problems within the industry as a whole, and Smathers wanted to portray the railroads as a vibrant, cost-effective form of transportation for the future shipping needs of the nation. "Railroads will play an even more valuable role in meeting the challenges of tomorrow than they do today," the report optimistically declared.[23]

Yet Smathers recognized that the railroad industry was beset with problems, far greater than when he held hearings on the "railroad problem" a decade earlier that culminated in the passage of the Transportation Act of 1958. Their working capital had declined precipitously from $955 million in 1955 to $58 million in 1970, with thirty-four railroads, including the Rock Island, having negative balances of working capital, which resulted in more borrowing to fund equipment needs. "Interest rates and other 'fixed charges' of the industry consumed 27 percent of railroad earnings before taxes in 1955. They now take up 73 percent."[24] The ICC recognized in 1969 the dismal state of the industry, with the report stating "after 83 years of regulation, it [ICC] could only conclude of the railroads: given competitive pressure, continued inflation and unsatisfactory rates of return, the general financial condition of the railroads may be expected to remain poor, capital expenditures to remain minimal, and reduction in employment extended."[25] It was a dismal forecast; how could it be changed?

The Astro Report called for creative federal government policies, including the alleviation of local taxes on railroad property and rights-of-way. Railroads were the only shipping entity that paid taxes on property, a significant disadvantage to profitability. It called for a federal crossing-gate program to alleviate maintenance of railroad crossings throughout the country (eventually a program that fell under the sway of the National Transportation Safety Board). Finally, the authors called for a federal transportation fund that would allow for government funds to rehabilitate railroad roadbed and track, paid for by federally backed loans (the report called for $400 million) to help railroads improve rights-of-way.[26]

The final section of the report dealt with inequities in government regulation of transportation, tracing the history of regulation and showing how railroads were regulated far more than trucking (less than 50 percent regulated) and barges (unregulated). It then suggested that the government look to abolish the ratemaking powers of the ICC, arguing that "railroad managers are blocked at almost every turn in managing their business with imagination and enterprise."[27] Calling for the elimination of unfair rate discrimination on the part of the government, Astro fell short of backing complete deregulation of railroad rates, but it was clear that the industry and its trade association were moving in that direction.

The Nixon administration was caught in between the growing demand for government assistance to aid the railroad industry and a growing number of economists and businessmen who sought to deregulate transportation. In the end it chose to do both, splitting the difference with a Democratic Congress that favored a government program to aid railroads—leading to the creation of Amtrak, the National Passenger Railroad Corporation, in April 1971, and passage of the Regional Rail Reorganization Act (3R Act) in January 1974. The Nixon White House also encouraged studies on deregulation of the industry.[28] It was this latter viewpoint that continued into the presidencies of Gerald Ford and Jimmy Carter after the failure of government bailouts became readily apparent with both Amtrak and the federally funded Consolidated Rail Corporation (Conrail), created in January 1976 to take over the properties and operations of seven bankrupt northeastern railroads.

The first railroad problem Nixon faced was the collapse of the private passenger train system. Journalist Fred Frailey has written that "the passenger train was wounded by competition, technology, unfair treatment by government and management indifference or ineptness and labor's refusal to change, and then put out of its misery by the postal service."[29] Few Americans were riding passenger trains in the post–World War II era, even as railroads invested in streamlined equipment and improvements in service. By 1960 only 29 percent of travelers went by rail, a decline from 74 percent who traveled by rail during World War II. During the 1960s, in spite of the best efforts of some railroads to preserve service, the hemorrhage of passengers continued, reaching less than 6 percent by 1970.

The end of government subsidies to carry mail by train in the late 1960s put the final nail in the coffin for even the most prestigious passenger trains. The Rock Island, as we have seen, dropped its best trains in 1967 and 1968 with the *Rocky Mountain Rocket, Twin Star Rocket,* and *Golden State* all ending service. A railroad losing money could hardly afford to keep passenger service. It was difficult enough in the climate of the late 1960s and early 1970s for most railroads to keep freights operating.

What was to be done about the passenger train? Secretary of Transportation John Volpe and members of Congress proposed to save what remained of the system, to rationalize service, and to promote passenger trains through federal subsidies. Congress was already at work on a plan to fix the passenger train network, labeled Railpax; the Democratic-controlled House of Representatives favored direct subsidies by the federal government to railroads to keep the passenger trains running. As Volpe told the White House in a memorandum, "Railroad management is almost universally opposed to remaining in the passenger business, with or without subsidy. If they are required to stay in the business, they want 100% subsidy, nothing less."[30]

The Senate's Commerce Committee had been working for a full year on developing a bill by the time the Nixon White House started to pay attention. Fearful that the Senate bill would subsidize 100 percent of remaining passenger service (close to 500 intercity trains were then operating), Volpe proposed legislation that would offer a partial subsidy of $40 million to establish the National Railroad Passenger Corporation (Railpax), far less money than potential legislation that would come from Congress, which totaled as much as $500 million over four to five years.[31] Volpe told Nixon that DOT had developed a proposal—rejected as infeasible by members of the Nixon White House—"which we feel has a good prospect for substantive success and which would keep federal costs to a minimum ($40 million of grant and $60 million of loan guarantees in the aggregate over five years)." "In the absence of an Administration proposal," Volpe continued, "it is highly probable that the Congress will take the initiative and will act. The potential courses of action Congress will be expected to take range from economically undesirable to fiscally injudicious. No action at all will simply impose further very serious damage to our Nation's rail network."[32]

Nixon aide John Erlichman was skeptical of the administration's involvement, informing the president that Volpe "feels under some pressure from the Senate to come up with an alternative [to 100 percent subsidy]. However, his staff work has been quite mediocre and incomplete and we will continue to press for a satisfactory submission before we move the matter to you." He continued: "At this writing it would appear that the Federal government should not get involved in this. If the Senate acts on some kind of 100% subsidy, we will probably recommend to you that you veto it."[33] Before a scheduled meeting with Volpe on March 5, 1970, Erlichman told Nixon that the bill was not ready and that no decision should be taken on it at the time.[34]

The Senate acted instead. On March 12, 1970, it submitted a bill calling for subsidy of remaining passenger trains for four years, at a cost of $435 million. The Nixon White House did nothing, stonewalling Congress and bottling up the Railpax bill in the White House. Then something strange happened. A Railpax bill was sent to Congress on the night of April 30, 1970. "The delivery was totally unofficial, never officially approved by the White House, and if anyone knows who delivered it, they're not talking to this day," *Washington Post* transportation journalist Don Phillips wrote. On the very next day, the Railpax bill was submitted as a replacement bill for the Senate version and was quickly approved without debate by a 78–3 margin.[35]

It would take another five months for the House to pass the bill creating the National Railroad Passenger Corporation. A slew of last-minute memos crossed Nixon's desk. Volpe urged its passage and was joined by several other government agencies. The Council of Economic Advisors (CEA) and Office of Management and Budget (OMB) recommended a veto due to economic considerations. The OMB director, George Shultz, told Nixon that the legislation had "high costs and limited benefits." White House political assistant William Timmons urged White House counsel Ken Cole that Nixon should sign it for political reasons. "A veto could embarrass some of our political friends," Timmons wrote. "It could hurt some of our candidates who favor signing it (Lowell Weicker, Hugh Scott and Jim Prouty)." He continued: "In light of these factors, I recommend signing from a Congressional/political viewpoint."[36] There was concern in the administration that if Nixon did not sign the bill it would cause DOT Secretary Volpe to resign. Peter Flanigan, Nixon's assistant for transportation in the White House, opposed the bill on economic grounds, stating that the proposal was too optimistic regarding the new railroad's profitability and that he feared continuing federal government subsidies into the future.

> I do not believe it is sound administration practice or politically credible for the Administration in the absence of overwhelming new evidence now to reverse its principal spokesman for transportation policy. To do so on the eve of a Congressional election would seem particularly undesirable. Therefore, unless the President is prepared to risk Secretary Volpe's resignation, I would recommend that he sign the Railpax bill.[37]

Nixon signed the bill into law on October 30, 1970, with a projected start-up date of May 1, 1971. The new corporation placed a freeze on passenger train service for six months until the May 1 commencement date. It also called for railroads operating intercity passenger trains to join the new company according to one of three formulas: either paying cash or rolling stock equal to 50 percent of the railroad's passenger deficit for 1969; 100 percent of the avoidable loss for passenger train operation in 1969; or 200 percent of the avoidable losses for service between points in the new network created by Volpe and DOT.[38] Outside the Northeast Corridor (the route between Washington, D.C., and Boston), the new passenger corporation would operate a paltry network. Out of 259 passenger trains operating in March 1971, only 110 would still be in operation under the new Amtrak system ("American Travel and Track") created on May 1.[39]

The Rock Island could not afford the Amtrak entry fee and on April 1, 1971, opted out of joining the new passenger corporation, being the first railroad to do so. Under the law railroads that did not join the new corporation were required to operate their passenger services for two years.[40] The Rock Island had only two operating intercity trains by that point: from Chicago to Peoria and from Chicago to Rock Island. Losses on the determined formula in the law would have required the Rock Island to pay $4.5 million for Amtrak operations. Rock Island CEO Ted Desch stated, "While the annual loss experienced by the two pairs of trains is great, the cost to Rock Island of joining Railpax, payable over the next three years, is very high."[41] The decision proved costly for the Rock Island. Keeping the trains in operation drained revenues. The Rock Island had annual losses topping $1 million through the end of service on December 31, 1978. The State of Illinois provided a subsidy of $1 million, increasingly to serve a declining number of riders on wobbly track. Nicknamed the *Peoria Rocket* and *Quad Cities Rocket* by railfans, the trains were anything but, with slow orders providing a leisurely ride of more than five hours over the 150-mile trip, hardly the two-and-a-half hours it took in the 1960s to reach the Quad Cities from Chicago.

The creation of Amtrak likely would not have occurred without the bankruptcy of the Penn Central, which crystallized the White House's response to the railroad problem. Nixon was concerned about the growing problems on the railroads for some time, but he wanted to avoid direct government assistance. On March 5, 1970, he recommended that the administration pursue studies about deregulating railroads and trucking, and he instructed Volpe to take up the matter with the Council of Economic Advisors.[42] An interagency subcommittee of the Cabinet Committee on Economic Policy—consisting of members of DOT, OMB, the CEA, Labor, and Justice—held working meetings to craft suggestions for improving the regulatory impact on railroads. Nixon assistant Peter Flanigan played an active role in focusing the group's discussions and working papers on deregulation.

Volpe was feeling like the odd man out. On June 12, 1970, he wrote to Erlichman suggesting that various groups, both in Congress and in the administration, were taking the lead on regulatory reform. "Peter Flanigan has brought together representatives of the various agencies . . . with the idea of developing changes in regulatory policy," Volpe wrote. "A committee has been formed under the Council of Economic Advisors to look at various possibilities and some tentative ideas have been circulated. Except for the latter, we have not been privy to these endeavors and know very little about their character, objectives, or interim findings."[43]

The Federal Reserve had issued a report on the financial condition of the Penn Central in May 1970. "Penn Central requires loans of about $263 million over the next seven months," the report stated, "of which $100 million is needed immediately."[44] Efforts by the Nixon administration to negotiate a $200 million "V-loan" with the Department of Defense under the Korean War–era Defense Production Act fell apart when the New York Federal Reserve concluded in its report that "the proposed V-loan financing in the amount of $200 million maturing on October 31, 1970, of itself, would provide inadequate assistance to the Company, and, in all likelihood, merely postpone the institution of proceedings under the bankruptcy act." Congressman Wright Patman, the prickly populist Texas Democrat, told the House: "The $200 million or the $225 million being sought under the guarantee was only the beginning of the welfare program for this giant corporation." With no chance of repaying the terms of the loan, Patman asked, "how could the Administration go this far down the road in a plan to throw hundreds of millions of dollars out the window? What prompted public officials to act in such a manner with public funds?"[45] The V-loan was not granted.

Groups within CEA and OMB had also been busy working on the railroad problem, and their interest accelerated in the wake of the Penn Central bankruptcy. Paul McCracken, chairman of the CEA and a University of Michigan economist, told Nixon that a plan should be supported to allow railroads with financial problems to "be exempt from Interstate Commerce Commission regulation for a given period of time or until the road was financially strong again." Coupled with the White House's loan guarantee program for ailing railroads, this could contribute to a "freer transportation system." McCracken argued that "it would be inaccurate to say that the heavy hand of regulation was the sole or even the major cause of financial difficulty of the railroads, but it has certainly contributed to their problems." "The example of railroads operating free of regulation might well indicate that some of the reasons for regulation have long since disappeared." OMB director Shultz agreed and suggested that the proposal took a long-term look at solving the railroad problem. "If it could be demonstrated that selected deregulation produces stronger and more efficient transportation systems," Shultz wrote, "the trend towards more Federal involvement and ever-increasing Federal spending in transportation might be reversed."[46]

The path toward deregulation kept getting derailed by the crisis of the Penn Central and the plight of other northeastern bankrupts. What had been a long-term economic goal now was sacrificed to short-term political considerations as pressure was mounting on Washington to take substantive action on the bankrupt railroads. Since the PC bankruptcy filing in June 1970, the Penn Central had brought on board new management, hiring William H. Moore as president in September 1970, replacing Stuart Saunders (who was fired by the trustees). Moore was an operations man who had success running the Southern Railway. David P. Morgan of *Trains* magazine wrote, "The man who brings the PC back onto high iron will rate and will receive a splendid press. He will be bigger than E.H. Harriman who brought the Union Pacific back from the dead [in 1898]."[47] The Trustees told a Senate Commerce Committee hearing that "there is a reasonable prospect that the Penn Central can be restored to effectiveness and made viable again within three or five years." They wanted a joint private and public partnership to secure $175–250 million over the next four months "and possibly that much more over the next 36 months." The private capital wells for the railroad were dry, however, and Congress took the point that the railroad was asking for a bailout from the federal government.[48] The Nixon administration had proposed a bill authorizing $750 million in short-term loan guarantees for the railroads, but Congress had not yet debated the proposal.

Although Congress was not yet willing to act, the administration was. The railroad crisis in the Northeast was spreading, and there was fear that the bankrupt Central Railroad of New Jersey, a coal hauler and commuter line between Newark and Scranton, Pennsylvania, would cease operations entirely by the end of the year.[49] Justice Department officials urged the use of trustee certificates for the CNJ, and mention was made of getting the State of New Jersey to assume operation of the commuter lines on the property. Meanwhile the Penn Central's fortunes rested on an Emergency Labor Board determination concerning retroactive wage rates payable to labor unions on the bankrupt line. The board's recommendation was for wage increases of between 5 percent to 8.5 percent, which would cost the PC an additional $260 million by 1973. "May knock out Reading and some others," according to notes from one meeting. What if the PC refused the increase? A strike was predicted, and discussants needed to plan for that eventuality. "Maybe CNJ disaster will job Congress into loan guarantee bill that will save PC. DOT is convinced $750 million fund is enough to save PC *if* lending institutions will come forward. . . . PC says, look, with high deficits and negative cash flow, no bank will lend money."[50]

The financial difficulties of the PC forced the Trustees to tell a House committee in December 1970 that if loan guarantees were not granted to the railroad "there is the prospect, bordering on certainty, that unless emergency action is taken immediately, the Penn Central railroad will have to shut down within the next 30 or 45 days for lack of funds." The wage increases to labor forced the hands of the Trustees, they told the House committee, negating a 7 percent rate increase allowed by the ICC. "We proceed with the conviction that the answer is not nationalization. That would only mean embalming all the mistakes which have been made, preserving them by passing on a tremendous continuing bill to the taxpayer." But some emergency help was needed or the entire railroad would cease operations. "No one can really bring himself to recognize the fact that the Penn Central railroad may actually have to stop running. . . . But this is the fact, and it would be worse not to say so."[51]

The Federal Reserve also studied the possible impact on the economy of a shutdown of the PC. The report concluded that "the loss of the Penn Central's facilities for even a short time would obviously deal a severe blow to the orderly functioning of the economy and to those persons who rely upon its passenger facilities for commutation to work or other purposes." The shutdown might lead to rationing of electrical power as coal could not be moved, and "it is not inconceivable that developments could occur, in both the real and the financial markets, sufficient to create an economic recession of a greater magnitude than that experienced at any time in the postwar period."[52] Undersecretary of the Treasury for Monetary Affairs Paul Volcker told a Senate hearing that no current statutory authority for providing assistance to the PC existed. However, the Nixon administration's bill to provide loan guarantees to the PC and other bankrupt railroads should be supported, Volcker testified, if "such legislation is unambiguous, cover[s] the full risk, and provide[s] means of promptly discharging the Government's obligations should recourse to the guarantee become necessary."[53]

DOT Secretary John Volpe told the Senate Commerce Committee that "in the short term, there appears to be no substitute for Federal financial assistance. Without substantial infusions of cash, the roads now in reorganization face the possibility of liquidation. . . . So long as there is a reasonable prospect of recreating a viable, privately-owned carrier through the process of reorganization . . . we should make every effort to do so." Volpe proposed a bill with loan guarantees of $500 million, but these were short-term measures.

> I cannot overemphasize the need to deal with the more basic problems confronting the entire railroad industry. . . . We must squarely face the long-standing problems affecting rail transportation and look for solutions in such areas as: revising Federal and state regulatory

policies; removing the discriminatory taxation and reviewing the tax laws for other inequities; increasing the productivity of the industry through improved labor and management practices; improving railroad operating efficiency; and exploring other areas of railroad operations where new concepts or new technology might lead to greater efficiency.[54]

There the matter sat. The loan was not allowed—yet. The darkest hour for Penn Central and the other northeastern bankrupts was still to come. For the next year Nixon aides and the president himself worked to gain support for a partial deregulation of both railroads and trucking, securing commitments from railroad executives, labor officials, and a few shippers that railroad deregulation would be beneficial. Flanigan prepared a bill that the administration submitted to Congress in October 1971. However, politics intervened, and the administration backed away from supporting the bill. Truckers and their powerful Teamsters Union were not interested in deregulation, and they had great clout in Congress and within an administration seeking political support for its program from working-class Americans.[55]

Meanwhile, support for a bailout of the northeastern railroads intensified. Not only did Amtrak relieve the PC of passenger train operations; northeastern states were in the process of working to create municipal commuter transit agencies to take on the burden of commuter operations from the struggling railroads. New York, Connecticut, and Pennsylvania all entered agreements to lease track and pay the PC to operate commuter operations. The railroad sold its New York City–Connecticut line to the New York Metropolitan Transit Agency for $7.2 million, relieving the PC of the headache of operating and maintaining the former New Haven line.[56]

But none of this ended the deficits, which continued to accrue. Even with better operating men on board; even with a growing rationalization of the system and improvements in computer systems for car relocation; and even with federal assistance totaling $150 million between 1971 and 1976, the railroad still ran up substantial deficits totaling $600 million in the three-year period ending in 1975. In 1971 alone, with an improving economic picture from previous years, the railroad lost $550 million. In part this was due to the intractable political problem of securing abandonment of significant portions of redundant and unprofitable track. The ICC refused to consider the abandonment of 6,000 miles of track as proposed by bankruptcy Trustee Jervis Langdon in a core proposal submitted to the commission. "Even the smallest segment required a separate application, questionnaire, hearings, briefs, and oral arguments (if requested), with final ICC decision later," Langdon said.[57] Labor costs were extraordinary, and every effort to cut back on costs met with sarcasm from labor, with the president of the United Transportation Union (UTU), Al Chesser, blaming "the bloodthirsty, stinking tactics of mismanagement" for the PC's problems and refusing to negotiate with the Trustees on constructive solutions.[58]

Federal Railroad Administrator John W. Ingram (who would become president of the Rock Island in October 1975) showcased the difficulties railroads faced in getting rid of unnecessary track. He told one audience in a speech about the railroad crisis in the Northeast:

> Let me tell you a little story about the abandonment of unprofitable branch lines. One weekend last summer I was headed for Rehoboth Beach, Delaware, to enjoy the Atlantic Ocean. You have to drive across the Eastern Shore of Maryland to get there, and I asked my staff to list a few of those Eastern Shore branch lines that the Penn Central wants to abandon. I wanted to see them for myself—perhaps count the boxcars on the sidings to see if there really was a shortage of business. I drove to the area, checked my maps, and simply *couldn't find* anything that looked like a railroad. On Monday morning, I hollered at my staff for having sent me off on a wild goose chase, but they stuck to their guns. So we went back—this time with property maps and a surveyor.
>
> We found the branch line, all right. At one place it was directly under a junkyard full of wrecked cars. At another point the highway department had covered the tracks with at least eight inches of pavement. And just off the road we found a six-inch wide tree growing between the rails. That line had been completely forgotten, yet grown men were arguing before the ICC that that stretch of track was vital to the Nation's economy![59]

Not every abandonment procedure was that ridiculous, but many were. And as the profitability of the entire industry seemed at stake, railroads quickened the pace of abandonment filings, with experts predicting that by the end of the 1970s about half of the existing track in the nation would be abandoned.[60]

The railroad crisis worsened in June 1972 when Hurricane Agnes devastated the northeastern states, hitting Pennsylvania and New York especially hard. The Erie Lackawanna experienced losses of $11 million and had more than 200 miles of track washed out in southern New York. That was the last straw for Dereco, which pushed its subsidiary carrier into Section 77 bankruptcy as a result.[61] The other bankrupt carriers did not fare well either, with losses of all four carriers totaling an estimated $40 million. More than 4,400 freight cars and 1,400 locomotives had been destroyed by the flooding. EL president Gregory Maxwell told Congress that "prior to the storm, we anticipated we would show a breakeven income statement at the end of the year. Instead, due to Agnes, we will have a $20 million deficit." The storm washed out major bridges along the PC's mainline between Philadelphia and Pittsburgh, causing "an operational nightmare," William Moore told Congress. Asking Congress for money to deal with the costs of the flooding, the bankrupt roads all stated that if aid was not forthcoming they would have to stop operating by winter.[62]

Congress appropriated the requested money for weather-related repairs. Under the Emergency Rail Facilities Restoration Act of 1972, railroads could apply for generous low-interest loans, and a fund of $40 million was created to help alleviate the damage from the hurricane.[63] But the railroads' problems were not solved. The PC was on the verge of collapse by the end of the year. Trustees told U.S. District Court Judge John Fullam that the railroad could not be reorganized on an income basis without significant financial help. After itemizing expenses, the Trustees were set to request $600 million from Congress through 1976 to allow the railroad the ability to repair and rehabilitate track and equipment. After that the railroad would need an additional $200 million until earnings improved and it could make it on its own.[64]

Congress asked the Nixon administration to come up with a plan to address the northeastern railroad problem and to do so by March 25, 1973. But Nixon was distracted by other pressing issues, including the peace treaty in Vietnam, as well as the Watergate hearings that began in March. In February the Penn Central was shut down by a massive strike, and Nixon ordered striking workers back to the job the next day. Fearful of an entire industry collapsing, and in light of the possibility that the government would take action, Judge Fullam delayed a PC filing of a plan of reorganization until July, arguing that "it has long been apparent that the particular problems of Penn Central cannot be completely divorced from problems of national transportation policy. . . . It would obviously be premature, therefore, for this Court to make final proceeding on the basis of the existing legislative and regulatory framework."[65] He ordered the Trustees to file a workable plan for reorganization—or else a plan for liquidation.

Nixon had embraced Trustee Jervis Langdon's July 1972 reorganization plan, which called for a reduction by half of the Penn Central's track and of its workforce. Nixon wanted to make sure that the Penn Central survived as a private corporation and had the new U.S. secretary of labor, George Shultz, plan for a new company (nicknamed "De Nova" within the White House), which would operate Penn Central lines.[66] De Nova would require current bondholders and creditors to invest in the new company, a dicey prospect at best, and it depended on a waiver of all ICC regulations should it succeed (there would be no hearings on abandonments). Not surprisingly, the concept went nowhere.

Congress had waffled as well through the spring of 1973, until the Trustees reported on June 29 "that unless government financial assistance is made available by October 1 the railroad's freight and passenger services would terminate beginning October 31, 1973." "In the absence of government aid the financial condition of the estate has become so perilous that prudent stewardship requires immediate attention to an orderly cessation of service before the end of the year."[67] This was the shock to the system that Congress needed to take action.

Two proposals were put forth. Senator Vance Hartke (D–Ind.), better known for his long and vocal opposition to the Vietnam War, proposed a solution known as ConFac (Consolidated Facilities). The idea was to make the Penn Central right-of-way publicly owned, that is, after a 1 percent tax on all surface transportation was collected and used to rehabilitate the track. Then any railroad would be able to use the line for a fee paid to the U.S. Treasury. There were problems with such a proposal, including the issue of compensation for taking the property itself, but through the 1970s some type of government ownership of the nation's railroad right-of-way kept being discussed as one solution.[68]

The second proposal came from the Union Pacific's Frank Barnett. Barnett was concerned that if the Penn Central was liquidated, and if nothing was done for the other bankrupt roads in the Northeast, then the UP would have significant trouble, as 25 percent of its interchange business was through those carriers. So Barnett and UP general counsel William McDonald wrote a bill themselves and solicited a sponsor, whom they found in Republican Representative Dick Shoup (R–Mont.). The bill seemed workable and it gained support after Representative Brock Adams (D–Wash.) loaned his name to the bill after Barnett had Stephen Ailes of the Association of American Railroads take the bill to shop around Congress. In December 1973 the Shoup-Adams Bill—the Regional Rail Reorganization Act —passed Congress.[69] Nixon signed it into law on January 6, 1974.[70]

The 3R Act called for the creation of a national nonprofit corporation, eventually called the United States Railway Administration (USRA). The USRA could issue loans and loan guarantees outside of budget constraints in Congress, similar to the role of Fannie Mae, the national mortgage asso-

Photo 5.1 Representative Brock Adams (D–Wash.), seated left, and Representative Richard Shoup (R–Mont.), seated right, at a 1973 dinner. Both men would sponsor passage of the Regional Rail Reorganization Act (the 3R Act), a bill drafted largely by Frank Barnett and William McDonald of the Union Pacific Railroad. Photo from Brock Adams Photo Collection, used with permission of University of Washington, Department of Special Collections.

ciation created in the 1930s. The USRA—not Congress—was given the task of creating a new railroad corporation in the Northeast, to rationalize the system, and to prepare a final system plan leading to the creation of a private railroad corporation (Conrail), which could operate the new northeastern railroad network. The cost of the proposed startup and operation of Conrail was expected to be from $1.5 billion up to $2 billion to rehabilitate track and modernize plant and equipment, a significant expense and one that caused the most consternation as the bill was finalized.[71] Furthermore, loans under the provisions of the act were to be made available to all northeastern and Midwestern railroads, not just the northeastern bankrupts.[72] (See Photo 5.1.)

The decision to provide assistance for all bankrupt and ailing railroads in the northeastern and Midwestern regions signified to executives at the

Rock Island that federal aid would be made available to the railroad should the unthinkable occur: the merger with the Union Pacific did not go through. Provisions to secure a loan from the federal government through the USRA were being discussed by Rock Island management after the passage of the 3R Act in January 1974. As it turned out, even though the merger of the Rock Island and Union Pacific had been approved by the ICC in the final version of the Klitenic Report, released in February 1973, the UP no longer wanted the Rock Island. Only federal assistance could save the Rock Island. Whereas the Penn Central was too big to fail, the Rock Island proved to be too small to save—or to succeed.

ACT TWO

BANKRUPTCY

SIX

BANKRUPTCY BLUE(S)

> Paralysis on the Rock Island benefits other railroads who see either elimination of competition or—more importantly—an opportunity to serve our market at taxpayers' expense with a guaranteed profit. It is a situation that would have brought a gleam to the eye of the old robber barons. I don't think the Congress wants this unfair and expensive prospect to become fact.
>
> —John W. Ingram, Senate Testimony, March 10, 1975

The long delay by the Interstate Commerce Commission to approve the merger between the Rock Island and the Union Pacific helped kill the smaller company, which had declined since the merger was first filed with the commission in 1964. The decision by ICC Rail Examiner Nathan Klitenic to redraw the western railroad map as a condition of approving the merger, and the piecemeal release of the three-volume report over a span of two years, contributed to UP's declining interest in the Rock Island. The physical condition of the Rock necessitated slow order operation on most mainline routes; the condition of most branchlines was deplorable, with speeds reduced to 10 or 20 miles per hour on wobbly track, which in places sank into the ground beneath it. The financial condition of the company prevented any maintenance or improvement of its track. And it would eventually be forced to stop running altogether unless it could improve the balance sheet demonstrably.

The ICC's final announcement approving the merger came on November 8, 1974. "By its order," ICC Commissioner George Stafford announced, "the Commission will conditionally authorize the UP to acquire the Rock Island by merger, provided that certain portions are transferred to the Denver and Rio Grande Western, the Southern Pacific Transportation Company and the Atchison, Topeka and Santa Fe Railway Company." The DRGW would acquire the Rock Island mainline between Omaha and Denver, while the Santa Fe would be required to purchase the line from Memphis to Amarillo. As a further condition, the Santa Fe would be required to purchase the Missouri–Kansas–Texas Railroad, and other railroads would be offered relief in the form of traffic rights and interchange agreements with railroads like the C&NW, Milwaukee Road, Kansas City Southern, and Frisco.[1] The details of these acquisitions would be negotiated by the railroads themselves subject to ICC ratification.

What to do about the merger between the two railroads had produced some striking disagreements within the ICC about the impact of their decisionmaking on the western railroad map. The "Godfather" approach to the merger—make an offer the railroads couldn't refuse—came about through discussions among staff and commissioners in late 1973.

> Competing carriers will force one another to accept the relief proposed by the Commission out of fear of destruction should a competitor by accepting Commission relief pose a threat of substantial diversion of traffic. The problem with this approach is that applicant, UP, may say the hell with the whole thing. . . . Personally, I would not worry about the parties rejecting the Commission's decision. The worst thing that can happen to RI is that it goes bankrupt, and we get another shot at the reorganization stage. . . . It is certainly not the Commission's fault for the failure of the Rock Island.[2]

Another approach was voluntarism—making carriers agree among themselves regarding the conditions specified in Klitenic's report. The end result would be the formation of four major western systems (which is what Klitenic had called for), but with the railroads cooperatively making this happen, not through ICC order.[3] Commissioner Daniel O'Neal responded favorably to the suggestion but reminded staff that "there does not appear to be sufficient motivation evidenced by the critical carriers to move voluntarily even in their own long range self interest."[4]

O'Neal personally favored denying the merger at the end of 1973 so that the railroads could be compelled to rework the western region in their own interest. "A grant of the application [for merger] could result in improvement of at least a part of Rock Island's track and service and, if it is soon enough, protect it from possible bankruptcy," O'Neal wrote. "In my view, if no substantial service improvement would follow from the merger there would clearly be no justification for approval. Approval simply to avoid the Rock Island's bankruptcy thereby endangering other carriers would not be in the interest of the public."[5] Commissioner Kenneth Tuggle responded: "This case has been here more than ten years. A most meticulous study was made by Klitenic. If the Commission proposes a restructure not geared to the UP-RI application, and not relying on the leverage given it by that application, it might just as well [accept] Klitenic's work instead of starting anew and soliciting 'voluntary' conclusions." O'Neal wrote in the margins: "I think he means staff approach is attempting to come up with an offer they won't refuse."[6] In the end, the ICC's decision to allow the merger with conditions split the commissioners. But the decision itself, plus the conditions, were a product of real effort over the course of the previous year to achieve consensus on the merger.

Rock Island management, of course, was not privy to such discussions. One of the few alternatives it possessed for raising cash was to present the railroad's desperate case before the ICC and its merger partner, the UP. On March 7, 1973, CEO Ted Desch, Kirkland & Ellis attorney E. Houston Harsha, and board chairman Peter Kiewit met in Washington with ICC Chairman George Stafford and Kenneth Tuggle of the ICC's Finance Division. Desch presented the bleak financial news and pleaded for some resolution of the merger. "Speedy denial of its application was preferable to the current situation," Desch argued. Tuggle "seemed sympathetic to the Rock Island's situation," Desch reported, but Stafford "said very little in the meeting."[7]

The Rock Island executives traveled to New York that afternoon for a meeting with Frank Barnett of the UP. They discussed the exchange agreement and its termination if the merger was not effectuated by the 1974 date. Barnett stated that the UP was still interested in the merger as proposed but that he had seen maps, in reference to the western railroads, in the Department of Transportation "showing extension of the Southern Pacific to Pittsburgh, of the Santa Fe to Detroit, and some truly coast-to-coast transcontinental railroads." Barnett revealed that the UP was to propose a solution to the eastern railroad crisis and hoped for a settlement of the merger proceedings in the West "within four months." "Desch then observed that Rock Island might not last that long. William McDonald [of the UP] was visibly shocked, Barnett less so, but attentive." Desch proposed deferring payments on leases of equipment, to which there was no commitment. McDonald asked whether the Rock Island could raise cash through unissued bonds, but Desch replied that he wasn't sure of the value of the bonds. The two sides parted with "Barnett expressing sympathy for the Rock Island's position, but [without] suggestions for any interim help."[8]

Three months later, on June 26, 1973, Rock Island's management team—including Desch, William Dixon, and Kiewit, along with board members Henry Crown, John D'Arcy, and Bruce Norris—met in New York with Union Pacific executives Frank Barnett, John Kenefick, and William Cook. The discussion centered on the Rock Island's precarious finances, which were "at the lowest level in the modern history of the company," as Desch had reported to the Rock's executive committee.[9] Crown asked if the UP could extend a $10 million loan to be secured by first mortgage bonds with a par value of $15 million. "Mr. Barnett replied in the negative." Crown suggested instead that perhaps the UP could provide a moratorium on equipment lease payments from the Rock Island for 18 months, which would amount to a $10 million loan. The UP would check with its board in late June and then telephone Desch with a reply. It, too, was negative.

Discussion then shifted to the merger agreement with the UP. Peter Kiewit "stated that the Rock Island was like a boxer with his hands tied behind his back under the current circumstances, and might be better off without the burden of the merger agreement." Barnett replied that the deferred maintenance on the Rock Island would necessitate a renegotiation of the exchange ratio given changed circumstances and that "until the full commission [ICC] issues its report in the Rock Island merger case, Union Pacific is unwilling to commit current dollars to sustain Rock Island's viability." Desch hesitated to go that far, instead arguing that the UP owed Rock Island stockholders at least a partial consummation as outlined by the ICC; Barnett agreed to that but pledged no further financial support. Crown then suggested that "in view of Union Pacific's unwillingness to help, perhaps Rock Island's board would be impelled to call a special meeting of stockholders to apprise them of the situation and perhaps then to vote on whether to abandon the merger agreement or not." Crown asked whether "Union Pacific would be willing to terminate the merger agreement right now; Mr. Barnett said yes."[10]

The Rock Island was running on embers by 1973, its finances in disarray; unable to attract private investment capital; its merger awaiting final approval by the ICC; barely staying afloat. With all the problems surrounding the merger deal, UP was backing away, leaving the Rock without support from its chief partner for the previous decade. Rock Island management discussed its options through the remainder of the year. At a July 16, 1973, board meeting attorney Houston Harsha advised management to issue a press release about the financial problems and the discussions with UP. When talk shifted to further financial options, it was suggested that short-term borrowing be explored, secured by company bonds, or accounts receivable, or even guarantees "from certain directors" of the company.[11] The next day Desch issued a press release stating that discussions with UP to secure capital had been unsuccessful "and had been terminated."[12]

What had changed the UP's mind? The financial condition of the Rock Island was clearly one reason. Estimates to rehabilitate the track were placed at more than $100 million in the mid-1960s; by the early 1970s the repair bill would have been astronomical even for a railroad like the UP with the resources to dedicate toward reconstruction. The changing nature of the industry was another reason. The Chicago and North Western Railway under Larry Provo pushed for an improved relationship with its major exchange partner at Fremont, Nebraska. Provo contacted John Kenefick, a protégé of Alfred Perlman and brought over to UP as president in 1968 before his former company, the Penn Central, slid into bankruptcy. Provo reminded Kenefick that the old C&NW operators, such as Ben Heineman, were now retired or had left the company. "There are four railroads across Iowa and they really only need one. My strategy is to have the [C&NW] be the survivor and I think the survivor is going to be the one with the most support from the UP." Kenefick agreed, visited Provo in Chicago, "and we kind of had an extramarital affair, if you will, with the North Western, from that time on."[13] The C&NW coordinated freight sales and rates with the UP and, in effect, provided single-line service into Chicago. The Rock Island was no longer needed by the UP.

Rock Island's press release on its financial problems alarmed three New York investors in the railroad: Justin Colin, a senior partner with the firm Colin & Hochstein, who asserted that he owned or controlled 200,000 Rock Island certificates of deposit; Lewis Harder, president of International Mining Corporation, told Rock Island executives that "he and people I represent" owned 500,000 Rock Island CDs; and Patrick Cestaro, vice president of institutional sales for Colin & Hochstein. They met in New York with Desch and Harsha and expressed concerns with the timing of the July press release, with Harder saying that "he would have done everything possible to talk us out of issuing it. He said that the press release had knocked the Rock Island stock down." Cestaro discussed his knowledge of the UP situation, saying that there was a divide between management of the corporation (Lovett, Barnett) who wanted the merger versus the "young Turks" John Kenefick and William Cook who did not. While none of the men offered financial assistance to the railroad, they all offered personal assistance in helping the Rock Island secure aid for improvements. A couple of days after the August 1, 1973, meeting, Desch received a phone call asking about board seats for the men; it was dutifully granted, and Cestaro, Harder, and Colin were all named board members in the fall of 1973.[14]

Through the fall of 1973, while Congress and the Nixon White House debated the 3R Act, the Rock Island debated how to address its pressing financial problems. One of the few alternatives left, aside from the massive austerity measures already being taken, was federal government loan assistance. Desch sent a missive to Secretary of Transportation Claude Brineger and other Washington officials pleading the Rock Island's desperate circumstances. "Rock Island is in imminent danger of collapse primarily because the Congress, the ICC, and other federal agencies have bloated the Rock Island's expenses, while simultaneously refusing to permit higher rates, thus forcing Rock Island to curtail service drastically." Desch laid out the bad news concerning the costs to railroads of problematic regulations: $40 million lost to delayed or disallowed freight-rate increases while inflation in the economy increased costs; passenger service deficits on commuter service in Chicago and intercity trains of $16.4 million over four years; and the ICC's decade-long delay on the UP merger while other rail mergers were approved that diverted traffic away from the Rock Island. All told, Desch concluded that federally mandated expenses took an average of more than $10 million per year away from the coffers. "The Rock Island has not paid dividends or interest on debentures for several years; it has devoted all its financial resources to service," and yet it continued to decay, with 1,700 miles of track on slow orders, and with hundreds of desperately needed and immovable heavy bad-order cars out of service. The only solutions: federal loans and financial assistance to help bridge the gap until the consummation of the merger.[15]

Desch's honesty was refreshing, but going to the federal government for assistance after criticizing it for the railroads' problems was indelicate diplomacy to say the least. But railroads never had to worry as much about massaging Washington politicians before then. Most railroads did not retain a lobbyist in Washington (Rock Island would not hire its first until 1978).[16] Rather, railroad corporations relied on the Association of American Railroads to make their case as an industry; they also relied on home-state politicians. Robert Michel, a Republican congressman from Illinois, took the Rock Island's issues to the FRA administrator, John W. Ingram, in November 1973 and received an icy reply. Under then-current laws, the Rock Island could not qualify for federal assistance, although Ingram pointed to the pending legislation working its way through Congress (the 3R Act). "Should this legislation be enacted in its present form, the Rock Island would be eligible to apply for financial assistance." Ingram also said that the Rock Island should seek aid from the UP, and if that failed the only federal option open to it was "a petition for reorganization under Section 77 of the Bankruptcy Act."[17]

Desch informed the board of the critical financial situation in November 1973. He summarized the steps that had not yet been taken but might have to be, especially with serious financial imbalances projected for 1974. He suggested "a deferment of payment of various items such as taxes and equipment lease rentals for the applicable grace periods. . . . He went on to say that the railroad needs $3 to $4 million in the form of a short-term loan in order to keep going, and that without such an infusion of funds, the railroad in all probability will run out of cash at the end of January 1974, and possibly even sooner." The Rock Island had two sources of such cash: "through the use of the Company's mortgage bonds to collateralize a loan; and through the sale and lease-back of worn-out equipment."[18]

The other alternative was a loan from the federal government under the terms of the 3R Act, signed into law by President Nixon on January 2, 1974. Immediately, the railroad filed a preliminary application for a $100 million loan to provide reconstructive assistance to rebuild the mainlines and branchlines of the railroad. The final loan application was submitted in the spring of 1974. By the time of the signing into law of the 3R Act, the Rock Island's cash position had sunk further, and it ended 1973 with $265,701 in the till.[19]

These desperate straits mirrored the U.S. economy in the mid-1970s. The end of what historian Robert Collins has called "growth liberalism," with its emphasis on economic growth via Keynesian stimulus and cheap and abundant energy, contributed to an almost decade-long economic stagnation that hit older industries like railroads and steel particularly hard.[20] Spending on the Vietnam War and on Great Society social programs led to inflationary pressures in the U.S. economy by the end of the 1960s. Richard Nixon took office in 1969 dedicated to controlling inflation. In 1971 he introduced a phased wage- and price-control program, which helped alleviate some inflationary pressures. But in 1972, with Nixon seeking reelection, some of the controls were lifted, and by the end of 1973 the Consumer Price Index (CPI) had soared 8.3 percent, mostly driven by food prices when Nixon allowed the sale of wheat to the Soviet Union.[21]

The oil embargo from October 1973 to March 1974 added to inflationary pressures. Shortages of oil and gasoline led to energy prices skyrocketing by 74 percent in the last quarter of 1973. This led to reduced demand for other manufactured goods as Americans spent more for fuel and for home-heating during the winter months. Declining demand led to the start of a recession and rising unemployment. In the first quarter of 1974 GNP fell 3.9 percent.[22] Although the end of the embargo dropped fuel prices significantly, for businesses and industry the energy crisis led to price increases that further weakened the economy.

While energy costs were not the primary cause of the recession of 1973–1975, inflation accelerated from a combination of energy price increases and the removal of Nixon's price controls from the economy in mid-1974. Nonfood and energy prices soared by 14 percent, even as energy and food prices finally came down from 1973 levels. The combination of recession and inflation confounded Keynesian economists and confused policymakers. Which policy tools should one use and which was more important to address—rising unemployment or inflation? With Nixon distracted by Watergate through spring and summer, the administration chose to focus on inflation. The result was a widening recession that, in the first quarter of 1975, saw unemployment jump to 8.7 percent, the highest to that time in the postwar period.[23] Well after Nixon had resigned (on August 9, 1974), President Gerald Ford signed a $23 billion tax cut into law in March 1975, too late to address the recession and not enough to provide for a stimulus for recovery. By the time of the presidential election in 1976, unemployment still hovered around 7.8 percent, dooming Ford in the election and helping elect Governor Jimmy Carter of Georgia.

Railroads like the Rock Island were hard hit by inflation and the recession. Fuel shortages reached a critical level in the winter of 1974, but the problem had materialized even before the OPEC embargo. In late 1972, according to John Burnett, the director of purchasing and stores for the Rock Island, "our fuel supply became so critical that at times we had less than 48 hours of fuel available. Several times it appeared we might run out of fuel completely. . . . Last December 1 [1972], we only had 121,000 gallons of fuel at Goodland [Kansas], about enough for one weekend. So we had to protect ourselves by hauling fuel up all the way from Houston, 1,112 miles away." The Rock Island used about 108 million gallons of diesel fuel per year to power its locomotives, and "before the crisis we were buying an adequate supply at about 11 cents per gallon at delivery point. Now we don't know from day to day what the price will be, but it has risen at times above 20 cents. . . . One yardstick we might use is the fact that each penny per gallon price hike costs the railroad one million per year."[24]

The added costs of fuel came at a time when the railroad was hauling more grain and corn from Iowa and other Midwestern states than at any time in its history. Nixon's decision to allow grain exports to the Soviet Union helped immensely, but the Rock Island had developed new marketing arrangements for hauling unit trains of grain from country elevators to barges on the Mississippi or in longer consists to Gulf ports. In 1973 the company moved 204 trains under this new arrangement and a year later moved 228 unit trains. While carloads sunk with the softer economy in 1973 and 1974, the grain-traffic increases showed some promise, enough for the railroad to work with the State of Iowa in a partnership program to rehabilitate branchlines dependent on Rock Island service.[25]

Governor Robert Ray, an Iowa Republican, helped establish the Iowa Energy Policy Council in 1973 after the onset of the oil embargo left the state with limited energy reserves. Part of the commitment of the council was to help railroads rehabilitate branchlines in the state. The council reached agreements with the Rock Island, Milwaukee Road, and Burlington Northern to provide $4.5 million in state assistance to rehabilitate branchlines. Iowa Department of Transportation head Martin Van Nostrand told the press that "while $4.5 million is a lot of money, a state that spends a quarter of a billion on roads certainly ought to be willing to spend $4.5 million to consider more energy efficient modes of transportation than we're now using."[26] The Rock Island had asked Iowa for assistance in July 1973, seeking help from the state in the form of tax relief to allow work to progress on rehabilitation, the purchase and leaseback to the railroad of locomotives and cars to move grain, and the state purchase and leaseback of branchlines. The *Des Moines Register* editorialized that "a century ago states gave away public land to help railroads get started. Equivalent help to keep them may be in the public interest today."[27]

The Rock Island used state and shippers' money to rehabilitate numerous branchlines throughout Iowa. In many cases, funds were provided by shippers who wanted to save the line from abandonment. One such example was the work of the Audubon-Atlantic Branch Line Improvement Association, linking Atlantic, Iowa, on the Rock Island mainline with Audubon to the north. The contract called for funds to be provided by the shipper group and Iowa DOT to "rehabilitate the branch line to FRA Class II standards by 1977." The contract called for Iowa DOT to spend $740,000 with the shippers spending $260,000 until the work on improving the line was completed. However, the expected carloads never materialized. Per the contract, the railroad was supposed to move 1,000 carloads per year on the branch, but by April 1977, according to Rock Island vice president of operations Richard Lane, "only 218 (or an estimated 327 for the year) moved on the line (almost exactly the same number which moved in 1975)."[28]

Midwestern states provided other assistance to keep the Rock Island operating during the early 1970s. Illinois subsidized two Rock Island passenger trains, dubbed by fans of the railroad the Peoria and Quad Cities *Rockets*. In 1971 the railroad had requested $976,000 in state funds to help subsidize the trains. The Rock Island lost $1.2 million on the two trains that year and more than $1.8 million on Chicago commuter service as well. At a May 1972 board meeting a request for a $1.3 million operating subsidy was approved, and a few weeks later Governor Richard Ogilvie (who would later serve as the federal court–appointed trustee in the Milwaukee Road bankruptcy) secured a total of $1.5 million to keep the trains in operation.[29]

Each year the board reviewed the passenger train problem. In February 1973 Desch showed a study conducted by the Rock Island that reviewed "the cash effect of joining Amtrak as compared to continuing intercity passenger train operations . . . over the next four years." "Out-of-pocket deficits," Desch argued, "resulting from the continued operation of Trains 5-6 and 11-12 will total approximately $3,393,000 as compared to an out-of-pocket deficit of $5,517,600 during the same period if the Rock Island joined Amtrak at this time."[30] Unsurprisingly, the board postponed a decision to join Amtrak.

The Rock Island was required to continue its two intercity passenger train runs until December 31, 1978, when the last train pulled out of Chicago's LaSalle Street Station, ending more than a century of continuous passenger service on the Rock Island Railroad. By the end the trains were in bad shape, with ridership limited to a handful of patrons in each direction. Sometimes, according to Rock Island president John Ingram in a 1978 television interview, the train would pull into Chicago without a single passenger. Losses continued to mount, and the railroad sought to abandon the service.

Illinois also provided assistance to Chicago-area railroads hosting commuter service by passing a law in 1973 to create the Regional Transportation Authority (RTA) in a five-county area of northeast Illinois. Approved by a referendum of voters in 1974, the RTA initially provided financial assistance to the carriers involved in commuter service, including the purchase and lease of new locomotives and cars to replace worn-out equipment. For the Rock Island this meant the retirement of 1920s-era commuter coaches and their replacement with bilevel equipment, some of which had initially been purchased by the railroad in the 1960s. The RTA also provided a subsidy to help Rock Island continue to operate commuter service, a centralized fare structure, and improvements in service for commuters in the Chicago area. However, the Rock Island still provided the crews and most of the equipment and was responsible for the upkeep of track and stations in its commuter district. This proved especially costly, and after the railroad's bankruptcy filing in March 1975 the Rock Island consistently threatened abandonment of the service, which brought as many as 14,000 people into Chicago on a daily basis.

While Midwestern states acted to save vital railroad service in their region, the federal government was focused on saving the railroad situation in the Northeast. After the resignation of Richard Nixon, Gerald Ford set out to complete the restructuring of the northeastern railroad map as envisioned by the 3R Act. The act stipulated that the United States Railway Association (USRA), in cooperation with the FRA, would develop a final system plan for the reorganization of bankrupt lines in the Northeast. The final system plan envisioned a government-subsidized corporation to take over the operations of freight and passenger services in the northeastern region from seven bankrupt railroads. Debate centered on the cost to the federal treasury of the railroad and how the new system would work to bring rationalization of lines and resources to the region.

The Rock Island's loan application to the USRA seemed in jeopardy by the fall of 1974 as government officials debated a substantial loan to the troubled railroad. The Rock Island had been encouraged to file a preliminary loan application in February 1974 by John Barnum, an undersecretary at DOT, and FRA head John Ingram. "Ingram recommended that Rock Island file a preliminary loan application as quickly as possible," and Barnum was encouraging in his view that section 211 of the 3R Act was meant for railroads like the Rock Island.[31]

In its application for the loan, Ted Desch plainly argued that "the requested loan from the USRA is the sole remaining source of funds to enable Rock Island to avoid reorganization under Section 77." The loan money would go to repairing mainline track, of which 2,000 miles were operating under slow orders (at average speeds of 20 miles per hour). The main segment for rehabilitation would be the line between Chicago and Rock Island. Desch proposed that about $86 million of the loan would be used for betterments and rehabilitation of the tracks, yards, and sidings. An additional $10 million would be spent on rehabilitating cars and rolling stock, and $4 million would be used for unspecified miscellaneous betterments.[32] The Rock Island pledged collateral in the form of first mortgage 10 percent bonds, which "have as their security, property valued at $123,760,000, representing 29.4 percent of the value of the railroad's assets."[33]

The loan application helped seal the fate of the Rock Island–Union Pacific merger. Desch informed Frank Barnett of the loan application and asked UP to sign a waiver and consent to allow the request for assistance under terms of the merger agreement. Barnett replied that the request was "premature" before delivering the death blow long feared by the Rock Island. "I believe the extensive disclosures set forth in your loan application," Barnett wrote, "make it incumbent on me to furnish you on behalf of the Union Pacific with the notice that I do herewith . . . that at the proper time it will be necessary for the Board of Directors of Union Pacific to consider, in addition to the clearly foreseeable needed reevaluation of financial terms, whether or not . . . our long hoped for merger should be regrettably abandoned by Union Pacific."[34] A further letter from Barnett to Desch on September 25, 1974, spelled out how the UP "clearly believes that the circumstances in which the Rock Island today finds itself, and even more importantly may in the near-term future find itself, fall well outside the ambit of 'changes occurring in the ordinary course of business' within the intendment of our merger agreement." Desch followed with a press release stating UP's intention "to keep its options open" and "defended the Rock Island's financial and physical condition as occurring within the ordinary course of business."[35]

The debate over the futures of the merger agreement and the loan application spilled over during a board meeting on October 10, 1974, at which Theodore Desch and William Dixon resigned and Federal Railroad Administrator John W. Ingram, who had referred to the Rock Island as a "basket case" a year earlier, was brought on board as president and CEO of the railroad. The minutes read:

> Following numerous informal discussions among the directors in recent weeks it had been unanimously concluded that the Company should seek to attract a new Chief Executive Officer who would have a strong background in railroad marketing and, if possible, also in railroad regulatory affairs. . . . The names of several candidates had been discussed, and Mr. [Lewis] Harder had been asked to review the credentials of those candidates to report his recommendations to the board. Mr. Harder subsequently had informed the directors of his recommendation in favor of John W. Ingram.

Effective November 1, 1974, the Rock Island board hired and appointed what turned out to be its last CEO and president.[36]

While the hiring of Ingram surprised many observers, rumors concerning the change swirled since January 1974. The two principal actors, according to Rock Island counsel Houston Harsha's detailed memoranda, were Ingram himself, who "was advancing his own candidacy as Chief Executive of the Rock Island from the vantage point that he would be in a position to influence favorably the granting of a loan to the Rock Island," and John W. Barriger, a former Rock Island vice president and onetime assistant to Ingram at the FRA. The question centered on whether Ingram and Barriger were acting alone in pursuing a change of management or were being encouraged by certain members of the board of directors to make a bid for the presidency of the railroad.[37]

The inference that Ingram was pushing his own candidacy for president began in January 1974 when Ingram and Barriger met board member (and former U.S. senator) Harry Darby in Kansas City. The two men "stated that the Rock Island was in bad financial shape because of poor management and that consideration had been given by the directors to bringing in new management." Darby gave the men no encouragement and dutifully reported the meeting to Desch. The following day Barriger called board member Salvo Arias, and on April 8, 1974, Arias and Morton Weiner met in New York. What transpired at the meeting is unclear. Weiner told Harsha that "there had been a long monologue by Barriger about the Rock Island . . . that the property was being badly managed and new management was needed, and, in his opinion, Mr. Ingram or somebody else ought to be installed to run the railroad." Weiner told Harsha that Ingram did not make his hiring a quid pro quo on whether the Rock Island would secure a government loan, but "the inference was created that loans would be available if new management was brought in."[38] Harsha dutifully informed Undersecretary of Transportation John Barnum about Ingram, and Barnum expressed his concern over the revelations. But Barnum revealed something else as well: "He had known that Ingram was going to New York for a meeting inasmuch as Ingram had told him that he had been approached by the directors representing large financial interests in the Rock Island, with the inquiry as to whether he would be interested in assuming the presidency of the Rock Island."[39]

A story in the *New York Times* confirmed Barriger's role in promoting Ingram for the Rock Island's presidency. It also revealed that "several directors of the Rock Island have been urged by a consultant to the Federal Railroad Administrator, John W. Ingram, to appoint Mr. Ingram, 45 years old, to the post of president of their railroad. The directors have asked not to be identified, but they say they have asked for a meeting next week with John Barnum, Under Secretary of Transportation, to inform him of the proposal. . . . Mr. Ingram confirmed yesterday that Mr. Barriger had nominated him for a position with the Rock Island."[40]

The unnamed directors were, most likely, Lewis Harder and Patrick Cestaro, both of whom attended the meeting on April 29 with John Barnum. Barnum was interested in getting the story about whether Ingram had attempted to use his influence as FRA administrator to secure appointment as president of the railroad, a clear violation of federal law. Harsha was also in attendance and noted that Harder "was upset about the new leak and wondered what could have been done to stop it. He stated that Mr. Cestaro had flatly denied giving the story to Mr. [Robert] Bedingfield [the *Times* reporter]. Mr. Arias reacted to this statement by stating that he wanted to rebut any implication that he was responsible for the story." Harder spoke to Barriger twice in April, the second time telling him that "Barriger and Ingram were getting into a delicate area with a possible conflict of interest, particularly with the Rock Island loan application pending, and he thought they should have no further discussions. Barriger acted somewhat surprised, but then said 'perhaps you are right' and the conversation ended there."[41]

It appeared from available evidence that while there was an inference made that the pending loan application would be secured if Ingram was brought on board, there was no direct evidence linking a quid pro quo for hiring Ingram. One interesting revelation made by Salvo Arias was that *Times* reporter Bedingfield had revealed to him that Barriger had spoken with Union Pacific president John Kenefick and that "Kenefick was reported to have agreed that Rock Island's management should be replaced. Mr. Arias said that this angered him and he immediately called Frank Barnett, who flatly denied that Kenefick had made any such statement, although he agreed that Barriger had made a call to Kenefick." That very day, "by chance," as Harsha recalled, "we met Frank Barnett and William McDonald," and after several minutes of discussion Barnett stated that the claim by Barriger of Kenefick approving a change in Rock Island management was "absolutely false." McDonald went further and "stated that he was shocked to learn of Ingram's activities; that he found it difficult to believe that the man had actually been present at meetings where a change in the Rock Island management was urged and replacement by Mr. Ingram was suggested."[42]

It was an extraordinary event in the Rock Island's history. Ingram was hired in October 1974, and his supporters on the board were Harder, Cestaro, and Arias. In a later interview, Ingram nonchalantly, and without specifics, described the events leading to his hire:

> While I was at the FRA [John W. Barriger] decided I should work for the Rock Island. And he went and talked to a bunch of people on the Rock Island and a bunch of people on the Union Pacific who were involved in merging with the Rock Island at the time, at least that was the theory [and] got approvals here and there and everyplace and what do you know somebody asked me if I would like to come and work for us. I wasn't too sure I really wanted to go. The Rock Island not being my idea of a dream railroad. But anyway, I finally said yes.[43]

John Barriger's interest in hiring Ingram was owed to his argument that Rock Island's management since the departure of Downing Jenks in 1960 was inadequate and was responsible for the railroad's decay. As Ingram's special assistant at the FRA, Barriger produced a memorandum in April 1974 titled "Current Situation of the Milwaukee and Rock Island Railroads." Barriger labeled the management of the Rock Island "since Jenks' departure," including Ellis Johnson, Jervis Langdon, William Dixon, and Ted Desch, as the Rock Island's "four horsemen of the apocalypse, blindly taking that once fine railroad to the brink of disaster over which it will plunge this year unless either or both the Union Pacific and USRA-FRA come to its rescue." Barriger argued that "Rock Island has suffered from massive deferred maintenance and development," but the "removal of Desch and Dixon and their replacement by a thoroughly competent president will justify federal loan guarantees adequate to restore [CRIP] to efficient standards of operation."[44]

Barriger was a respected railroad executive and advocate for modernizing the nation's rail lines. He began his long railroading career while a student at MIT in the 1920s, working summers on the Pennsylvania Railroad before joining it as an executive. He also served as an analyst at Kuhn Loeb before joining the Reconstruction Finance Corporation as a manager on railroad rehabilitation. Following World War II, Barriger was chosen as president of the bankrupt Chicago, Indianapolis and Louisville Railway (the Monon), which he rebuilt substantially and modernized.[45] Barriger developed his concept of "super railroads," publishing a book advocating the modernization principles he adopted at Monon, including getting rid of curves and developing track that could haul more freight at faster speeds.[46] Barriger left the Monon in 1952 and served as a vice president for a short time with the Rock Island before assuming the presidency of the Pittsburgh and Lake Erie, a New York Central–owned company that he also turned around. Forced to retire at the mandatory age of sixty-five, Barriger was not finished railroading and served as president of both the Katy and the Boston and Maine, implementing his modernization principles at both lines. In 1973, he joined Ingram as a consultant at the FRA.[47]

Many fans and devotees of the Rock Island in its last years might disagree with the sagelike qualities surrounding Barriger's recognition of John Ingram's talent, for Ingram was, next to Henry Crown, the person most blamed for the Rock Island's bankruptcy and eventual liquidation. Such an assertion might seem ludicrous, as the railroad was on the cusp of bankruptcy several years before Ingram's arrival and there was little anyone could have done to stem the decline. Nevertheless, Ingram is not well liked among Rock Island fans and among those who worked on the railroad during those years.

Ingram, however, was an experienced railroad executive with more skills in marketing than in operations. He could be abrasive, acerbic, and arrogant, and these personal qualities did not endear him to many people—but he had a vision for how railroads should progress in an era where managerial initiative was stymied by regulation. While little Ingram did could turn around the railroad, he was hardly the reason for the Rock Island's quick descent into bankruptcy only five months into his presidency.

Ingram was born in Cleveland in 1929 and grew up on Long Island, New York. During high school he worked summers on the Long Island Railroad as a brakeman on passenger trains, attended New York's Pratt Institute to study engineering, then left there and majored in business at Syracuse University. He served in the Army Signal Corps during the Korean War and entered Columbia University to pursue an MBA, which he received in 1954. His first job was with the New York Central as an assistant to Alfred Perlman. Ingram spent his time at the NYC implementing a computerized car-location punchcard system and also gained experience testifying in ICC rate cases. In the late 1950s, he was recruited to the Southern Railway and worked on the Big John hopper-car case. In 1964 he went to the Illinois Central Railroad to be assistant vice president for marketing. Ingram developed the rent-a-train concept (to haul grain) while at the IC, the idea being that the IC would supply locomotives to pull someone else's cars (an early unit train idea), which survived in spite of strong opposition due to questions about the tariff rate. The IC also used it to haul sludge from Chicago's sewer processing centers to central Illinois to be converted to fertilizer. Tank cars were hauled back and forth at a set tariff; crews nicknamed the run "the Polish Panama Limited," which Ingram recognized was a "kind of a slur on the Panama and the Polish race."[48]

Ingram was appointed as head of the Federal Railroad Administration in 1971, just in time to supervise the northeastern bankruptcies of that era. One of the key changes he fought against as head of the FRA was nationalization. "There were two groups that really wanted the railroads nationalized," he recounted later. "The railroad unions at the time were very interested in doing it [and] a substantial number of shippers thought that might be a good idea too. So, one of the things we did rather quietly was to make sure that didn't happen and that the railroads stay as private companies."[49]

Ingram went to work immediately on the marketing of the railroad. (See Photo 6.1.) He changed the Rock Island's paint scheme (featuring a shade of crimson and yellow) to a light blue and white, cheaper to maintain and "a more economical paint than vermillion [sic]." Throughout 1975, "with a thousand new and rebuilt cars coming to Rock Island, and also more than 100 locomotives, it was decided to change the railroad's basic image to a more distinctive, more contemporary look, and one that would be less expensive, too. Accordingly, we have retired the old colors and symbol, honorable though they were, and symbolically announced a new Rock Island." For Ingram, the new scheme was about the "Rock Island's desire to rise again" with a "bold new 'R' trademark and designation 'THE ROCK' being applied

Photo 6.1 John W. Ingram, former head of the Federal Railroad Administration and controversial last president of the Rock Island, 1974. Photo in author's collection.

to locomotives and cars."⁵⁰ Fans immediately objected to the new scheme, which when clean was attractive and bright—but bankrupt railroads seldom had the ability to keep their cars clean. The new paint scheme was dubbed "bankruptcy blue" within the first few months of its appearance. Employees also complained about the new name for the time-honored railroad: "The Rock is an insurance company. This is the ROCK ISLAND railroad!"⁵¹ One employee news bulletin, published surreptitiously, said it best: "The blue paint will cover the red engines and other equipment but it won't cover the red ink."⁵²

Ingram brought to the railroad several of his former associates from the Illinois Central, including John Mitros, named vice president in charge of personnel, and Dr. Paul Banner, who was named executive vice president in charge of marketing, a new post that suited the holder of a doctorate in economics. Christopher Knapton, a young attorney, was made a vice president and served as a legislative representative in Washington and in the states the Rock Island served. The changes bristled some of the older managers on the railroad who found themselves at odds with the new structure of the company. Ingram made changes in operations as well, instituting mini–grain trains of twenty cars to shuttle grain from dilapidated branchlines in Iowa to Mississippi River ports for shipment to New Orleans. While grain moved on the Rock in record amounts, it did so while running on increasingly deficient track, with slow orders plaguing almost the entire system.

There were two larger problems. In November the ICC recommended, at long last, a final approval of the merger between the Rock Island and UP, subject to conditions: the Union Pacific selling the Tucumcari line to SP, selling the Memphis to Amarillo line to the Santa Fe, and the Omaha to Denver line to the DRGW. The report also urged the Santa Fe to purchase the troubled Katy. These were the subject conditions of ICC Examiner Nathan Klitenic, whose lengthy report had highlighted such conditions two years earlier.⁵³

This was good news for the railroad, and Ingram was cautiously optimistic, telling employees "the whole tenor of the ICC's press release . . . is encouraging. But we must keep in mind that all the ICC did was come out with a press release."⁵⁴ The release of the entire order, an additional 302 pages counting appendices, came out several weeks later. Houston Harsha suggested, in light of reports concerning the termination by UP of the merger agreement and the renegotiation of the terms of the stock-exchange ratio, which had already expired a few months earlier, that the Rock Island should seek direct negotiations with the three other railroads in order to "smoke out" the Union Pacific. "If the Union Pacific intends to terminate the merger agreement, certainly Rock Island has nothing to lose by directly negotiating with the other three railroads."⁵⁵ The ICC released its full report on December 3, 1974, and gave the parties ninety days to respond. The Union Pacific board of directors took the whole time awaiting the final outcome of the Rock Island loan application to USRA, announced in February.

The USRA loan decision was the second pressing issue before the railroad in Ingram's first several months as president. Rock Island managers had asked for $100 million to substantially rebuild the line, but the USRA awarded a paltry $9.1 million, which John Mitros called "puzzling." The amount was granted in a request by the Rock Island for working capital to oversee the line's rehabilitation. The USRA stated that the loan would allow the management "to fully take hold of railroad operations and to assert itself in turning around the company." It promised that the $100 million loan was still under consideration but that a determination as to that amount would be made at a later date.⁵⁶

The failure to secure the larger loan led Ingram and the board to consider shutting down the railroad, which would run out of funds by mid-March. Ingram met with congressional leaders at the end of February, pleading for assistance in the style of loan guarantees that had been granted to the Penn Central. Illinois Senator Charles Percy arranged for Senate subcommittee hearings into the matter, which were scheduled for March 10 in Washington. Board members met on February 28 and March 1 to discuss emergency measures to keep the company operating. One of the chief concerns was that shutdown would strand more than 14,000 commuters in the Chicago area who depended on the railroad for transportation to work in downtown high-rises. While the Regional Transportation Authority, which had been created in 1973 to coordinate mass transit on area commuter railroads, assured commuters that service would continue, the Rock Island reported that Texaco Oil Company had stopped providing diesel fuel out of fear the railroad would not be able to pay for it. "Texaco told us Friday [March 1] that they want cash on the barrelhead before they deliver any more oil." Only 15,000 gallons of fuel remained at the railroad's commuter yard in Joliet, enough to last four additional days.⁵⁷

Concern over stranded commuters in Chicago led the news coverage during the last days of the prebankruptcy Rock Island. Outside of Chicago the concern was on how farmers would get grain to market, and how small towns and elevators in rural Midwestern communities would be able to survive a shutdown. "The impact would be gigantic. I don't think anyone can even begin to realize what would happen if the Rock Island shuts down," an Iowa grain elevator manager told the *Des Moines Register*. "Right now, we can ship grain by rail all the way to the Gulf for 31 cents a bushel. It would cost 25 cents a bushel to ship it to the Mississippi River and another 15 or 18 cents a bushel for barge transportation. In an average small town business, if you take from 5 to 15 cents per bushel from the farmer, it cuts down on the buying power of everyone in town." Another elevator operator added: "If the Rock Island closed down in Iowa, I think you'd immediately increase prices 5 to 10 percent."[58]

To save cash, Ingram entered talks to sell the commuter fleet to the RTA (the same week the Chicago and North Western Railway, which operated three commuter lines in the city, entered talks to do the same). But the RTA lacked the funds to purchase the cars, and to raise the cash necessary would have meant an increase in the gasoline tax by five cents per gallon. Ingram also met with union leaders to secure 10 percent wage cuts from 10,000 workers on the railroad; management had already agreed to similar salary reductions to save the railroad about $1.5 million per month.[59] Union leaders were unhappy, complaining about the lack of dialogue between the railroad and labor, and only 2,500 workers had taken up the offer a week later. A former employee showed more generosity. A man living in Topeka, Kansas, who had worked for the railroad in 1916 and 1917, and who had once pilfered coal from the Rock Island, sent a $100 check to Ingram to cover his debt. "I hope you will forgive me as I know the good Lord has. I pray your railroad will come through its trouble." Ingram framed the check rather than cash it, adding that it would be better for the federal government to aid the railroad rather "than nice old guys like him."[60]

The railroad was getting little assistance from the federal government. The cashflow situation had reached a critical point; Ingram checked with accountants three times a day to get updates on the cash on hand. The railroad had less than $1.5 million in its coffers, not enough to cover payroll and other expenses; unless some aid was secured from the government the railroad would fail. The Interstate Commerce Commission met with Rock Island officials in Washington to discuss ways to avert a closure. ICC Chairman George Stafford told the press that "it would not be our intention to see the Rock Island shut down" but offered nothing to the management of the line after the meeting in March.[61]

Fortunately, $2 million in interline payments from the Canadian Pacific, Canadian National and Trailer Train Corporation came into the accounts receivable office on March 4, allowing Ingram to say that the railroad gained a reprieve until at least March 14.[62] There was also news that the USRA would reconsider the $100 million loan in order to keep the railroad running.

Senator James Pearson (R–Kan.) introduced Senate Bill 917 on March

3, 1975 (the "Railroad Temporary Operating Authority Act") to amend the Interstate Commerce Act so that when a pending merger was before the commission, the commission "may . . . grant temporary approval, for a period not exceeding 180 days, of the operation of all or part of the railroad properties or property rights sought to be acquired by the party or parties" seeking to merge with a troubled railroad. Under section 601(e) of the Regional Rail Reorganization Act of 1973, which amended the Interstate Commerce Act, a carrier that was determined to be cashless and ceased operations could have directed service over its property administered by the ICC for sixty days, with extensions granted for an additional 180 days. Department of Transportation general counsel Rodney Eyster testified before a Senate committee on March 10 that "the service order mechanism was designed to meet the situation which may be presented by the Rock Island—termination of operations due to a lack of cash." "Given the redundancy of lines in the area served by the Rock Island, it is our preliminary estimate that well over half, and probably as much as 70 percent of the traffic can easily be diverted to other available rail carriers by the end of the 60 day period."[63]

Pearson's bill had one large problem, identified by John Ingram in his testimony before the Senate committee.

> [Senator Pearson's bill] authorizes the ICC to *allow* the Rock Island and the Union Pacific to pretend that they have merged. For this legislation to be effective, someone is going to have to ask the Union Pacific if they want to do this. We have asked them, and we have not received an answer. Our answer is "yes, we want a merger." We have been kept waiting at the altar for 12 years; and if the Congress wants those two railroads to live together for a while without benefit of ICC clergy, that is acceptable to us. The legislation would provide for an unconstitutional taking of property, however, if the Union Pacific did not pay for the assets and operating rights received.[64]

Ingram also pointed out that while directed service could provide some relief for shippers in Rock Island's territory, and discussions had been held with the ICC to provide a smooth transition to directed service in the event of a cessation of operations, "the out-of-pocket cost to the American taxpayers could be as much as $60 million in money down the drain." Why? "We will get paid for this—it's our property. The incoming railroad (or railroads) will get paid for this—the act indemnifies them from a loss. In addition, the incoming railroads will be guaranteed a profit." "At the end of the eight months [of directed service], the treasury will be $60 million short, and

Rock Island territory will be left with an inoperable railroad in no better shape than it is today. You can buy time," Ingram told the committee, "at an expensive price—but you can't solve the problem this way. It reminds me of Penn Central—money spent but no solution."[65]

The Senate committee, chaired by Vance Hartke (D–Ind.) heard testimony from a variety of politicians from states served by the Rock Island. Senator John Culver (D–Iowa) stated, "the people of my State . . . know that the government has provided funds to assist other railroads in similar distress. Why should the Rock Island be singled out for euthanasia?"[66] Representative Glenn English (D–Okla.) added a twist when he argued how much legislative attention and bailout money had been given by Congress to railroads in the Northeast. "Just a few weeks ago," English commented, "the Congress was asked to provide an additional emergency grant to a major railroad company serving the northeast corridor. . . . In many parts of the country railways like the Rock Island are by far the most efficient and least expensive means of transport available. In some communities, it simply wouldn't be possible to find another way to ship the harvest of wheat, cotton, or corn at any cost." The railroad "carries about 21 million bushels of wheat per year out of the wheat belt and into the consuming states."[67]

Ingram also testified as to the long and contested nature of the Rock Island loan application to the USRA as well as the rehabilitation program he proposed to undertake should funds be appropriated. "What we want to do is to rebuild the Rock. The first year drawdown on that project would only be $37 million of loans. With that program we could start solving the problem—rather than perpetuating it." The $9.1 million loan from USRA would get the railroad through May, Ingram told the committee; an additional $37 million would gain the Rock Island the ability to begin addressing the track problem and securing needed revenues.[68]

Edward Jordan, president of the USRA, testified to counter Ingram's charges about the Rock Island loan application and to defend the granting of the $9.1 million for working capital expenditures. The main fear of the USRA was that the railroad would not be able to pay back a $100 million loan under any circumstances. "The Association's primary concerns were that traffic predictions did not reflect the substantial economic downturn commencing in the last quarter of 1974, that Rock Island was projecting over a 5-year period a $17 million annual net income improvement resulting from rate increases in excess of cost increases and that Rock Island may have been too optimistic in forecasting a substantially more favorable ratio for equipment-rent expenses."[69]

The cash situation was more dire than anyone realized, and after further discussions between Rock Island management and the USRA board it was determined that even the $9.1 million loan to provide the railroad with working capital should be delayed. Jordan did not rule out that the Rock Island could reapply for the $30 million that Ingram suggested would keep the railroad operating through 1975, but that figure was not part of the original $100 million loan application.

The last person to testify was C&NW president Larry Provo. Provo told the committee that "the problem we are faced with is excess plant. There's just too much plant for the business in the Midwest.... From our own knowledge of the Midwest and our own operations, we would estimate that 80 percent of the Rock Island traffic could be very conveniently handled by existing rail service under [directed service] orders and this would be at no cost to the Government."[70] "What we are saying is that there ought to be a private enterprise solution to this situation," Provo continued. He demonstrated that the C&NW had invested as much as $200 million in private capital to rebuild and to reconstruct its lines.

> In the last five years, we have invested $20 million to upgrade our line from Des Moines to Kansas City. This has made us more competitive. I am sure we have taken some business away from the Rock Island. Any money that goes into [the Rock Island's] Kansas City line, when they talk to you about benefits and getting benefits from these programs, they are talking about getting business back. They may try to cloud it, but they are talking about getting business back from us that we have gained from them under the free enterprise system.[71]

Instead, Provo directly recommended liquidation of the Rock Island.

> Liquidation would be in the interest of Rock Island's creditors and shareholders. The Rock Island has been suffering financial losses for years, and these losses have been increasing in magnitude in recent years.... Liquidation of the Rock Island would also benefit the public by increasing the utility of the remaining rail plant. The traffic now handled by the Rock Island would be handled by some 15 remaining railroads, thus strengthening the viability of those remaining carriers. ... So long as the Rock Island remains an entity, it is a time bomb. No strong carrier or carriers can acquire the Rock Island without extending their operations into new territories and, in the process, destroying connecting carriers whose services they no longer need. Liquidation . . . would permit the time bomb to be defused safely.[72]

It was stunning testimony; Larry Provo had completed the guerrilla campaign begun by Ben Heineman twelve years earlier in his war against the Rock Island–Union Pacific merger. (See photo 6.2.) The Rock Island responded, with attorney Martin Cassell arguing that "the North Western stands in remarkable contrast to other railroads, competitors or otherwise, in its bald attempts to capitalize on the misfortunes of the Rock Island. It is nothing more than an attempt to achieve by this stroke what it could never do directly. The North Western has dropped its effort to acquire the Rock Island by merger or control, but now seeks the destruction of the Rock Island so that it can have all the benefits with none of the burdens." Cassell went on to discuss how, in an acquisition, the C&NW would have to take over the entire operation "and then justify abandonments." "This is indeed a remarkable stroke to bring off: an instant takeover at no cost whatsoever—not a burden, only benefits." He added that the Santa Fe was also in favor "of this scheme," implying that the division of the Rock Island between the two railroads would have assured them of gaining what they could not in the merger agreement. "This stratagem is no longer transparent; it is naked."[73]

In the week between the hearings and a USRA meeting to determine the fate of the Rock Island's loan, employees flooded Washington offices with phone calls urging the White House and Congress to avert a shutdown. The White House received around 600 phone calls in two days. Most of the focus was on how the loan could be secured and that employees had taken pay cuts to save the railroad. Some reflected on how "Penn Central and other rail services, along with airlines and other modes of transportation are subsidized by the US government, so why discriminate against the Rock Island?" "If the US can support foreign countries with generous aid grants, it must surely take care of its own people's needs first (Cambodia and Vietnam were mentioned in particular)." The staff member noted that "most ended their conversation by saying, 'anything the President could do would be appreciated,'" adding, "Every caller was polite. It was the first and only time a group has called the Comment Office and presented themselves in such a civil and even pleasant manner."[74]

But civility and fears of a collapse of the Midwestern economy with the railroad's shutdown were not enough. On March 14 the USRA rejected the Rock Island's loan request for the final time. Only four days after the hearings concluded, the USRA concluded that the loan for $100 million could not be paid back and that a $30 million loan request to keep the railroad operating through the year was unfeasible given the Rock Island's current economic condition. Rock Island management was stunned. John Mitros

Photo 6.2 Larry Provo, president of the Chicago & North Western, who completed Ben Heineman's guerrilla campaign against the Rock Island by arguing for its liquidation in March 1975. Photo courtesy of Chicago and North Western Historical Society.

told the *Chicago Tribune* that the Rock Island "obviously expected to get the loan." "There is no way known to me that the railroad can go on," Mitros stated.[75]

On Monday, March 17, the Rock Island board of directors held an emergency meeting, where it was decided to seek bankruptcy protection in the U.S. District court Northern Illinois District, Eastern Division.[76] The next day, Henry Crown, the longest serving board member, who had been ill for much of the previous year and who had not participated in a board meeting for some time, told James Cannon, an aide to President Gerald Ford, in a telephone call to "cut it up into pieces" and urged that "what has been done in Federal Court should be undone." When asked about solutions, Crown revealed that the RTA in Chicago and its director, Milton Pitarsky, "wants to buy" and that the "track could be leased." Cannon's notes on the phone call are sketchy, but Crown wanted out, and given that Cannon wrote how many shares of stock Crown owned (200,000 shares) and how many bonds he controlled (50 percent of outstanding total), there was little doubt that Crown would not support reorganization of the railroad but rather urge its liquidation.[77]

At 5:00 P.M. on St. Patrick's Day, March 17, 1975, Norman Nachman of the Chicago firm Nachman, Munitz & Sweig; John Bordes and Houston Harsha of Kirkland & Ellis; and Rock Island VP for law Thomas Megan appeared in the courtroom of Judge Frank McGarr in the Everett McKinley Dirksen Federal Building. The lawyers had just filed a bankruptcy petition under Section 77 of the Bankruptcy Act and were asking Judge McGarr to approve the petition and to authorize the railroad to continue operations for the time being. The attorneys were also asking for a decision on the appointment of a trustee (or trustees) for the railroad at a hearing on March 28— just three days before the Rock Island would embargo service.[78]

The March 31 date for an embargo was "to enable shippers to make any other arrangements which they think they would want to make" and to allow a trustee, if appointed, "to express their views with reference to this embargo." "Because the financial problems of this railroad have been advertised in the press for such a long period of time," Nachman continued,

> some of our creditors have become a little scared; some are on the verge of trying to levy executions on some of our properties. . . . It would be a very unfortunate thing if creditors in these various states took separate and independent action against this Railroad and its assets. It is the opinion of the president of this company that these assets, at salvage value, are worth about $480 million. The liabilities

are slightly in excess of $200 million. The directors of this corporation are convinced, that with the protection of this Court, the very substantial equities which reside in these assets can be saved and that the shareholders of this corporation will receive a substantial return on their investment.[79]

After some discussion about the RTA making a deficit payment to the Rock Island of $600,000, which would allow Chicago commuter trains to continue operating, Judge McGarr asked for assistance from the counsels present in "finding a trustee who is appropriate." With the good humor that marked his handling of the case for the next decade, Judge McGarr stated "that except for riding commuter trains, my knowledge of railroading is limited to my Lionel [train set], when I was a boy." With the signing of the order recognizing the petition for bankruptcy, the search for a trustee had begun and the last chapter of the Rock Island's storied history was about to begin. No one present in the courtroom that day—and few outside it—would have thought that the railroad would last another month, let alone five more long and difficult years.[80]

SEVEN

STAYIN' ALIVE

> We call it [the Rock Island] a cigar box operation. If we don't have the money in the cigar box, we don't spend it.
>
> —William Gibbons, Bankruptcy Trustee, October 1975

In 1976, the Rock Island publicity department sent shippers and friends of the railroad a pamphlet consisting of a reworked children's story and contemporary morality play. Titled "The Little Engine That Did," the booklet showed a happy Rock Island train on its way to deliver important goods for the nation. Suddenly, it stopped dead, facing a hill it could not climb. Along came BIG SHINY ENGINE, sporting a herald unmistakably resembling the Union Pacific Railroad crest. Would it help the stranded crew? Of course not. "I'm big time! I get around to oceans and forests and real big mountains. Bug off, Buster!" A few minutes later along came a red, white, and blue BIG DADDY ENGINE, its patriotic garb unmistakably a metaphor for the government-run Conrail. Would it help? No. "Buzz-off buster! I just hauled a big load in the East and I gotta go back for more. That's more important. Get a horse." Finally, along came BRIGHT NEW BLUE ENGINE, sporting its blue-and-white livery and The Rock logo. Could it help? "I think I can," and of course it did. The pamphlet concluded with the appropriate theme for the nation's bicentennial: "The Rock Island *is* the spirit of '76!"[1]

The message was clear: The Rock Island was alone. No other railroad was willing to save it—in fact many were waiting for it to fail.[2] The government was not going to provide assistance, except in the form of trustee certificates to use while in bankruptcy. Only the Rock Island, with help from its loyal shippers and friends, could save itself.

One of the more iconic newspaper headlines in modern American history appeared in New York's *Daily News* on October 30, 1975. After President Gerald Ford had rejected a federal bailout of New York City, the paper ran this headline: "FORD TO CITY: DROP DEAD."[3] The president, who had stalwartly rejected federal money to prevent a default on the city's debt, sounded the tocsin for principled economic reform: "Every family which makes up a budget has to make painful choices," Ford lectured.[4] Why shouldn't politicians in urban areas?

Or, for that matter, why shouldn't private businesses live by painful choices? That was what Ford and the United States Railway Association seemed to be saying to the Rock Island Railroad by refusing federal aid in March 1975, forcing the line into bankruptcy court for the third time in its history. And while the *Chicago Tribune* and other Midwest newspapers were not as clever as the *Daily News* editors in their parsing of words, in effect the outcome was the same. Ford seemed to be telling the Rock Island to drop dead.

While the executive branch denied assistance, Congress still provided some hope. Senator John McClellan (D–Ark.), who chaired the Senate's powerful Appropriations Committee, met with Ingram and ICC representatives to investigate whether a loan could be secured. "I do not want to see this railroad go down the drain," McClellan stated.[5] Two bills were proposed to help the Rock Island. Senate Bill 1306, sponsored by Dewey Bartlett, and joined by McClellan and a host of other Midwestern senators from Rock Island states, would "authorize the Secretary of Transportation to make a loan of $100 million to the Rock Island, subject to certain conditions."[6] The loan would allow for the physical rehabilitation of the property, not for operations. The bankruptcy Trustee, William Gibbons, urged hearings on a bill in a letter to several congressmen, arguing "it is in the nation's best interests to loan sufficient funds to the Rock Island to upgrade those portions of its lines that would survive as active portions of a national rail system."[7] John Ingram testified in favor of bills working through committees in Congress to support the Rock Island, defending the essentiality of Rock Island routes after criticism from DOT that "everywhere the Rock Island goes, other railroads go as well." "In a number of cases, our routes are shorter, flatter and straighter than those in the competition. Unfortunately, they are also slower—because the physical structure of the track was neglected for such a long time," Ingram stated. "Let me be clear. I am not talking about the essentiality of the Rock Island as a corporate entity; I am talking of the essentiality of our routes."[8]

The second bill, Senate Bill 917, sponsored by Senator James Pearson (R–Kan.), which had been reported favorably out of the Commerce Committee, would give authority to the ICC to allow railroads interested in merging with the Rock Island permission to operate over its track until a merger could be effected. This was a different arrangement than ICC-directed service, which would allow the ICC to permit railroads to operate over a bankrupt carrier's track for a maximum of 240 days, which the ICC was working to implement should Judge Frank McGarr determine that the railroad should cease operations. Neither bill wound up receiving a vote in Congress.

Judge McGarr had not yet determined what he would do. At March 29 hearings in Chicago, he announced the appointment of a single Trustee, his former law partner William M. Gibbons, of the Chicago firm Moses, Gibbons, Abramson & Fox. Judge McGarr had consulted many people about whom he should appoint. He refused suggestions to appoint more than one Trustee, "because I don't believe you can run some complicated operation . . . with a committee." He also rejected appointing a railroad man. "Crosscurrents of conflicting interests, the competing railroads, the accusations, counter-accusations, and emotions that I have already heard in this case, concerning the other railroads trying to cannibalize the Rock Island—and I mention that without any indication that I believe it or I think it is true, I just simply do not know—but these all create a climate or environment from which it would be difficult to extract a detached, independent trustee." Given the complex nature of the case, "and after considerable contemplation," Judge McGarr had "determined to select a single trustee, in whose legal competence, integrity, and good judgment I have complete confidence."[9]

Rock Island attorney Norman Nachman had submitted a list of possible trustee names to the court, including William Karnes of Beatrice Foods, William Huttig, vice president of operations for the Illinois Central Gulf Railroad, and Morton Weiner, the executive vice president of Norris Grain Company. The Rock's list also included its president, John Ingram, as a potential trustee.[10] Gibbons was not a Rock Island candidate. Other people had evidently solicited the judge about the position and had given their opinion about whom he should choose, drawing a mild rebuke from the court about "the impropriety of *ex parte* communications, suggesting the proper outcome of this case." Those individuals "attribute to me much more power and much more control over this situation—the future of the Rock Island— than I have." Reminding the large crowd in attendance that "this is a bankruptcy case" and "the principal purpose of this proceeding, as I see it, is either continuing operation, under some plan, which will benefit the creditors and protect their interests or liquidation for the benefit of the creditors. . . . And if I can't make re-organization for the benefit of the creditors work, I have no option but liquidation for the benefit of the creditors."[11] (See Photo 7.1.)

Neither Judge McGarr nor Gibbons knew anything about railroads, which is what appealed to the judge in his appointment of Gibbons. Frank McGarr was a native Chicagoan, born in 1921, the son of a plumber. He

Photo 7.1 President Gerald Ford discussing the fate of the Rock Island aid bills in Congress, April 17, 1975. Ford, seated middle, speaking with Senator James Pearson (R–Kans.), seated to Ford's right. To Ford's left are Secretary of Transportation William Coleman, Ford aide James Cannon, and Representative Dewey Bartlett (D–Okla.) (seated facing Pearson). Others unidentified. Photo courtesy of Gerald Ford Presidential Library.

attended Saint Ignatius High School, a Catholic prep school on Chicago's southwest side, and received a bachelor's degree from Loyola University in Chicago in 1942. He joined the U.S. Navy and was appointed executive officer of his ship, the U.S.S. *Howard F. Clark*, a destroyer escort named after a naval flyer who went missing in the Battle of the Coral Sea. The ship saw action in the Battle of the Philippines Sea, and at Iwo Jima, and was attacked by Japanese kamikaze planes while escorting ships to the Battle of Okinawa.[12] He returned to Chicago after the war, received his law degree from Loyola in 1950, remaining to teach at the law school until he was appointed first assistant U.S. attorney for Chicago in 1954. He went into private practice in 1958 until appointed to the federal bench by Richard Nixon on September 22, 1970.[13]

William Gibbons was born in Chicago in 1919. Like Judge McGarr he had attended Loyola University Law School after serving in the U.S. Navy during World War II. He remained in private practice until appointed Trustee of the Rock Island, a position he held until the company's reorganization in

1984. He had extensive corporate law experience, including bankruptcy and real-estate law, two areas that would prove important to the Rock Island's reorganization. He had also been a special hearing officer under the U.S. Justice Department, presiding over conscientious objector cases from the Vietnam War. But he had never been affiliated with a railroad; knowing his own limitations, Gibbons decided to keep John Ingram as president to handle railroad operations.[14]

Gibbons hired Nicholas Manos as his legal counsel. Manos was born in Chicago in 1922, the son of immigrant parents. His father, George Manos, was a restaurant owner, and Nicholas attended public schools before matriculating at DePaul University and then DePaul Law School. He was drafted into the U.S. Navy short of graduation and received an appointment with naval intelligence, going back to DePaul to complete his legal training in 1943, while also learning Japanese. However, he was sent to London and assigned to be a legal officer for Admiral H. K. Hewitt at the postwar Nuremberg Trials. Upon his return he entered private practice in Chicago, running as a Republican for Cook County Circuit Court judge opening in 1968. In 1975, he joined Gibbons as counsel to the Trustee in the Rock Island bankruptcy, a position he held until the company's reorganization in 1984.[15]

Appointing a trustee for the bankrupt railroad signaled a desire to reorganize the property, not liquidate it. (See Photo 7.2.) But vexing questions needed to be sorted out. How should the reorganization proceed? Should the Trustee attempt to save the entire railroad? Should he sell or abandon a significant portion of the railroad in favor of preserving a core operation that could restore profitability? Should he seek a merger with another railroad? These were all open questions as the Trustee assumed management of the railroad.

The court first had to determine whether the railroad would continue to operate. Judge McGarr had postponed shutdown until May 15, 1975, and many individuals working for the railroad, as well as shippers, continued to accept that date as inevitable. But the Trustee and staff continued to operate the line and to act as if the line would continue. The Rock Island had secured a grant of $840,000 from the Regional Transportation Authority in Chicago to allow the railroad to continue to operate commuter service. "This grant will enable the Rock Island and the trustee to operate this commuter service without having to use any of the other funds of the corporation."[16] A proviso in the contract with the RTA allowed the state to purchase the line should the railroad quit operations. Gibbons added that "it is the present intention of management and the trustee designate to increase the freight

Photo 7.2 *Judge Frank McGarr, in a picture from the 1960s. McGarr was the judge in the nine-year Rock Island bankruptcy case. Witty, professional, ethical, and fair-minded, McGarr set high standards for his handling of the complex legal issues in the case. Photo courtesy of William McGarr.*

operations and not to reduce or eliminate them." Judge McGarr cautioned: "If it is possible, that is the way I would like to see it go, but it's too early to make any determinations."[17]

Rumors mattered more than fact in the weeks after the Rock Island filed for bankruptcy. Many individuals expected that the railroad would be liquidated. The railroads were preparing for this eventuality and wanted to operate key portions of the railroad with the intention of securing the track after the Rock ceased operations. John Ingram told one correspondent that "it is our present intention to sell off our principal lines to connecting carriers." The approach of "various large railroads who support the so-called 'bits and pieces' approach . . . would destroy the asset value of the Rock."[18] The ICC staff put together a contingency plan in the event of a shutdown.

The uncertainty over the railroad's future was broached by Nicholas Manos at a court hearing on April 15, 1975.

> Unfortunately, your honor, there has crept into the mind of the public the image that the Railroad is going to discontinue its service—and indeed, is going out of business, perhaps, on May 15, 1975. For that reason, we are placed in a very precarious and prejudicial relationship, insofar as our shippers are concerned. There is a great uncertainty that they have in their mind as to our capabilities of receiving their orders after May 15th; and consequently, your Honor, our revenues are being threatened.

Manos described how the cash situation had improved since the bankruptcy filing due to deferred payments on taxes and other items, "which gave the Debtor greater flexibility in the operation of the Railroad."[19] Judge McGarr gave his assent to Manos' request to remove the embargo date, contending that

> it is not my intention to order the cessation of railroad operations at any time in the foreseeable future. I think the title of the statute we are operating under tells us what we are supposed to be doing here. The primary goal of the proceeding is the reorganization of the railroad, which means to keep it going, if it is possible to do so, consistent with the interest of the creditors. So unless it is demonstrated to me that this goal is unsustainable, and that the continued operations will be seriously detrimental to the creditors, I intend that we continue to operate the Railroad and work toward a plan of reorganization which will make its permanent reorganization possible.[20]

The Rock Island had just been given a green light.

Gibbons developed an all-encompassing strategy designed to restore the railroad to profitability. He was willing to sell significant portions of the railroad if it replenished the coffers of the Rock Island. (See Photo 7.3.) He contacted John Reed, the president of the Santa Fe, in May inquiring about its interest in "any offer on your part to acquire any part, or all, of the railroad." Reed expressed some confusion in his reply, especially given comments by Gibbons that he wished to "maintain the integrity of the Rock Island's system. On that basis," Reed continued, "I would think that the portions of your system that might be of interest to us or other railroads would be the very same portions that would be essential to you in maintaining your system's integrity." Gibbons replied that he needed to explore every option in maintaining a viable railroad for both the public's and the creditors' interests. He also lectured Reed, who had recently referred to the Rock Island in

Photo 7.3 Rock Island bankruptcy Trustee William Gibbons, left, with attorney Nicholas Manos, right, in front of a newly painted ROCK diesel locomotive in Des Moines, Iowa, August 7, 1975. Photo by Jervas Baldwin, © 1975, The Des Moines Register and Tribune Company, reprinted with permission.

Business Week as dead and a relic of the past: "Relic it may be but dead it is not; and I hope to maintain a viable line."[21]

Gibbons also continued cost-cutting measures begun under Ingram's administration, with the first cuts coming to management in April.[22] He also pursued the remedy of trustee's certificates from the federal government in order to invest more money into equipment leases and track repair. But still the Rock Island experienced a deficit in the first quarter of the year at $18.9 million, double the size of the previous year's deficit.[23] By the end of the first year of bankruptcy, 2,100 jobs had been eliminated on the railroad.

In order to proceed as efficiently as possible with reorganization, Gibbons needed an accurate appraisal of what the railroad was worth should liquidation be necessary. Rock Island attorney Norman Nachman, representing the interests of the board of directors in the bankruptcy case, had stated that the assets of the railroad were worth $200 million at an April 15 court hearing. The railroad's own accounting department put the figure significantly higher. To ascertain the true value of the property, Gibbons secured the engineering firm of Ford, Bacon & Davis to assess the property and the assets contained therein. The news was quite good: "In our opinion the methodology and values used by the Rock Island in estimating the net value of its assets by liquidation to be $401.6 million dollars are reasonable and tend to conservatively state the value." Track and equipment were valued highest, at $366 million, with real estate placed at a net worth of $41 million.[24] The value of the property would support Gibbons in his efforts to improve the railroad and to help it reorganize.

Many investors remained unimpressed and regarded the efforts of the Trustee as a dangerous infringement on creditors' interests under the bankruptcy laws in place at the time. One creditor who had an intimate connection with the Rock Island now sought to intervene in the case. On July 30, 1975, Henry Crown and the Crown family filed a motion to intervene. Crown counsel Robert Bombaugh of the Chicago firm Jenner & Block described the significant interests at stake: "These interveners hold approximately $10 million in first mortgage bonds; approximately $24 million in income bonds; and approximately two-hundred and thirty thousand shares of stock in the Rock Island." Judge McGarr worried that if he granted the Crown interests the ability to intervene that any bondholder and shareholder could thereby also be compelled to intervene; he asked whether there had been any attempt to form committees of bondholders and shareholders, but Bombaugh had no knowledge of such efforts. In resignation and in recognition of the significant holdings Crown held in the railroad, Judge McGarr granted the motion to intervene. This proved a key decision in the bankruptcy proceedings for the Rock Island.[25]

The Crown intervention was caused in part by Gibbons's desire to secure $19 million in trustee certificates available to the railroad through the Emergency Rail Services Act of 1970. After Gibbons and Manos were appointed as trustee and as the trustee's attorney, respectively, to the case, Crown had lunch with both men and urged an orderly liquidation of the railroad. But Gibbons now was moving in a different direction, intending to use the funds to lease new cars and locomotives to keep the railroad operating.[26] Any additional borrowing would necessitate a claim against the estate should liquidation occur; borrowing from federal funds would push back the bondholders from securing their investment in the property. Crown had every reason to be concerned, believing—even before the Rock Island had been declared bankrupt—that it was not salvageable as an operating railroad.

The Rock Island's application for trustee certificates hit some bureaucratic snags in the summer and fall of 1975. The Federal Railroad Administration, which controlled the remaining funds the Rock sought to acquire, demanded that the application contain a number of additional points in order to be complete, including "full and complete information on offers received from other railroads for the acquisition of any portion of the Rock Island"; the projected costs of rehabilitation of major segments of the line; "a strategic business plan for the Rock Island which will explain in detail how and on what timetable you presently anticipate the Rock Island being able to restructure its operations for purposes of reorganization"; a projected income statement; and "a list and analysis of potential coordination programs with other railroads."[27]

Gibbons responded to each question raised by the FRA. In regard to lines under consideration for sale, "discussions are in very preliminary stages" with both the DRGW regarding sale of the Denver line and with SP regarding the Golden State route, but Gibbons cautioned that "it would deleterious to our bondholders' interests to reveal the actual 'bid and asked' details that occurred to date." Regarding the business plan, Gibbons responded that "the first priority of the Trustee and management has been to stabilize the cash flow and put it on a positive basis." He showed how efforts to promote efficiencies by reducing employees, repairing cars and locomotives and returning them to service, and recapturing traffic lost to other railroads during the uncertainty plaguing the railroad in the previous year. It was too soon to determine precisely how the reorganization would work out. "This, however, is not important for the disposition of the $19 million in Trustee Certificates. These funds will be spent for track and equipment maintenance in areas which will be included in each of the reorganization alternatives." In the end, without the $19 million, "major aspects of service that would suffer . . . would be speed, capacity and reliability." The ICC had recognized that "Rock Island services are essential" in a telegram attached as an exhibit, and various states, such as Iowa, have "taken official action of similar impact."[28] In a telegram to Secretary of Transportation William Coleman, the ICC signed off on the trustee certificates for the Rock Island.

It took some convincing to get Secretary Coleman to go along with providing assistance for the Rock Island. In preparatory responses for testimony by Ingram, Rock Island lawyers quoted Coleman on a range of issues having to do with assistance for the Rock Island. Coleman had preferred to let the railroad die, arguing that "80% of the Rock Island's business could be picked up by other carriers. That's not really endangering the public welfare."[29] Coleman had stated that he "didn't like the idea of risking government money on a railroad whose necessity is in question anyway," to which the Rock Island responded:

> Fair enough. I think all of us have been burned pretty badly by the way we've had to pump cold hard cash into the Penn Central and other lines in the Northeast. But remember, the appropriation here is not a government grant. It is for the very simple expedient of having DOT guarantee $19 million worth of borrowings. . . . Government has done a lot more—with far less security—for other railroads and other industries than what is being asked for here.[30]

The Trustee faced a more difficult problem stemming from a Crown petition for immediate liquidation, which argued "that the Debtor is not reorganizeable on an income basis, within a reasonable time, under Section 77 of the Bankruptcy Act. . . . What Henry Crown and his interests are saying, by this allegation, is that the Chicago, Rock Island and Pacific should be liquidated."[31] Manos raised the question of conflict of interest stemming from the Crown investments in other railroads, including substantial holdings in the Frisco—a major Rock Island competitor—and sole ownership of the Mississippi River barge company—in direct competition for grain shipments with the Rock Island. Manos would return to this theme throughout the course of the bankruptcy hearings. After lengthy proceedings on whether there would be a hearing on the Crown intervention, Manos made a final statement "to dispel anything in this public record . . . that there is anything wrong with the Chicago, Rock Island [and Pacific]. I make this publicly, because we are serving many, many thousands of shippers." Albert Jenner of Jenner & Block, who now appeared in the case as counsel for Crown for the first time, replied to the court: "I am disturbed by that statement, if your Honor pleases, because I disagree with it." Judge McGarr replied that

> Mr. Manos' concerns, I am sure, stem from a problem which was created much earlier, when the public impression, that the Railroad's operations were to be suspended, created some great difficulties. . . . I don't think there is any basis for any public concern that the Railroad is going to be liquidated soon. . . . We may someday liquidate the railroad—I don't know—he doesn't know [Manos] and I don't know, but in the meantime, let us not bury it before it is dead.[32]

The Crown petition for immediate liquidation relied on a report prepared by Richard J. Barber, an economist and head of his own consulting firm in Washington, D.C. Barber had extensive experience in economic and financial analyses of railroads, including experience with DOT and other work on behalf of the Senate's Commerce Commission leading to the formation of Amtrak and passage of the 3R Act. A former professor with economics and law degrees from Yale and the University of Michigan, Barber was retained by Jenner & Block "to conduct an intensive examination of the Rock Island forecasts and to arrive at an opinion as to their adequacy for determining the future condition of the Rock Island."[33] Barber studied the Rock Island's July forecasts contained in the filing for trustee certificates with the DOT; a more detailed forecast sent to DOT in September (pursuant to a request for more information from the FRA); transcripts of depositions from Rock Island employees; and materials prepared for the 1974 USRA loan application.

The picture Barber painted was devastating. "After a period of growth between 1964 and 1970, traffic (as measured in revenue tons) has tapered off significantly. In 1974, the railroad moved 48.6 million tons or 3.6 million *less* than in 1970." Due to declining traffic and reduced receipts, the Rock Island was forced to lease more cars and locomotives. "The Rock Island's net rental payments have soared 251 percent from $15 million in 1964 to over $53 million in 1974," Barber wrote. "Of the 537 locomotives in service at the end of 1964 only four were leased, but by the close of 1974 more than half of the road's locomotives were leased."[34] The current year was no better. Carloads had fallen to 24.9 percent through the first two quarters of 1975, and tonnage hauled to 20 million, the lowest in the five-year period dating back to 1970.

The most devastating section of Barber's report was its conclusion that

Rock Island forecasts of both traffic and finances were not only grossly inflated but also in error. Forecasts of carloads for 1975 were consistently revised downward by the railroad but were still highly inflated when based on actual data. "The large gap between Rock Island 1975 reality and Rock Island 1975 projections," Barber wrote, "provide[s] an important reason for challenging the validity of its forecasts for 1976 and beyond."[35] Barber also summarized Rock Island's forecasts extending to 1980 that showed expanded traffic and revenue unsustainable in the recent history of the railroad or in the methodology employed to come to such figures. The railroad was predicting, due to an unspecified economic recovery in the nation, 1976 levels of 48.62 million tons hauled.

> Given the decline in Rock Island traffic this year, the traffic forecasts for the rest of the decade are unrealistically optimistic. . . . Except for the World War II experience the Rock Island has never achieved the rate of traffic growth contemplated in the current company forecasts. . . . I can discern in the projections of such accompanying company explanations as exist no rationale and no persuasive evidence to support the steep and sustained traffic recovery that the railroad has portrayed.[36]

After an exhaustive survey of the Rock Island's commodities, as well as its income and revenue forecasts, Barber concluded that "based on my analysis [and] the projections, prepared by the company and by the trustee, are highly and inexplicably optimistic. The Rock Island forecasts paint a bright picture. . . . It is my opinion that the Rock Island forecasts are unreliable and unsubstantiated and hence should not be accepted for purposes of determining the future economic and financial condition of the railroad."[37]

The report was not submitted to the court until after the trustee certificates had been approved by the FRA and ICC, so even though it became the basis for the intervening attorneys on behalf of Crown to make the case for liquidation, the court continued to allow for the postponement of a plan for reorganization and for the rehabilitation of the railroad.

Along these lines, the Rock Island Trustee sought inclusion in a pending merger between the Missouri Pacific Railroad and its subsidiary companies, the Chicago & Eastern Illinois and the Texas and Pacific Railroad. Gibbons argued that "a merger would create a strong regional system for the middle third of the country" and that it would strengthen both roads.[38] The debtor company, represented by Nachman, as well as intervening interests (Crown, Continental Bank, and First National Bank of Chicago) all opposed the inclusion of the railroad. Nachman told the court that "there are no facts asserted in this petition to apprise the Debtor as to why this relief should be granted." The Missouri Pacific attorney, Patrick Mullin, stated:

> I think I can say, unequivocally, that there is no intention on the part of any of those three railroads to agree to the inclusion of the Rock Island Railroad as part of the merger. It is, essentially, a family-line merger.
> ... I think that to permit the application to be filed is to permit the Trustee to pursue a will-of-the-wisp and to divert attention from ... pursuing a direct plan of reorganization, instead of an attempt to come in on our coattails.[39]

Judge McGarr allowed the petition, but the ICC did not allow the railroad's inclusion in the new MoPac system, whose merger was approved on September 29, 1975.

Instead, the ICC was debating the larger issues still unsettled from the failed Union Pacific–Rock Island merger. On October 24, 1975, the ICC Office of Proceedings issued a report deferring further consideration of the merger, recognizing the UP's self-removal. However, the report went on to argue for "possible conveyance of Rock Island lines to other carriers which might be made to facilitate reorganization of the Rock Island. . . . All in all the report sets policy for which no guidance was given and certainly for which none would be given. . . . The report discusses the breakup of the Rock Island in a gratuitous manner."[40] There were ongoing discussions by the Trustee to sell parts of the railroad to the SP, and DRGW and these matters would be left open, but the idea of the Rock being split up was rejected by a majority of the commissioners.

The ICC Office of General Counsel argued that

> if the Commission chooses, after due consideration, that the best "reorganization" plan for the Rock Island is one of partial or complete reorganization, it should have the opportunity to make that position known in a carefully written and clearly stated report. . . . By acting as a matchmaker in outlining different conceivable marriages of bits and pieces of the Rock Island with other carriers, the draft report echoes earlier combination efforts . . . which aroused such intense criticism.[41]

Given the long history of ICC intervention in the Rock Island's affairs, the best advice was benign neglect. "There is no need at this stage to even talk about the possible dismemberment of the Rock Island and who should get what since there is no consensus or unanimity anyway. And it appears that the Rock Island is doing better and will get some DOT loans. Let's let the trustee see what he could do without the Commission breathing down its neck."[42]

The Trustee was attempting to rebuild the railroad and to gain profitability. By the end of November some 2,000 jobs had been slashed at the Rock Island. Negotiations were ongoing between the SP to buy the Golden State route and with the Rio Grande to purchase the Denver–Omaha line. In late October the Trustee received news that DOT had approved the trustee certificates. But the railroad needed to restore its ability to gain revenue. Toward this end, the Trustee appealed to the court on October 28, 1975, to allow for the lease of twenty-five air-slide hopper cars (specialized to haul flour), 300 covered hopper cars for hauling grain, and fifty-six locomotives from GM's Electro-Motive Division. Manos argued that if the Rock Island did not lease the cars and locomotives at this time, the builder would allow for their sale or lease to another carrier. "These cars have an inherent value," Manos stated, "even after years of use that I believe would survive any type of proceeding in Section 77, or successful reorganization."[43] The problem was the leases themselves, which would cost the railroad a relatively small amount, about $5 million per year in fixed charges over fifteen years. Robert Bombaugh argued that this was a significant amount given the rate at which the railroad was accumulating leases—totaling some $20 million (a figure from the Barber report).

Manos argued that the Rock Island's needs were immediate and reflected the fact that even in bankruptcy the public interest needed to be served. "This is not a dying enterprise, this is a living enterprise. . . . A few days ago our cash position was $22 million, a figure that the Rock Island has not seen since the late fifties and since the early sixties." Manos told the court that the railroad made a profit in September and "that in my opinion we have turned the corner. . . . This railroad has pulled itself up by its bootstraps since the Trustee was appointed."[44] Bombaugh asked for time to consider the impact of the leases on the creditors, but Manos argued for a quick decision in order to ensure the railroad did not miss out on the ability to lease the equipment necessary to make revenue. Judge McGarr agreed in part with Manos: "I will not allow an encumbrance of the railroad's assets to the extent that it seriously impairs creditor's rights," he stated. "But on the other hand if equipment enables the railroad to make money while this [Section 77] proceeding is pending . . . then I think we ought to utilize new equipment to make money while we can."[45] On November 3, the court approved the leases of

300 covered hopper cars. The intervening parties had dropped their objections to the leases of the cars, and additional time was granted to study the issue of locomotive leases.[46]

In January 1976, Judge McGarr approved the railroad's request for trustee certificates totaling $22.6 million, as well as the lease of the fifty-six locomotives. Convinced that improvements in operations and in revenue had arrested the "slide into financial disaster," Judge McGarr argued that the positive cash flow in recent months "makes it clear that the recent ten year history of the Rock Island can provide no basis or reliable indication for projections as to losses in the future."[47] Crown attorneys insisted that an outside expert be named to assess how much the Rock Island repair bill would be. Robert Bombaugh cited a UP/SP report saying it would take $1.7 billion to $1.9 billion to repair the track "to their standards," but Nicholas Manos called such a figure ludicrous, arguing that the estimate of the Rock Island at $300 million to $400 million was more realistic.[48] In May, Crown attorneys filed suit in Washington, D.C., federal court to block the trustee certificates, but Judge Howard Corcoran denied the request for a temporary restraining order and remanded the decision back to Judge McGarr. By the early summer of 1976 the Rock Island began to receive the federal money.[49]

The Rock Island's operations did improve throughout the bicentennial year. In the first half of the year the railroad lost $11.5 million, a 64 percent decline from the previous year, when it lost $32 million in the first six months of 1975. The Rock posted a small $357,000 profit in June 1976, appreciably better than the previous year, when it lost $3.4 million.[50] While much of the change was due to improved efficiencies and operations, as well as a diminished labor force, a significant part of the improvement owed to the fact that in bankruptcy the Rock Island avoided paying taxes to states and localities and was also freed from paying debt obligations accrued before bankruptcy.

One of the chief difficulties for the railroad remained its passenger operations. The Rock Island's commuter service between Chicago and Joliet necessitated a substantial commitment of funds from the railroad in equipment, crews, and maintenance of track. About 14,000 riders from southwestern Chicago suburbs depended on the Rock Island to make it into work each weekday. The railroad suffered from a $2.3 million loss in 1976 from commuter service, in spite of subsidies from the Regional Transportation Authority. The RTA board had voted to extend an emergency grant of $1.7 million to the railroad in June 1976 in order to keep the commuter service operating. The cost of rehabilitating the track on commuter lines throughout Chicago was estimated at $7 million to $10 million, and Nicholas Manos told the court that the grants, while helpful, covered only half of the railroad's projected loss on commuter operations for the year. With an upturn in business and a cash position holding steady at $16 million, Manos said, the commuter operations were a potential drain on reorganization.[51]

The Rock Island released to the press a sharp warning to Chicago area commuters that

> failure of the RTA to pay $3,356,069 in financial assistance to the Rock Island covering deficits from commuter operations for fiscal year 1976, is threatening essential transportation service to thousands of Chicagoland commuters. Unless we have affirmative action on our request, followed by payment forthwith, I shall take immediate action commensurate with my obligation as a trustee to alleviate the railroad's cash drain from commuter operations. . . . There is no way we can allow this to continue.[52]

Gibbons discussed suspending operations entirely and shutting down the line between Chicago and Joliet. He also broached the idea of requesting a substantial increase in fares from the Illinois Commerce Commission, which would have driven many commuters away from riding the railroad.

The RTA board countered with threats to end service on the railroad and replace the commuter trains with bus service. That was hardly a serious option, but the RTA board agonized about what to do. As board member Patrick O'Malley told the meeting of the board on August 10, "The question is how much money do we want to continue to pour into a broken down railroad?" Jerry Boose from the far-western suburb of St. Charles argued, "Faced with this crisis, about the only thing we can do is to buy it and enter into a purchase-of-service agreement with someone to run the railroad." The board did not conclude what to do at the meeting, scheduling hearings in southwestern Chicago to solicit citizens' responses and hoping that an agreement could be reached to avoid a shutdown—even if that meant temporary grants to the Rock Island.[53]

Chicago Tribune transportation reporter David Young wrote a series of articles on the plight of the Rock Island commuter operations. Rock Island commuters had tolerated years of bad track, declining service, and aging and dilapidated equipment. The Rock Island possessed fifty-eight cars built between 1923 and 1929; dubbed Capone cars, they were single-level and not air-conditioned; twelve of those cars were out of operation. It also had seventeen single-level Pullman-Standard cars, which were acquired in 1949, in serious need of updating. The newest cars in commuter service were thirty bilevel cars acquired when Jervis Langdon was president. The Rock's engines were decrepit, with twenty locomotives in passenger service, including the oldest Electro Motive Division E-6 locomotive in operation, with the majority of the passenger units dating back to the early 1950s. While the RTA had placed an order for twenty-one locomotives and fifty passenger cars, delivery was not expected soon, and not all the locomotives were to be allocated to the Rock Island.[54]

The RTA studied the costs involved in rehabilitating or abandoning service and, in a 66-page report released in July 1976, concluded that rehabilitation costs were less than abandonment. The cheapest alternative was for the RTA to rehabilitate the line and move the terminal to Chicago's Union Station, connecting with the Rock Island at Englewood on Conrail's mainline. Moving railroad operations out of its costly and antiquated headquarters at LaSalle Street Station was already occurring. And moving passenger service to Union Station had been discussed dating back to the late 1960s. The RTA study showed how that would be the most feasible and inexpensive alternative, with a projected cost of $61 million versus abandoning parts or all of the system (pegged between $119 million and $123 million). Negotiations between the railroad and the RTA over purchasing the line were hamstrung not only by the price of the railroad mainline but also in the costs to rehabilitate it.[55]

The Rock Island was seeking $40 million from the RTA to purchase the right of way and equipment from the railroad, as well as to transfer service out of LaSalle Street Station. The RTA was negotiating with Gibbons about the price, and a final decision would be several years away. In the meantime, the RTA, after receiving a favorable ruling from the Illinois Supreme Court concerning its $177 million budget for 1976, offered the Rock Island $7 million to keep the commuter operations running until June 1977, with $1.6 million dedicated to wiping out the deficit from 1976 and the remainder applied to operations for the next calendar year. Gibbons was hesitant, arguing that the full amount necessary was $7.5 million; in effect the RTA wanted the Rock Island "to make a donation to us of the depreciation in Rock Island equipment. I said we're not in a position to make donations. We're responsible to our creditors."[56] But as the *Tribune* editorialized, Gibbons's position was "a little like a man dying of thirst pushing away a glass of iced tea because it contains too much lemon and not enough sugar."[57] (See Photo 7.4.) Judge McGarr agreed with the position stated in the newspaper and ordered the Rock Island to accept the money; the RTA even upped the ante, paying the railroad $7.5 million to operate the Rock's commuter lines.

The Rock Island was also struggling financially with the continuation of intercity service between Chicago and Rock Island and Chicago and Peoria. The four trains had an out-of-pocket loss of $1.8 million, with an average daily total of sixty-six passengers. The Illinois DOT had provided the railroad with $1 million per year, a subsidy paid out in four quarterly installments. But on June 7, 1976, Manos informed the court that Illinois had not paid two quarterly installments and that there was disagreement within the legislature concerning the subsidy. Given the losses and the failure to provide payment, Manos was requesting the court to allow the Rock Island to discontinue service, a process the attorney knew had to work its way through the Illinois Commerce Commission. Manos asked the court for a thirty-day cutoff of service should the State of Illinois not provide the subsidy.[58]

Attorneys for the Illinois Commerce Commission and for Butterworth Tours, which contracted with the Rock Island to haul an observation car on the back of its trains, complained that the hearing before the court was designed to circumvent the process of having hearings before the Illinois Commerce Commission. "We believe that this should be set aside and this should be directed to go before the Illinois Commerce Commission," ICC attorney Hercules Bolos told the court. "If the ICC decides it's adverse to their claims, then they can either go to the appellate court, or if they feel that interstate commerce may be affected as a result of the Commission's decision, then they can go to the Interstate Commerce Commission." Judge McGarr often gave his opinion outside of the constraint of the law, and in regard to this matter he held forth, concluding:

> The procedure that you gentlemen describe is the reason why the railroads in this country are in the trouble they're in today, because when they have a losing operation, in this instance $4,500 per day, they're required to run the bureaucratic gamut and lose money and bleed from every pore for months and years while the agencies involved horse around with these things. I think the time has come to put an end to that in any way I can put an end to it.[59]

Judge McGarr also lectured the attorneys present that given the Rock Island's financial problems the passenger service hardly constituted "a vital public interest."

> I want my remarks to serve notice to the Illinois Commerce Commission, if they aren't going to act fast, I am. You can tell me I don't have jurisdiction but I think that all the equity and all of the public interest is to be served by the discontinuance of this operation,

Photo 7.4 Commuter service remained a headache for the Trustee, who wanted to sell the commuter operations to the newly created Regional Transportation Authority. The RTA would purchase the property from the Trustee in 1983. Two photos show a Rock Island commuter train in Mokena, Illinois, in 1977; and right, Rock Island E-units and a new RTA locomotive waiting for the evening rush at LaSalle Street Station. Note the weeds and platform condition of the commuter station. Both photos by Mark Llanuza, used with permission.

or, if the State doesn't want it discontinued, they've got to come up with the money to run it. The Rock Island is not going to continue to afford this service and I'm going to shut it down.[60]

The pressure worked. A few weeks later, at a bankruptcy hearing scheduled by Judge McGarr every six months in order to update the court on the progress toward reorganization, Manos reported that "as a consequence of the Court's order" the State of Illinois had appropriated $500,000 on an emergency basis and would soon provide the remainder of the subsidy for 1976. "We anticipate further that we will be able, we hope, to achieve a favorable contract with the IDOT relative to fiscal 1977 and if we don't, as the Court has mandated, we will then proceed to the Illinois Commerce Commission to achieve a discontinuance of this service."[61] The intercity

trains would continue to operate over the Rock Island until December 31, 1978.

The federal ICC decision to keep the Rock Island–UP merger open allowed the Trustee to negotiate with other railroads about purchasing parts of the property without the necessity of having lengthy hearings before the Commission for approval. Two negotiations were ongoing by the end of 1976. Gibbons had been talking with Ben Biaggini of Southern Pacific about purchasing the Tucumcari line, from Santa Rosa, New Mexico, to Kansas City, and the Kansas City–St. Louis connection as well. Some studies had been made to determine a purchase price. In the 1960s the SP was to pay $98 million for the southern half of the railroad; the final price announced by the two parties in April 1978 was $57 million, a crucial indication of the physical decay of the property.[62]

An interesting memo to Gibbons and Ingram should have led the Trustee in a different direction. Newton Swain of the Rock Island studied the effects of the purchase offer by the SP and concluded:

> The SP's proposal to purchase the Tucumcari to Trenton, Missouri and the Kansas City to St. Louis line of the Rock will result in two separate systems (Rock North and Rock South) which will have combined losses $7.4 million greater than the Rock experienced in 1975. The SP

proposal will cause carload reduction of 112,265 or 14.7 percent. Revenue will be reduced by $66 million, or 20.5 percent, and operating and rent expenses will only fall by $55.3 million or 13.1 percent. Neither the southern or northern systems will make a profit. The North will lose $26.4 million, while the South will lose $12.5 million.[63]

But the Trustee could not afford to keep the line with rehabilitation projections well above $100 million. If the Rock could rid itself of the expense of upkeep on a line whose profitability had long been suspect, the reorganization could proceed, and a core system might be able to sustain profitability for the corporation.

It was a good thing that word of this estimate never reached the Crown attorneys, who consistently used the six-month status hearings to challenge the Trustee's estimates about the railroad's profitability. For the remainder of the bankruptcy proceeding, the attorneys sparred over investments to the property, cost estimates, salaries of the Trustee and his attorney, and whether the railroad could be saved. Crown had concluded long before the bankruptcy that it could not. And while the first year of the bankruptcy had shown the potential to turn things around, the railroad faced a dreadful future.

EIGHT

THE OMEN

Distraught Woman in Train Station: I must get to Chicago in the *worst* way.
Ticket Agent: I'm sorry, ma'am, but the *Rocket* just left.

—*Peoria Rocket* joke, 1970s

The Rock Island Railroad had long been a staple of popular culture—and remains so. It isn't one of the four railroad properties in the iconic Monopoly boardgame, yet it is featured in song and film, making an indelible mark on music culture with John Lomax's folk/blues/country "Rock Island Line," recorded in 1934 by Lomax and a group of Arkansas state prisoners. Three years later, Huddie William Ledbetter, known as "Leadbelly," recorded his own popular arrangement, and the song has been put on vinyl (or disc) numerous times, most famously by Johnny Cash, whose deep baritone anchored the most successful and best-selling version. In 1955 in Great Britain, Lonnie Donegan revived the song and popularized a form of music known as skiffle, going number one. Donegan's skiffle band—guitar, standup bass, and washboard—would influence legendary British Invasion performers such as Keith Richards of the Rolling Stones, Eric Clapton of the Yardbirds, Jimmy Page of Led Zeppelin, and Pete Townshend of the Who. Each of them attributes his early interest in guitar-playing to the 1950s skiffle craze in Great Britain.[1]

On screen, movie fans can spot the Rock Island's former Chicago commuter line in *Source Code* (2011), starring Jake Gyllenhaal as a soldier transported into a commuter train to prevent a terrorist bombing. The train is filmed on Metra's Rock Island District track just south of downtown Chicago as it passes by the landmark Armour Institute building on the Illinois Institute of Technology campus.[2] In one scene, after the bomb explodes, the train hurtles off the track over 35th Street near U.S. Cellular Field, home of the Chicago White Sox baseball club.

One film, which takes a few liberties with the railroad's history, was the 1950 western *Rock Island Trail*, starring Forrest Tucker and Lorna Gray. The movie premiered in the Quad Cities, attended by John Wayne, Roy

Rogers, and Dale Evans. The story combined a lot of fiction—the Rock Island Trail Company was a railroad seeking to expand to the West but ran into trouble with steamship companies and stagecoach lines. The heroic Reed Loomis, played by Tucker, with the assistance of Constance Strong, played by Adele Mara, helps to fight against the manipulative and corrupt business practices of Kirby Morrow (Bruce Cabot in the role), who will stop at nothing to prevent the railroad going through. There are even Indians (even though when the Rock Island was built there were none in the territory). One of the few truthful elements in the film centered on the depiction of the railroad winning a case argued by Abraham Lincoln in 1856, which allowed the line to build a bridge over the Mississippi River.[3]

Perhaps the most eerily accurate portrayal of the Rock Island on film was the 1978 release of *Damien: Omen II*, the sequel to the popular and critically acclaimed horror classic *The Omen* (1976). In the sequel, teenager Damien Thorn is being raised by his uncle Richard Thorn (played by William Holden) and his wife (Lee Grant). The couple have their own son, Mark, and after a series of strange incidents and deaths involving close colleagues of Richard Thorn, and a journalist and doctor suspicious of the young man, Damien comes to find out who he really is—the son of the Devil, the Antichrist prophesized to usher in the end of the world. (In the first *Omen* film, Robert Thorn, played by Gregory Peck, discovers who the adopted Damien is, and tries to kill him with the knives of Meggido, but is killed himself by police.)

In the sequel, one of the men who learned of Damien's origins is the curator of the Thorn Museum, Richard Warren (played by veteran character actor Nicholas Pryor). After collecting the discoveries of the deceased archeologist Bukenhagen, including Yigael's Wall (a fictional stone that depicts the Antichrist's image), Warren goes mad when he realizes that Damien's picture is on the wall. He informs Richard Thorn of what he saw, but Thorn refuses to believe it until his own son, Mark, mysteriously dies at Damien's hands after threatening to betray his cousin's secret.

Warren takes up refuge at a church purportedly in New York City (but really a church near the Cabrini Green public-housing project in Chicago), and Thorn flies there to have Warren show him the wall. Nervously, Warren takes Thorn to a railyard holding a piggyback container with Yigael's Wall inside. The scene was at the Rock Island's 12th Street piggyback yard just south of LaSalle Street Station. A yard locomotive, Electro-Motive Division NW 2 4901—in the crimson and yellow Rock Island paint scheme—is switching the yard and the crew parks it to take lunch. Meanwhile, Thorn unlocks the container to see the wall while Warren huddles in fear behind the flatcar. Ominously, as Thorn views the wall and sees that his adopted son is indeed the Antichrist, the Rock Island locomotive, empty of a crew, begins to move slowly toward the parked flatcar. A switch is thrown, and as the locomotive picks up speed it slams the flatcar, pushing Warren into the coupler knuckle, where he is crushed when it collides with a Rock Island boxcar in the siding. Yigael's Wall is destroyed by the impact; like his brother in the first film, Thorn is killed by the knives meant to kill the boy; his wife betrays him and professes her loyalty to Damien, who then blows up the Thorn Museum building, ending the film.[4]

The metaphor of a possessed Rock Island switcher locomotive in *Damien: Omen II* was uncannily on target, for the railroad itself seemed possessed by demons throughout 1977 and 1978, victimized by incredibly harsh winters, spring storms that washed out big segments of track, and an indifferent—if not outright hostile—federal government. While the Trustee and his attorney argued that the railroad was on track for reorganization, the Rock Island began to suffer from the vagaries of long-neglected maintenance and the problems of running a railroad during an era of high inflation. Coupled with a declining national economic picture, these were more than signs of trouble ahead—they were omens of what was yet to befall.

Railroad operations are consistently subject to the uncertainties of weather, a depressed economy, weak commodity markets, and declining industrial productivity. In the late 1970s all of these conditions hit the railroad industry particularly hard and practically all at once. In the fall of 1976, in spite of the third best grain harvest in history, granger railroads like the Rock were hauling less grain than they had expected to ship. For the Rock Island, grain carloads represented 14 percent of its carloads, which accounted for 25 percent of the company's revenues. Exports were not the problem, as the Russian grain deal struck in 1973 still was producing sizeable exports of grain; the domestic market was weakened by low prices for corn and grain. Farmers stored their crops rather than shipping them, and even with the efficiencies of unit grain trains and more jumbo hopper cars available on railroads like the Rock Island, the price of corn and grain dictated the supply in the market.[5] The result for the Rock Island was a third-quarter loss of $3 million in 1976 during its peak shipping time, better than the previous year, but still providing ammunition for Henry Crown's attorneys to challenge the claims of William Gibbons that the railroad had rebounded.

Nevertheless, Nicholas Manos and the Trustee made optimistic claims of progress toward reorganization in bankruptcy hearings. "Phenomenal" was the adjective Manos appended to the progress, arguing that the Rock Island's path toward profitability was assured if conditions continued to improve. Manos made this statement in a contentious status hearing on December 28, 1976. Citing the downturn in grain shipments and verifying that while the Rock Island had decreased carloads of 6 percent in the third quarter of the year (to the tune of a decrease of fully 10,000 cars loaded), Manos nevertheless took an optimistic view. He explained that the farmers had been storing grain for a long period of time, close to two-and-a-half years, and that once the farmers start selling grain the railroad would have the capability of moving it. Manos also argued that the Rock Island had been engaged in the long-delayed rebuilding of the track, with equipment and machinery acquired the previous year. Some $14 million was being spent on this rehabilitation, with a half-million new ties and 100 miles of new rails being laid; additionally, more than 600,000 tons of ballast had been placed on Rock Island track. "It's quite evident, your Honor," Manos argued, "that the management of the Rock Island now is in a position where cyclical declines in the economy have no effect on it, and if one is to project for the future.... I think now we're at the bottom and we're going to start now on the upturn, and the Rock Island is now leveraged where profitability is going to be achieved."[6]

Manos based his argument on the fact that since the property had been taken over by Gibbons, the decade-long slides in profitability and maintenance had been reversed. He went over the history of paying dividends in the early 1960s rather than putting money back into the railroad and reiterated that "whatever monies are being generated, or will be generated, will go back into this plant, where they belong, to preserve the vitality of a road to serve the public interest."[7]

A second issue in the hearing was the filing of a plan for reorganization by the Trustee. On this matter, Manos begged for a delay, arguing that there were several important issues still pending regarding the sale of parts of the Rock Island to the Southern Pacific Railroad; talks with the Denver & Rio Grande Western regarding the purchase of line segments; and continuing negotiations concerning the sale of Chicago commuter facilities to the Regional Transportation Authority. But there was a new wrinkle. The passage of the Railroad Revitalization and Regularity Reform Act (the 4R Act), signed into law by President Gerald Ford in February 1976, allowed for railroads to apply for loans from the federal government to rehabilitate track and equipment. The Trustee was applying for $160 million, half of which would go to rehabilitation of key segments of the Rock Island with the extra to be spent on equipment and motive power. "The Quadruple R Act was

The Omen

designed for railroads such as the Rock Island," Manos argued. "It wasn't designed for railroads which were in the affluent position of the Union Pacific or the Burlington Northern." Manos was preparing an application to the Federal Railroad Administration for a loan and was also preparing to make the argument that any such loan would be subordinate to the bondholders and junior creditors in the Rock Island bankruptcy.[8]

Albert Jenner, the senior partner in the firm Jenner & Block, challenged Manos's assertions of progress toward profitability. Jenner had been involved in the case from the beginning, making his first court appearance in the fall of 1975. Born in 1907 in Chicago, the son of a policeman, Jenner was raised in the working-class neighborhood of Canaryville on the city's South Side. He earned his undergraduate and law degrees from the University of Illinois, making his way through law school as a professional boxer, paid $50 per fight; he also served as a circulation manager at the *Daily Illini*. He graduated from law school in 1930 and three years later joined the firm that would soon bear his name, becoming a partner in Poppenhausen, Johnston, Thompson & Cole in 1939. Jenner had developed a reputation as a gifted litigator, "superbly prepared, one of the greatest lawyers I ever met," as Chief Judge William Bauer of the United States Court of Appeals for the Seventh Circuit described him.[9]

Jenner was also a dedicated public advocate, a long supporter of civil rights and the NAACP Legal Defense Fund. He served on several distinguished committees, even being appointed by Harry Truman to serve on the National United States Loyalty Review Board; he was senior counsel for the Presidential Commission to Investigate the Assassination of President Kennedy (better known as the Warren Commission). In 1968 Lyndon Johnson appointed Jenner to serve on the National Commission of the Causes and Prevention of Violence.[10] In 1965 he defended Jeremiah Stamler before the House Committee on Un-American Activities, attacking the committee for its long history of abuse of witnesses. In the 1968 case *Witherspoon v. Illinois*, Jenner argued before the U.S. Supreme Court against the death penalty for his client on the basis that potential jurors had been excluded from serving after they revealed their moral qualms about the death penalty. The Supreme Court ruled in favor of Jenner in this case.[11]

A remarkably gifted counsel and a man of impeccable character, Jenner had been an attorney for Henry Crown since the two men met back in 1934. (See Photo 8.1.) He helped Crown in an investment case involving the defense firm General Dynamics in 1965 and later was appointed to the executive committee of General Dynamics by Crown. Given their long association, it was not surprising that Crown turned to his good friend to handle

Photo 8.1 Albert Jenner, Henry Crown's attorney in the bankruptcy case. Courtesy of Jenner & Block.

the Rock Island intervention. Along with Jenner, Daniel Murray, a Harvard Law School graduate, handled the bankruptcy matters on the case along with Thomas Sullivan, Carter Klein, and Robert Bombaugh. All made appearances in court on behalf of the Colonel, as Murray affectionately referred to him thirty years later.[12]

Jenner challenged each of the claims Manos made concerning the railroad's progress, consistently challenging the accounting practices of the railroad as opposed to federal ICC accounting rules, which showed larger losses. He also raised the issue of how the Rock Island's decline in carloads during the fall harvest season was a cause for concern, doubting that it was entirely a result of farmers deciding to withhold grain from the market. He showed instead that other western railroads, with the exception of the Milwaukee Road, all had significant increased carloads while the Rock Island experienced a decline. Jenner also challenged the claims that the Rock Island was doing anything more than simply standing pat on maintenance, using figures from the 1974 FRA loan application, which showed that Manos's figures for rehabilitation were what the railroad claimed was a necessary maintenance expense.[13]

The most serious issue for the creditors was the pending application for $120 million with the FRA. Jenner argued that the amount being requested, when added to "the new leases for cars, locomotives and purchases and contracts, you get up to $200 million ahead of the bondholders, let alone the junior creditors. And I suggest to you your Honor sincerely that hasn't the point been reached in this application in which the burden is on the Trustee to establish before your Honor, that the tremendous expenditures are not going to impair the capital of this railroad."[14]

Manos defended the progress and responded that the railroad was now doing what it hadn't done in the past, arguing that "Mr. Crown is at the stage now where he finds it difficult to admit the errors of the past because in so doing he admits the correctness of today's Rock Island Trusteeship." Jenner had complained about the decline in equity at stake in the increased borrowing, to which Manos responded: "Do the shareholders have the audacity to complain about a decline in equity when they are the ones that brought this Railroad into the Section 77 protection? Are they the ones that are entitled to the protection of this Court to the extent that we now are being pressured to file a plan of reorganization? For whom? The shareholders, whose board of directors brought us to this posture? So much for that statement."[15]

As for how long the reorganization would take, Manos referred to the lengthy Missouri Pacific reorganization, which "took twenty-five years," to which Judge Frank McGarr replied dryly, "I haven't got that much time, Mr. Manos." The judge also reiterated that

> the whole current operations I view as excellent. I can't praise the Trustee and his attorney too highly. The question is not whether they're doing a good job, however, but whether it is possible to do a job that is good enough. Despite their best efforts, it may not be. I can't help but reflect on the question of why car loadings are falling off. . . . All the capital investments that I've authorized over the past twenty-odd months have been justified as necessary to maintain or increase car loadings and revenues, and they've not yet clearly begun to do so.

> . . .
> I look for better revenues, I look for reduced losses, reduced erosion of the assets available to the creditors, and the time left to achieve this is not unlimited. I'm not going to say it's two years or five years or twenty-five years, but it's not unlimited and it is measured not by the calendar, but by the erosion of assets available to creditors. The time is not unlimited, but neither has the time come to conclude that the reorganization is not possible.[16]

The status report set the tone for the remainder of the hearings, with Manos providing optimistic updates and projections of income and Jenner and his attorneys categorically challenging each contention put forth by the Trustee. Judge McGarr approved of the status updates, scheduling them every six months, sometimes with updates at three months. The pattern was established early in the proceedings as Judge McGarr waited patiently for signs that the railroad was turning the corner financially, even as the performance was not keeping up with the optimistic projections of the Trustee.

The best chance for speeding up reorganization lay in two significant deals being negotiated with the Southern Pacific Railroad and the Denver and Rio Grande Western Railway. In July 1976, the SP had submitted a proposal to purchase the Rock's line from Santa Rosa, New Mexico, to Topeka, Kansas. Included in the proposal was an offer to purchase the railroad's line from Kansas City to St. Louis as well. The SP president was Ben Biaggini, and as the two sides discussed the offer—including how much traffic the Rock would lose from the deal—Biaggini was increasingly nervous about losing the line to his rival, John Reed of the Santa Fe. In a phone conversation with Gibbons at the end of 1976, Gibbons recounted that "his voice could be characterized as tinged with anxiety, urgency and a willingness to patronize." Gibbons told him the offer of July 1976 was still open, but "I was going to court to seek leave to reject his offer and I would not give him the traffic and revenue information unless the court ordered him to do so. . . . I told him that any deal that cut the heart out of us would not fly and that a north and south Rock was calculated to lead to liquidation." Biaggini asked for a chance to rebut the Rock's data on the losses to occur should the sale go through, but Gibbons warned him that "he and Crown could take depositions and attempt to get discovery and that we would be tied up for months. 'Oh, no,' he said, he didn't want to wind up with Crown and if that there was any way that we could get him [SP] to Kansas City, we would work it out."[17]

In order for the purchase to work, the SP needed trackage rights between

Topeka and Kansas City over the Union Pacific, but relations between the two giant western roads were strained. Gibbons related that the Rock Island had a lease problem and was meeting with UP CEO John Kenefick soon "about both problems." "Biaggini said that anything he could do to screw Kenefick and John Reed would be fine. I asked him if he was going to screw me. 'You,' he said, 'I'll put an umbrella over you to protect you.' I told him that Reed was interested in something. 'In what?' he asked. 'Ben, you know what my problem is if I get a better offer.'"[18]

A few weeks later, fearful that the Santa Fe would act quickly if he did not, Biaggini, Gibbons, and John Ingram held a conference call to finalize the details of the purchase. Part of the problem with SP's initial offer was that it would include access to Herington, Kansas, which was the point where Rock Island track diverged south to Gulf ports. If the railroad was split into a North Rock and South Rock, as analyst Newton Swain informed Gibbons in November 1976, the Rock Island "will have combined losses $7.4 million greater than the Rock experienced in 1975. Revenue will be reduced by $66 million or 20.5 percent. Neither the southern or northern systems will make a profit. The North will lose $26.4 million, while the South will lose $12.5 million."[19]

The men discussed the track condition between Topeka and Herington, Kansas, including an offer by the SP to take over one track and assume maintenance expenses on the line, while the Rock Island employed the other track to reach its southern line. Biaggini then stated: "We're talking about Santa Rosa to Topeka, including the Dodge City branch," with the Rock keeping a Salina branch and a line to Amarillo. "All right," Biaggini continued, "we'll give you five-and-a-half million dollars for the Saint Louis line—cash." "That's a new one," Ingram responded. "$15 million," Gibbons responded. "What?" Biaggini asked. "$15 million." "I'm offering you five and half million cash for the St. Louis line. . . . Okay?" "Yeah, all right," Gibbons replied. "All right," Biaggini concluded, "the deal on the Tucumcari to Santa Rosa to Kansas City—that is, including the two tracks through Armourdale [yard] and so forth—is still the same as it was. We'll make the tender offer on the bonds, hinge it on getting 80 percent, we deposit a sufficient amount of cash with you to pay the rest of them off at maturity . . . and we pay off the Union Pacific and the Small Business Administration loan." "And then you make your own deal with the UP from Topeka to Kansas City," Gibbons asked. "No, we need your help on that deal 100 percent. . . . This gives you the best of everything—it gives you everything you've ever wanted—gets rid of the Tucumcari line and relieves you of a major worry in connection with rehabilitating the line between Herington and Topeka, gets rid of your first mortgage bond, it leaves you in Kansas City, keeps you in Salina, Kansas and gets rid of a dog in the St. Louis line so what else can I do for you on Monday morning," Biaggini concluded. "It's starting out to be a good year, Ben," Gibbons concluded.[20]

The terms of the deal were favorable for the Rock Island. The mortgage bonds were worth an estimated $51.4 million, and the deal would have left the railroad without any mortgage indebtedness (the *Chicago Tribune* reported that it would still have $50.3 million of corporate debentures, $8 million in equipment trust debt, and $19 million it owed for trustee certificates to the federal government). Crucial for the Rock Island was its ability to keep one track in operation between Topeka and Herington, the point of departure south for the Rock Island's crucial grain movements. This was what Gibbons had referred to when he said that Biaggini's original proposal would have cut the Rock Island in half.[21] Of course the sale had to be approved by both the court and by the ICC, and it was not brought into effect until late 1980, by which time the railroad itself had ceased operating. Henry Crown, who owned one-fourth of the Rock's first mortgage bonds, was not happy about the sale price, balking publicly in both the *Wall Street Journal* and *Forbes* in April 1978 that the Rock Island was asking $120 million for the same piece of railroad in the merger proceedings in the 1960s. Gibbons tersely replied in a letter to Crown that "your recollection is faulty. My understanding is that the SP was to buy all of the railroad south of Kansas City (about 40 percent) from the Union Pacific. According to our agreement in principle, SP will purchase about 10 percent of the railroad. The extrapolated price for the 1966 deal would be about $225 million."[22]

Unlike the SP agreement, a long-discussed deal with the DRGW never came to pass, although the railroad would be one of the directed-service operators over the line it long wanted to purchase from the Rock Island. As part of ICC Rail Examiner Nathan Klitenic's redrawn western rail map, the Rock island would have been forced to sell its line from Council Bluffs, Iowa, to Denver to the DRGW. The DRGW wanted access to Chicago and proposed a new operation that was being called Rock Island Western. In May 1976, Gibbons had discussions with Sam Freeman, vice president and general counsel of the DRGW, and reported to Ingram that

> the DRGW would like to structure a deal whereby it could get to Chicago rather than stopping at Kansas City and Council Bluffs. I suggested that they first give us a proposal on the Kansas City and Council Bluffs segments. . . . I told him it would most certainly have to be a joint trackage agreement rather than a sale. I suggested the

possibility of a merger because of the extension of the route, and he said that a merger involved too much track for them. He was under the impression from last year's discussions that we could survive as a north-south route alone and I disabused him of this notion.[23]

In March 1977 the DRGW made an offer to purchase the "line segments between Denver and Council Bluffs/Kansas City." Gibbons found it "unacceptable because it does not adequately compensate the Rock for the possible reductions in cash flow," so Gibbons extended several options, including a higher price than being offered by the DRGW in lieu of diversion of traffic.[24] Freeman accepted the idea of having further discussions on purchasing the line, but nothing materialized over the course of the next year. Traffic studies by both railroads yielded completely different diversion numbers: The Rock showed traffic losses of $21 million, whereas DRGW showed $12 million in lost traffic to the Rock Island. Neither was acceptable given the perilous nature of Rock Island's finances, and the proposal to purchase the line went no further.[25]

The condition of the railroad's track and finances remained dominant topics in the courtroom as to whether it could be reorganized on an income basis. A report on track conditions to the court dating from December 1978 showed the main problems the railroad faced. "The Rock Island, in 1975, the year of bankruptcy, was found to have the second *lightest* average weight of rail." At an average of 102.3 pounds per yard, the Rock was the second lowest in the western district, with only the C&NW possessing a lower track weight (averaging 94.3-pound track). But that figure did not tell the whole story. On many segments of the Rock Island, particularly branchlines in Iowa and other states, 60-pound rail was not uncommon. The Trustee claimed installation of 129 miles of 115-pound rail and 28 miles of 132-pound rail, which were better suited to heavier carloads, but on a 7,300-mile system, hardly the type of progress to restore profitability.[26]

Responding to claims that the Trustee was not putting enough money into track rehabilitation, the report seems defensive, claiming that "the deferred maintenance on the property, particularly in areas of light rail, inadequate anchorage, and poor drainage, is a time bomb which is very difficult and slow to defuse. . . . Overcoming deferred maintenance is a lengthy process." The other problem was one shared by all railroads. The increased use of heavier cars, including the 100-ton jumbo hoppers common in Rock Island territory, placed a heavy burden on the track and required more continual maintenance. Slowing down was not necessarily a bad thing, the report argued, when it came to the use of heavier equipment. (See Photo 8.2.)

Photo 8.2 From the cab window of a Rock Island locomotive, one can see the deterioration of the track conditions in Dallas, as the end of the railroad approaches. In April 1979 the locomotive waits on a spur, which is used despite its decrepit condition. Copyright by Lewis Raby, from the collection of Tom Kline. Used with permission.

"Speed hasn't always been our goal. In some rehabilitated areas, notably the Northeast Iowa grain-gathering branch lines, light rail often keeps even rehabilitated speeds down to 10 or 25 MPH." "In areas where rehabilitation has been concentrated, notably Chicago-Omaha, Memphis-El Reno, Oklahoma and select portions of the Chicago-Houston spine, speeds are higher (up to 60 MPH) than they were at the time of bankruptcy."[27]

A lot of the money to maintain and to rehabilitate branchlines came from an innovative state program in Iowa, one of the few states that tried to save railroad track mileage in the mid-1970s. There was reason for concern in the state, which during the early 1970s ranked fourth in railroad mileage, with more than 7,000 miles of line. As a commemorative history of the bill establishing the Iowa Rail Assistance Program argued, "deferred maintenance, inefficient use of freight car and the inability of some carriers to cope with the increased shipping brought about as a result of the 'Russian Grain Deal,' finally took its toll on Iowa's rail system." In 1974, the Iowa General Assembly created the Rail Assistance Program, administered within the Iowa DOT and the Energy Policy Council, a state organization created in 1973 to advise the legislature and governor on energy issues. By 1982, the Rail Assistance Program wrote twenty-nine contracts to upgrade track on seventeen branchlines totaling 1,191 miles at a cost of $79 million, split between taxpayers, shippers, and railroads.[28]

The roots of the Rail Assistance Program lay in the 1972–1973 energy crisis, which impacted the state drastically, particularly in shortages of propane and natural gas to dry out a wet corn crop in the fall of 1972. Iowa governmental officials created the Energy Policy Council "to plan and to coordinate Iowa's energy efforts." "Government has a prime opportunity to conserve energy in the field of transportation, which consumes one-fourth of the energy used in Iowa as it does in the nation," a brochure stated. "The railroads are potentially the most energy efficient carrier of goods on long-distance, inland trips. The deterioration of rail service in Iowa, as in other states, shows the price being paid for the nation's failure to have an energy-related transportation policy. Iowa has initiated an innovative branch line improvement program, but no state can solve this problem by itself." The legislature appropriated $3 million to help rehabilitate branchlines, identifying seven that held first priority, and seven more secondary branchlines, for rebuilding.[29]

The Rock Island was a willing partner with Iowa, negotiating contracts to rebuild three branchlines.[30] One, from Indianola to Carlisle southeast of Des Moines, was one of the first contracts broached by the authority. In September 1974, the Energy Policy Council entered a contract with the railroad to rebuild the line for $598,000. Rock Island said it was unable to come forward with any money. Energy Policy Program director John Milhone stated that "looking at their financial statement, I am inclined to believe them. According to the proposed agreement, the State would provide two-thirds of the money, or $400,000, and the shippers, one-third, or $200,000." Richard Lane, of the Rock Island, called to say "the terms of the agreement were favorable to the Rock Island." But no formal action was taken until the next year, following the inauguration of bankruptcy proceedings.[31]

The branchline was in deplorable shape. An 11-mile line through Warren County, the Indianola branch served a total population of 19,000 and had two major shippers: grain elevators that shipped 600 hopper cars and 2.1 million bushels of grain per year. The Rock Island provided data showing about sixty cars had shipped on the line in 1973. But the track conditions were barely able to sustain the heavy weights of hopper cars.

The load limit is 200,000 pounds, and it is therefore embargoed to cars over 70 tons. The timetable speed is 10 mph over the entire line with numerous locations where speed is limited to 5 mph. Derailments occur frequently even at these speeds and the line is out of service for several days at a time. . . . Approximately 5 miles of the line is laid with 65 and 75 pound steel that is from 67 to 79 years old. . . . Tie condition is extremely poor and ballast consists largely of dirt and cinders.[32]

Two other branchlines on the Rock Island were given state assistance as part of the program, including the Iowa Falls gateway, some 130 miles of track extending from Iowa Falls northwest to Estherville. In 1974, the line hauled $23 million worth of grain, most of which was destined for Gulf ports. This was the heart of the Rock Island's territory, and as the *Des Moines Register* reported, "[you] see track laid before 1906 which is in deplorable condition." West of Rodman, the track was so bad that wooden ties dating to the 1930s were common, as well as rails stamped with the date 1904. Kinks in the track, where one rail was higher than the other, caused frequent swaying, and derailings were common on the branch. Needless to say, the experience of the reporter on the Iowa Falls branch was a common experience throughout Iowa.[33]

No wonder the Rock Island was eager to accept the assistance of Iowa officials and businessmen. The Audubon-Atlantic Branch Line Improvement Association, a collection of shippers on a 25-mile branch in western Iowa, loaned William Gibbons $100,000 to provide service on the branch; a state contract to rehabilitate the line to FRA Class II standards (up to 20 mph), was approved in 1976 with the goal of moving 1,000 carloads of grain on the line. In 1977, the railroad had moved only 327 for the year, "almost exactly the same number as we moved in 1975," Richard Lane, the Rock Island traffic manager, stated. The state and shippers had spent close to $750,000 to upgrade the line—and the results were not too impressive.[34]

The Rock Island continued to lobby for funds. John Ingram wrote Governor Robert Ray and the state legislature about the continued commitment of the Rock Island to the program. "Because of our present financial condition," Ingram wrote, "it is indeed possible that the Rock Island's treasury could not produce the railroad's cash share of a particular project; we have learned through experience, however, that our share can be advanced by shippers or can consist of contributions in kind—labor and materials instead of cash."[35] And the money came. With the support of shippers and the state, the Rock Island secured roughly $2.5 million to rehabilitate 500 miles of branchlines in Iowa. By the end of summer 1977 the *Des Moines Register* optimistically declared that the Rock Island had revived. "Thanks in large part to help from the State of Iowa and from Iowa shippers, the Rock Island seems to be making a go of it." "The apparent revival of the Rock Island is good news for the many Iowa farmers and businessmen who depend on it."[36]

Not all Iowa railroads were as interested in receiving help from the state. C&NW's Larry Provo objected philosophically to the necessity of rehabilitating marginal branchlines in the state. Commenting on a plan to rehabilitate a branchline on the C&NW at Roland, a few miles from the C&NW mainline at Nevada, Provo argued, "Surely, if this line were not there we do not believe that anyone would seriously consider making an investment to construct the line today. We do not feel that the line should be kept and maintained simply because it is there." There were not enough cars shipped per mile to justify the $700,000 expense, "which would merely permit operations at 10 mph." Provo asked for authority to support abandonment of the line.[37] In 1976 he reiterated the desire of the C&NW to abandon 1,500 miles of unprofitable branchlines in Iowa. "The small country grain elevators will have a different function. They will become intermediate points between farmers and larger grain elevators." Provo also condemned Iowa's action to invest in saving Rock Island track, whose "elimination would be a good way to get rid of some excess railroad capacity."[38]

Branchlines in Iowa may not have excited the imagination of politicians thinking of railroads, in robber baron–like terms, of coast-to-coast enterprises serving large industrial cities and concentrated population centers, hauling coal, iron ore, finished manufactured goods, and the flotsam and jetsam of industrial production. But the Rock Island and other Midwestern lines teetering on bankruptcy were vital to the economy of Midwestern towns, many of which featured their own product of industrial farming—the grain elevator, a towering co-op along the railroad tracks in just about every Midwestern town. "Up through here," a Rock Island clerk in Dows, Iowa, told one *Trains* magazine correspondent, "is a very rich grain area.... And these elevators, I mean, they're big business in their town. Klemme's elevator [in Dows] is the biggest thing in town. It keeps the town. It's the main employer. If you kill the railroad, you've killed the whole town."[39]

Yet politicians in Washington representing Rock Island territory seemed almost incapable of articulating how the demise of railroads like the Rock Island and, later, the Milwaukee Road—all in the desire for efficiency and rationality in the route structure—would impact their region. Midwestern taxpayers were subsidizing the government-run railroad freight system, Conrail, which primarily served the industrial Northeast, and the passenger service Amtrak, which in its politicized route structure bypassed Iowa's largest population corridor and traveled on the southern route of the Burlington Northern. There was no federal aid coming to Midwestern railroads like the Rock Island, apart from the trustee certificates provided in 1976. Not until the railroad was forced by the ICC to be operated under directed service, in the fall of 1979, did politicians begin to take notice and to mobilize sentiment to save the railroad. Out of fear of having another Midwestern Conrail on its hands, Washington did very little to help the Rock.[40]

Little is more illustrative of continued government indifference to the railroad, and the perils of continued regulation for a company in bankruptcy, than the Trustee's effort to eliminate the Rock Island's intercity passenger service. Since deciding not to join Amtrak in 1971, the Rock Island had continued to run four intercity passenger trains, Numbers 11-12 (the *Peoria Rocket*) and Numbers 5-6 (the *Quad Cities Rocket*). The four ramshackle trains were remnants of a once-proud *Rocket* fleet; and though the railroad throughout the early 1970s tried to provide better service and attract passengers, this became impossible during bankruptcy and given the physical decline of the property. As Anthony Haswell (head of the Washington-based lobbying firm the National Association for Railroad Passengers whom Ingram brought to the Rock in 1975 and installed as managing director of passenger services) argued, "Physical disabilities of both the commuter and intercity services were a major discouragement to imaginative marketing."[41]

Gibbons made his initial case for discontinuing the trains in September 1976, arguing to the federal court in Chicago that the service cost Rock Island $1.7 million in 1975; for the first quarter of 1976 the loss was $407,000.[42] Even with subsidies from the State of Illinois ($750,000 in 1974, $1 million in 1975, and $250,000 in 1976), losses still topped $1 million annually, and the state's payment (made in quarterly installments) was often late, causing even more expenses for Rock Island.[43] A railroad in reorganization, as Gibbons stated, could not afford the luxury of passenger service that was not patronized and was not in the public interest.

A second argument the Rock Island made concerned the declining number of passengers. The daily average of passengers carried was 235 in 1974, declining to *sixty-six* in the first quarter of 1976, producing a "daily out-of-pocket-loss for the period of approximately $4,500."[44] The trains were not necessary, as Gibbons explained, due to the presence of regular air service between Chicago and the Quad Cities, regular bus service provided by Trailways, and nearby Amtrak stations in Chillicothe, Illinois, on the Santa Fe, only 18 miles from Peoria. There was no compelling public interest for the service, and, as Gibbons argued, the loss of $4,500 per day put the railroad in a serious bind when it came to maintaining revenue-producing freight operations, which *were* in the public interest.

Judge McGarr determined that "in the emergency situation now faced by the Rock Island, the threat to its assets, continued operation, and reorganizability is of a dimension such as to constitute a taking without due process." Instead of going before the Illinois Commerce Commission, which typically had jurisdiction in such cases, Judge McGarr pointed out that unless the State of Illinois restored its subsidy immediately "the emergency nature of this situation" would dictate that the federal court assume jurisdiction "and order a hearing" to discontinue passenger service.[45] Within a month the state paid what it owed to keep the trains running.

Gibbons next turned to the Illinois Commerce Commission, filing a petition to end the service. Hearings were held in Rock Island, in Peoria, and in Chicago that commenced in late 1976 and continued through February 1977. The Rock Island's argument was much the same as before: that the cost of providing the service was detrimental to a railroad in reorganization; that the public was not using the service; and that there were plentiful alternatives for transportation in the region. A total of 7,000 passengers rode the train between the Quad Cities and Chicago in the first six months of 1976, down from more than 50,000 in 1974. (See Photo 8.3.) Slow-orders on the track extended train schedules by as much as three hours versus 1970, and the railroad was paying twenty-four crew members and more than sixty ticket agents and support personnel (including a dining attendant) who could be utilized elsewhere on the line. A Rock Island TV station aired a special (*Last Ride for the Rocket?*) in 1977 documenting problems aboard the trains, interviewing Gibbons and Rock president John Ingram, who spoke candidly about how it was not uncommon for no one to be on the train when it pulled into Chicago. "Like today," reporter Paul Meincke stated. "That was the case today?" Ingram wearily chuckled. "It used to happen once in a while, but now it is a regular occurrence."[46] The viewers also met the veteran engineer Danny Signore, who discussed how *Rockets* used to blast through Illinois at speeds up to 90 mph; but due to decaying track conditions, they were lucky to make a consistent speed of 40 mph, extending the journey from the Quad Cities to Chicago from three hours to a consistent five or six. Signore said, "It makes me sick, especially when cars pass us by."

The service may have been ramshackle, but it was also quaint, and one could get a little romantic seeing a dirty, rundown Rock Island diesel pulling two coaches across the Illinois countryside. Conductors and crew on the *Peoria Rocket*, which was the low-priority train of the two remaining *Rockets*, delivered a newspaper from the open-coach vestibule to an elderly man in

Photo 8.3 *Two passengers on board Train No. 12: Joe Pierson (taking the picture) and George Strombeck. Photo by Joe Pierson. Used with permission.*

Putnam, Illinois, who had once pointed out a broken rail to the crew. The crew would make unscheduled stops if it was more convenient for a patron. The crew was friendly, professional, and caring, even if the equipment they used was rundown, Spartan, and old. (The newest coach was thirty years old at the end of the service, and the locomotives, all EMD E-8 units, including one painted in a bicentennial paint scheme by Chicago's 20th Century Railroad Club, were ancient as well.)[47]

The hearings held throughout the state produced several counterpoints to management's contention that the trains were unprofitable and did not serve the public interest. The City of Chicago's brief to the Illinois Commerce Commission contained charges that the Rock Island had willingly neglected the track, using comparisons of schedules from 1959 and 1970 to show the lengthened travel time, concluding that the "Rock Island, through deliberate acts, negligent acts or failure to act as required by law, has allowed its intercity passenger service to deteriorate to such a degree that there has been wholesale abandonment of this service by the riding public." The corporation counsel for the city argued that case law before the ICC was clear that willful neglect of service was not a means by which railroads could discontinue passenger service and argued that the Rock Island be ordered to continue service.[48]

The United Transportation Union also filed a brief insisting that the operation was sustainable, pointing a finger at the Rock Island for letting service decay. Citing the same ridership figures as Rock Island, the UTU claimed that hauling a daily average of about twenty passengers on the Quad Cities run and twelve on the Peoria run was sustainable. The union also argued that future prospects for "the trains appear very good." Repair of the mainline was under way, and "the anticipated speed will be 60 mph" as stated in testimony by the railroad's chief engineer. The Rock Island also needed to protect the twenty-four workers who would be impacted by discontinuing service, which the railroad was not interested in doing. Finally, the UTU challenged how much the railroad was impacted financially by the operation of the trains, arguing that "Rock Island's asserted losses are *de minimis* when compared with its overall operations. The railroad has assets of $437,587,000"; and "its total revenues were $384,835,000 and $336,523,000 for the years 1974 and 1975 respectively." "The carrier's losses were $21.8 million and $30.4 million for the two respective years. *We cannot understand the Trustee's assertion that discontinuance of this operation is an important part of the process of reorganizing the Rock Island.*"[49] The UTU's short-sightedness and unwillingness to recognize the railroad's losses as severe—to protect, in this case, twenty four jobs—would wind up costing labor thousands of jobs a few years later.

The Illinois Commerce Commission continued to keep the trains running. The election in 1977 of Republican James Thompson as governor did not change the funding, which continued to subsidize a service that went unused by the public. In August 1977, after the state refused to allow discontinuing operations, the Rock Island petitioned the federal Interstate Commerce Commission to do so. In testimony before Administrative Law Judge Paul Cross in February 1978, Gibbons reiterated the harsh financial penalties befalling the railroad for operating the four trains. Under cross-examination from UTU attorney Gordon MacDougall, Gibbons was directly asked about his compensation as Trustee of the Rock Island. He was also asked about pending sales of lines and the negotiations between the Rock Island and the Regional Transportation Authority concerning RTA's purchase of a track operating between Chicago and Joliet. MacDougall also asked about the movement of Rock Island passenger operations from LaSalle Street Station to Union Station in Chicago. Gibbons was coy on his answers, but it was clear what labor's strategy was regarding the high compensation Gibbons and Manos received to handle the bankruptcy case.[50]

This was shown most clearly in blistering testimony by John McGinness, a Conrail brakeman and legislative director of UTU's Illinois division.

McGinness had testified in the Illinois proceedings and now joined in the federal ones, arguing he was opposed to discontinuance of the trains, "not only for railroad employment, but because we believe there is a genuine public interest in a revitalized passenger train operation." McGinness pointed to improvements in the line and the rehabilitation that in the future would raise track speeds. But his most forceful testimony concerned the "alleged deficit" of the Rock Island: Using data from the ICC, McGinness pointed out how the passenger deficit of the Rock Island was "only $181,000," most of it presumably from commuter operations. The freight deficit for 1976 was $24 million. "There are means available to Rock Island to cure an alleged fully-distributed passenger deficit of $181,000," McGinness stated. Gibbons and Manos were each making around $180,000, according to ICC filings. "The high fees of Messrs. Gibbons and Manos have been previously publicized in railway labor circles as indicating excessive management plunder of this railroad in reorganization. . . . Rock Island's management is by no means underpaid." "Accordingly," he concluded,

> even assuming the viability of the $181,000 asserted deficit for all passenger service the public interest asserts that if a choice is to be made between the expenses of the Trustee and the passenger deficit, that it be the services of the trustee which should be discontinued, and other economies undertaken in his office. If there is a $180,000 misunderstanding, it should be resolved in favor of the passenger trains, and against the inflated fees of the trustee and his staff.[51]

The Railway Labor Executives' Association (RLEA—a federation of railroad unions that emphasized policy development and was a lobbyist for various brotherhoods) also protested discontinuance of the four trains, especially because it "would result in adverse effect to certain employees of the carrier or carriers involved." The Illinois Brotherhood of Locomotive Engineers (BLE), citing the poor performance record of the railroad, pointed out the "Rock Island's failure to conduct an aggressive marketing program," which "leads one to believe that the railroad further intends to discourage ridership of its trains." The BLE recommended a reduction of 50 minutes from the average run and cited track improvements being made as a possibility for future improved operations.[52]

In the end, after two years of hearings, briefs, and filings in court and before the ICC, the Rock Island was granted the right to discontinue the trains in May 1978. Paul Cross gave the order, which stipulated that the ridership would not be inconvenienced by such discontinuance and that Amtrak

Photo 8.4 The Peoria Rocket *had seen better days by 1978, shown rounding the curve at Morris, Illinois. Note the condition of the track and the pockmarked nose of E-8 diesel locomotive 654; the persisting decay of the property by this point is obvious. Photo by Mark Llanuza. Used with permission.*

should be encouraged to take over the route if continued service was desirable.[53] The Rock Island could not provide effective service, and Cross agreed that it constituted a hardship amid the reorganization. Gibbons had won a war of attrition, but appeals and delays meant the trains would continue for a time until the last intercity passenger train left LaSalle Street Station for Peoria at 6:15 P.M. on December 31, 1978.[54] A blizzard had closed O'Hare International Airport and Midway Airport that evening, had stranded motorists on the interstate, and had delayed Amtrak trains by several hours—yet here was the decrepit *Peoria Rocket* on its farewell run, hauling nine passengers (three of them migrants from Amtrak, bound for Chillicothe, Illinois), through miserable weather, leaving on time. There were no bands, little fanfare, not even press coverage in Chicago.[55] The inglorious end of the *Rockets* after forty-three years of operation came with a whimper. (See Photo 8.4.)

The last run of the *Rockets* through a blizzard magnified the problem the railroad industry faced with some of the worst winters in the country's history. During the winter of 1976–1977, Chicago experienced forty-three consecutive days of below-freezing temperatures. Lake Michigan nearly froze over, some 90 percent of its surface covered by ice. And from November

1977 to March 1978 Chicago was covered by snow for 100 days. The snow depth in Chicago was 29 inches in January 1979. Other Midwestern cities and rural areas were hamstrung by these three incredibly cold and difficult winters.[56] The winter of 1977 was one of the worst of the twentieth century (but pales in comparison with 1978 and 1979, which remain number one and two); Rock Island connections with Conrail and other eastern roads suffered tremendously. A mile-long, fifteen-foot snowdrift plagued Conrail's Buffalo line; rotary snowplows, more common in the western mountains, were employed by Midwestern railroads to cut through mammoth drifts.[57]

Operations under extreme conditions are always difficult. The trifecta of three of the worst winters in a row hit the railroad industry particularly hard. But William Gibbons claimed the challenges were met, telling employees "almost every part of the railroad suffered from subfreezing temperatures, blizzards and drifting snow. Employees and managers were hard pressed to keep the Rock rolling. Frozen switches, broken air hoses, mechanical difficulties with equipment and locomotives, snow plowing and other weather-related problems presented challenges which Rock employees met head-on."[58] Altogether, the Rock Island performed well in the winter of 1977. Yet the winter was cruel to carloads and to traffic. "January's car loadings were barely 51,000—a level not seen even during the depression of the 1930s, when territorial population was half of what it is today. Cash melted away as revenues dried up with the drop in car loadings, and as expenses skyrocketed when the cold weather froze track, engines, and people everywhere."[59] The rebuilding of one-third of the Rock Island's fleet of locomotives, by selling the locomotives to Precision National Corporation and then leasing them back, had allowed the railroad to be power-ready when winter hit. "The unprecedented winter months of December 1976, and January and February, 1977 could have had disastrous consequences for the Trustee's operations except for the new and rebuilt power which supplied great availability under severe conditions," Manos told the court.[60] This was reiterated in a newsletter to employees: "Rock Island was staggered by the costs generated by its unbroken service to its territory. By March [1977], the railroad's working capital had eroded to half of what it had been when Rock Island closed its books on December 31, 1976. Rumors that the ROCK would cease operations on March 1 circulated over the railroad," but due to planning and efficiencies being built into the operation "the Rock Island was able to survive yet another peril." Yet it had been a close call, and in a cheeky conclusion Ingram gave away a bit too much: "Winter almost accomplished what the bondholders, the US Railway Administration, the US DOT and the neighboring railroads had failed to do in 1975 and 1976—close down the Rock Island forever."[61]

Even without bad winters, the Rock Island remained an operational trainwreck during 1977. That year it hauled 714,557 cars of freight but lost an estimated 14,500 carloads due to shortages of freight cars, particularly jumbo hopper cars and 50-foot boxcars (it would be far worse in 1978, when the Rock lost 33,600 carloads of freight). In one week during March alone, the railroad could not provide 5,200 cars for shipping; accordingly, the railroad permanently lost 613 carloads of freight traffic to trucks or other railroads, "and this is only what we know about. Shippers don't usually bother to tell us when they divert business to others. Do everything you can to keep the cars moving."[62] "At the beginning of 1975, the Rock had a fleet of 25,139 freight cars," but on average these cars had to be replaced (1,000–1,250 per year). They were not. Lenders were not interested in providing the Rock with funds at reasonable rates, and "as a result, the freight car fleet declined in 1975, 1976 and 1977." In 1978 the railroad was able to negotiate favorable leases with companies to provide freight cars, but the damage of the previous three years had taken a toll and the loss, or deferral, of business due to freight-car shortages was staggering, with 33,960 carloads lost and 448,820 deferred.[63]

At the last court session of 1977, Manos and the Trustee continued to make the case that the railroad could be reorganized on an income-producing basis, which, given the declining carloads and revenues of the Rock Island, seemed in dispute. Manos reported that the request for funding under the 4R Act had been delayed "for about a year. Other railroads around us have received interim financing," including the Illinois Central Gulf, the Milwaukee Road, and the Katy. "The only railroad that has not received any interim financing is the Rock Island Railroad, unfortunately."[64] Why didn't the Rock Island receive the money? Manos charged that it was a deliberate action on the part of both the Crown interests and the intervenors representing the interest of subordinate bondholders by the First National Bank of Chicago. In each case, intervening attorneys contacted the FRA to scuttle any money for the Rock Island. "I would expect this of Mr. Crown to proceed with objections before the FRA. . . . His announced purpose . . . is to liquidate the Rock Island for his own purposes," one of which concerned Crown's "substantial interest in the Frisco Railroad that competes heavily with the Rock Island," as well as his ownership of "all of a barge line that competes heavily with the Rock Island."[65] Robert Bombaugh objected, arguing that Crown had never opposed federal financing provided it was subordinate to bondholders as a lien against the estate.

The issue of Crown's Frisco ownership had been raised by Manos before, but it was particularly important now in light of the revelation that the Frisco and Burlington Northern had begun merger discussions. Manos consistently argued that Crown was a major owner of stock in the Frisco, a merger that the Rock Island vehemently opposed, representing a conflict of interest in the Rock Island proceedings and explaining Crown's interest to force a liquidation.

Manos raised concerns about a conspiracy in the hiring of a consultant, Temple-Barker & Sloan, by First National Bank of Chicago (representing indentured bondholders in the case) and Continental Bank (representing stockholders). The consultant was to study the financial condition of the railroad in order to reveal whether it could be reorganized. Crown's attorneys had not participated in the study, relying on the Barber Report, which was filed in court in early 1976. Manos questioned why First National was opposing the FRA money, as the initial $2 million requested was to be subordinated to bondholders in the bankruptcy. "What hurts here, your Honor, is that we have not received the interim financing," Manos glumly concluded.[66]

Terry Moritz of the Chicago firm Isham, Lincoln & Beale, who had represented First National as an intervenor in the case, defended the bank's opposition to the FRA financing. "We see a railroad that in the last three-quarters has lost 20 million dollars," he stated, "and that persists in losing money at an accelerated rate. We have a fiduciary obligation to the bondholder to see to it that if and when this railroad is liquidated there is a significant amount of assets sufficient to pay off approximately 53 million in debt obligations. Mr. Manos will exhort us that the money will always be there. We aren't that confident." Continental Bank's lawyers concurred with Moritz.[67]

Judge McGarr was caught off guard by the banks' opposition to the financing, recognizing for the first time that their interests were similar to Crown's. "I can understand the Trustee's chagrin when he goes to Congress, or to the federal agencies for money, to find that those persons whom he would hope would join him in achieving reorganizability, are fighting him on the other hand. . . . The federal programs, depending on how you look at this, are vital to the reorganization of this railroad, if there is going to be a reorganization," Judge McGarr concluded, before determining that "while he finds it unfortunate with relation to the future of the railroad, the parties are entitled to their position and to their activities."[68] Judge McGarr went one step further, arguing "if you knew how little I regard the opinions of these agencies you wouldn't worry about that [concerning the FRA's participation in Court proceedings]. I am beginning to get a glimmer of the processes behind the scenes to determine whether the grant will or will not be made. The determination is rarely objective, it all depends on which senator on behalf of which railroad makes the loudest noise."[69]

Very few senators, or government officials, or members of the executive branch were making much noise about saving the Rock Island. As 1977 dragged into 1978, and another punishing winter dealt the Rock Island yet another blow, Secretary of Transportation Brock Adams made it abundantly clear (if it was not clear already to anyone paying attention) what he thought of the Rock Island. Whereas Manos may have seen conspiracy among the intervenors in the case to kill the railroad, in Washington the take was very different. If the Rock Island was a "walking dead man," as Adams called it in January 1978, then why try to save it?

NINE

WALKING DEAD MEN

It's Not My Place to Run the Train / The Whistle I Can't Blow /
It's Not My Place to Say How Far / The Train's Allowed to Go.
It's Not My Place to Shoot Off Steam / Nor Even Clang the Bell /
But Let the Damn Thing Jump the Track . . .
And See Who Catches Hell.

—Brock Adams, "My Job," January 1978

The December 19, 1977, bankruptcy filing of the Chicago, Milwaukee, St. Paul, and Pacific Railroad in the Dirksen Federal Building in Chicago—the same courthouse where the Rock Island filed bankruptcy—made for a glum Christmas in parts of the upper Midwest. The Milwaukee Road was the twelfth-largest railroad in mileage in the nation, with more than 10,000 miles of track stretching from Chicago northwest to Minnesota and west to Iowa and South Dakota. In 1915, in what was seen then as an ill-advised move, the railroad completed a Pacific extension to Tacoma, Washington, over the Cascade Mountains through Snoqualmie Pass. The route was later electrified, the haunt of General Electric box-cab electrics and "Little Joes" (electric locomotives produced during World War II for the Soviet Union, the nickname a tribute to Josef Stalin). The locomotives were never sent, spending their careers instead on the Milwaukee Road and the Chicago, South Shore, and South Bend Railroad. The construction to Puget Sound was the last great transcontinental extension of the railroad building era. The Milwaukee Road was unique as well in that it possessed a southeastern line from Chicago to Louisville, Kentucky, the only western road with a route east of Chicago.[1]

The Milwaukee Road had always been a weak line in producing traffic, nowhere more than in the northern Plains and Iowa; heavily dependent on grain shipments over a vast network of branchlines, it could no longer compete after the formation of the Burlington Northern Railroad in 1970. Indeed, it was because of that pending merger in the 1960s that the Milwaukee sought a merger of its own, initially with the Rock Island in 1960 and 1961, and then with the Chicago and North Western Railway from 1964 to 1969 before the Interstate Commerce Commission pulled the plug. When C&NW offered to sell to the Milwaukee Road in 1970, the latter refused, instead seeking inclusion in the Union Pacific–Rock Island merger. That was not allowed either. The rejection of the C&NW offer was a fatal decision that sounded the death knell for the Milwaukee Road.[2]

It was one thing for government officials to treat the Rock Island's bankruptcy as an anomaly, a result of long-delayed merger proceedings between it and the UP; or as a failure of the corporation to maintain the property while it waited for the Union Pacific to take over; or simply a result of having too many railroads running in the same place—all common explanations of the Rock Island bankruptcy. But the Milwaukee Road's bankruptcy crystallized a wider problem in the Midwest, similar to the collapse of the northeastern railroad system in the early 1970s. How would the government respond? Would nationalization be necessary to bring about stability and order in the western region? Or would some other solution, such as widespread abandonment and liquidation, be necessary? These were vexing questions for the government as yet another major Midwest railroad sought bankruptcy protection.

Before the federal government could respond, John Ingram proposed one of the more interesting solutions to the Midwestern railroad crisis. Called Farm Rail, Ingram sought a consortium of five Midwestern railroads—the Rock, the Milwaukee, the Illinois Central Gulf, the Katy, and the Kansas City Southern—to "combine some of the trackage where they operate; consolidate freight yards in some major transportation centers; pool equipment; combine some sales offices; centralize their computerized payroll functions; and perhaps even pool revenues." The Rock Island and Milwaukee Road had started such a process in the summer of 1976, operating trains on 243 miles of Rock Island track between Kansas City and the Mississippi River moving 28 million ton-miles of freight over the line; traffic has been so heavy "the track is wearing out," Ingram told the *Washington Star*.[3] It was not a Midwestern Conrail, Ingram noted, but "a consortium of railroads operated in their joint best interests."[4] Ingram did not detail how this would work out, nor had he approached other railroads about the concept, but he was confident that if labor unions and other interests could be brought on board Farm Rail could stave off "service collapses that would seriously affect the future of many hundreds of communities and industries" throughout the region.[5]

The government did not see the problem in the same way as Ingram. Rather, Secretary of Transportation Brock Adams and the Carter White House thought the solution was to rationalize redundant mileage and bring weaker lines under the control of stronger ones—not necessarily through merger but through operating agreements and control. Their goal was a "private sector solution" to the problem.⁶

Adams was a former Democratic congressman from Washington first elected in 1964 and served on the House Budget Committee and the Interstate and Foreign Commerce Committee. Known for supporting regional business interests such as the Boeing aviation company, Adams had been a vocal critic of the Vietnam War, supported the War on Poverty, supported Robert Kennedy for president in 1968, was liberal on social issues, and as a board member of the International Council of Planned Parenthood favored abortion rights and even population control. He was also a strong supporter of organized labor and particularly friendly with United Transportation Union president Al Chesser. Long interested in transportation issues, Adams in 1973 helped draft the Regional Rail Reorganization Act (3R Act; originally called the Shoup-Adams bill). He was a natural choice for Jimmy Carter to become head of the DOT in 1977.

Brock Adams outlined the administration's position regarding the railroad industry's problems in a December 2, 1977, memorandum to the president. In discussing the railroad industry's problems, he described "a vicious, declining cycle from loss of traffic, to loss of revenues, then profits, then capacity to provide service, then more losses of traffic and so on. The railroads' ordinary income today is only one-quarter of its 1947 level, after adjusting for inflation. For the industry as a whole, internal cash generation is insufficient to meet capital requirements, and return on investment is too low."⁷ The factors that caused this decline were outside of the railroad industry's control, and Adams pointed out several issues: "basic changes in traditional rail markets" due to industrial decline; "regulation, which had constrained management's ability to adjust rates, merge corporate entities and abandon obsolete facilities and services; inability of labor and management to agree on methods for improving productivity; government provided highways, locks, dams and other facilities"; and "insufficient R&D and slowness in adapting to new technology." Carter added in the margins of this memo: "also, too many railroads, too much track, too many employees, increasing dependence on gov't. bailouts, too much past (present?) use of RR money for non-related investment."⁸

Adams stated that "the department's policy studies will continue to place high priority on keeping the industry functioning as a vital business within the private sector. We wish to minimize the degree of public involvement—especially public financial involvement—in the industry." He also argued that financial assistance could be made only after a careful examination of each particular circumstance. But more was needed industrywide, including institutional and management changes that would go a long way toward improving profitability. Not mentioned as a major area for recommendation was deregulation, which eventually was how railroad profitability rebounded.[9]

Following the Milwaukee Road bankruptcy declaration, Adams scheduled a meeting in Chicago on January 18-19, 1978, to discuss the Midwestern railroad crisis. Before that, he fired off another memo to Carter on administration policy on assistance to Midwestern railroads, arguing that only a private-sector solution was amenable for the Midwest. "Your marginal notes on my December 2 memorandum" (where Carter indicated there were too many railroads and too much track) impacted Adams, who quoted the lines for the president and stated: "I want you to know that I am taking direct action based on the memorandum and your assessment. If we do not have a strong, innovate railroad policy, Congress will move on its own traditional type of bailout solution."[10] Adams told Carter that he wanted to authorize constructive private-sector solutions using "existing statutory authority of Section 401 of the 4R Act by having the railroads (both in and out of bankruptcy) restructure through market swaps, joint use arrangements, and abandonment proposals. . . . Again, I want to avoid having a Conrail-type solution in the Midwest."[11]

What Adams said at the conference in Chicago was not well remembered—except that there would be no government bailout similar to Conrail. What he said a week before the meeting about the Rock Island has been long remembered, however, and drew the ire of the Trustee in response. In a lengthy story on the Midwestern railroad problem and how he and the administration might respond, Adams told the *Wall Street Journal*: "The Milwaukee Road's situation is only the tip of the iceberg" in the Midwest. He described the Rock Island as "a walking dead man." Adams added that both the Milwaukee and Rock Island may not necessarily survive: "They would like things to be as they have been, but they are never going to be as they have been."[12] The last quote was particularly unfair to the Rock Island, as the Trustee had been taking action to salvage whatever could be and to get rid of lines through sale or abandonment. Gibbons responded in the paper the next day, telling Adams that he should "keep his cool and refrain from pushing a rapid fire panic button." Gibbons then stated that 10 percent of Rock Island track had been rehabilitated, the railroad had modernized its locomotive fleet, and it had rebuilt and purchased new freight cars. "This and other recent railroad statements," Gibbons concluded, "are a disservice to the public and to the entire railroad industry. A continued attitude such as his will contribute nothing towards the solution of the Midwest railroad problem. It will only exacerbate it."[13]

The meetings on January 18 and 19 involved officials from DOT, Daniel O'Neal of the Interstate Commerce Commission, Lawrence Sullivan of the Federal Railroad Administration, as well as executives of Midwestern railroads, labor unions, shippers, and state officials. Adams told the assembled press that "I am not wed to the concept that every railroad corporation should survive. We must be very careful about a commitment of public funds. We have to make sure that the public investment can be paid back."[14] In his public comments, Adams argued that the Midwestern railroads would not be bailed out as in the Northeast, arguing the distinctiveness of the collapse of the Penn Central in a declining industrial area. "The Penn Central was far more dominant in the Northeast than any single carrier is in the Midwest," he argued. "The reorganization of northeastern carriers required a major governmental planning process, during which funding of $660 million in trustees certificates, grants and rehabilitation loans were required to keep them alive."[15]

Why were the Midwestern railroads different? Adams argued that the Midwestern economy was far stronger, not as reliant on the movement of heavy industrial products, and did not possess the dense network of lines competing for declining traffic. What was needed in the Midwest was not a Conrail West but a restructuring of the rail network—not necessarily through mergers but through rationalization or new competitive arrangements. Here, Adams singled out the Rock Island, which "as you know, has already proposed a plan calling for the consolidation and coordination of its freight services with those of four other Midwest railroads. Under this plan, the consortium of privately-owned railroads would jointly share terminals, rail yards, equipment and revenues. I would reserve judgment on this specific plan, however, until the costs and prospective benefits can be fully assessed."[16] In the end, all Adams offered was assistance already available to Midwestern roads under section 401 of the 4R Act.

Trustee William Gibbons directed his remarks at what Adams had told the press, saying "I am sorry, Mr. Secretary, we are not a walking dead man. Your report on our demise was grossly exaggerated." However, what Rock Island officials revealed to the hearing seemed to justify Adams's comments, as the railroad reported 1977 losses of $35 million, higher than the year the railroad went into bankruptcy. Gibbons blamed the other railroads in the territory the Rock Island served, arguing "we are surrounded by those who would cut off our oxygen for their own selfish interests and not for the purposes of solving the railroad problem." That prompted James Wolfe, the new president of the Chicago and North Western Railway, to whom Gibbons addressed his comments, to renew calls for the liquidation of the Rock Island.

"This second Midwestern bankruptcy petition demonstrates, if any further proof were needed, that there is not enough rail traffic in the Midwest to support the number of routes and railroads being operated." He argued that the Rock Island should have been split up years ago and parceled out to competing carriers. "Sad though the bankruptcy of the Milwaukee Road is, its demise offers another opportunity to rationalize the Midwestern rail plant."[17]

Conrail haunted the conference like an apparition. There was good reason so much reference was made to *avoiding* the creation of a Midwestern Conrail. The northeastern Consolidated Rail Corporation had turned into a corporate welfare case, sucking up $2 billion in federal assistance in its first year, with projections of billions more over the course of the next decade. Railroad operations over the 24,000-mile system were made worse by difficult winter weather during Conrail's first two years of operation, by the failure to secure needed cuts in its labor force, and the failure to abandon significant segments of unprofitable branchlines.

Brock Adams, who had a hand in the creation of Conrail in what became the 3R Act in 1974, could state unequivocally that the federal government, now under a Democratic administration, did not want yet another government-run railroad corporation. (With some irony—for most Americans see the two political parties and their views of government programs in the opposite manner—the impetus for a government solution to the railroad problem occurred under Republican administrations.) Both Richard Nixon and Gerald Ford authorized a bailout of the northeastern railroads. Carter, more interested in cutting government spending, wanted to pursue a private-sector solution for the Midwestern railroads. Conrail was one of the main reasons for this: It had become an albatross.

Expectations were high for Conrail improving on the performance of the northeastern bankrupts on conveyance day, April 1, 1976. The railroad ran a full-page advertisement in the *Wall Street Journal* announcing a "different type of railroad." The only difference, however, was that Conrail arose from not one but seven bankrupt northeastern railroads, none possessing the revenue-generating traffic necessary for the new railroad to prosper. The United States Railway Association was given the task of developing a final system plan (FSP) for conveying the private railroads into the government-supported Conrail. When the FSP was released, in July 1975, it called for the formation of Conrail, the offering "of all economically self-sufficient [Erie Lackawanna] freight services east of Akron, Ohio and most Reading services" to the combined B&O, C&O, and Western Maryland (now called the Chessie

System); the Delaware and Hudson gaining "route extensions"; Southern Railway's "purchase of the Penn Central main lines on the Delmarva peninsula and car float from Cape Charles to Norfolk"; and Amtrak's "acquisition of the Northeast Corridor from Boston to Washington for the development of high speed passenger service." The USRA had considered two government-supported lines in the East, called MARC-EL (comprising the Erie Lackawanna lines and a separate Conrail composed of Penn Central), but it rejected that alternative and chose to support a single Conrail approach.[18]

Penn Central's bankruptcy trustees released a blistering response to the FSP. "The FSP would, in our judgment, produce exactly the opposite result of the stated purpose of the 3R Act of 1973 under which it was prepared. Instead of creating a self-sustaining Conrail in the private sector, the FSP would remove the distressed railroads from the private enterprise system for the foreseeable future, if not forever, with most of the disadvantages of nationalization and few real benefits." It also stated that the "present conditions of the distressed railroads" were "primarily as a direct result of unfair handicaps imposed by governmental fiat."[19] The terms of the nationalization of the properties "are so blatantly unfair as to amount to a confiscation of those assets," a PC press release stated. Even more disturbing, the USRA had determined that the PC's assets were worth $471 million "on the fictitious assumption that the rail properties are worth no more than what would be realized if they were scrapped." The Trustees made it clear that should the FSP pass Congress they would immediately file "a claim against the US government under the Tucker Act, a law enacted in 1887 that allows liability claims against the federal government under a slew of provisions, including liquidation under the Fifth Amendment takings clause, for the fair value of the estate's assets that are being taken for public purposes—for the $7.4 billion that the Trustees believe in all fairness that these assets are worth."[20] The discrepancy would scare away potential buyers, like the Chessie System, which refused to be part of the new FSP (in the end it might have to cough up billions of dollars should the court determine the worth of the lines it took over was higher than the USRA's calculation).

Congress acted on the FSP hurriedly, drawing a rebuke from House Minority Whip Robert Michel (R–Ill.) about "backdoor legislation" and cutting off debate on the proposal. Under the FSP, Conrail was going to need $6.9 billion in government funds, Michel stated. But there was not to be a debate about the options available to Congress. Instead, House leadership was rushing headlong into Conrail before vexing issues—such as the discrepancy between the valuation of the lines, as well as labor costs—could be

Photo 9.1 President Gerald R. Ford signing the Regional Railroad Revitalization and Reform Act (the 4R Act) in February 1976, with William Coleman, DOT Secretary, to his right; Ford aide James Cannon is to his left. Courtesy of Gerald R. Ford Presidential Library.

resolved. Michel discussed several alternatives not considered in the FSP (a few of which had been rejected by the USRA), including deregulation, an auction of lines, ConFac (the purchase of the track by the government similar to the Interstate Highway System), and even, "though it goes against my philosophical principles," nationalization.[21]

The concerns over cost, and of how any valuation might burden the new corporation, led Congress to adopt a specific piece of legislation to deal with these and other railroad issues. The Regional Railroad Revitalization and Reform Act, signed into law in February 1976, was written partly to provide Conrail with the funds and rehabilitation dollars needed to begin operating. (See Photo 9.1.) It also provided a $1 billion fund for other railroads to apply for rehabilitation grants and assistance—funds that the Rock Island and other railroads sought. Most important, it provided the beginnings of deregulation by placing a two-year limit on the ICC's consideration of mergers and by allowing rate flexibility (7 percent up or down on tariffs) if a railroad controlled no more than 70 percent of the traffic in a given area.[22]

"By the end of 1980," Jervis Langdon wrote, "Conrail's net operating loss amounted to $1.4 billion, or seven times greater than had been projected in the FSP."[23] Rush Loving Jr. argued that "Conrail was losing money at the same rate Penn Central had hemorrhaged cash—$1 million per day."[24] Langdon claimed, "By its [the USRA's] own estimates, additional federal financing (above the $3.3 billion already consumed) of from $900 million to $3.7 billion would be needed to cover even presently known contingencies." Langdon cited a 1980 USRA report that said "it was unclear whether [Conrail] can ever become self-sustaining in its present form." Freight traffic had gone down from levels the bankrupt Penn Central hauled in the mid-1970s, and its per-ton miles of freight hauled was below PC's as well.[25] Yet the federal money was restoring track to prior standards and rehabilitating equipment, particularly locomotives and freight cars. Federal funds did make a difference for Conrail, but it was clear from the amount of money spent, and the uneven returns by 1980, that further federal money for bankrupt railroads like the Rock Island and the Milwaukee Road would not be forthcoming. Conrail's failure had pointed the way to deregulation as a solution, even though that was not a clear path in either 1978 or 1979.

A month after the conference in Chicago, following another devastating winter, Ingram appealed to Brock Adams for loan credits to help defray car shortages due to the weather. "Our current car shortage has skyrocketed to over 5,000 cars and is growing," he said. "We need anything we can get on wheels. . . . If loan credits could be made available to us to put light bad order cars back into service immediately, the advance could be quickly repaid from revenues earned by the cars. A maximum of $2 million would create considerable increases in available needed equipment for the ROCK's customers to use during the truck-barge crunch." After January 20, Ingram reported, "we started to experience a great increase in car loadings. . . . While this increase in on-line business may sound like a windfall for the ROCK, it is not. Cold weather is reducing our margins and we are forced to finance increased business in a declining cash situation, caused by the previous periods' costs and traffic declines."[26]

The Rock still had its application for $160 million pending with the FRA, mainly to fund track work on the core of the railroad. It seemed unlikely it would secure any of the additional money, and liquidation rumors spread yet again. A *Business Week* article in March 1978 seemed to suggest that the venerable line was at its end, focusing on the court battle between Crown's lawyers and the bankruptcy Trustee.[27] But in April, when the $57 million deal between the SP and the Rock was announced, Judge McGarr once again allowed a six-month reprieve for the railroad. The *Des Moines Register* worried that the ICC would drag its feet and not approve the sale quickly. "The Rock Island has put up a plucky fight to improve its facilities and service.... We would like to see it survive and thrive." But the editors knew chances were slim unless regulators speedily approved this and other line sales and the FRA provided assistance to rebuild the lines.[28]

In September 1978, the FRA did allow the Trustee to borrow an additional $33.5 million to rebuild 2,915 freight cars, to buy or rebuild seven locomotives, to construct a new paint facility, and to enlarge repair shops at Little Rock, Arkansas. None of the additional money went to track rehabilitation. And while Gibbons signed the paperwork for the certificates, it came with a warning from FRA Administrator Thomas Sullivan, in a letter to Brock Adams, that the Rock Island could not be reorganized on an income-producing basis and that if it continued to lose money on FRA projects "we believe liquidation would be ordered." The FRA also showed losses between 1978 and 1981 of an additional $122 million should the railroad keep operating.[29]

Why, then, did the FRA grant the money? Sullivan had little faith that it would do any good, and it was hotly contested by Crown lawyer Albert Jenner, who brought the FRA memo to the court's attention. The FRA even took issue with the Trustee's report that carloads were improved by 9.5 percent from 1977, showing Association of American Railroads data that showed the Rock's carloads were down 1.15 percent from the year before. Why give the railroad additional money if no one believed it could be reorganized?

There may be two reasons, and both had to do with innovations that Rock Island was exploring to address its competitiveness in the Midwest. The first innovation had no chance of working: John Ingram's scheme to renegotiate work rules with the Brotherhood of Locomotive Engineers. The Rock Island had about 650 engineers on its system, making $23,000–$25,000 per year (about $16 million per year total in salaries). They were limited to an eight-hour workday, or 100 miles, whichever came first. Ingram wanted to have two five-man crews board a train that would work nonstop for 30 days at a time. The "off crew" would sleep in a Pullman car attached to the train. In return they would be paid $30,000 per year for working only six months, as the railroad would allow a month off after 30 days on the road. The reduction in crews would save the railroad money even after paying the additional amount in salary. "Our employees seem willing to listen to new ideas because they need the job security as much as we need the profits," Ingram said.[30] Nothing came of the idea, as the BLE and the Rock Island agreed to retroactive wage increases guaranteed by national labor negotiations. The BLE agreed to reduce to three-man crews on what the Rock was calling shuttle trains—trains hauling one commodity less than 100 miles—in order to maximize car use and to keep loading cars at a rapid pace. This was a three-month experiment in Dallas that the union had agreed to in order to recapture shipments going by trucks.[31]

"It's unheard of for a railroad to hold a sale," an advertisement airing on late-night television in Denver stated. "We think it's about time someone in this business did the unheard of."[32] John Ingram had convinced the ICC to allow the Rock Island to hold a freight sale, offering shippers a 20 percent discount between Thanksgiving and New Year's Eve 1978 on eastbound trailer traffic between Denver and assorted cities on the railroad. Trailers headed west were full, but eastbound freight was 90 percent empty, an expensive proposition for a bankrupt railroad. A blitz of newspaper advertisements in the *Rocky Mountain News* and the *Denver Post* accompanied the sale, with a new name (yet again) being used for the railroad, ROUTE ROCK (which began to appear on new freight cars in late 1978). A new slogan, "Creator of America's First Freight Sale," was placed underneath the new image. Full-page newspaper advertisements nationwide hawked the Rock's new image and showed the innovation on the railroad. "We've stopped operating in the old-fashioned, traditional way. To be competitive, we're challenging the *status quo* and responding to nationwide shipping needs with innovative and unique services"; it listed Farm Rail, boasted about the use of shorter trains to keep cars full and moving, and touted that "some of our best service ideas come from our people, our unions, our sales reps, our shippers."[33]

The innovations proposed and enacted may have been gimmicks, but they pointed to a change in railroad operations—the use of short-unit trains to haul commodities and keep shippers happy; smaller crews; and rate sales—all of which were allowed under the regulations. For the moment, however, Ingram and Rock Island management faced their biggest problem: Bad track was continuing to hamper revenues and forcing shippers to look elsewhere to get commodities and freight to market. The FRA released data from 1977 showing how the Rock Island far outdistanced the pack in accidents, with 568 accidents that year, 59.7 percent of them caused by bad track. This was measured as 42.4 accidents per 1 million train miles, three times higher than the U.S. average of 14.7.[34]

As the Rock's track decayed, some of its neighbors received assistance from the federal government to rebuild their lines. The C&NW received $90 million in funds from the FRA to lay 136-pound welded rail on its mainline from Clinton, Iowa, to Fremont, Nebraska. The Rock Island was seeking to block funding for an additional $35 million so that the C&NW could upgrade its mainline between Chicago and Clinton.³⁵ In August the *Chicago Tribune* reported on a run-through agreement between the UP and C&NW, allowing UP freights into the Chicago area on C&NW track, "the forerunner of an eventual attempt by the Union Pacific to acquire the smaller North Western." While UP's John Kenefick disagreed with that assessment, it was quite clear that an eventual merger made sense for both parties, even though the UP was cautious after the Rock Island merger attempt failed. "We'll think twice before we do it again."³⁶ Somewhere, Ben Heineman had to be smiling.

Rock Island executives knew that the FRA money for the C&NW would hurt the railroad, giving C&NW "a clear-cut service advantage" in Iowa's east-west corridor. A conclusion in a memorandum from Rock Island's Christopher Knapton was that "absent a coordination [of service] project within the corridor . . . it is now imperative that we file an application for Trustee certificates for the rehabilitation of our route from Silvis, Illinois to Council Bluffs, Iowa." Gibbons had contacted Wolfe about the Rock gaining trackage rights over the C&NW between Cedar Rapids and Council Bluffs, but Wolfe denied the request.³⁷

The Missouri Pacific had also become a profitable railroad after consolidating its three-way merger with the Texas and Pacific and Chicago and Eastern Illinois in 1976. Relying on shipping chemicals from the Gulf to northern cities, with 16 percent of its traffic coming from grain, MoPac had developed into a well-run and well-managed railroad, ever since Downing Jenks took over as president in 1961. By rehabilitating track, buying new equipment, and investing in the plant, Jenks was able to bring about a rebuilt railroad, unlike his tenure at the Rock Island in the late 1950s.³⁸

In the court battle over the future of the railroad, the Trustee continued to put forth optimistic projections about progress. The banter at the start of a status hearing on September 18, 1978, was positive, prompting Judge McGarr to comment, "I gather that the jovial atmosphere in the courtroom foretells agreement on all issues," to which Nicholas Manos replied, "Your honor, President Carter and [Menachem] Begin and [Anwar] Sadat can do it. I see no reason why Mr. Jenner and I and the Trustee can't accomplish the same thing." Manos told the court that, while the first half of 1978 had been bad, with winter weather and car shortages producing a deficit of $12.8 million through April, the summer months showed an upturn in traffic—"nine or ten percent ahead of last year." Manos reported that negotiations with the DRGW to purchase the Kansas City–Denver line were ongoing, that the railroad was still in talks with the FRA about securing federal assistance to rehabilitate the track, and that the additional new freight cars allowed by the court, as well as the 2,200 cars being rehabilitated, were improving traffic and revenues. Manos ended his status report by asking for an additional six-month extension to file a plan of reorganization, adding, "prospectively, and cautiously optimistically, I say to this Court that prior to the next status hearing, we will be in a position to have sat down with the creditors and their representatives and to have displayed to them an outline of a Trustee's plan; and hopefully, by next December we will present the outline to the Court; and perhaps, even—shortly thereafter—a defined program."[39]

Albert Jenner responded for the Crown interests, referencing a comment about the Trustee believing there is light at the end of the tunnel with a witty riposte: "The only remark against that is that the tunnel keeps extending in length, making it more difficult to see the light."[40] Jenner countered the claims made by the Trustee in every category: carloads, maintenance, operating revenues, and expenses. He concluded: "The Rock Island is suffering from insufficient traffic and revenues, increasing operating expenses, inefficient and unprofitable operating ratios, deteriorating and under-maintained physical plant considering net losses in enormous proportions." "One of the problems in looking down a long tunnel, your Honor, is that you get tunnel vision, you don't see to the right or to the left, and you get very little perspective."[41]

His detailed presentation should have been enough to raise doubts about the possibility of reorganization. But his presentation in a memorandum of the FRA's Thomas Sullivan was equally damning, for it was Sullivan who predicted that by 1981 the railroad would lose $121 million. "Now let's say they [Sullivan's projections] are too gloomy—let's cut that by twenty-five percent—that over those four years, the Rock Island will lose $91 million," Jenner argued. Either way, the losses would be severe. But he quoted more from Sullivan's memo:

> FRA's financial profile of the Rock Island is that of a railroad which meets anticipated operating cash deficits through deferrals of maintenance and consuming of assets, and is unable to generate a turnaround. Specifically, on the basis of our financial analysis, we conclude: one, Rock Island cannot reverse the trend of continuing operating losses; two, Rock Island cannot finance rehabilitation without Federal assistance; three, Federal assistance will not measurably alter Rock Island's financial performance, although it will improve service. Rock Island in its current physical structure cannot achieve an income-based reorganization in the foreseeable future.[42]

Attorney Terry Moritz, representing First National Bank of Chicago and the holders of first mortgage bonds, echoed Jenner's claims, producing even more details of the decline of the property and challenging the optimistic claims of the Trustee. "As we see it," Moritz explained, "the Federal Government has rejected, in two separate applications, any justification for further Federal funding." He continued: "In effect, the Federal Government has told the Rock Island the Federal well is dry. We think that fact is very significant. What the Government has told the Rock Island is that it is willing to provide funding, if the Rock Island is prepared to participate in the piecemeal disposition of lines owned by the railroad." Moritz added that the government was not in favor of the Rock Island continuing as a railroad. "We believe that the myth of the Rock Island's importance to the national rail system has been rejected by the Federal Government. We believe, further, that the Court should, similarly, reject that myth." The court should allow a six-month extension for the Trustee to file a plan for reorganization, but there should be no further extensions, Moritz concluded.[43] Susan Getzendanner, representing first mortgage bondholders of Continental Bank, concurred, arguing that the time had come for a proposal from the Trustee showing how the railroad could be reorganized.

Oddly, it was the U.S. government that called for some respite in the demands for a swift liquidation. John Broadley, an attorney with the Department of Justice, spoke regarding the FRA memorandum. Broadley pointed out that while the memorandum was grim when it came to the Rock Island's chances for reorganization, it did say "in its current physical structure." "To date, we have had no analysis or—as far as I am aware—no study has been made by the Trustee to identify or to determine whether there is, within this railroad—within the Rock Island—a profitable core railroad, which could be reorganized on an income basis." Broadley joined Jenner in calling for the filing of a preliminary report on a core reorganization plan by March 1979 and possibly sooner. He was joined by Iowa's DOT, which argued that there was a viable core that could be restructured; Iowa was interested not in maintaining the Rock Island as a corporate entity but as a viable railroad serving important shippers in the state.[44]

Norman Nachman spoke on behalf of the corporation, arguing that the Trustee was left in a difficult position when he took over a railroad that had seen a decade of losses. And while the Rock Island's attorney was complimentary toward the Trustee, Nachman told the court, "For the first time since this case started, very serious consideration must be given by this Court, within a reasonable period of time, as to how much longer this railroad can continue with these ongoing losses."⁴⁵ Nachman agreed that the Trustee be given six months to file a reorganization plan.

Nicholas Manos defended the efforts of the Trustee, pointing out the progress that had been made on car acquisitions and rebuilding and asking for the time necessary to turn around the financial condition of the railroad. He spoke of the negotiations with the SP and the DRGW to purchase significant line segments; he spoke of the rehabilitation of track, adding that the railroad had made progress in that regard since the petition was filed. Manos also questioned the motives of Henry Crown, arguing that his interests in the railroad had been singularly defended in the court, but not a word had been heard from other bondholders and creditors. He also revealed that Crown had sold $5 million worth of Rock Island debentures just that week, wondering what the motivation was behind the sale. (Albert Jenner told the court it was due to the tax expenses from holding the debentures and that he had been advised not to sell any more.) When it came to the filing of a plan of reorganization, Manos told the court, "We feel that the entire balance of the Rock Island system is a viable system on an income basis; and we are prepared to demonstrate it. And, in realistic terms, it is going to demonstrate itself, in the next six months."⁴⁶

Judge McGarr had been the biggest supporter of Gibbons and Manos, and while he allowed a six-month extension, he understood that by doing so he was entering a looming endgame for the railroad's prospects. "I foresee problems of horrendous complexity and difficulty down the line," Judge McGarr stated. "I've determined that the income reorganizability issue of the Rock Island must be decided by the anniversary of these proceedings, or very shortly thereafter." Judge McGarr continued the case until the end of the year, telling the lawyers that he needed to see further evidence of income growth, as Manos had argued was occurring. "They may be a flash-in-the-pan and they may be the beginning of a real upturn in car loadings and income and in hope for the Rock Island. We can't wait forever to find out, but I am willing to wait until the end of the year or such sufficient days beyond the end of the year to get the figures for December." He then commended the attorneys in the case "for the caliber of their representation," adding "I must confess, the judging business gets pretty irritating and pretty dull—but it's a pleasure to listen to good lawyers argue a case and it's a pleasure I have had today listening to everybody address themselves on the issues."⁴⁷

The central argument in the Rock Island bankruptcy case was coming down to a single question: How much longer could the Trustee delay filing a plan of reorganization? Manos and Gibbons had long postponed the filing of such a plan, arguing that the process of negotiations with other railroads in the sale of lines, other mergers in the western territories, the bankruptcy of the Milwaukee Road, and the lagging application for federal funding necessitated the delays. Creditors argued that the delay in filing a plan, and the continued losses on railroad operations, pointed to the futility of an income-based reorganization, the only alternative being liquidation. Labor unions pointed to the steep fees charged by the Trustee and his attorney to the estate (each made $180,000 per year), as well as the appointment of Gibbons by Judge McGarr as Trustee, as evidence of a conspiracy to defraud the railroad, to prevent it from being reorganized in the first place. None of these excuses or theories for why the Trustee delayed filing a plan for reorganization was necessarily wrong, but none of the evidence supports any of the propositions either. In the end, the delay in filing a plan hurt the Rock Island's chances to survive. No one could have envisioned, even as late as 1979, that the only alternative would be complete liquidation and the piecemeal sale of lines to other railroads, states, and shippers. That was the consequence of the failure to develop a core concept that could have been acceptable to creditors, shippers, and the government. By the time the core proposal was finally put forward, in December 1979, the Rock Island was being operated under ICC directed-service orders after a strike shut it down in August 1979.

As William Gibbons summarized 1978 in his annual report, he explained how he "felt increasingly encouraged by our efforts to prove that the Rock Island is reorganizable." The railroad had made progress, with a "third quarter profit of $918,000. October was $1.4 million in the black, and our ten-month loss was $9.2 million compared to $20.8 million for the same period in 1977. Carloads, which were 14,500 below 1977 levels for the first seven months of 1978, began a dramatic upswing. By December 1, we had made up the deficit and were 4,000 ahead of 1977." The Trustee thanked the court for its assistance in allowing the Rock to acquire needed freight cars, and the FRA for providing the $33 million to rebuild cars and repair locomotives. "Our fortitude and our will to prevail were tested on many occasions in 1978: another extra severe winter belted us; the lawyers for Henry Crown, the First National Bank and Continental Bank continued to press for liquidation.... The testing, however, did not find us wanting."[48]

But as 1979 arrived, the worst winter in a century would grip the Great Plains, with blizzard conditions and freezing weather contributing to a shutdown of thousands of miles of railroad throughout the region. Between November 1978 and March 1979 the most severe winter weather of the twentieth century gripped the Midwest, hitting northern Illinois and Iowa particularly hard, and dampening any remaining chance that the Rock Island Railroad could be reorganized. This was the third successive brutal winter—and the worst one yet—with new records for snow depth, major snowstorms, and lasting cold than any previous Midwestern storm in recorded history. Northern Illinois received an average of 68 inches of snow (38 above the typical winter), and the air temperature averaged 7.8 degrees below normal for the two-month period from January through February.[49] Chicago received a record 16 inches of snow between January 12 and 14, 1979, on top of a 7-inch accumulation on New Year's Eve. The slowness of the response by city plow crews led to the defeat of Mayor Michael Bilandic and the election of reformer Jane Byrne as Chicago mayor later that year. Elsewhere on the Rock Island system there were weather problems. Cedar Rapids and the Quad Cities received similar large blizzards in January, with each metropolitan area averaging record snowfall of 58 inches in the winter.[50]

The impact was devastating to the economy and surface transportation; most roads were buried, trains and airlines were delayed and cancelled, and city services were interrupted. The Rock Island lost $36.7 million during the first four months of 1979, the Chicago and North Western Railway lost $30 million, and the Milwaukee Road lost a devastating $40 million.[51] Even for healthy railroads, the weather was enough to cause staggering losses; for railroads in bankruptcy, it was a catastrophic blow, one from which the Rock Island never recovered.

An already bad track situation was made worse by the winter weather. According to a statement by Thomas Schmidt, chief engineer of the railroad, of 6,326 miles of track in service in May 1979 fully 4,027 miles were Federal Railroad Administration Class II (maximum speed of 25 mph) and Class I (maximum speed of 10 mph) standards. Only 208 miles of Rock Island track supported train speeds of up to 50 mph and 2,090 miles of train speeds up to 40 mph. "Track condition in the Class II, I and less than I categories generally consist of poor tie conditions, light (less than 110 lb. rail) and inadequate and fouled ballast. . . . 819,923 crossties and 84,291 rails would be needed to bring the RI up to at least Class I standards," Schmidt stated, "with an estimated deferred maintenance on the RI to exceed $200 million."[52] It was already clear that the government was not going to provide funds to rehabilitate the property, and Bankruptcy Trustee William Gibbons could only point to piecemeal improvements of the track on the mainlines of the railroad, some 150 miles of which had been rebuilt since the bankruptcy began.

Compounding matters for the Rock Island during the first quarter of

1979 was the use of cash to pay for operating expenses due to the harsh weather, a measure that led Nicholas Manos to report to the court on March 13, 1979, that the Rock Island's cash situation was desperate. "In the month of January, the Rock Island lost a sum of approximately $9 million." "There has been a loss of cash of approximately $10 million in February," Manos stated. Fearful that after making payroll on March 15 and March 30 that the railroad could dip below $1 million in cash, Manos requested that the Trustee be granted access to borrow up to $5 million from escrowed funds accumulated from real-estate sales. Believing the carloads would pick up after March once the winter weather abated—as happened in 1978—Manos promised that the funds would be immediately restored upon a positive cash balance.

Manos was granted $2.5 million by the court, for sixty days, and forced to pay interest back into the account, but he wanted more, arguing that "the possibility of a flood or a 100-year flood . . . we would like the availability of the protection of funds out of the escrowed account to the extent of $5 million."[53] After lengthy objections from the creditors and assurances that the fund would be paid back, on the next day Susan Getzendanner, representing Continental Bank, drew up the order allowing the borrowing to proceed. Getzendanner and other creditors' counsel were not willing to let the railroad go under as a result of the weather-related crisis, but they did want to ensure that the funds would be placed back into the escrow account with interest—to which Judge McGarr agreed.[54]

A month earlier, a major breakthrough had occurred in court after all the principal creditor attorneys, the Trustee, and the federal Justice Department counsel agreed to appoint an independent consultant to analyze the Rock Island's financial and operational data, including studies of line segments to assess whether the railroad could be reorganized. Gibbons had been directed to do an in-house study at a September 1978 hearing and had been working on such a document, but the outside consultant would produce a separate report to assess three questions: "First, can the Rock Island be reorganized on an income basis in its present structure. The second part would be an effort to determine whether there is a viable core system. If the answer to the first question is no, what are the viable alternatives for the estate in these proceedings and where do we go from there."[55] In April the parties agreed to hire the accounting firm Peat Marwick Mitchell as the outside consultant. The Trustee would prepare his own plan and the consultant would produce its own. The FRA agreed to fund the cost of the consultant at an expense to the government of $500,000.

The dire economic picture was also complicating efforts to reorganize the railroad. Jimmy Carter had taken office in 1977 intent on cutting government spending, balancing budgets, and rejuvenating a weak economy. He was not a conventional liberal or a Keynesian comfortable with deficit spending, a product of his background as small businessman and southern governor, and was seen as a departure from previous Democratic presidents. *Business Week* magazine asked, "How would you categorize your economic views? Are you a Keynesian, a monetarist, or what?" His answer: "How would you categorize me? I don't know." Chairman of the Council of Economic Advisors, Charles Schultze, labeled Carter a "reluctant Keynesian" who pushed and obtained a modest stimulus package in 1977, but thereafter he pursued a fairly conservative blend of policies to limit spending and deregulate significant sectors of the economy, especially transportation.[56]

Carter's biggest nemesis continued to be inflation, which dominated the economy between 1968 and 1983. A result of economic, political, and psychological forces, the "Great Inflation" of the 1970s, as economic journalist Robert Samuelson has called it, led to annual double-digit price increases in the CPI in 1975 (up 12.3 percent), 1979 (up 13.3 percent), and 1980 (up 12.5 percent). The years in between were not sharply lower, with CPI annual increases averaging around 7 percent.[57] Keynesians argued that there was a tradeoff between high unemployment and inflation; but in the 1970s both rose simultaneously. University of Chicago economist and Nobel Prize winner Milton Friedman had argued that the tradeoff was a myth and that the evidence in the 1970s economy seemed to prove the point of monetarists, such as Friedman, who pinned the blame for inflation on Federal Reserve Board monetary policy.

Robert Samuelson has argued, compellingly, that the Great Inflation was partially the result of the victory of a set of ideas that viewed fiscal and monetary policy as useful in promoting a political agenda; creating a full-employment economy (anything under 4 percent unemployment); preventing recessions by fine-tuning the economy; and taming the business cycle. This intellectual revolution began with John Maynard Keynes, the British economist whose *The General Theory of Employment, Interest, and Money* (1936) revolutionized the economics profession. In the 1960s, with John F. Kennedy as president and fighting a recessionary economy, economic adviser Walter Heller argued that an economy could grow and the harshness of recessions could be prevented through mechanisms designed to encourage inflation.[58] The "new economics," as it was dubbed, seemed to work. By 1965 unemployment decreased to 4 percent, inflation remained at less than 2 percent, and the economy grew by 5.5 percent. Business and government had seemingly found a way to coexist, as business prosperity was not diminished by government intervention in the business cycle. Then came the inflationary spiral of the late 1960s, with Lyndon Johnson's Great Society spending, the increased spending and borrowing on entitlements, and the war in Vietnam all adding to fiscal problems and a gold liquidity crisis in 1968.[59]

The lesson of the new economics was that politicians who failed in their responsibility to tame the business cycle, and to make recessions less severe by spending money and creating new federal programs, met with punishment from the electorate. Both political parties after 1965 played a game of providing for a full-employment economy. Richard Nixon, Gerald Ford, and Jimmy Carter all sought wage and price controls to try to tame inflation as the scourge of rising prices (with energy and food labeled the two culprits by politicians) dealt blows to the cost of living for workers and middle-class Americans. Anxiety about cost of living was one of the main issues reflected in polls during the decade. Not doing something to address inflation—even if the means by which inflation was addressed ultimately did greater damage to the economy by contributing to more of it—was out of the question as a political response during the 1970s.[60]

The Federal Reserve Board played a huge role during the onset of the Great Inflation. Traditionally, since its creation in 1913, the Fed's role had been to support the banking system and the money supply especially after its powers were broadened during the Great Depression. Its board remained conservative, dominated by bankers and businessmen, not economists. After Richard Nixon removed the United States from the postwar Bretton Woods gold standard in August 1971 (at which gold was pegged to the U.S. dollar at $35 per ounce) in favor of a system of free-floating exchange rates where currency was traded like any other commodity, Fed policy was tied into managing the money supply and preventing inflation. It did the job poorly—influenced by the politics of the new economics—and allowed for the expansion of credit by cutting interest rates and the printing of more money, especially as the economy entered a recession in 1974 and 1975.[61]

High inflation hit the railroad and transportation industries particularly hard. Railroads saw labor costs go up as companies negotiated national labor agreements with the unions that applied across the board for all operating trades. Wage costs were a significant portion of railroad operations, and they escalated through the decade. Fuel costs, particularly after the 1973 Arab oil boycott and during the 1980 embargo during the Islamic revolution in Iran, struck transportation hard. Due to price controls on American-produced oil, diesel fuel shortages were common throughout the nation, especially in the Midwest. Carter lifted the controls on American produced energy in 1980, but in a compromise with Congress he instituted a windfall-profit tax on energy producers that sapped their interest in producing more oil and natural gas.[62]

In the summer of 1979, independent truckers shut down highways and fuel depots in the Midwest in a wildcat strike aimed at protesting high fuel prices. Seventy-five thousand truckers blocked highway interchanges, circled gasoline stations, and blocked access to fuel depots. Some simply refused to ship anything, leading to the shutdown of meatpacking plants and the rotting of fruits and vegetables in the fields. Some people engaged in violence against truckers who refused to strike, slashing tires and smashing windshields.[63]

The pickets and blockade of fuel depots had a profound impact on the railroads. On June 26, 1979, ICC Chairman Daniel O'Neal was briefed about the diesel fuel situation. Unable to deliver the fuel, oil companies were cutting allocation of fuel to railroads, with Amoco reducing the Rock Island to 60 percent of its needs. "As a result of these and many other reductions in fuel allocations, the railroads have purchased additional fuel on the spot markets at exorbitant prices. Our reports indicated that spot market prices range from $.73 to $1.15 per gallon." O'Neal was told the "fuel supply situation has been exacerbated by independent truckers blocking railroad fueling stations. Such illegal actions have been caused by serious disruptions in rail operations at many locations."[64] As reported to O'Neal, on July 3, 1979, the Rock Island had a seven-day supply of fuel and had been cutting service on branchlines; the C&NW had a three-day supply.[65]

Higher revenues and market-based rates would have alleviated these two cost drivers for railroads. But government regulation remained the bête noire to profitability in the industry. Rate increases granted to railroads by the ICC during this period, with inflation annualized at 10–12 percent per year, were quickly absorbed by rising costs of labor, material, and equipment. William H. Dempsey, president of the Association of American Railroads, told the House Subcommittee on Transportation and Commerce that "railroads had been experiencing cost inflation of about 11 percent per year. [The industry] had used the general rate increase device for the most part, not to improve its revenues, but simply to cover part of its cost increases. In effect, the general rate increase has been used *simply to maintain* a 1 percent return on investment."[66] What could be done to help the industry as it faced a cash crunch due to inflation?

One option, embraced initially by Gerald Ford and put into policy with the 4R Act, was deregulation of the railroads, allowing them to control rates and abandon unprofitable lines and services. Another was nationalization, but the Conrail and Amtrak experiences had already underscored the problems inherent to that option. The debate raged throughout the industry in the decade; most railroad executives feared both options—the world they knew was often more comfortable than the uncertainties of deregulation. Labor unions also favored continued regulation.

Deregulation was long discussed as a solution to the growing cartelization in the railroad industry. It was a significant discussion item during Senate hearings in 1958. In the 1960s, academic economists began to study the issue, including the University of Chicago's George Stigler and Richard Posner and others intent on disproving the public-interest benefits of regulation. These economists showed instead that claims of regulators to protect the public interest from rapacious industries often led instead to "regulation as a device used by relatively small subgroups of the general population, either private corporations or geographic or occupational groups, to produce results favorable to them which would not be produced by the market."[67] The ICC and other regulatory agencies promoted cartelization with minimized competition and were protected by powerful and vocal beneficiaries: labor unions, shippers, and regulatory bureaucracies.[68]

President Carter wanted to promote the deregulation of transportation and appointed Alfred Kahn as chairman of the Civil Aeronautics Board (CAB) to help bring about airline deregulation. Kahn was an economist at Cornell University and had long studied the effects of regulation. A liberal New Deal Democrat by background, Kahn's two-volume *Economics of Regulation* (published in 1970 and 1971) outlined a marginal cost function that Kahn had successfully applied to utility rates while head of the New York Public Service Commission between 1974 and 1977.[69] Working with Congress and especially Senator Edward Kennedy (D–Mass.), Carter signed the Airline Deregulation Act into law on October 24, 1978, which completely deregulated a cumbersome fare and pricing system, allowing for competition and the entry of new players into the market (CAB had controlled where airlines flew and controlled access to key markets). Airline companies had initially feared deregulation but came to embrace it late in 1978.[70] Carter's bill to deregulate the trucking industry was also signed into law in 1980. (See Photo 9.2.)

Railroad deregulation was next on the list, but a bill was not expected to pass until late 1980. Even then, railroad deregulation appeared to be a hard slog, with impacts on rural areas; service reductions and abandonments; the new rate system's effect on captive shippers (industries located on only one railroad line); and a myriad of problems related to labor unions. All threatened to delay the legislation, which Carter wanted passed before the 1980 presidential election. In the background was the fate of the Rock Island,

Photo 9.2 Discussing airline deregulation: Brock Adams, seated on couch with, L to R: Stu Eizenstat, President Jimmy Carter's domestic policy adviser, Mary Schumann, Adams, Frank Moore, Jack Watson, President Carter, and Charles Schultze (back to camera), in the Oval Office, May 4, 1977. Used with permission of University of Washington Department of Special Collections.

along with Judge McGarr's order on January 25, 1980, to liquidate the line, which made it imperative that deregulation be secured. While the Rock Island's collapse was not the main reason for the passage of railroad deregulation—rather it was the culmination of the massive financial, operational, and regulatory problems emanating from the previous two decades—there is little doubt that it was central to the development of a deregulated railroad industry.

Unfortunately for the Rock Island, the railroad would not benefit from deregulation; when the denouement passed, it was remarkably fast. Over six months from March to August 1979 there was marginal hope the railroad could be turned around. But after a debilitating strike by the Brotherhood of Railway and Airline Clerks, joined by the United Transportation Union (UTU), began on August 28, 1979, the fate of the railroad was sealed. The ICC ordered directed service on the line by the Kansas City Terminal Railroad (KCT) in September 1979, ostensibly ending the Rock Island's operational control of its own property. The railroad was declared cashless by the ICC at that time, providing the ICC a legal basis to appoint an operator. For the Rock Island, the second half of 1979 was its *Götterdammerung*.

TEN

THE ROCK IS DEAD

> It begins the long and regrettably last chapter of the Rock Island. There comes a time in any course of events when the end is inevitable.
>
> —Judge Frank McGarr, January 25, 1980

John Ingram, like many railroad executives, wished to end the stranglehold of labor union agreements on the Rock Island and pointed to the Florida East Coast Railway's (FEC) success at breaking its operating unions as the way to advance the goal.[1] The FEC was struck on January 22, 1963, after the railroad, which had emerged from bankruptcy in 1960, refused to uphold a nationally negotiated agreement to raise wages for nonoperating union members. The operating unions joined the strike and shut down the railroad. Supervisory managers operated the trains along the 800-mile route beginning on February 2, 1963, and hired nonunion employees to work on the railroad. Some 200 acts of sabotage were reported to authorities in 1964 alone, the worst being the dynamiting of two freight trains on February 27, 1964, which was investigated by the FBI (four former employees were convicted of the action).[2] Agreements were eventually reached with nonoperating unions, but the engineers and other operating unions stayed off the job. FEC changed its work rules to reduce crews from five men per train to two, and the result was a profitable operation that by the late 1970s was keeping cars moving and reducing costs.[3]

Labor still had enormous clout politically in Congress during the 1970s, and railroads typically balked at the demands of unions. While historians today look at the 1970s as an era in which labor unions declined precipitously, railroad unions remained strong.[4] In railroad labor negotiations in 1978, when Jimmy Carter imposed voluntary price and wage controls (not wanting to see wages go above a 7.5 percent to 9 percent guideline), unions were able to extract wage increases of 35 percent, which would exacerbate the inflationary spiral. Troubled railroads like the Milwaukee Road and Conrail negotiated with individual unions for lower wage increases, but the Rock Island held to the national accords, much to the consternation of Judge

McGarr, who often complained in court about whether labor unions were interested in the Rock Island's future.[5]

The Brotherhood of Railway and Airline Clerks refused to accept the new national agreement. Its 235,000 members were threatened by automation and computerization in the industry; BRAC's leader, forty-two-year-old Fred Kroll, who had been a computer clerk with the Pennsylvania and the Penn Central, wanted assurances in the new contract that BRAC members who lost jobs due to technology would be granted five years of protection. A simmering controversy between BRAC and the Norfolk and Western Railway concerning the road's classification of 1,000 clerks as supervisory personnel, not as workers eligible for membership in the unions, led to a BRAC strike that Kroll ordered on July 10, 1978. Norfolk & Western supervisory personnel took over the trains, close to 3,500 managers, and shipments moved.[6] As Richard Saunders argued, "Here was proof that the FEC solution was universally applicable."[7]

The strike spread to other railroads in September, after Kroll contended that a mutual-aid fund to support railroads during strikes was allowing the N&W an additional $800,000 for its operations. Kroll went to court and secured the support of a federal judge, who allowed BRAC members to broaden their strike against other railroads that contributed to the fund. On September 26, 1978, BRAC shut down the nation's rail system, striking forty-three railroads, including the Rock Island. Commuter service in Chicago was shut down, with the exception of the Rock Island's commuter line. A Chicago judge ordered the strikers back to work on the commuter lines.[8] After four days Jimmy Carter called for a 60-day cooling-off period under the Railway Labor Act, which returned BRAC workers to the job. The Norfolk & Western strike ended a week later.[9]

On the surface there did not seem to be a huge labor union problem on the Rock Island. William Gibbons reported to the court in his Trustee's Report that "Rock Island's people *increasingly* recognized their obligation to themselves and to their families and the railroad which employs them and became increasingly determined to save the railroad which provides their jobs." He reported that the railroad had negotiated agreements with twelve unions, with most agreeing to work-rule changes aimed to increase productivity. In return, the railroad increased wages at the nationally negotiated level. "Before he entered those negotiations, the Trustee was determined that his employees could share in any wage increase that was negotiated nationally. He was determined that his employees should not be second class employees, even though the Rock Island was engaged in a struggle to reorganize."[10]

However, Gibbons had not reached agreement with either BRAC or the UTU. "The only outstanding issue with these organizations," Gibbons reported, "is 'retroactivity' which Rock Island cannot pay. Since the Trustee is not receiving retroactive benefits on work rules, he cannot grant retroactive pay."[11] Under the terms of the Railway Labor Act, BRAC filed so-called section 6 notices on the Rock Island, notifying their intention to negotiate changes to the contract. Throughout negotiations in 1977 and most of 1978 no agreement was reached between the parties, with no resolution on the question of retroactive pay. BRAC called for the National Mediation Board to look into its claims that BRAC members had been denied $2.2 million in retroactive pay dating from January 1, 1978, for 1,800 Rock Island employees represented by the union (the Rock Island rejected mediation). On April 2, 1979, Fred Kroll informed the press that the union had voted to strike the Rock Island but had not yet set a date.[12] After repeated failed negotiations, BRAC walked off the job on August 28, 1979.

The UTU was also interested in resolving the issue of retroactive pay. The UTU represented 2,500 employees on the Rock Island in three branches (firemen, switchmen and conductors, and brakemen). Both the railroad and UTU rejected mediation in April 1979, but after threats of a shutdown in late May the two parties agreed to establish a Special Board of Inquiry, which issued its recommendations on August 27, 1979; two days later the UTU struck the Rock Island.[13]

Before that strike, the threat of a work stoppage on the morning of May 23 led to a plea in court by attorneys of the Regional Transportation Authority to keep the Rock Island's commuter lines open. Jeremiah Marsh, the RTA's attorney, filed a complaint with the court, asking for a temporary restraining order against the Rock Island, allowing for the continued operation of the commuter service. "The RTA has been in contact with the Trustee who has informed us that he will run some of the freight service and none of the commuter service" should a strike occur. This violated the service order between the railroad and RTA, which stipulated that service could not be denied unless all operations were shut down by a strike. Manos reported that Gibbons was planning a greatly reduced freight service should the strike occur. "With 650 people, we are going to try to run 20 percent of our total freight operations. And, incidentally, in doing that, we are not going to be running any hazardous materials. We are going to limit our freight operations to coal, grain and sand." Manos worried about the safety of the 14,000 commuters should the railroad be required to run passenger service with inexperienced personnel. He also raised the issue of possible violence by strikers against the railroad.[14]

Marsh asked for an injunction against shutting down commuter service, but Judge McGarr refused to grant relief, stating that he joined with counsel for the Trustee "when he mentions the debt of gratitude that the Rock Island has to the RTA for taking over the commuter service. . . . I think that I would have ordered the abandonment of the commuter service had the RTA not come in and saved it because I don't think the Rock Island could have survived any other way. In the presence of this strike I am not sure it is going to survive anyway." He was deeply concerned about the safety of riders. In denying the temporary restraining order, he would consider the injunction on Tuesday, May 29, after the intervening Memorial Day weekend. "I don't know how this strike is going to turn out," Judge McGarr stated. "Maybe we can survive it; it may mean the end of the Rock Island as a reorganizable railroad." In addition: "Maybe my prayer is that some ray of intelligence will descend upon the union leaders who are threatening to call it, because I think it is a suicidal strike as far as the Rock Island is concerned and you cannot divorce the interest of the members of the union from the interest of the Railroad itself."[15]

Judge McGarr had directed counsel for the Trustee and the RTA to work out an agreement should a strike occur, and on the next day the court convened again to discuss the solution. Michael Schneiderman, an attorney with the Chicago firm Hopkins, Sutter, Mulroy, Davis & Cromartie, representing the RTA, stipulated that the RTA would operate the Rock Island commuter service with crews it would recruit from the operating unions. Judge McGarr: "The Rock Island would run the same way it's always run except that the provision that the operating crews on the commuter lines would work for you instead of the Rock Island. I gather that is what you envision?" "That would be the practical effect," Schneiderman replied. "I think it might be necessary for us to take control of the property and the equipment under a lease or some kind of arrangement."[16]

Gibbons still raised concerns about operating the commuter lines, particularly as it would require all supervisory personnel to maintain a minimum freight operation. He made reference to how the Norfolk & Western had operated 43 percent of its railroad with 15 percent of its workforce, citing a book published by the railroad documenting the strike. "I don't want to disadvantage or inconvenience the public of Chicago any more than the RTA does, but this is a strike and as your Honor so aptly put it yesterday it is a strike which may very well spell the end of the Rock Island." It was the first time in the bankruptcy proceedings that Gibbons, who had always been optimistic, actually admitted the possibility that the railroad might not carry on.[17] After lengthy discussions of whether the RTA could get the unions to agree to operate the commuter lines—RTA attorneys assured they would—the RTA was granted the right to operate the commuter lines and to pay indemnities that might arise, as well as the full cost of operations in excess of what they were already paying as the service provider. Judge McGarr approved, ending: "For the time being the commuter line and services of the Rock Island Railroad will become the RTA Railroad Company, and if they have problems with the Commerce Commission they will be the RTA's problems and not the Rock Island's."[18] It was all for naught. The UTU gave mediation one last try and cancelled the strike authorization just before midnight on May 23.[19]

The special board of inquiry and the efforts of the National Mediation Board could not find common ground between Rock Island, BRAC, and UTU. The two main issues continued to be the Rock Island's insistence that its precarious financial condition did not allow it to provide pay retroactive to January 1, 1978. BRAC and UTU insisted that this principle, which was normal in railroad union negotiations, be continued. The two sides dug in, and the mediation board could find no compromise position. On August 17, 1979, BRAC postponed a strike for a week after a 30-day cooling-off period had expired.[20] The mediation board had proposed binding arbitration, with a three-member panel consisting of one management appointee, one labor appointee, and one neutral member acceptable to both sides; Fred Kroll accepted the proposal for binding arbitration, but the railroad did not (convinced by Judge McGarr, according to the *Chicago Tribune*, to reject it).[21] Judge McGarr believed that if the railroad went to binding arbitration and was forced to accept the retroactive pay proposal, it would cost the Rock Island "millions of dollars" and might lead to other unions asking for similar retroactive pay increases. The Rock Island had placed a figure of $2.5 million on the BRAC retroactive pay, while the official report of the Emergency Board authorized by President Carter to look into the dispute put the figure significantly higher, at $14 million.[22]

Kroll was angry and undiplomatically told the *Chicago Tribune* on August 25 that "the Rock Island Railroad will be struck without advance notice in the next several days." Kroll complained that "every plan we have offered they have rejected. They [the railroads] got a 7 percent rate increase in view of wage increases and they're due another 9 percent October 1." He continued, "We agreed to hold off on retroactive pay until then and then take it in monthly installments. They refused. They won't arbitrate. They won't accept any offers. So, we have no other alternative but to strike in the next several days." Kroll refused to give the railroad advance notice on the strike saying, "These are the worst people I've ever had to deal with."[23]

Kroll was not privy to Rock Island financial statements, but his claims that the railroad industry had benefited from rate increases of 7 percent, followed by a projected 9 percent increase, especially when weighed against the national labor agreements reached in 1977 (which gave labor unions a *35 percent increase* through 1981 and which the Rock Island agreed to pay), is a bit disingenuous. There is no way the railroads could have made money from rate increases of 16 percent during an inflationary period when wages had gone up significantly. Kroll also suggested that the "railroad could also pay the clerks from the proceeds of a recent $57 million sale of equipment [actually lines, not equipment] to the Southern Pacific."[24] Of course, the sale had not yet received ICC approval and the money was to be used, under Section 77 of the Bankruptcy Act, to pay off the mortgage debt of the estate, not for current operating expenses.

There is not much evidence explaining BRAC's decision to strike the Rock Island, which was joined a few days later by the UTU.[25] The unions may have misunderstood the bleak financial situation of the railroad, or thought, given the situation in the Northeast, that federal intervention would bring in a new Midwest Conrail and that the railroad—and their jobs—would be spared. But the strike turned out to be the end of the line for the 1,800 members of BRAC who walked out on August 28, 1979, and the 3,500 members of the UTU who joined them on August 30. In effect, BRAC's strike had already shut down the entire railroad as pickets were respected by other unions. Given Kroll's harsh statements to the press about Rock Island officials, there does not seem to have been a sound understanding of the dire financial situation. This strike would kill the Rock Island.

Operations ceased, the yards were quiet, and the track devoid of traffic. Commuter operations in Chicago were shut down as well, causing havoc for 14,000 daily riders. Midwestern governors, led by Illinois Republican James Thompson, wrote President Carter urging him to use his authority to end the strike, but no response was forthcoming from the president. Rock Island executives put their plan of operation into effect to move freight using 650 supervisory personnel beginning in early September. The executives planned operations in a war room on their fourth-floor headquarters at 332 S. Michigan Avenue in Chicago, with a map showing where trains were located on the system. Gibbons said, "We're handling this thing one day at a time. Right now, we're just trying to get the railroad cleaned up." They did so by moving freight trains abandoned on the line when the strike began and getting priority service restored (such as a daily General Motors parts train, which the Rock Island handled between Chicago and Omaha and which brought in $50,000 a day to the railroad; GM shifted the train to the C&NW on September 5).[26] The Trustee hoped to expand service to move grain beginning in a week's time. Officials were confident they could duplicate the success of the N&W managers who operated 43 percent of the railroad after a BRAC strike in 1978 (the difference being that the N&W had 3,500 management personnel and was profitable, whereas the Rock Island had 650 and was bankrupt).

The creditors were unappeased and filed a 72-page petition in court on September 6 to declare the Rock Island cashless and to plea for cessation of freight operations. "The Debtor's estate has become cashless with no realistic prospect of reversing that situation and achieving positive cash balances," it stated. "In the first six months of 1979, the Trustee suffered net losses of $45.1 million on an ICC accounting basis and $46.7 million on his own depreciation accounting basis. These massive losses, the worst in the Rock Island's history, resulted in the elimination of treasury cash and irreversible deterioration in net working capital," a deficit of $52.2 million. "Recent events have made the question of a possibility of a reorganized Rock Island academic. . . . The Rock Island's cashlessness is symptomatic of its inability to be reorganized on an income basis."[27] In closing, the lawyers for Crown used punctuation uncommon for legal documents—exclamation points—to make their case: "The course of action pursued by the trustee has proved catastrophic! The Rock Island's 1979 losses are out of hand! Putting it bluntly, the trustee has lost control!"[28]

A day after the strike against the Rock Island, Gibbons and John Ingram met with Daniel O'Neal in Washington to propose a new system pared down to 2,200 miles linking St. Paul with Galveston, Texas, and encompassing the Chicago–Omaha mainline and the Iowa branches. Essentially, this new system would make the Rock Island a grain hauler exclusively and would reduce the system by eliminating the Tucumcari–St. Louis line (being sold to the SP), the Omaha–Denver line (interest being shown by DRGW), and the Choctaw Route from Memphis to Tucumcari, as well as southern routes in Arkansas and Louisiana. While this reduction was not yet an official plan for reorganization, Gibbons had produced a core that would form its basis.[29]

At the first status hearing since the strike, on September 10, Nicholas Manos asked the court for an additional six-month extension to file the plan for reorganization. In doing so he stated that the basic plan was for a north-south orientation and that the FRA and Crown had said that "the North-South line of the Rock Island is a potentially viable configuration." "It will be a strong agricultural railroad and with a possible addition of some of the Milwaukee Lines, if they are available in Iowa, to enhance the grain gathering activities. We believe that the income based reorganization would be a reality."[30] Albert Jenner took exception, saying that "I am thoroughly amazed with some of the statements that Mr. Manos has made. Never at any time have the creditors agreed that the north-south spine of the Rock Island is subject to an income-based reorganization." Indeed, Jenner continued, nowhere in the case until now had the Trustee made the argument that anything but the *entirety* of the railroad was reorganizable on an income basis.

Jenner then moved on to introduce the petition for liquidation of the railroad. "We think the cessation of operations is occasioned by the fact that the Rock Island has exhausted its reserves of cash. Recently, the Trustee has advised us that he is about to apply to the FRA for a loan of $30 million to replenish his working capital before the winter months. That has alarmed us tremendously." "Truly," Jenner continued, "the creditors have suffered enough in four and a half years. In the face of over 150 million in losses they have seen the continued erosion [of the estate]. . . . But this railroad has reached a serious state in which it just can't carry on when it can't pay its bills, when it is looking for money to pay its payroll, and when it cannot maintain the roadbed of the railroad."[31] The motion to end freight operations was supposed to be entered in camera (only to the judge), but the clerk had filed it in the system on September 6; by then, DOT officials in Washington and a story in the *Des Moines Register* had already reported its contents. The Trustee begged for time to prepare a response to the motion, and Judge McGarr allowed the railroad until October 10 to do so (if the railroad even existed on that date).

There was doubt among creditors that it would remain viable. On September 18, after receiving news that the Trustee had taken $2 million from the $7.5 million escrow fund without the consent of the creditors and Judge McGarr, the court held a hearing on the matter that spilled over into whether the railroad was cashless. (Manos did admit he was wrong in his interpretation about informing the creditors, and the Trustee was to pay back the account with interest, which he did on October 9.) The strike and the need to continue operations with management crews was the reason given for raiding the escrow account. Manos responded to whether the Rock Island had enough cash on hand by stating: "It is quite obvious we have never been in a strike posture before so we can't tell you what is going to happen if this strike is prolonged for a time. . . . Our present projection is that we will be even [in] cash through October and November, on an average, and we won't need any further funding."[32]

There was tremendous uncertainty surrounding the Rock Island. What would the government do? Would Carter order the strikers back to work by using his authority under the Railway Labor Act? Would the ICC declare the Rock Island cashless and authorize directed service by other carriers over its lines? Would the Rock Island even have the ability to start up again should the strike end? Judge McGarr humorously stated that the railroad was saving a lot of money on payroll during the strike, but could it afford to become an operating railroad once the strike ended? All of this uncertainty plagued the Trustee in mid-September. Operations continued in reduced form, but Manos realized that "with respect to cashlessness or the availability of cash to continue an operation during the pendency of the strike—we just don't know yet."[33]

This led to an opening for the creditors, and Daniel Murray, a partner at Jenner & Block, took it, arguing that "based on what Mr. Manos has said today in court, it appears to me very clearly, your Honor, that the Rock Island is cashless today. . . . I must say that if Mr. Manos had called us in advance to seek our approval for use of the funds . . . we would have strongly objected to that." He continued: "And the reason we would have strongly objected to that is quite simply that there is no prospect at all at this point that the Rock Island is reorganizable, either in its present structure, whether it is on strike, not on strike, whether there is a reorganized core— there is simply no possibility."[34] Murray demanded the money be paid back to the escrow account immediately, before any anticipated directed-service order made the amount unrecoverable as assets of the estate, severely prejudicing the creditors.

Judge McGarr gently scolded the Trustee for borrowing the funds and ordered that they be paid back as "cash permits." But that led to another problem: How much cash did the Rock Island have? What were the financials, and how was the strike impacting them? Was the railroad cashless? A status hearing on the creditors' motion to end freight operations was scheduled for October 10, at which time the Trustee would respond to the motion; however, Judge McGarr felt like the answers to the questions he raised had to be answered before that date, especially given the fact that the Trustee had been forced to borrow from the escrow account to conduct operations. "The affairs of the Rock Island are coming to a crisis and to a head in a very near future. No later than the hearing on October 10th these matters will be decided, if they haven't been decided beforehand by the Commerce Commission. The issue of cashlessness, the issue of a cessation order, will all be decided at that hearing."[35]

The federal government had been closely monitoring the situation. On September 14, Stu Eizenstat, President Carter's domestic policy adviser, sent a memorandum to Carter about a strategy devised by a group of officials, including Neil Goldschmidt (who had replaced Brock Adams as secretary of transportation in August after Carter demanded the resignation of his entire

Cabinet on July 17), Dan O'Neal, and representatives of the Justice Department and OMB. Eizenstat told the president that there would be "discussions with the bankruptcy judge and union leaders" about when they might return to work; "a series of legal steps leading to an order by the ICC directing another railroad or railroads to take over the operation of the Rock Island Lines"; and "a process beginning immediately to restructure the railroad over the next eight months." It was an election year, and Carter was dealing with a terrible economy and the Iran hostage crisis, so after Eizenstat announced that he would draft a statement about the situation he gently reminded Carter, "As you know, this is a highly visible issue throughout the Midwest."[36]

On September 20, Carter made a statement from the White House briefing room. Carter announced he was appointing an emergency board under the Railway Labor Act to intervene in the dispute between the unions and the railroad. "This strike is having a severe adverse economic effect on farmers throughout the Central United States," Carter said. "The purpose of this action is to get the trains rolling again in a matter of days, and to start moving grain that has already been piling up in the large areas of the Midwest served by the Rock Island Railroad line." He also asked the ICC to take the steps necessary "to permit other railroads to employ Rock Island employees and workers to maintain service." At the end of his statement, Carter urged passage of the railroad deregulation bill "so we can avoid further bankruptcies and further dislocation in our rail industry throughout the country."[37]

Goldschmidt followed Carter in the briefing, giving a few details on the need for directed service and showing, inadvertently, how vital the Rock Island still remained to the transportation infrastructure of the nation:

> Fifteen percent of the nation's grain elevators currently are without service; grain elevators are already full or close to being full, a record harvest of corn, milo, and soybeans is due in two or three weeks; interior flour mills are operating at 50 percent of capacity and at substantially increased costs because millers cannot get grain shipped by the Rock Island; rail cars stranded on the Rock Island serve to aggravate the current national rail car shortage; U.S. grain exports have been reduced over the last three weeks due in part to the lack of Rock Island service.[38]

Goldschmidt announced that the FRA administrator, Thomas Sullivan, had met with Judge McGarr, Gibbons, and creditor attorneys in a closed meeting in Chicago the previous week. (But he did not disclose that at the meeting FRA told the railroad that it would no longer be eligible for federal funding and that estimates of $40 million would be necessary to start up the railroad once the strike ended.)[39]

The unions defied the president's directive and did not return to the job. The UTU wanted to return, but Fred Kroll of BRAC remained the obstacle, and as long as the clerks remained on strike, other unions would not cross the picket lines. Kroll did not believe the order mandated that the clerks return to work and wanted assurances that the workers would be paid at prevailing wages. Until he received these assurances, the clerks remained on strike. *Chicago Tribune* editors ripped the union, calling its defiance of the president's order "indefensible." "The Carter administration may now have to seek a court order to end the strike, although it is not at all clear whether the union has any more respect for the federal judiciary than it does for the federal executive branch." "Outright defiance of the government in this setting is not only disgraceful, it is a repudiation of the legal scheme which gives the unions a good deal of their strength."[40]

In a hearing on September 21, the subject of Rock Island's finances was on the docket, particularly what the railroad's cash position was at that point and whether it could continue to operate until October 10. With union attorneys present in court, Manos made a lengthy plea for an in camera hearing, given that the Rock Island financial condition was to be discussed. Judge McGarr rejected the motion, and the creditor attorneys bitterly condemned the attempt to suppress the public hearing on the matter. Still, Manos told the court that "the railroad does have the cash ability to continue its current operation under the strike posture. And to meet its obligations without adding, by the way, to the unpaid cost of administration which have already accumulated and remain unpaid at this time." He stated that the escrow account would be repaid in November, and Gibbons agreed. Without giving much financial evidence whatsoever, the Trustee and his attorney seemed to satisfy the judge, who was expecting the answers he received.[41]

The creditor attorneys were alarmed about what they did *not* hear. John Broadley of the Justice Department was surprised that there was no responsible financial officer testifying. He told the court that "we have information that raises very serious questions concerning the ability of the Rock Island to operate until the end of next week, let alone to the 10th of October." "Excluding the [FRA] program funds," Broadley continued, "the 511-505 funds [from the FRA], and funds advanced by shippers for car repairs and funds advanced by the Southern Pacific for work on the Tucumcari Line, and excluding the two million drawn down from the escrow account—the information was that the cash position was less than a million dollars." The Rock Island had several lease payments on equipment coming due in the next couple of weeks, an officers payroll due of $800,000, and "we have information that the Trustee is holding vouchers [payables] in excess of $22 million."[42]

Albert Jenner gently chided the judge for asking for facts but not receiving them. "As a distinguished federal Judge, you ask for the facts. You have received no facts. We haven't received any facts except for a statement of Mr. Manos and Mr. Gibbons that they think this and they think that." Jenner then reminded the court of promises the Trustee had made over four and a half years in the case. "Not a single one has come to pass. We don't hear anymore about the Rock Island turning around the corner. . . . Yes, they have turned the corner into an abyss, not into an operating railroad." "The cash position hasn't been stated to your Honor," Jenner continued. "Generalizations have been said to your Honor—well, we think we will be able to keep the railroad running. Now [what] we want to know, and I am sure your Honor wants to know, is how—are they going to keep it running by not paying bills as they have been, not paying them—some 22 million now. . . . If the employees return, how will they pay them?"[43]

Scott Bannister, an attorney for the Iowa Department of Transportation, "was flabbergasted and greatly distressed by the Trustee's position today." Bannister recalled how in the past Iowa has continually supported the Rock Island "in both financial terms and in legal terms before this Court." But "after a great deal of soul-searching we have reached a difficult decision, and that decision is that the time for the Trustee to reorganize this railroad has run out. . . . We no longer see any light at the end of the tunnel." Other states, which Iowa had represented as an intervenor in the case, agreed. The question of the inability of the Rock Island to reorganize meant it was now time for the railroad to cease operations.[44]

Pressured by the creditors, John Ingram took the stand to relate the railroad's financial statements. The Rock Island was not cashless. Instead, Ingram reported that its cash balance, in the strike posture in which it was operating, was $3 million and that the railroad was going to make its lease payments on time without hindrance, with estimated receivables of $6 million in the month of September. Ingram also reported that in September the Rock Island moved 14,000 carloads of freight, and "based on our estimate, in October we will move 22,000 cars."[45] Ingram also showed data that depicted how the Rock Island was moving 500–750 cars per day. "We have had a startling increase in productivity since the strike has started." He continued: "We have today a few more than 100 men on board the trains, where pre-strike we had 2,800 men on board the trains running them. This startling increase in productivity is brought about, I might say, by some very long hours and some very tired people. . . . Approximately 100 people are handling 25 percent of the volume it took 2,800 people to handle pre-strike."[46] Ingram also related that the strike posture operations could continue, telling the court about some vandalism to bridges in Iowa that the FBI was investigating, and ending as follows: "It is pleasant to note that the people that came to do the bridge burning in one case made a mistake and burned one of the bridges of the Chicago North Western, so I guess it is not all bad."[47]

Judge McGarr finally ruled "in the context of the strike operation the cash flow continues to be fairly positive. Operations can continue in their present posture until October 10th." However, he warned that

> if the predicted financial chaos which some people fear ensues in the startup [operations after the strike] . . . it may justify an immediate cessation order. . . . I can't lose sight of the fact that the application of the creditors for cessation of operation of the railroad filed not too long ago, was a drastic and dramatic attempt to bring to a climax the drama of the Rock Island and the Trustee has been given as short a time as my conscience will allow to respond to that. I can't shorten it anymore.[48]

Jenner posed one last question to the witness: How much cash on hand was there at the end of September 20? Ingram replied that there was $6 million, but after subtracting payroll, dedicated FRA program funds, and payables, there remained a negative working capital balance of $1.9 million. Jenner wanted $2 million restored from cash on hand to the escrow fund, and while Ingram said that was possible, "it would leave us out on a limb" as the railroad approached October and the resumption of full service. Broadley made one last-ditch legal appeal to rule the Rock Island cashless. The Justice Department lawyer argued that the "employees and suppliers who have advanced their labor and their supplies to this cost of administration to the extent of $26 million have an equal right to the assets available, the cash available. And could I read something that leads, as I see it, to the inevitable conclusion that something should be done now?" Citing Judge Henry Friendly's ruling on cashlessness in the Penn Central case, Broadley read: "If after all reasonable efforts a reorganization trustee was faced with an eminent depletion of cash that will make it impossible for him to pay current bills for wages, supplies, interline balances, and similar expenses, and still leave an amount sufficient to permit an orderly liquidation." Judge McGarr postponed a ruling on Broadley's argument until October 10, finally agreeing to a status report on the cash position of the railroad as of September 28, 1979.[49]

The ICC acted before the court hearing and instituted a Directed Service Order (DSO) over the railroad to begin on September 26, in effect declaring the Rock Island cashless, necessitating operations over the line by other carriers. The government appointed the Kansas City Terminal Railway, a switching railroad owned by twelve other railroads, including the Rock Island, as the directed-service operator. Its management would assume responsibility for operating the Rock Island for 60 days, with the option of extending it an additional 180 days if necessary; an end to the strike would assure that operating crews were members of BRAC and UTU. Vice President Walter Mondale and ICC Chairman Daniel O'Neal announced the DSO at a press conference in the White House briefing room. Mondale informed the press that UTU members would return to work immediately, but Fred Kroll wanted to negotiate with the Kansas City Terminal about wages and work rules.

Dan O'Neal was asked about Judge McGarr's finding that the Rock Island did have the cash to operate. O'Neal replied that "the federal judge's order. . . . was looking at whether the railroad had cash in terms of erosion of the estate." The ICC was looking at whether the railroad had cash to "operate and to provide service over the whole system. Today the railroad, by their estimate, is providing about 20 percent of the service that they are required to provide under the Interstate Commerce Act. We feel that they are actually providing much less than that. So the railroad is not meeting its obligation to the public and in fact does not have the cash that would allow it to meet that obligation."[50]

This was a curious argument. Ingram had shown that the railroad had sufficient cash to conduct operations during the current strike. The government was now concerned about the movement of grain as a national economic issue, which was, of course, not an inconsiderable issue, especially politically, but that argument did not get at the heart of whether the railroad was cashless. The strike had been ended a week earlier by President Carter's executive order, but the workers had ignored it and did not go back to work. There were concerns about whether the Rock Island could have possibly afforded the start-up costs, estimated at $30 to $40 million should the workers return, but they had not returned, and that possibility was still in the future when the DSO was declared. There was also the cost of directed service itself. Here is a quote from the press-briefing transcript: "What was your estimate of the total cost to the taxpayer of this operation? O'Neal: Well, for 60 days, we feel that $50 million will cover it. Q: And beyond that? O'Neal: Well, if it goes beyond that to 240 days, it is going to be in the neighborhood of eighty, ninety million total."[51]

If the Rock Island was claiming start-up costs (should the strike end) of $30 million to $40 million, and the federal government had loaned that money to the railroad, the costs to the estate would have gone up considerably. The creditors would have vehemently objected to such a development, especially as the reorganization plan had not yet been submitted. Once again, much like in the Penn Central debacle, the taxpayer was on the hook for the money, in this case conducting operations on a railroad that had 25 percent of its lines in service and was moving about 500 cars a day. The *Chicago Tribune* editorialized that the ICC-Carter decision "instead of simply letting a failing, redundant carrier fold up so that its lines can be bought by other, healthier, railroads . . . has elected to go the route of costly government intervention in the name of saving the farmers and the grain harvest. That may be a mighty good road to take—but only for presidential politics."[52]

There was some confusion in the initial days after the government intervened about how the process would work. Gibbons had met with officials from the Kansas City Terminal to discuss guidelines concerning the property. There were issues raised by creditors about the condition of the property after directed service and whether the estate would be compensated for damages to the line and equipment. All of the complex issues had to be decided, for at no time in history had the ICC ever ordered directed service on a railroad larger than 240 miles; in fact a DSO had been implemented only once before. The Rock Island remained, even with all its problems, a large railroad system—7,020 miles in length serving thirteen states.

The ICC began to make progress in early October, reaching an agreement with BRAC to pay the prevailing industry wage rates and finally getting the union back to work. On October 3, Judge McGarr ordered the Trustee to give up control of the property to the Kansas City Terminal, forcing Gibbons to relieve six management officials from their positions, including John Ingram, who was fired on that date. The RTA was inspecting the commuter lines in anticipation of restoring service by October 6.[53]

But the court still had to deal with the Trustee's response to the creditors' motion to liquidate the railroad and cease freight operations. The latter point was now moot; for at least sixty days, the Kansas City Terminal was in control of freight operations. But the first point was more than relevant. The Trustee responded in a 16-page brief filed in court on October 9, which stipulated that planning toward a reorganized core was under way. "I am preliminarily of the opinion that a profitable core exists. . . . This core consists of rationalized Iowa lines with extension to Chicago, Minneapolis, Omaha and Kansas City. . . . The proposed modest-in-size core system as the basic element of planning for Rock Island has advantages for all interested parties, public or private."[54] Gibbons also related that the sale of nonviable lines to other railroads would be examined. In essence, the planning for the core proposal was to liquidate about two-thirds of the railroad if it could not be sold. Finally, the Trustee announced the full restitution of the $2 million to the escrow account, which occurred that day.

The penultimate court hearing on these matters occurred as scheduled at a lengthy session lasting most of the day on October 10. Nicholas Manos presented the Trustee's planning toward a reorganizable core and asked for cooperation among all parties in bringing this about. He worried about the 60-day period of directed service and thought it would be difficult for the railroad to complete a plan in that amount of time. Albert Jenner countered by going through the creditors' motion to liquidate, arguing that once the DSO ended the railroad would still be cashless and would not have the funds to restart operations. He called for an order from Judge McGarr to force the Trustee to file either a total liquidation plan or a partial liquidation plan by the end of directed service in December. He also asked that the Peat Marwick study be recast to study the Trustee's plan. Finally, Jenner asked for a report on the railroad's financial status as of October, which was very similar to the report a week earlier.[55]

Justice Department attorney John Broadley gave a concise report about the facts before the court. First, the court had a limited amount of time. Second, of the $25 million in accounts payable reported by the Trustee (and earlier by Ingram), "most of these would have to be paid before the Rock Island could ever run the railroad again." Third, there would be no further federal funding for the Rock Island. Neil Goldschmidt had written a letter delivered to the court that day stating this and also blasting the Trustee for his failure to propose a plan to reorganize the railroad over four years.[56] Finally, Broadley stated that the viability of a core does not exist, and the fact that the Trustee had not proposed or shown a viable core in four years showed this. "Given these circumstances the Rock Island rail properties should be liquidated as quickly as possible." The Trustee should also work as soon as possible with the FRA to find buyers for the railroad's lines.[57]

Given the long and tortured history the Rock Island had endured with the ICC, it was ironic that the only lawyer in attendance that day defending the Trustee's right to submit a plan of reorganization was Henri Rush, the counsel for ICC. "I sense the frustration of the groups that have lived with these proceedings a great deal longer than I have," Rush began. He could understand and supported the idea of selling off lines under section 401 of the 4R Act. "But at the same time I would urge that it is not so late and time is not so short that we ought to throw out the fundamental principle and basis of Section 77 of the Reorganization Act. It is clear that [Section] 77 preferred reorganization to liquidation." Rush knew the tight deadlines, but he argued that this could be accomplished within those deadlines and that the law favored this approach over immediate liquidation.[58]

Judge McGarr determined that the Trustee should be granted 60 days to develop a reorganization plan; agreed that the Trustee had identified such a core; and that he should be granted time to develop a plan for it. He also authorized the Trustee to seek sales of lines to other railroads, including the RTA's continuing discussions to purchase the Chicago commuter lines. He agreed with the creditors that the railroad not be allowed to borrow more money to fund any purchases that would add administration costs against the estate, and that this represented an unconstitutional taking of property under the Fifth Amendment.[59]

One of the more important decisions made in court that day was to recast the Peat Marwick study, and a committee was appointed to do so, including creditor attorneys and Scott Bannister from Iowa DOT. Judge McGarr wanted the study to help the Trustee isolate and identify a viable core, as well as to help coordinate the sale of lines by studying the economic potential of those lines. The original study was to be delivered to the court by March 1980; now Judge McGarr and the attorneys believed it should arrive shortly after the Trustee's reorganization plan was submitted in December. "When we started this morning," Judge McGarr said, "I felt so bad that I had worried about whether I would live through it. When we got to the middle of it, when I saw how complex it was, I began to wish I would last through it. Right now I am back to my first position. I really haven't got enough strength to hear anything else. I will go home and go to bed."[60]

It was not until November that the Kansas City Terminal was operating most of the Rock Island, and in one sense it was miraculous that directed service was occurring at all. The track was in "deplorable" shape, and while the Rock had a significant number of freight cars (about 24,000), the locomotive fleet was in bad shape, with 27 percent of the fleet under the designation "heavy bad order." Track speeds were slow, which drove up crew costs, as a crew on a mainline freight could take a train only 80 miles (versus 100–120 on most railroads) because of slow orders. Supplies were lacking on the property, especially fuel, and vandals had also impacted the property. The costs of the operation through November were estimated to be $40 million.[61]

The ICC held field hearings throughout the Midwest to assess operations under directed service and to discuss options should the Rock Island ultimately be liquidated. "The ICC held twenty four days of hearings in seventeen cities in order to elicit comments and information regarding the impacts on the various interests of the geographical area served by the Rock Island." The hearings wanted to assess the essentiality of Rock Island service, how the strike impacted local communities; what alternatives shippers possessed during the strike; the cost of alternate transportation; shipper traffic volume by line; impact on labor; public views on which lines could be dropped; preferences as to other railroads operating under directed service; and what recommendations those testifying had for restructuring the railroad.[62]

"The public consistently deemed the Rock Island services essential and supported the continuation of service for the additional 180-day directed service period.... The Kansas City Board of Trade testified that in 1978 the Rock Island moved 10 percent of the US grain moving in the western United States," one report stated. Shippers testified to the economic consequences of the strike. "At the Oklahoma City hearing, one grain elevator company testified that interest of 16 ¾ percent per year is being paid on grain which is still in its facility and that is preventing them from paying cash to the farmers for their crops." In Phillipsburg, Kansas, a small north-central town that saw the largest attendance among all of the hearings (seventy witnesses), "the citizens of eight northern Kansas counties served by the Rock Island stand to lose over $10 million."[63]

The Phillipsburg hearing showed how the Rock Island's collapse would impact much of the rural Midwest. The hearing had "a remarkable turnout, considering that the weather turned from very heavy rain/sleet the first day to blizzard conditions on the second day." People wanted to continue service in northern Kansas, arguing that "the very existence of many of these communities is threatened by cessation of Rock Island service . . . without the railroad some towns simply have no reason to exist." The drop in rural population would be even worse without local rail service to haul grain to market.[64]

Companies along the mainline outside Chicago testified that "should rail service be discontinued to Morris [Illinois] and our plant manufacturing facilities, our company would be forced to curtail operations, and most likely would have to cease operations entirely." A paperboard company in Morris testified that without rail service alternative service would "raise costs of manufacturing and shipping to such a point that both our operations could not exist or stay competitive in the paper industry." Bellrose Silica, located in Utica, was "solely dependent on the Rock Island. It is either rail service being retained or we go out of business. It is that simple." These examples were common among all shippers who testified.[65]

The ICC now faced a question: whether to extend directed service beyond the original 60-day limit, which expired on December 5. Field reports showed that the KCT was doing a good job of providing service, and there was deep concern that if directed service was not extended the impact on the economy would be devastating. Meetings held in Washington between the ICC and congressional staff on November 14 pointed out that of the $50 million approved under DSOs, $34 million had been spent by the KCT and $6 million had been spent by a DSO on the Milwaukee Road, leaving $10 million to be expended. If projections about spending by the KCT until the end of the year held true, the KCT would be left with a $1 million cushion. Staffers told the ICC that "Senate House Conference on Appropriations would appropriate an additional $76 million, but would require the ICC to go back to the Appropriations Committee for additional authority to allocate funds to RI directed service after $70 million has been spent on the RI." Dick Schiefelbahn of the ICC explained that the commission was meeting to consider alternatives to the DSO, including having other railroads operate other sections of the Rock Island "without compensation" if they expressed interest in acquiring the lines. He suggested four alternatives: a reduction of 740 miles of the system; pick up and delivery of all traffic, except where it is serviced by other carriers; a 10 percent reduction in the line with options north of Kansas City and originating and terminating traffic south of Kansas City; and a restructured core north of Kansas City only, with the reduction of 4,200 miles.[66]

The ICC met November 19 to discuss the options, in what Nicholas Manos later told the court was a "garbled meeting." Various ideas were discussed, with the consensus being that directed service should be continued and that the option of reducing the Rock Island by 740 miles would be the best approach. Neil Goldschmidt proposed that directed service be continued with the KCT as the provider for 90 days, until March 2, 1980. At that time railroads that had expressed an interest in buying parts of the Rock Island could assume directed service under emergency agreements until May 31, 1980. This would allow DOT to arrange for selling parts of the railroad to carriers interested in buying various lines (i.e., the section 401 process under the 4R Act that was already under way). This was ultimately the process agreed upon by all parties. Goldschmidt also announced that railroads would have until February 1, 1980, to notify the FRA of their intent to buy Rock Island lines.[67]

The growing complications for reorganizing the Rock Island were immense. Gibbons and his staff were preparing a reorganization plan with tremendous uncertainty and new surprises virtually every day. The president's Emergency Board established to investigate the strike ruled that the Rock

Island would have to pay retroactive wages to BRAC and UTU, as well as wages equal to nationally negotiated wage agreements to the other unions. That meant an additional $12–$14 million which would be charged against the new company (should it be reorganized) or against the estate (should the Rock Island be liquidated). Manos reported this news to the court on November 1, 1979, prompting Judge McGarr to comment that "every day we learn of new burdens this viable core is going to have to carry. They seem to be mounting in alarming numbers." Negotiations would have to commence between unions and the Rock Island anyway depending on how many employees the reorganized railroad would need, or depending on the success of sales to other lines. But certainly the ruling was more bad news for the Trustee.[68]

The Carter administration's response to the Midwest rail problem could not be separated from politics, as Carter faced a tough reelection fight in 1980. The Iranian hostage crisis had begun in November, with Iranian students kidnapping fifty-six hostages at the U.S. embassy in Tehran. He was being challenged by liberals in Congress who were backing Senator Edward Kennedy for the Democratic nomination. Double-digit inflation and fuel shortages made the economy the most crucial problem, and the cure—the appointment of Paul Volcker as chairman of the Federal Reserve Board—was austerity, as Volcker drove interest rates to an incredibly high 21 percent by 1980. With all of these problems swirling around the president, handling the railroad crisis delicately—and with an eye toward the upcoming Democratic caucus in Iowa and the primaries thereafter—was imperative for the president's campaign.

Neil Goldschmidt reminded the president of the political effect of railroads in a memo outlining his strategy for the Midwest rail crisis. Goldschmidt wanted to "appoint a special rail representative for the Midwest whose primary role will be to listen to affected shippers and communities" and to express their concerns to Washington. He proposed close interaction between the federal government and the states, as the government's policy was based on the assumption "that a Conrail-like solution should be avoided." Finally, he stressed to the president the need

> to make sure that your own political organization is fully up-to-date on our efforts in the Midwest and to provide a means for us to deal with rail problems which come to the attention of members of that organization [Carter's reelection committee]. . . . Senator Kennedy's misguided concern with the Wabash Railroad notwithstanding, I am

concerned that legitimate efforts of the Administration to rationalize the rail system in the Midwest will continue to surface as campaign issues.[69]

On December 28, 1979, Gibbons finally submitted his reorganization plan to the court, sending a copy to the ICC. Manos had secured yet another delay at a court hearing on December 7, but this time—pressured by events and the impatience of the judge—the plan was presented three weeks later. The plan proposed that the new company would continue as the Rock Island Railroad and conduct operations over a 1,934-mile system stretching from Chicago to Council Bluffs, and from St. Paul to Kansas City. It would include the major northwest Iowa branchlines and the Peoria branch. The Trustee projected a labor force on the new railroad of 3,200 workers. The remainder of the railroad would be sold to interested parties, or abandoned and sold for salvage, to reduce the debt of the estate.

The Trustee placed the value of assets in the company at $530.5 million, "including a valuation of $220.6 million for the assets of the proposed Core subsidiary and $309.9 million estimation of net liquidation proceeds of the Non-Core Assets." The total claim of creditors was estimated at $386.6 million. The operations plan was incredibly optimistic, showing carloads increasing from 415,115 per year in 1980 to 509,282 by 1985, with total revenue of $217 million by 1985. It showed gross ton-miles growing significantly on each segment of the core, without any substantiation of how this was to be done considering the loss of traffic that affected the railroad in 1979. It also projected a total of $119 million for rehabilitating track through the five-year assessment of operations. All of this would produce "a net income of $6.7 million and a cash flow of $18.7 million in 1980. In 1985 the net income will be $27.3 million and the cash flow is $38.5 million." "The study reaches the conclusion that the Core is viable."[70]

The plan provided for a retirement of the administration claims arising from the bankruptcy by selling off noncore assets, even considering the sale of the core itself if it could be negotiated with an interested party. It also considered a freight-car leasing program that would put the Rock Island's cars in service on other railroads (so in effect the railroad would become a car-leasing operation). The Trustee listed the claims it would pay through administration claims, back taxes, trustee certificates, claims for track work, and federal government claims. It provided for the secured bondholders who would receive non–interest bearing certificates equal to half their financial worth and new Class A preferred stock in the new company. Unsecured creditors would receive non–income bearing certificates equal to half their claims and a new Class B stock equal to half their claims. General stockholders would receive a new issue of common stock.[71]

There was little comment by creditors about the plan in the month after its release as the creditors awaited the Peat Marwick study, which was presented to the court on January 23, 1980. Donald Hill, a principal accountant with Peat Marwick, presented the plan to the court after Manos vigorously defended the basis of the Trustee's plan. Hill stated that Peat Marwick "analyzed two key cases. We did a detailed analysis of the core as presented in the Trustee's plan. . . . We completed an independent analysis to determine the economic return, what we call the internal rate of return, and we did a loan repayment analysis based upon what we projected the cash flow would be over the period of 1980 to 1986." "To essentially summarize the findings," Hill stated, "it is our finding that the internal rate of return in loan repayment capability of the adjusted Trustee's core . . . we find that [they] are clearly unfavorable."[72] Operationally, there were problems with assessing carloads, which Hill concluded were too optimistic, and uncertainty about the connection the new railroad would have at Council Bluffs. (The Trustee's study depended heavily on a friendly connection at that city, but the UP and the C&NW had been operating through-trains to Chicago, and it was doubtful that the Rock Island could reestablish traffic flows over its railroad.) In every analysis measured by Peat Marwick's own data and study of the core, the proposal came up short and would not deliver on the promises in the Trustee's reorganization plan.

Manos begged for time for all parties to study the plan. "A review of the Trustee's plan, even on a cursory basis, demonstrates that the plan is geared for a total liquidation if that is what the public and the private domain desire," he stated. "Your honor, only God knows whether [Peat Marwick] is right, or whether the Trustee is right, but there is an agency that has the expertise to look at all of the operational, financial and engineering matters. That agency is the Interstate Commerce Commission."[73]

John Broadley responded to Manos: "I suggest that we have come to the end of the road with the independent core railroad." Reiterating that Peat Marwick was the agreed-upon outside consultant hired by the court, Broadley concluded that "based upon the conclusions reached by Peat Marwick, it is a waste of everyone's time to refer this plan to the ICC, since there is a fundamental defect in its underlying assumptions, that there is a viable core railroad which can be operated by the reorganized company." Broadley asked the Trustee to withdraw his plan "as fundamentally flawed . . . and that the Court direct the parties to submit by February 11th proposals for

Photo 10.1 Joliet, Illinois: A seemingly healthy Rock Island freight consist moving company property to staging yards to prepare for shutdown in March 1980. Photo by Mark Llanuza, used by permission.

the sale of the entire Rock Island. . . . The government is willing to work with the present creditors' committee to devise some guidelines for the structuring of the sale of all of the assets of the Rock Island, and if necessary, a repackaging of the Core."[74]

Judge McGarr responded, wondering if any railroad would be interested in notifying the ICC of its interest in purchasing the Rock Island by February 1. "I would sort of wait and see what would happen at a distress sale some time later rather than make a serious bid on an operating entity . . . hoping I would get a better bargain." He worried that time was too short and that the February 1 deadline might pass without any interested parties stepping up to purchase the Rock Island.[75] Broadley responded that the sole focus should be on the liquidation of the Rock Island and that time was indeed running out to find buyers. Cheekily, Manos replied that the Trustee and he would have to reschedule the next court hearing because they would be in Denver "pursuing the liquidation of a sizeable portion of the Rock Island."[76] (Compare Photo 10.1.)

On Friday, January 25, 1980, the most consequential hearing in the Rock Island bankruptcy case occurred. At the end of three-plus hours of discussion, Judge McGarr determined that the Rock Island was not reorganizable and should be liquidated. His decision was the culmination of nearly five years of bankruptcy hearings and the Trustee's failure to present a plan that would fulfill either the public interest or the interest of the creditors, who had seen the debt grow an additional $150 million since March 17, 1975. It authorized the largest liquidation of any railroad and, to that time, one of the largest liquidations of any corporation in American history.

Manos defended the Trustee's plan and refused to agree to the motion made by Broadley to withdraw it from consideration. He continued to argue that the plan should be submitted to the ICC as Section 77 of the Bankruptcy Act allowed, yet—strangely—the ICC counsel, Henri Rush, was not present in court that day to back up Manos (Judge McGarr was surprised that the ICC had skipped the session). Daniel Murray of Jenner & Block presented a well-crafted argument on behalf of the Peat Marwick report's conclusions that the core proposal was not viable, urging that the Trustee withdraw the plan.[77] Terry Moritz did the same, providing facts on how, since March 1975, "the Rock Island suffered continuing and accelerating severe deterioration of its financial condition. Carloads had declined from 760,000 in 1975 to 332,000 in 1979; losses were $31 million in 1975, $25 million in 1976, $34 million in 1977, and $21 million in 1978." "Current liabilities of this estate as of September 30, 1979, are $116 million. That is twice shareholders' equity of $58 million." "I am very concerned, your Honor," Moritz concluded, "that the Trustee's plan is simply a blueprint for another reorganization.... That situation cannot be allowed to occur." Moritz joined Murray in arguing for the liquidation of the Rock Island.[78] Broadly concurred and discussed other issues pertinent to liquidation and the government's sales of lines. Norman Nachman, the attorney representing the railroad company's board of directors, also concurred with the creditor attorneys concerning the Peat Marwick report and the inadvisability of going ahead with a core proposal. He was hesitant to do so, as he had always supported the Trustee's efforts, but he had been informed by board chairman Lewis Harder that the core proposal would not have the board's support. Only the State of Iowa, representing all states' interests in the case, sided with Manos about submitting the plan to the ICC for public discussion on the status of lines, but Scott Bannister's presentation was half-hearted; he understood and sympathized with what some of the creditor attorneys were arguing.

Judge McGarr was thoroughly impressed. "I think I have heard enough of what have probably been the best oral arguments I have had the pleasure of listening to from the various attorneys involved in this case." Judge McGarr engaged in a bit of reminiscing, beginning with his total faith in the Trustee and how he believed that the railroad was reorganizable. He praised

Manos, who had filed "a plan of reorganization to the point that where when I saw him on the street and noted his declining weight, I had a severe attack of conscience because I was afraid I was driving him into bad health."[79]

Then, he decided: "I have listened to the Trustee for four years through his counsel argue that I authorize and continue to be patient with the attempts to bring about a cash-based reorganization. Mr. Manos argues with some emotion today that I should not decide based on four hours of hearings. I have in fact thought of very little else for four years." He continued,

> we went through a lot of travail, all of us, spent a lot of hours, missed a lot of dinner dates, in constructing the framework for the final Court's witness to determine the possibility of reorganization. . . . I have studied the plan of reorganization and I have studied the [Peat Marwick] report. I am satisfied that the witness that the parties have recommended to me has done a fine job. It is a good study and I am compelled to accept its conclusions. That being so, I am compelled also, if logic prevails, to accept the conclusion that the plan of reorganization prepared by the Trustee has no hope of success.

He then instructed the Trustee not to file his plan with the ICC and to begin planning for a complete liquidation of the property.[80]

> Before I finalize the order, I would like to say that this ruling, in my judgment, means only that the final and inevitable decision that I have just made will have little effect on the public interest. It does now what would inevitably be done in a matter of a few months and it starts now rather than later the process of private sales or Commerce Commission reorganization of railroad service in order to patch together the best possible compromise between the public interest and the creditors' interests.

"And I guess," he said with much understatement and some inevitability, "it finalizes the last chapter in the long and regrettably sad history of the Rock Island."[81]

For 133 years, since it was chartered by the State of Illinois as the Rock Island and LaSalle Railroad Company in 1847, the Rock Island Railroad had provided freight and passenger service in its territory. It boasted a colorful history: The railroad's right to build a bridge over the Mississippi River was successfully argued in court by the attorney Abraham Lincoln, and it was one of the first railroads victimized by a train robbery as Jesse James and his gang held up a Rock Island train at Adair, Iowa. It had been one of the strongest Midwestern railroads until its corporation was plundered by a financial syndicate, necessitating its first bankruptcy in 1909. It had survived two world wars, and the Great Depression in between, but it could not survive the new competitive posture brought about by automobiles, trucks, highways, and airlines. And it could not survive without a stronger partner in the form of a merger with a major western railroad. That opportunity had been denied, and as a consequence the last act of the Rock Island was written in a federal court. While it was a sad occasion for those who worked for and loved the railroad, it nevertheless opened up what would be one of the most successful acts in the railroad's history.

ACT THREE

LIQUIDATION

ELEVEN

TOO LATE THE HERO

> In these three and a half years, we have carried out the most fundamental restructuring of the relationship of business and government since the New Deal.
>
> —Jimmy Carter, Signing Statement, Staggers Rail Act, October 14, 1980

One could wax nostalgic about the death of the Rock Island. The company that had helped to shaped the Midwest suddenly disappeared, its lines sold, abandoned, torn up—crumpled in the dustbin of history.[1] The end of an enterprise that seemed so permanent is never easy, either for those who depended on it for its livelihood or for those who were sustained in any number of ways by its operation. But the collapse of a railroad as large as the Rock Island was simply stunning. Its death had not been unexpected, as anyone who witnessed its recent operations could have attested. Certainly the government would save it, many thought. Why would the government spend all that money on Conrail but not on Midwest lines like the Rock Island?

The end of its operations left a gaping hole in the hearts of thousands, people who toiled to keep the railroad operating, as well as those who could no longer rely on the steady presence of trains for employment and travel. "So sad, so strange, the days that are no more," Alfred Lord Tennyson wrote, a paean to memory and to the deep wellspring of regret, nostalgia, and pain associated with loves and times lost. So it was for many a Midwesterner with the death of the Rock Island.[2]

Nostalgia and sentiment did not hinder the Rock Island's creditors, the Trustee, and Judge Frank McGarr from engaging in their work, shifting from operating and reorganizing a railroad to liquidating the estate to achieve the highest possible return for creditors and investors. At no time in the nation's history had a railroad as large as the Rock Island ceased operations. In one way, the task ahead was easy: Sell the assets and maximize the value of the estate for creditors. In another way, it was a project fraught with political and economic implications. The battle over liquidation revealed major differences between the federal government, state governments, labor unions, shippers, and the court, which took more than a year to be worked out. Relying on a reduced staff of close to 250, William Gibbons engaged in what turned out to be one of the more successful corporate liquidations in history.

The first problem was to get the property back under the control of the Trustee. The Directed Service Order governing the Kansas City Terminal's operation expired on March 2, 1980, (eventually it was extended to March 23 with a final date of March 31).[3] The Interstate Commerce Commission had determined that the Rock Island would be embargoed for inbound shipments on February 15, with outbound shipments and local loads forbidden after March 2. Preparatory work involved the KCT collecting Rock Island freight cars and locomotives, securing equipment on the property, locking up buildings, and completing accounting functions related to the DSO. All outbound freight cars were to be secured and delivered to interchange points by the end of February. The Rock Island possessed 24,000 freight cars and close to 500 locomotives, which also had to be located for return to lessees or sale by the estate. Nicholas Manos often said early in the liquidation proceedings that if all the cars were gathered in one spot they would stretch for 250 miles. It was an immense undertaking for the KCT to deliver what Manos called a "buttoned down railroad" to the Trustee.[4]

Meanwhile the Secretary of Transportation and the Federal Railroad Administration worked to secure potential buyers under section 401 of the 4R Act. One proposal by the FRA was to find bidders who would continue emergency service orders on key segments of the property. But this was complicated by the end of directed service itself. Some carriers were willing to operate without compensation from the government—which was providing a subsidy on losses from operations—but what about those carriers unwilling to risk losing money? The FRA recommended possible Emergency Rail Services Assistance Act (ERSA) loans to the Rock Island Trustee, who would then pay the carriers, or even allow "the free use of the properties on an initial temporary basis so as not to lose an eventual sale." This drew a shocked margin note from William Gibbons, who wrote, "Nick, did you see this?!!" The FRA described that "for Rock Island properties, 17 bids covered 65 percent of present mileage and 88 percent of present traffic."[5] But none of these bids had, as of yet, reached the stage of a contract. Neither would the Trustee allow operators on the property for free, a source of some contention in court between the railroad and the government.

Congressional representatives, senators, and state governors were also concerned about ending service. Some wrote Judge McGarr to pressure him to keep the Rock Island operating beyond the March 2, 1980, deadline for continuing directed service. Congressman Thomas Railsback (D–Ill.), whose district included the Quad Cities and who had helped secure federal assistance for the railroad—the Rock Island named a GP-38 locomotive in his honor—wrote the judge about keeping the Rock operating. Judge McGarr, besieged with phone calls and requests from politicians, answered somewhat intemperately:

> I do not mean to be disrespectful when I wonder aloud where you have been. The Rock Island has been besieging the federal agencies and Congress for financial help for five years. If the Rock Island had ten percent of what Congress has wasted on Conrail, the road would be solvent. The Milwaukee Road Restructuring Act (MRRA) was passed with commendable haste. The Rock Island could never even generate a discussion of a Rock Restructuring Act.[6]

The Milwaukee Railroad Restructuring Act to which Judge McGarr referred was passed in November 1979 out of fear that total cessation of freight operations on the Milwaukee Road would "have serious repercussions" on states in the northern Plains. The statute included a deadline for the railroad to negotiate sales and leases of its property and allowed the federal court in Chicago the ability to determine the finality of sales; it sped up abandonment procedures; it allowed terminated employees to receive preference on hiring by other rail carriers; and it provided labor protections and supplemental unemployment insurance to any employee separated from the railroad who was unable to find a new job in the industry by April 1, 1981, through the period ending on April 1, 1984. The MRRA also stipulated new borrowing, as an administrative claim (a debt incurred by the estate after bankruptcy was declared) against the Milwaukee estate, of up to $200 million from ERSA.[7]

The federal government sought the same labor protections guaranteed in the MRRA for Rock Island employees impacted by a shutdown. Neil Goldschmidt said that "there is a need for legislation to provide assistance to Rock Island employees who are not offered employment by interim operators and acquiring carriers. We will be working with Congress on an accelerated time schedule to develop an appropriate legislative proposal regarding labor protection." He also claimed that the "labor question has loomed as a stumbling block for an orderly transfer of Rock Island properties."[8]

By the time of the first status report on the liquidation on February 19, the labor question had become central to the Rock Island bankruptcy case. Judge McGarr had received comments, not a formal motion, on his liquidation decision from the Railway Labor Executives' Association. Judge McGarr said that "I don't know what to do with 'comments' but they suggest that I did not have the authority to reject and to refuse to forward to the Commission the plan of partial reorganization proposed by the Trustee."[9] Justice Department attorney John Broadley argued that part of the confusion rested in the idea that Nicholas Manos had raised the notion that "the Trustee is no longer required to serve the public's interest in this proceeding." Broadley reminded the court that this was still a Section 77 hearing and that until the Rock Island was declared abandoned by the ICC it still possessed public-interest and common-carrier obligations.[10]

What were those obligations, and how could the railroad continue to operate in the public interest after the end of directed service on March 31? Several emergency DSOs had been authorized by the ICC and permitted other railroads to operate segments of lines. Judge McGarr questioned this idea, stating to Henri Rush, an attorney for the ICC, at a March 19 hearing:

> You are interested primarily . . . in the public interest [and] in the continuation of certain operations. . . . But the Rock Island, subject to the order of liquidation, is really now the creditors' railroad, it's the creditors' property and the Trustee's role is not to operate it, but to liquidate it, and to do so for the benefit of the creditors and if anyone buys or operates over lines of the Rock Island from now on, it's obvious that the interest of the creditors demands that they pay fair compensation for it.[11]

Rush "took violent exception to the notion that this railroad no longer has any public interest obligation." "Until a certificate of abandonment is obtained from the Commission, a railroad, even though it has a constitutional right to cease operations," must still file an application with the ICC. John Broadley agreed, stating that the railroad still had common-carrier obligations under the law, and he asked the judge to sign an order allowing for emergency directed-service operations on the railroad through May 31.

Creditor attorneys Daniel Murray and Milton Fisher expressed surprise at this mention of continued common-carrier obligations. Murray reminded the court of recent history, arguing that since the strike in August 1979 the ICC and DOT had opposed a plan of reorganization; the ICC had declared the railroad cashless; and the ICC had stated the view that the railroad could not be reorganized. "So, it seems to me that it just simply does not make any sense to suggest that there is any kind of common carrier obligation of the Trustee at this time," Murray concluded.[12] Judge McGarr, while agreeing with the creditors' position, realized he had no authority in the matter and allowed the emergency DSO to take effect. After KCT finished its winding-down of operations on March 31, twenty-one different railroads took over operations on segments of the Rock Island.[13]

The question of compensation to the Rock Island estate for operations on its property became a key theme in courtroom hearings. On April 1, Nicholas Manos argued once again that no one was sure what the twenty-one railroads were doing on the property, "what they are doing with the property, and what they are doing with our inventories and equipment." There was conflict between the Trustee and the ICC about the terms of compensation. Gibbons demanded that "the Rock Island be immediately compensated for the use of its facilities," arguing that the railroads "be directed to pay the Trustee in advance an estimated monthly rental" based on a formula employed in determining payments based on Rock Island traffic from 1978. Manos concluded that a new hearing on this matter should be scheduled soon, and "that unless the Trustee is satisfied and unless the creditors are satisfied that the Estate is being dealt with fairly, we will present to the Court the issues for its determination in the exercise of its summary jurisdiction . . . with the ultimate disposition of its liquidation and reorganization."[14]

Judge McGarr established the future parameters in the case:

"I will assert the authority of the Court in every area necessary to bring about an early realization of the maximum values obtainable for the assets of the Rock Island, or compensation for their interim use." He continued: "If this means cooperation with the Interstate Commerce Commission, it's a situation which I will welcome. If it means confrontation with the ICC, it's a confrontation that will have to take place quickly. This includes asserting my jurisdiction over the compensation decisions" and "insisting on the authority of the Court to review those decisions . . . in light of what I think is fair and just compensation." He was disturbed by the lack of interest in the purchase of Rock Island lines, and equally concerned by the slowdown in negotiations between the Trustee and the RTA for the purchase of the commuter property. But he knew that these matters took time, reminding the attorneys that every day he was "besieged by phone calls, telegrams, and letters . . . from businessmen who depend on the service of the Rock Island." He was disturbed by the economic harm his liquidation order had caused, but it "couldn't be helped," and "under the circumstances nothing else could have been done." But further delays on reorganization would continue to diminish the estate and hurt shippers; Judge McGarr wanted such matters resolved quickly.[15]

On April 11 the Trustee and the creditor attorneys filed a motion to confirm the discontinuance of railroad operations on the Rock Island. The motion gave the ICC ten days to respond under both the Bankruptcy Act and the MRRA.

> The Trustee and other Movants recommend that, to avoid further dissension on the issue . . . the Court should confirm the unconditional discontinuance and termination of the Rock Island's rail service obligations. It is particularly important in view of the end of directed service that there be no doubt that, both as a factual and a constitutional matter, no obligation to operate exists. The Court should make clear that this discontinuance and termination of rail service is and was totally unconditional.[16]

The Trustee had reached agreements with several railroads regarding compensation for operating on the property, but there were some notable holdouts, including the Southern Pacific's Cotton Belt subsidiary and the RTA. The RTA had long been in negotiations to purchase the commuter lines within the RTA's footprint, but Manos accused it of being a freeloader (using the system without paying compensation for the track and equipment) and of not responding to Trustee inquiries concerning compensation. Manos told the court, "There are railroads that want a free ride on the property of the Rock Island."[17] Michael Schneiderman disputed Manos's assertions and argued that from the very beginning the RTA had been negotiating in good faith with the Trustee, accusing Gibbons of "sitting there like a stone waiting for the RTA to make an offer and then another offer and to have nothing in response. The Trustee is trying to hold the commuters as hostage for an exorbitant price."[18]

There was a huge difference between the Trustee and the RTA concerning how much the commuter line's value, particularly given the necessity to rehabilitate track and the equipment running on it. One estimate placed the Trustee's value of the property, including real estate and equipment, at $40 million to $75 million; the RTA board was requesting a much smaller $17 million loan from the FRA to purchase the line.[19] The ongoing discussions were tense because of how the Trustee wanted to maximize value for the estate at the expense of private or state-run sellers. Gibbons drove a hard bargain for the sale of Rock Island property in order to ensure the liquidation was successful to all creditors and administrative claimants. And still, the RTA was divided about whether even to continue running commuter service on the Rock Island line, which was being accomplished under directed-service operations with C&NW crews. Throughout the spring and summer of 1980, many in Chicago assumed the line would close, forcing commuters into cars or nearby lines to the southwest suburbs.[20]

Perhaps the biggest stumbling block to a successful reorganization and liquidation was, as Neil Goldschmidt had identified, labor. In April and May, Congress considered and passed the Rock Island Railroad Transition and Northeast Corridor Improvement Act, sponsored by Senator Nancy Kassebaum (R–Kan.), whose state contained hundreds of unemployed Rock Island workers. It passed through the House and the Senate after major provisions were added to provide funds to northeastern railroads. President Carter signed it into law on May 31, 1980, protecting former workers on the railroad who could not receive positions with other carriers. (There were about 5,000 former Rock employees who would be idle as a result of the end of operations.) The statute provided $75 million "in Federal loan guarantees to the Rock Island to cover labor protection expenses associated with an agreement" between the Rock Island and labor organizations, which were given ten days to reach a deal concerning labor protections for nonhired employees. The stated condition is critical to this part of the story line: "*The Government will be assured of repayment because the loan has the highest priority lien on revenues received by the trustee during the liquidation process*" (emphasis added). In other words, Congress had just passed, and Jimmy Carter signed, a law stipulating that the federal government would loan the bankrupt Rock Island company $75 million for labor protection out of its own bankruptcy estate.[21] Carter praised the legislation, which also included a staggering $750 million appropriation to upgrade Amtrak's Northeast Corridor, plus another $38 million for Amtrak to study passenger corridors in the nation (DOT had just cut dozens of unprofitable Amtrak routes through a massive reduction in 1979).

Albert Jenner wrote Lloyd Cutler, the counsel to the president, opposing the bill. Jenner described the long bankruptcy case and how the creditors were victimized by having $150 million in claims added to the bankruptcy estate by the Trustee's efforts to reorganize. He then stated directly:

> The Rock Island Transition and Employee Assistance Act [RITA] is fatally flawed because it violates the Fifth Amendment rights of the creditors and shareholders of the Rock Island . . . in that it operates as an *ex post facto* law to deprive the creditors and shareholders of their

property rights, it violates the separation of powers doctrine by invading the exclusive province of the Reorganization Court in a pending case in order to effectuate an adjudication of a claim, and it functions as special legislation rather than as a uniform law in bankruptcy.

Jenner argued that the law was unconstitutional on all these points and concluded that "it represents unsound public policy insofar as it seeks to provide labor protection to employees who have steadfastly resisted essential productivity improvements and who have defied Presidential orders."[22] But Carter, facing a tough reelection campaign versus the Republican presidential candidate, Ronald Reagan—and struggling with an economy mired in recession—kept his nose to the political winds and secured more labor-union support.

Two issues—abandonment of the property and labor protection—were on the docket at a lengthy court hearing on June 2, 1980. Manos led, arguing for complete abandonment: "The Rock Island no longer has any common carrier obligations . . . and by precedent, there is no labor protection to be imposed as a condition upon this estate." He hoped the workers could find other jobs, but "as far as this Estate goes," "there can be no labor protection" with the millions owed to creditors and claimants.[23] The RLEA attorney, Michael Clarke, opposed total abandonment, arguing that the court did not have authority to make such a decision, and also that the Rock Island Transition Act provision for a ten-day period of negotiations between the Trustee and labor unions had to be honored. (Clarke had filed a motion for a stay in the abandonment procedures, which was heard by Judge McGarr.)[24]

The states of Iowa, Kansas, and Texas also argued against total abandonment. Previously, the states called for liquidation but, fearing the end of service for shippers and having very few railroads in place to purchase lines, now worried about the prospects of losing even more rail service. The State of Kansas Railroad Working Group had been meeting since January to plan for liquidation and how to attract service into the state to serve shippers by using five major Rock Island lines. None of the Kansas lines had been included in the Trustee's core reorganization proposals, so the state was threatened with the shutdown of more than 500 miles.[25] Each state worried about a general order of abandonment of the value of Rock Island properties and urged the judge not to accept the motion to abandon the entirety of the Rock Island until various sales could be worked out in the states.

Daniel Murray gave a succinct summary of the main issues in the bankruptcy case and how the court had come to its conclusion to liquidate the property. He praised the ICC for acting with uncommon haste in making the same conclusion that the property be abandoned, arguing that while it was true that some of the property would be sold and operated by other carriers, the Bankruptcy Act referred to the abandonment of the Rock Island as a corporation and as an operating railroad. He also argued against labor protection on the estate: "I concede that labor protection, your Honor, has an emotional appeal to all of us, because we all share sympathy for the many workers who have dedicated themselves to the Rock Island over the years and who find themselves out of a job," Murray began. But looking at the proceedings over five years, the Trustee was hampered in his ability to reorganize the railroad by labor-union intransigence in changing even the most minor work rules to gain more productivity from the workforce. During the strike and under the DSO, "the jobs of Rock Island employees continued to be protected at a cost to the Government of over $70 million or $80 million." Reiterating his sympathy once again with the workers, Murray argued instead that "we have no sympathy for the leadership of the unions to which these workers belong, because they did not cooperate in helping to make these reorganization proceedings successful, and we do not believe as a matter of some public policy, as well as a matter of law, that they should be rewarded for their intransigence."[26]

Judge McGarr stated that he had protected the public interest for five years and he was still cognizant of whatever role he had in doing so now. He also stated, "This is a bankrupt business, and private creditors cannot forever support the ongoing operations, at a loss, of a railroad in service of the public interest." "The Rock Island," he continued,

> is operating nothing, and it hasn't been operating anything for some considerable time because it has been my decision, and continues to be, that the continued operation of the Rock Island has passed the point where it is mandated by the public interest and is such a serious financial disservice to the creditors that it was terminated and had to be terminated.[27] So, the motion to confirm the discontinuance of the Rock Island Railroad operations will be granted. The abandonment of the operations is ordered, and by that I mean a total system abandonment.[28]

Judge McGarr also refused to grant labor protection and rejected the RLEA's motion for a stay of the order pending an appeal.

The Trustee and creditor attorneys asked for a temporary restraining order and preliminary injunction against the ICC and DOT to prevent federal action under the Rock Island Transition Act. Both were necessary, Manos told the court on June 9, 1980, because "unless the injunctive relief by way of a temporary restraining order is entered today, the power of this Court to consider the Constitutional aspect of the Act" will be taken away.[29] Daniel Murray reiterated his position a week earlier regarding Congress protecting labor unions that had acted contrary to the best interest of the reorganization efforts by the Trustee: "What is special and so unusual about this legislation is the impact that it has on private property, and that is the reason why I think it is so critical to the history of the relationship between private property and public use."[30]

Murray then added an important discussion about motives behind the statute:

> I think we are all accustomed in an election year to efforts to appropriate large-sums of hard-earned taxpayers' money from the public till to fund politically opportune projects, the proverbial legislative pork barrel. But, what I think is so extraordinary, and I submit also deeply troubling about this legislation, is that it backs up not to the public till, but private property, so that the administration and Congress can win the favor of labor unions in an election year, and it's that kind of abuse of Government again which the Fifth Amendment is designed to prohibit.

The government was now supplying, Murray stated, the Rock Island employees a sum of money unavailable to any other unemployed worker in any other industry. "And why? Because the Congress has determined that the Rock Island services are essential to Midwest rail transportation and to the Midwest economy, even though, in the last five years, neither the Administration nor the Congress has been willing to put any significant sum of money into the Rock Island Estate to preserve the Rock Island operations in the Midwest."[31]

Other creditor attorneys agreed, raising the constitutional issues and focusing, much like Murray, on the political calculus behind passage of the statute. The government attorneys for the ICC—Henri Rush and the Justice Department—defended the law. But it fell to the RLEA's Michael Clarke to spell out the issues. He stated that the Trustee, in filing its motion, was violating the Rock Island Transition Act and the Railway Labor Act by refusing to meet with labor to negotiate a solution to labor protection issues. Clarke also stipulated that the United States Court of Appeals for the Seventh Circuit would soon hear the case, so there was no reason to grant a temporary restraining order.[32]

Judge McGarr ruled that the Rock Island Transition Act was illogical and determined that the Rock Island—a bankrupt corporation not making any claims about operating in the public interest—indeed had a public interest deriving from labor claims against the estate. "That Congress believes it can legislate a $75 million labor protection burden on the assets of the Rock Island comes to me as a startling concept."[33] In addition, the judge stated:

> It seems to me clear, without the necessity of a great deal of comment, that the Rock Island Act, which is the subject of our deliberations today, is an unconstitutional taking, an unconstitutional deprivation of the property rights of the creditors. It seems to be thus in two respects at least, and probably more, but the labor protection aspect of it, which has been argued today at length, and in addition, the curious procedural deprivation of the ordinary rights of application and appeal decisions affecting the property rights of creditors in a bankruptcy case.[34]

Judge McGarr ordered an injunction, stipulating that the negotiations called for between labor and the Trustee would not take place and that the court would await the appellate ruling on constitutionality being argued before the Seventh Circuit.

U.S. Supreme Court Justice John Paul Stevens, who was "riding the circuit" at the appellate court in Chicago (i.e., sitting on assigned panels for appellate review), denied the request of the RLEA to stay the injunction as ordered by Judge McGarr against the Rock Island Transition Act. He stated that the bankruptcy judge was right on the merits of the law and that the Rock Island Transition Act did indeed authorize a taking of the Rock Island property without just compensation.[35] Stevens stated that it wasn't clear from the new law if the Tucker Act applied in this case; if Tucker was applicable, it would allow a remedy against the government if any payments made under the new law were declared to be unconstitutional. Congress had not and now was considering applying it through a joint resolution. DOT recommended instead that the payment of $75 million be made from DOT funds, rather than from the railroad, to the Railroad Retirement Board on behalf of unemployed workers. Doing nothing about the legislation in Congress stoked fears that the former Rock Island workers now employed by other carriers would strike, precipitating a nationwide work stoppage on the railroads.[36]

Government attorneys had made a similar argument in district court on June 29 in a motion to vacate the injunction. John Broadley argued that the act "was a quite reasonable exercise of [congressional] power under Article III, Clause II of the Constitution [the Commerce Clause]."[37] Henri Rush of the ICC argued that the injunction interfered with Congress's intent and was not necessary, from a constitutional perspective, to disallow labor negotiations between Rock Island and its unions. Union attorney Michael Clarke argued as to the irreparable harm the judge's injunction was having on the 6,000 workers who were not hired by other railroads and who would not receive the money in the bankruptcy. He also argued, as did other attorneys, that the U.S. Supreme Court would have to hear the case, which would cause further delay, and that it would not possibly act until the next term (in 1981), further harming employees.[38]

Nick Manos suggested that the government authorize a grant to the railroad's employees.

> Mr. Rush says the government is frustrated and he emphasizes this by shaking his head. . . . Mr. Rush's frustrations should be, and the frustrations of the United States should be taken care of by a grant. . . . Mr. Clarke says that we're at the end of the line. Mr. Clarke, we've been at the end of the line a long time ago. Unfortunately, there are no jobs. Mr. Clarke says there is an unequal treatment of employees in the railroad industry. What can I say about the poor employees of the Ford Motor Company? What can I say about the employees of Chrysler? What can I say about the poor employees of Pittsburgh [sic] Steel who have been out of a job? What can I say about the hundreds of thousands of workers who are now out of a job because of the economic climate?

Manos reminded the court: Of the $21 million in Rock Island coffers, all of it was accounted for by creditors and administration claimants before labor.[39]

Manos need not have evoked such passion to convince Judge McGarr that the motion would be denied, leaving the RLEA to seek an appeal in the Seventh Circuit or in the U.S. Supreme Court. Clarke asked, "So do we have a finding on constitutionality?" Judge McGarr responded, "Yes." The veteran jurist had already determined that "it was unconstitutional for more than one reason."[40] Then he made it clear that the attorneys for the government and the RLEA would have to seek relief in whichever court would hear their motion for injunctive relief. On July 1, those attorneys filed a motion for a stay of Judge McGarr's injunction with the U.S. Supreme Court: "As long as the injunction remains in effect, there exists a serious threat of a strike by the Rock Island employees that will result in cessation of necessary operations and service." This was the identical argument made before Judge McGarr. The Court refused to vacate the injunction, leaving the RLEA with no other alternative but to file a lawsuit in the Seventh Circuit against the Trustee, a case the U.S. Supreme Court would eventually decide.[41]

The process of disposing assets continued through the summer. The Trustee reported that "track leases have been executed covering approximately 2,016 route miles with rentals totaling $808,700 per month." The Chessie System completed a lease for 98 miles of the Blue Island, Illinois (the main Chicago yard), and Bureau Junction (central Illinois) for $135,568 per month, with an option to purchase the line. This was the mainline from Chicago to central Illinois and served silica sand and gravel quarries in the Illinois River valley. The C&NW was renting the line from Minneapolis to Kansas City for $410,000 per month, and the Katy was renting 960 route miles in Kansas and Oklahoma for $300,000 per month. The Trustee reported sales to the Missouri Pacific of 40 miles of track in Arkansas, with assorted shortline railroads for smaller segments of track. The final consummation of the sale of the Tucumcari–St. Louis line, to the Cotton Belt, was to be finalized on October 30 for $57 million. There was tremendous optimism about the sales and potential returns.[42]

The Trustee also reported several major real-estate transactions, including $24 million for all "owned locomotives and parts inventory as well as 80 acres of our shop facilities at Silvis, Illinois," to the Varlan Company. During August the Trustee had completed negotiations to sell-lease the LaSalle Street Station property in downtown Chicago, 50 percent of which was owned by Penn Central Corporation. The Rock Island concluded a 99-year lease of their interest with "put" and "call" options for potential sale with prices set between $1.7 and $2.6 million.[43] The Trustee also showed how his early objective was proceeding, that is: "To dispose of rolling stock under termination agreement which would result in limiting to the greatest extent possible the unsecured long term lease obligations." A total of 10,389 freight cars had been delivered to final destinations; 8,928 remained online, and 4,854 were offline. More than 200 locomotives had been delivered to final destination, and about 300 locomotives awaited disposition.[44] All told, some $6 million had been added to escrow accounts (which now totaled $18 million) in the three-month period ending August 31. (See Photo 11.1.)

Outside the courtroom, decisions were being made in Congress that could still complicate the reorganization. On October 11, 1980, Jimmy Carter signed into law the Staggers Rail Act, providing for partial deregula-

Photo 11.1 LaSalle Street Station in Chicago. The headquarters of the Rock Island Railroad, in a few months it would meet the wrecking ball. Photograph by the author.

tion of the railroad freight industry. It had been a long fight for the president to secure a bill that would achieve rate deregulation, allow for speedier abandonment procedures, and promote competition among a rail industry staggering under the weight of government regulation. Carter had delivered on his promise to deregulate key segments of the economy, securing the deregulation of transportation and communications and, ironically, promoting an agenda of market liberalization in the economy more amenable to the ideological predilections of his opponent in the presidential campaign, Ronald Reagan. For the Rock Island, Carter would be too late the hero, but for the railroad industry as a whole Staggers established a green light for innovation and profitability for decades to come.

Yet passage of the bill was never a sure thing, and it was hindered by congressional interests with ties to shippers, labor, and other interest groups concerned about deregulation. Carter submitted his proposals for deregulation of railroads on March 23, 1979. In his message to Congress announcing the proposed changes, citing a DOT study on the industry, Carter stressed that "without major changes in structure and operation, the railroads will be unable to generate the funds needed to sustain themselves. . . . The capital needed to sustain the freight rail system between now and 1985 will total $42.5 billion; it estimates that the industry itself is capable of generating or borrowing less than $30 billion. These figures do not include the federally-aided Conrail system in the Northeast which is losing $300–$400 million per year." Carter concluded that "deregulation presents the only viable option to either a massive increase in federal subsidies to the railroads or increased government intervention in their operation—both of which are highly undesirable."[45]

Carter proposed: that railroads be allowed to set prices without interference from the government, which would be established gradually over five years; the transfer of rail mergers from the ICC to the Justice Department under antitrust laws; new guidelines for abandonments so that railroads would not be forced to keep running money-losing lines; new rules on rate discrimination; labor protections for rail employees impacted by mergers and abandonments; and the elimination of most of the ICC's powers over rail operations.[46]

The previous DOT secretary, Brock Adams, had outlined the deregulatory goals in a memorandum distributed to the executive branch in spring 1979. Adams outlined the broad strokes, including a five-year adjustment period after which maximum rates would be terminated. To protect shippers during this five years, a "rate of reasonableness" would be established to determine effective competition by others in the industry. Adams also described changes regarding abandonments, rate bureaus, and mergers.[47] Officials within the executive agencies—including Labor, OMB, Justice, and the Council of Economic Advisors—concurred with the move toward deregulation but quibbled with specific proposals that might impact the president's anti-inflation programs regarding rate reasonableness and other issues in Adams's memo.[48]

The OMB director under Carter at the time, John White, provided a detailed and instructive dissent to DOT's proposals on abandonment. DOT was proposing a three-year window before a more liberalized set of rules would develop. OMB showed how imperative it was that abandonment rules be lessened immediately. The ICC had projected Class I railroads to lose $171.5 million in 1979 and that the rail system was operating close to 200,000 miles of lines. By abandoning 30,000–35,000 miles immediately,

White argued, close to $350 million per year in rehabilitation and operating costs would be saved.[49]

The Senate Commerce Committee crafted a bill that was distinctively at odds with the president's guidelines. Rush Loving Jr., an aide at OMB, produced a memo strongly advocating that the administration pay attention to the Senate on this matter. "The redrafted version of the bill not only fails to deregulate the railroads, it provides new controls as well." It made it more difficult for railroads to abandon lines and allowed for rate changes that barely kept pace with inflation. Loving had information from the committee staff that the bill would wind up costing an additional $2 billion for assistance and subsidies to the railroad industry. "The Administration has reached this impasse through default," Loving argued. "Thus far the Carter Administration has followed the quite unofficial line that any bill going under the guise of deregulation is all right. Not so." OMB officials responded by asking, "Which goal—passage of a bill in an election year or attainment of significant reform—is a higher priority if both cannot be achieved?"[50]

The main Senate stumbling block for the bill, which was reported out of the Commerce Committee in December 1979, was Senator Russell Long (D–La.), who wanted to place rate restrictions on coal shipments. Long thought that railroads would place "exorbitant prices for coal transportation, where they often are the only means of transport. He is concerned that higher rail coal rates may deter utilities from converting to coal. . . . His amendment would create a new (and second) revenue to variable cost threshold to be established by the ICC." "If a railroad set a rate for any commodity, including coal, which exceeded this new threshold, it would have the burden of justifying the rate increase if any shipper complained," thereby forcing an ICC investigation, which would place the burden of proof for the rate increase back on the railroad.[51] Long attached a *Business Week* article in a letter to his colleagues suggesting that the railroad industry was not suffering from low rates of return on equity but instead had averaged a healthy 12 percent return—negating the idea that deregulation was necessary to help the weak railroads. The problem with the article is that it ignored any but the most profitable railroads; when looking at all the Class I carriers, the rate of return was 2.5 percent.[52]

The administration and railroads endorsed Senator Howard Cannon's (R–Nev.) substitute amendment. Cannon's amendment, which proposed a compromise with Long and was entered into the final bill in the Senate, allowed ICC discretionary investigation in the rate freedom zone if a revenue to variable cost threshold was passed. It also required the ICC to state its opposition to a rate in writing. The bill sailed to passage through the Senate on April 4, 1980, by a 91–4 vote.[53]

In the House there were two areas of concern for the Carter White House. Harley Staggers (D–W.V.), who was retiring after the end of the session, was close to labor unions, and they had been lobbying him heavily to include significant labor protections in any bill passed. Staggers was not heavily involved in the debates on the bill—it would be named in his honor as a testament to his long activism on behalf of railroads—but there was some concern that he might push for amendments requiring labor protections onerous to the railroads and to the Senate.[54] Bob Eckhardt (D–Tex.) was another problem. He wanted to preserve a cap on coal rates for Texas utility companies who blamed the railroads for charging too much for coal shipments from the Powder River basin. Eckhardt proposed an amendment similar to Long's amendment providing caps on rate increases. The administration lobbied intensively in favor of the Senate bill throughout the summer recess.[55]

The Carter White House had two important allies who worked to get the Senate bill through the House: Representative Jim Florio (D–N.J.) and Representative Edward Madigan (R–Ill.). Their version of the bill was a lot closer to the Carter administration's proposals than even the Senate version with the Cannon compromise. But the problem was the Texas delegation, with Eckhardt favoring rate caps and Senator Lloyd Bentsen worried about captive shippers in the state, especially a San Antonio utility relying on coal shipments from the Powder River basin over Burlington Northern. Carter spoke about how the ICC was allowing the Chicago and North Western Railway access to the Powder River over a joint line so that competition to the region would be secured.[56] There were several other proposals and amendments being discussed to secure the Texas delegation's votes and support for rail deregulation.[57]

Compromise was reached in mid-August among shippers, the railroads, utility companies, and Congress, but then Florio balked, feeling that too many provisions in the bill had been weakened. Carter once again intervened to urge a compromise, and after lengthy negotiations between the parties a bill was submitted to the House that was finally signed into law on October 14, 1980. The main provisions of the bill were: the ICC was prevented from regulating a rail carrier's rate increase unless it exceeded a revenue to variable cost threshold set at 160 percent and to a maximum of 180 percent over a four-year period; joint line rates were revised for three years to allow carriers a surcharge to cover out-of-pocket costs; rail carriers could enter contracts with shippers for the first time; collective rate-setting procedures were curtailed and industry-wide rate setting was abolished; ICC procedures for rate investigation and restructuring (including mergers) were simplified; and railroad entry into new markets was made easier. Additional money for Conrail was authorized, with an additional $500 million for FRA to assist railroads in buying preferred stock; and the bill amended the Rock Island Transition Act to make it clear that the bankruptcy court could not refuse to implement the employee protection plan, and if the law was later found to be unconstitutional, the federal government would guarantee reimbursement.[58]

The provision regarding the Rock Island was debated in district court on October 7 as the government attorneys and Michael Clarke of RLEA filed a motion to vacate the preliminary injunction against the ICC in the enforcement of the Rock Island Transition Act. Describing the new section of the act related to labor protection, Broadley asserted that the new provisions of the Staggers bill (still two weeks away from Carter's signature) would obviate the need for the injunction and allow the Trustee to negotiate a labor settlement with former Rock Island employees. (In effect, Congress had instituted a remedy in the law under the Tucker Act, as Justice John Paul Stevens had recommended in July.) Henri Rush of the ICC argued that Staggers was really a new piece of legislation and thus the injunction was no longer in effect. Michael Clarke argued that time was of the essence for Rock Island employees and joined the government in asserting that Staggers made the injunction moot.[59]

After hearing from the creditor attorneys as to unconstitutional taking of the property of the estate, Judge McGarr put off making a decision on the motions, for the bill had not been signed into law yet. Judge McGarr was not persuaded that the new bill cured anything in the old one:

> The new bill does not address the basic finding of the Court that the whole program which has been changed only cosmetically, to borrow someone else's word, was an unconstitutional deprivation.... I share Mr. Moritz's comment, or argument, that you do not proceed, nor must the Court allow proceedings under what is patently unconstitutional legislation because there is a remedy somewhere down the line that may straighten things out. It really is not at all clear to me that to dispense the money now, to allow the claim against the assets of the Rock Island to accrue, to say to the Trustee that if this is all unconstitutional you can sue under the Tucker Act and get it back, is even to cure the irreparable harm argument.... So, as I said, my

initial impression without ruling on it is that the new bill does not cure the old problem.[60]

From these statements, it was clear that the judge was not going to accept the constitutionality of the Rock Island Transition Act, even if amended by Staggers.

While the Trustee waited for the proceedings to move through the justice system, the mundane task of selling off assets took up most of his time. Gibbons had a capable staff, including Richard Lane, the director of staff coordination and manager of assets disposition who was in charge of preliminary discussions regarding the sale and salvage of the track and property of the Rock Island. Lane spent the majority of his hours handling the initial contacts and discussions regarding potential leases and purchase of Rock Island property.[61] He was fond of hand-writing (not typing) incredibly detailed memoranda concerning discussions and meetings between him and representatives of railroads interested in the property.

Some of the negotiations got downright testy between the state interests—hoping to secure rail service on lines for which the Trustee did not feel he had a significant offer—and the Rock Island. One example is the fallout over negotiations to purchase an 866-mile portion of the Choctaw Route (also called the Sunbelt Line by Rock Island officials) between Memphis and El Reno, Oklahoma; Little Rock and Alexandria, Louisiana; and Mesa, Arkansas, to Stuttgart, Arkansas. The state interests, known as "A-OK" (Arkansas-Oklahoma Railroad) began discussions with Gibbons to purchase the line in the fall of 1980, offering a figure of $21 million to the Trustee. "The A-OK plan is a package; they have applied to the FRA for funding. Oklahoma has funds already authorized and Arkansas expects such authorization to be approved in the next session of the Legislature. They have 'substantial operators ready and willing to operate the lines,'" Lane wrote. When asked how they arrived at the figure of $21 million, Gordon Fay, who represented the A-OK negotiations, replied that this was the FRA salvage value. Gibbons replied that "this is a transportation corridor useful for railroad and other transportation purposes and it is pointless to discuss net liquidation value." Nick Manos countered with a price of $100 million—a staggering difference. "Mr. Gibbons pointed out that, even excluding our interest in the Harahan Bridge [over the Mississippi River], the value of the Memphis-Little Rock segment would exceed their entire offer."[62]

In June 1981, as negotiations continued, Lane took an inspection trip over the route and reported that he "was rather impressed with the condition of the 'Sunbelt' east of Calumet, Oklahoma (the main line between El Reno, a major Rock Island yard and Oklahoma City)." He also reported that the Rock Island's recent offer of $75 million "seems reasonable in light of $50 million in rehabilitation that would be faced by A-OK had not the Rock Island already reworked 424 miles" of the route. Still, the deal went nowhere. A reworked proposal to spin off part of the line from El Reno to Elk City on the Oklahoma-Texas border was discussed at a June 1981 meeting between the representatives. The offer from A-OK for that segment was $8 million, and for the total amount of track on the Choctaw Route the group increased the proposal to $45 million—half what the Rock Island expected. Gibbons agreed to sell an 82-mile segment of the former mainline to the State of Oklahoma in 1981, but the A-OK sale lingered, and only parts of the line (not the complete 800 miles discussed) were sold to the state, which contracted years later with the A-OK to provide service.[63]

While the possible sale of lines seemed to be dragged out by the Trustee, the liquidation of property was making progress throughout 1981. Between May and June the Trustee reported thirty-six separate meetings with railroads interested in leasing or buying line segments. Track leases on 2,545 miles of the railroad were in place, bringing in $1.3 million per month. Discussions with the C&NW to purchase the so-called spine line (the roughly 750-mile north-south line stretching from St. Paul to Kansas City) and with the Katy to purchase the southern spine from Herington to Galveston were ongoing. The railroad had recouped $83 million from real-estate sales, line sales, and leases through July 1981.[64] All told, the liquidation seemed to be proceeding very well.

Midwestern politicians and business interests thought the Trustee was proceeding as a proverbial tortoise, obstinately refusing offers to sell rail lines to shippers and to other railroads. After receiving letters from politicians complaining about Gibbons, and after news reports concerning businessmen demanding a Justice Department investigation of the Trustee, Judge McGarr wrote Senator Robert Dole (R–Kan.) defending Gibbons and Nick Manos: "I sympathize with those who complain of delay in the liquidation proceeding. At this moment, the greatest single bar to the formulation of a final plan of liquidation, is a problem arising from a recently enacted federal statute . . . the Rock Island Railroad Transition and Employee Assistance Act."[65] In response to Midwestern governors, Judge McGarr argued similarly, but added that Gibbons's main duty "is to maximize the return on the Rock Island real estate for the benefit of creditors." He continued: "It is necessary for the governors to recognize that expressions of interest of the states in obtaining and operating segments of the Rock Island have not been backed up with sufficient cash, or a viable prospect of obtaining cash. . . . I kept the Rock Island operating at substantial losses and over the objections of the creditors for six [sic] years in deference to the public interest," Judge McGarr explained.[66]

The frustrations and differences between the states and the estate were shown in the controversy over the Katy's attempt to purchase 900 miles of Rock Island track from Herington, Kansas, to Galveston. The Katy's subsidiary, the OKT (Oklahoma, Kansas, Texas) had been operating the track since March 1980 as a directed-service provider. After a real-estate appraisal conducted by the Rock Island, Gibbons informed OKT that the price for the line would be $160 million. OKT counteroffered with a ten-year lease with an option to buy for $50 million, which Gibbons rejected and re-countered with a price of $77 million (the net liquidation value). In May 1981, after meetings with the FRA and gaining guarantees of $30 million in support, OKT responded with a $45 million offer for the Herington–Dallas line; Gibbons rejected it, suggesting $57 million for the Herington–North Fort Worth track. The 34-mile Dallas–Fort Worth line, which the City of Dallas was interested in developing as a commuter line, was appraised at $50 million to $55 million alone (Gibbons referred to the appraiser's estimate of its value as a "goldmine"), and the mayor of Dallas was interested in purchasing it at that price.[67] Gibbons now balked at the price (960 miles of railroad for $57 million) and returned to the higher $77 million purchase figure. OKT refused and threatened to end the lease for the line by November 1981.[68]

Governor George Nigh (D–Okla.) accused Gibbons of refusing to negotiate in good faith, prompting the Trustee to reply that "bad faith or lack of good faith and irresponsibility are serious charges particularly when made by persons who are obviously not in possession of all the facts. Railroads are not priced by the mile as shelf inventory in a store is priced by the unit. Many factors such as real estate, quality of track materials, traffic and traffic potential and particular advantages to the purchaser go into the structure of the price." There was inflation in values, and "had I recommended the OKT offer for the Court's approval, I would have been irresponsible and in bad faith with respect to my creditors, among whom are numbered the State of Oklahoma and the KATY."[69] As Gibbons told the Midwest Governors' Conference in Oklahoma City on March 4, 1982:

> I recognize and share the disappointment and frustration of buyers who have not been able to reach agreement with me today. Portions of Rock Island's system do not have a sufficient traffic base so as to

Photo 11.2 The Katy's OKT subsidiary operating over former Rock Island track in Kingfisher, Oklahoma, 1982. The OKT would purchase the line from the Trustee in late 1983. It is operated by the Union Pacific, which acquired the Katy through merger in 1988. Photo by Tom Kline. Used with permission.

support profitable operations. It is therefore understandable that prices offered to me in those instances are driven by a thorough business-like approach to the bottom line for potential revenues. Such is undoubtedly the case in the instance of the MKT-OKT. My position has been clearly stated, and often, to be that I am in sympathy with their desire to serve the public interest, but that it cannot be at the expense of the estate which could do much better by dismantling and selling the parts and selling the underlying real estate where it is able to do so.[70]

Gibbons added that the FRA was helping to hold the states hostage to the demands of the estate by appropriating "a meager $38 million" to help purchase the various lines being auctioned by the bankruptcy Trustee. "The bottom line then appears to be that the public interest continues in certain marginal lines of the Rock Island estate but that there is no ability to purchase, except at the expense and sacrifice of the estate. . . . Moreover, it appears there is no prospect of increased appropriations in the foreseeable future."[71] (See Photo 11.2.)

Once again, like so many previous times in the Rock Island's history, the fortunes of the estate holders were being held hostage to the whims of government action, both in the pending arguments before the U.S. Supreme Court concerning the Rock Island Transition Act, and in the FRA's decision not to support (yet again) the sale of lines "in the public interest" to Midwestern states. Yet miraculously—and with sudden swiftness—this impasse would end—and favorably for the estate in almost every way. At the same time, with a revitalized economy, the end of the worst post–World War II recession, and the Great Inflation in 1983, the Rock Island's fortunes would turn decisively—finally—for the better.

TWELVE

LONG LIVE THE ROCK

> The Rock Island bankruptcy was the most successful railroad reorganization in history.
>
> —Nicholas Manos, January 8, 1984

On December 2, 1981, the case of *Railway Labor Executives' Association v. Gibbons* was heard before the U.S. Supreme Court. Michael Clarke argued the case for the RLEA and Daniel Murray for the Trustee. Clarke had a tough argument to make. In the district court, Judge Frank McGarr had determined that the Rock Island Transition Act was an unconstitutional taking of private property and twice issued injunctions against it. RLEA argued that the Commerce Clause determined the act's constitutionality and that the district court and the United States Court of Appeals for the Seventh Circuit in Chicago had incorrectly determined that there was an unconstitutional taking. Clarke received consistent questions from the Justices regarding takings under the Fifth Amendment. Clarke insisted that the "only issue before this Court" was the issue of compensation for the taking, though he had difficulty citing any specific cases where a taking of private property in a case like the Rock Island Transition Act was constitutional.[1]

Clarke argued that the act was a continuation of a preexisting obligation for labor protection under the Milwaukee Road Restructuring Act, not a new obligation on the Rock Island estate as claimed by the attorneys for William Gibbons and as the Seventh Circuit had determined in its ruling. The problem with that argument, as Judge McGarr and other attorneys said, was that the Milwaukee Road Act pertained to an operating railroad, whereas the Rock Island had been abandoned and no longer operated in the public interest.

Elinor Stillman, representing the government appellees in the case, argued that Congress had determined that the compensation granted to labor in the act should be stipulated as being in the public interest. When asked whether she thought that this was the same as a taking for public use, Stillman replied she thought it was, before Justice John Paul Stevens interrupted and asked, "supposing the Congress made a finding that General Motors could run the Ford Company better than Ford does, and that they should transfer their assets to General Motors because there would be a public benefit, would that be a taking for public use?" Stillman stammered and said, "I guess one reason why this is difficult is that this is a substantive due process test," to which Stevens replied: "It is difficult because there is no precedent to support your position."[2]

Daniel Murray of Jenner & Block spoke for the Trustee and framed the issue as a clear violation of the Fifth Amendment's takings clause. Murray outlined the history of the reorganization and the creditors' interests in keeping the railroad going for five years, paying out more than $100 million to the employees while the estate lost more than $200 million. He also argued that the Rock Island was no longer a common carrier and that other cases cited by Clarke and Stillman applied to operating railroads, not to abandoned railroads. The labor protection put on the Rock Island estate by the Rock Island Transition Act was retroactive; the Rock Island had paid labor and had paid health benefits and railroad retirement benefits in full during its bankruptcy. But once the property was ordered to be liquidated by the district court, its common-carrier and public-interest obligations ended.

Murray's argument was that the law was a violation of the constitutional prerogative against the rule of uniform standards in bankruptcy, as the act applied only to the Rock Island and not to other railroads in bankruptcy. It was this argument that won; on March 2, 1982, in a unanimous 9–0 decision, Justice William Rehnquist wrote that while Judge McGarr's injunction against the act after the passage of the Staggers Rail Act was moot, the labor-protection provision of the Rock Island Act was a violation of the uniform standards of bankruptcy in the constitution. "By its terms, RITA applies to only one regional bankrupt railroad. . . . The language of the Bankruptcy Clause itself compels the conclusion that such a bankruptcy law is not within Congress' power to enact."[3] The Supreme Court affirmed the Seventh Circuit's decision regarding the Rock Island Transition Act.

With that one decision, the Rock Island liquidation was able to hit high gear. Spared a $75 million administrative claim against the estate for labor protection, the Trustee now worked unimpeded on a reorganization plan designed to restructure the assets of the estate and to sell off and liquidate the remaining properties. The Supreme Court lifted a cloud on the Rock's reorganization prospects and allowed for what turned out to be a successful liquidation. (See Photo 12.1.)

Congress was still attempting to hinder the Rock Island reorganization. Concerned that the Trustee was not acting swiftly enough to sell rail prop-

Photo 12.1 Daniel Murray, who would argue the winning case for the Rock Island Trustee in Railway Labor Executives' Association v. Gibbons. *Photo courtesy of Jenner & Block.*

erties in states like Kansas and Oklahoma, Senator Nancy Kassebaum proposed a bill (S. 1879) to amend both the Milwaukee Road Restructuring Act and the Rock Island Transition Act to allow the ICC to make a valuation of rail properties for sale should there be an impasse between a Trustee and a potential buyer. She held hearings in the Commerce Committee on December 6, 1981, at which William Gibbons and Nicholas Manos, as well as creditors' counsel, testified. In his testimony, Gibbons explained the complexity of selling properties of such a vast rail system: "I have spent several thousand dollars on professional appraisers, both real estate and track structure appraisers, in order to obtain what I consider adequate tools to negotiate these sales." Gibbons hired the engineering firm Ford, Bacon & Davis to do track appraisals, which were based on the net liquidation value of the track (based on the weight of the rail, other associated equipment, and land values). The issue delaying sales was often a discrepancy between the price offered for the lines and the ability of the purchasers to pay. "In areas of negotiation, the purchaser or the would-be purchaser cannot justify paying my price primarily because the traffic base of a segment upon which the carrier is operating will not support the payment of a price equal to what I consider at least net liquidation value."[4]

Nicholas Manos argued that the bill as constituted was flawed. The prices to be determined for property were not a matter that the ICC should determine whatsoever. Pointing to the Oklahoma-Texas Railroad transaction, and one involving the sale of lines in northern Kansas to the Mid States Port Authority, Manos argued that "the problem is that there is a genuine dispute with respect to price." "There just is no money with which to fund the acquisition by so-called financially responsible entities. . . . It's almost akin, Senator Kassebaum, to the management of a shoe store that has a big quantity of size 4 shoes and a lot of size 6 customers, and it hires a strong shoe clerk to fit those 4s into the 6s. You just can't do it. What you've got to do," he told the committee, "is provide the money for the purchase of these lines from the Rock Island. Otherwise, I don't see any other solution to the impasse."[5]

The bill would languish in Congress, awaiting the final disposition of the Supreme Court decision. By the time President Ronald Reagan signed the bill into law in January 1983, it was moot. The new act provided, at government expense, some $35 million in assistance to unemployed Rock Island workers. The impetus for the bill in the first place—the claim that the Trustee was not negotiating in good faith—had already been dispensed with as the sale to the OKT Railroad of the line from Herington, Kansas, to North Fort Worth, Texas, had been consummated in October 1982.

Other line sales and leases were proceeding with greater dispatch. In February 1982, Gibbons announced a fifty-year lease between the Chessie System and the Trustee for the mainline between Blue Island, Illinois, and Bureau Junction in central Illinois. The freight railroad would share the line between Blue Island and Joliet with the Regional Transportation Authority, which had begun condemnation proceedings on the commuter line (which the agency was still operating under an ICC DSO). In 1983 the RTA would conclude a purchase agreement with the Rock Island, securing the property for $35 million.[6]

Other negotiations to sell lines sometimes met with surprising results for the estate. Beginning in February 1982, Gibbons had negotiated a deal to sell to the Milwaukee Road a 38-mile segment in Iowa between Washington and Muscatine. The railroads reached an agreement for $4 million. A second Iowa segment between Culver and Davenport was also being discussed, with the total amount settled at $10.5 million payable over time. The Milwaukee's Bankruptcy Trustee had approved the first sale, which was reported to Judge

McGarr on May 20. But then the C&NW got involved and wanted to purchase the entire 64-mile line, including trackage rights, for $16.5 million, with $5 million cash up front and the remainder paid over five years, a far better deal for the estate. Manos reported this to the court on June 2, 1982, urging that the C&NW bid be considered and that the Milwaukee Road be authorized to improve on its bid. The line was attractive due to the construction of a new coal-fired power plant at Fruitland, which the Milwaukee would be able to service with Powder River coal exchanged with the Burlington Northern at Ottumwa.[7] Eventually, a private sale became a bidding war and the Milwaukee wound up winning—as did the Rock Island estate—purchasing the line for $17.5 million a few weeks later.

Now that the Supreme Court had removed the uncertainty of the labor protection from the estate, and following the Court's rejection of a writ of certiorari from the Railway Labor Executives' Association in May, two problems emerged in the hearings. The first issue concerned the issue of post-bankruptcy administration claims against the railroad. When would they be paid? Manos kept asking for the district court for a postponement of payment, even though, as attorneys for the claimants argued, the Rock Island now had sufficient cash to pay some claims. The claimants were not all major corporations. One group of cooperative grain elevators from Estherville, Iowa, had loaned the Trustee $1.4 million to repair hopper cars and track to serve their elevators. The Federal Reserve Board's decision to drive up interest rates to end inflation depressed the agricultural economy, and the elevators in northwest Iowa, which had loaned the Rock Island money to serve their branchlines, needed to be compensated or face bankruptcy themselves. Manos was sympathetic but argued that the amount of cash in the Rock Island coffers "was sequestered for the use of the creditors." Judge McGarr continued to delay payments on administration claims, but this could not continue forever.[8]

Some of the complexities involved in filing a reorganization plan with the court involved how claimants were treated under bankruptcy law. Administrative claims (debts incurred by the estate after bankruptcy was declared) were dealt with first. The two largest administrative claims were the federal government (the Rock claimed it owed $51 million; the government claimed $56 million) and the Union Pacific Railroad (for equipment leased to the Rock Island, which owed $18 million). Next in line were the claims of bondholders and stockholders and others entitled to assets of the estate. With line sales, property sales, and leases, the Rock Island had about $80 million escrowed in the summer of 1982, not enough in and of itself to pay off secured creditors, tax obligations, and other debt.

Nicholas Manos and the Trustee's staff spent the majority of their time in negotiations to settle outstanding debt. In the summer and fall of 1982, Manos negotiated a settlement of $6 million on the UP's $18 million claim provided the funds were paid to the railroad immediately. He reported the deal to the court on October 3, 1982, and also reported favorable negotiations with the Federal Railroad Administration proceeding on the claim of $51 million.[9]

Price Waterhouse was the accounting firm for the Trustee. In annual reports filed in court, one can easily see the progress the Trustee was making in liquidating the property. At the end of 1980, the Rock had $28 million in income from rentals, interests, and sales of assets; by the end of 1981, that figure was $77 million. The Rock had expenses in 1980 of $70 million, which had been reduced by the end of 1981 to $61 million. The Trustee had reduced the net loss of the property from $172 million to $147 million in December 1981.[10]

A year later, with the problem of labor protection removed, and after further settlements achieved with creditors, Price Waterhouse showed the Rock Island making remarkable progress in financial statements presented to the court. The Rock Island's income on December 31, 1982, was $131 million, with a $44 million expense providing a net income gain of $87 million. The deficit at the beginning of the year was $147 million, which shrank to $59 million by the end of 1982—a staggering gain of $88 million over the course of the year. On the financial side, at the end of 1982 the Rock Island had $246 million (mostly in cash) and its net income per share of common stock had improved from a deficit of $14.98 in 1980 to a positive $29.87 per share at the end of 1982.[11] By any measure these were impressive gains on the balance sheet and showed the way toward a successful reorganization.

The filing of a reorganization plan was the next major debate in court. Manos had asked for a six-month extension of time to file a plan at a hearing on July 13, 1982, with Judge McGarr granting an extension to November in order to discuss progress, with the intention of having a plan filed in January 1983. In the meantime, the Trustee and attorneys for the creditors worked to complete the sale of the Oklahoma-Texas lines to the Katy, which was finalized on October 20, 1982, at a cost of $55 million. The OKT, a subsidiary of the Katy, now owned the former Rock Island line from Herington to North Fort Worth; it had been operating on the property under a lease since March 1980.

The attorneys also worked out the terms of settlement agreements that were mailed to former employees, creditors, and other administrative claimants, making offers that the recipients had a right to accept, refuse, or negotiate.¹² In most cases, the offers were accepted. Many of those who refused believed they were offered a pension or some salary adjustment that was not part of the settlement. The Trustee had restructured the pension plan of the company, canceling the old one and purchasing an annuity with Canada Life Company, which contained the same provisions and benefits as the original Rock Island pension (the company no longer had an operating pension plan). John Mitros, a former vice president of the company, did not receive a pension under the new plan because he was employed with the railroad less than the mandatory ten years. He wrote to inquire of Gibbons about the status of the pension, but Gibbons informed him he was not eligible for the pension and that it was Mitros who should know about the eligibility considering he was the official who established the pension. Under the terms of the new plan, John Ingram received no pension from the Rock Island either.¹³

It was not until January 19, 1983, that the reorganization plan for the railroad was filed with the court. Nicholas Manos introduced the plan by injecting "a little ancient Greek history. It was Ulysses, your Honor, who stormed Troy with the wooden horse and it became very well known in history later that one must beware of Greeks bearing gifts. But that admonition, I don't think should apply to this particular American of Greek extraction here today." Manos then reiterated the history of the reorganization and the development of a first plan of reorganization and the great successes experienced in the liquidation proceedings. He then stated, "In summary, and almost unparalleled in corporate reorganization history, if not railroad reorganization, and I can point to no other proceeding, I don't care what size, unparalleled, this estate is now poised at the projected date of December 1983 to consummate a plan, assuming nothing unforeseen, which would pay all creditors the principal of their claims 100 percent on the dollar." Manos then described how the plan would pay all claimants, grant stockholders shares of the new company which would be involved in the liquidation and leasing business and no longer in the railroad industry. "The only indebtedness that [the company] would have under this plan, your Honor, would be securities that would be issued for the equivalent value of the interest that certain of the creditors would not be receiving at consummation date."¹⁴

Judge McGarr allowed the Interstate Commerce Commission to review the plan and comment within twenty days, though he added, "The Commission has a very, very vital statutory role in the operation of a railroad. I am not very impressed with the Commission's role in the liquidation of one." Yet he allowed time for ICC review, recognizing the complexity of the situation.¹⁵ As Manos told the court on January 19, "The so-called Kassebaum bill, which has now been enacted, was delayed in its enactment for a long period of time. A sufficient period of time, I might add, for the marketplace, and the law of supply and demand, and the law that governs offers and acceptances, it gives everybody a chance to interplay."

However, Manos worried because "only one-third of the rail properties of the Rock Island have been liquidated to date. We are in negotiations, your Honor, for a couple of thousands or more of rail lines to sell to railroads." The Trustee was not sure what impact the legislation would have on the negotiations that were ongoing.¹⁶ Manos also pointed out some good news from the government with a piece of legislation granting the cities of Dallas and Fort Worth $24 million to purchase the 34-mile line in order to construct a commuter line between the two urban areas.

The creditor attorneys all pointed to how smoothly the process of developing the reorganization plan had gone, heaping praise on the Trustee and his attorney for their cooperation. Albert Jenner said that he had told a reporter that "I do want to tell you from history that in my time, and up to the present time, I know of no other instance in the reorganization of railroads in which there is really a consensual plan presented to the court." He praised Manos and Gibbons and Judge McGarr for their roles in making the plan possible and for the speed by which it was enacted and presented. Henry Crown had given Jenner the message to express his thanks and support to the court about the plan as well.¹⁷ Judge McGarr was quite pleased, calling for a status report a month later to hear from the ICC, then added, "I think you all deserve, even though it's early in the afternoon, the right to go out and have a drink in celebration of the filing of the plan. We will recess." Albert Jenner responded, "Your Honor, we can go into chambers on that issue," and Judge McGarr responded, "I don't think I have enough supplies."¹⁸

"The liquidation process to date," the Trustee wrote in the plan of reorganization itself, "has produced highly beneficial results for the estate and all parties in interest. The sale of lines to users, which approximates about one-third of the rail system, has produced $182.4 million. All other assets have thus far produced additional sales of $100 million." Claims against the estate, he reported, had been reduced by $100 million since June 1982.¹⁹ The plan established twelve classes of claims against the estate, with the administration claims being paid in full at interest of 7.5 percent, including personal injury claims, wages, state and local tax authorities, six-month claimants, and administrative claims otherwise not covered. The secured creditors were next, followed by unsecured creditors, prebankruptcy tax claims, income debenture holders, and finally stockholders. In each case the plan would pay in full, with interest, the administrative claims and taxes. Creditors would receive an amount of cash equal to the full principal and the secured contractual or coupon interest on bonds, with exchangeable notes equal to enhanced interest secured after March 17, 1975. Income debentures would receive the same with a different category of exchangeable notes. Stockholders would receive shares of stocks in the new company. When executed and confirmed, there would be the election of an eleven-member board of directors.[20] The total amount owed to claimants was $302.8 million, and Gibbons proposed to pay off all claims in cash with interest as part of the plan. The bondholder notes would be paid at a cost to the estate of $63.3 million.[21]

As the plan awaited final consummation under the court's supervision, Gibbons continued to negotiate the sale of Rock Island lines to other railroads. One of the largest of the sales involved a bidding war between the C&NW and the Soo Line Railroad for the spine line (from St. Paul to Kansas City). The court had encouraged "auctions" whenever beneficial to the estate, and in this case the Trustee oversaw a bidding war of tremendous value for the property.

The C&NW had been operating the spine line since May 1980, paying more than $1 million per month to lease the property. The line was crucial for Iowa, Missouri, and Minnesota, and its rehabilitation drew attention in a Minnesota Department of Transportation study in 1981, which recognized that the C&NW was interested in purchasing the property.[22] Iowa shippers, however, disliked the C&NW, recalling inferior service in the 1970s and the routine abandonment of branchlines throughout the state.[23] However, the C&NW had invested money in the property and expressed interest in purchasing the northwestern Iowa grain lines as well; the C&NW's offer of $76 million for the purchase of the line in early 1983 seemed like a forgone conclusion. The Trustee planned to request the court's approval for the purchase on March 15, 1983.

Over the previous six months, the Trustee had also been negotiating with the Soo Line but had not received a substantive offer from that railroad.[24] The press had mentioned a Soo Line bid in September 1982, but discussions about what that entailed were still being held between Gibbons and Soo president Thomas Beckley in January 1983. However, the Soo's financing remained a question mark to Gibbons. For the Soo Line, the purchase would provide service to "a Kansas City gateway which would open up direct and shorter routes for our customers and give the Soo the ability to interchange traffic with several railroads not presently reached."[25]

When Beckley was informed of the C&NW's offer for the spine line, the Soo countered with an $81 million offer on the morning of the hearing. Nicholas Manos told the court that, "having been apprised of the $81 million cash offer of the Soo," C&NW "contacted the Trustee this morning . . . and informed the Trustee that the C&NW bid, or contractual offer . . . was now being increased by an amendment to the contract to $85 million."[26] Manos told the court that the bids were fairly close (the Soo was purchasing about 650 miles and the C&NW the full 716 miles) and added that both were cash bids, with no prospect of financing arrangements delaying the sale. The Soo attorneys gained a nine-day window by which to submit a new offer, which they did on March 18, upping it to $88 million. The C&NW quickly countered with $93 million, which the court accepted and submitted to the Interstate Commerce Commission for approval.

After the court had accepted the C&NW's offer by sending it to the ICC, the Soo countered with a $100 million offer to purchase 770 miles. The ICC determined that the Soo bid had to be considered as a new proposal, which meant the reorganization court would have to hear the offer before the ICC could rule on the rival bids. The Justice Department favored the Soo's entry into the market for competitive reasons, but the C&NW countered at ICC hearings in May that should the Soo win control of the line, the C&NW would lose 68,000 carloads a year and would be forced out of competitive commerce in the area between the Twin Cities and Kansas City. The C&NW also told the ICC that it had spent $5 million upgrading the property while it leased it from the Trustee.[27] Iowa took no position regarding either bid, advocating that whichever railroad controlled the line should allow trackage rights to other railroads for competitive reasons.

On June 29, 1983, Judge McGarr scheduled a hearing on the rival proposals. Manos reiterated the history of the bidding, with the Trustee determining that while the Soo offer was $7 million greater than the C&NW offer, by comparison the properties being acquired by the C&NW meant that the Soo's bid was really only $2 million greater. The C&NW was paying cash for the property and the transaction could be closed immediately, whereas the Soo was still lining up its financing. "The Trustee feels compelled to support the [C&NW] application," Manos said. There would be no delay in financing; the C&NW had been operating the property since May 1980; and the delay proposed by a Soo acquisition would cost the Rock Island additional money. Manos urged acceptance of the C&NW offer "in the best interests of the estate."[28]

Most of the complaints raised by attorneys for the C&NW, Soo Line, and state interests centered on the ICC's decision, which seemed to waffle on a number of questions concerning trackage rights and which railroad would be more beneficial for commerce in the region. Henri Rush, the ICC's attorney, felt under siege as the commission was criticized by almost every counsel in attendance, even though the ICC had speedily pushed through its decision. Michael Clarke of the RLEA asked the judge for a delay in the decision pending sufficient labor protections, which Judge McGarr again refused to grant.

Judge McGarr had to determine if the ICC was within its bounds constitutionally to refer the matter back to the court for adjudication. Judge McGarr ruled it was and, by doing so, took up the matter of the Soo's bid of $100 million. He stated:

> I have to address the Soo offer as an offer to purchase an equity which has already been sold. . . . There was a contract of preliminary approval. The North Western was ready to perform, and that circumstance creates an equitable right in the North Western. And to ignore that equitable right, by at this eleventh hour accepting and considering a new bid, would destroy the integrity of the bidding process. The preliminary approval was a meaningful ruling. . . . So the Soo's participation in that process ended in March. The North Western bid, already approved at that time, is confirmed and approved finally by the Court at this time.[29]

Judge McGarr waxed a bit nostalgic at the hearings when he said, "I realize that when we talk about the spine line, we are addressing the last major segment of the Rock Island to be disposed of in the course of the liquidation of this 'mighty fine line.'"[30] Indeed, it was. The major lines of the Rock Island had been disposed of by summer 1983, allowing the Trustee to file an amended reorganization plan with the court in August. There were other lines that awaited final disposition, including the main east-west line through Iowa and western Illinois (which was finally sold to Heartland Rail Corporation for $31.5 million in 1984). But other sales would be part of deals arranged and secured by the successor company.

The Trustee reported sizable gains in the financial health of the estate. Through the end of June 1983, "the sale and long term lease of lines to rail users approximates 3,140 miles or 45 percent of the Debtor's rail system and has produced $290 million. All other assets produced additional sales of $108.6 million. Assets yet to be liquidated are recorded at aggregate net book value of $123 million and are projected to have larger realizable values." Gibbons also reported that "claims against the estate which totaled $450 million" a year previous "have been reduced in a twelve month period through settlements and payments approved by the Court to $196.5 million." Stockholder equity was approximately $137 million, and the escrow account and other funds totaled $267 million, which now allowed the Trustee to satisfy all the claims "in full and with interest." He also reported that negotiations for the sale of 1,450 miles of rail were ongoing and would be concluded in 1983 and 1984.[31] By any measurement, the liquidation was an outstanding success.

In putting the plan together, Gibbons relied on a creditor committee made up of representatives of every class of claimants against the railroad, with the Crown intervenors, First National Bank of Chicago, and Continental Bank playing significant roles. The Kansas state attorney general's office represented the tax claims of all the states; labor was also represented, as were interline railroads and other administrative claimants. Gibbons had previously settled the FRA's claims for $36 million (the Rock Island had owed $52 million), so the federal government was not a participant in the committee. The consensual plan produced what Gibbons called "fair and equitable" settlements of all claims, even though some creditors, including the Santa Fe Railway and Banker's Trust Company, were concerned about legal aspects of the plan.[32] Judge McGarr accepted the plan as conforming "to the legal standards established and required under Section 77 of the Bankruptcy Act" at a December 23, 1983, hearing on the matter. There were still a few exceptions to be worked out regarding the dates at which interest rates would accrue, but effective April 19, 1984, the Rock Island would be reborn as a new reorganized corporation.[33]

A *Chicago Tribune* story in January 1984 called the Rock Island's successful reorganization a "second Penn Central," referring to the investment corporation that had emerged from the wreckage of the Penn Central bankruptcy. The difference, as Nicholas Manos was quoted as saying, was that "in the Penn Central case, creditors sacrificed." In Rock Island's case, all creditors were to be paid and the new corporation would be vested with a $300 million reserve, mostly cash, which would leave it vulnerable to a hostile takeover. Henry Crown, interviewed for the story, lauded the reorganization and stated that while the new corporation would not be in the transportation business "bondholders will be surprised at the value of their securities." Aside from the track remaining to be disposed of, according to Gibbons, the value of Rock Island assets included about 4,000 railcars, coal properties in Colorado and Oklahoma, oil and gas leases in Kansas, Oklahoma, and Texas, and real estate in Chicago, New York, Des Moines, and elsewhere. Gibbons also told the *Tribune* that "we're negotiating now on some fiber optic ventures" by leasing utility easements on former Rock Island property to communications companies.[34]

Two major line sales occurred a month before the birth of the new company. In February 1984, the Rock Island sold its 450-mile line from Council Bluffs to Bureau Junction to the Heartland Rail Corporation, a Des Moines–based company. Heartland, which owned the tracks, leased them to the Iowa Interstate Railroad, also received trackage rights over the Chessie System and the RTA from Bureau Junction to the Blue Island yard in Chicago. Eventually, the Iowa Interstate Railroad would acquire the Peoria branch as well.

Heartland was a group of about twenty Iowa shippers, including Maytag Corporation, that wanted to restore rail service to central Iowa—most of which had been without service since the shutdown of the Rock Island in 1980 (the Iowa Railroad had operated over the line between Council Bluffs and Bureau until 1984). Negotiations with the group, initially called TRAIN, began in 1983. The original price Gibbons placed on the line was $81 million, which was far too steep; the two sides wrestled until a price of $31.5 million was agreed to in February 1984. The State of Iowa's Rail Finance Authority, established in 1981 by Governor Robert Ray to deal with widespread abandonments and bankruptcies in the state, loaned Heartland $15 million to help make the purchase. In October 1984, after approval of the sale by the Interstate Commerce Commission, the Iowa Interstate Railroad began operating on the track, which was in decrepit shape. (See Photo 12.2.) Its signaling system was not operational, and the railroad operated with old Illinois Central rebuilt locomotives. But service was soon restored, and the Iowa Interstate Railroad relied for support on loyal shippers like Maytag. By the 1990s, the 550-mile regional railroad was thriving. Due to the emergence of ethanol in the late 1990s, the Iowa Interstate Railroad has prospered into a healthy regional system.[35]

On April 19, 1984, the Rock Island's plan for reorganization was consummated with the formation of the Chicago Pacific Corporation, a firm that would be a diversified investment and real estate holding company. Judge McGarr named an eleven-member board of directors from a list of nominees solicited by William Gibbons. The board included Gibbons; Lester Crown (Henry's son and chairman of Material Services Corporation); Thomas Ayers, the former chairman of Commonwealth Edison and the father of 1960s radical Weather Underground member William Ayers; Newton Minow, partner of Sidley & Austin in Chicago and former Federal Communications Commission chairman who famously called television "the vast wasteland"; David Murdock, billionaire investor of Pacific Holdings (who

Photo 12.2 Two Iowa Interstate diesel locomotives await their westbound train to Council Bluffs in the Rock Island's former Burr Oak Yard in Blue Island, Illinois, 1997. The bilevel commuter cars in the background are owned by Metra and operated over the former Illinois Central electric branch to Blue Island. Photograph by the author.

had purchased Rock Island stock in earnest at its low point and was one of the largest stockholders in the company by the time of its liquidation); George Jenkins, former chairman of Metropolitan Life; Paul Judy, former CEO of A. G. Becker; Neele Stearns of the Henry Crown Company; and Jackson Stuart, former chairman of Central National Chicago Corporation. On April 20, 1984, the board elected Harvey Kapnick, former CEO of Arthur Anderson, as chairman of the new company. "This is a one of the finest opportunities to build a company and mold a company that I have seen in my business career," Kapnick told the *Chicago Tribune*.[36]

Judge McGarr was universally praised for his role in shepherding the railroad toward a successful reorganization. "You resisted all pressures to depress the value of the estate," Manos told Judge McGarr while presenting to him an old locomotive bell from the Rock Island. "Now, a newly reorganized company will emerge healthy and viable, with solid prospects for the future." Judge McGarr replied, "I say goodbye to the Rock Island with a touch of sadness."[37] On June 1, 1984, the transfer of the company's assets to the new Chicago Pacific Corporation occurred. There was one hiccup: According to the reorganization plan, upon consummation $52 million would be placed in trust with Continental Bank. But that bank was insolvent due to bad investments and the failure of oil and gas leases in Texas. Gibbons worried that Continental did not have significant assets to cover the deposit and that that would place the money at risk. A solution was found to allow First National Bank of Chicago to receive the funds but allow Continental the ability to draw on them until its asset problems were resolved. Eventually, the Federal Deposit Insurance Corporation gave Continental $4.5 billion in funds to stabilize its assets, the largest federal government bailout of a banking institution until the collapse of Washington Mutual in 2008 and yet another example of the tortured history of too big to fail in the Rock Island case.[38]

Chicago Pacific Corporation had a short yet prosperous history. Its coffers filled with cash—some $300 million on top of a $300 million bank credit line all from the sale of Rock Island assets—and it was the subject of takeover rumors. Kapnick, who led the company, was former CEO of the accounting firm Arthur Anderson and a deputy chairman at First National Bank of Chicago. Born in 1925 in Michigan, Kapnick attended Cleary College in Ypsilanti before serving in the U.S. Army Air Forces in the Southwest Pacific during World War II. After the war he received an MBA from the University of Michigan and joined the Chicago office of Arthur Anderson in 1948. Kapnick rose to partner in 1956 and from 1970 to 1979 served as CEO of the firm, whose culture and organization changed during his tenure. Charged with being arrogant and having conflicts of interests, which made the Arthur Anderson board suspicious, Kapnick went to First National Bank of Chicago and worked as a consultant on the Rock Island reorganization. Friendly with the Crown family and other Rock Island interests, he was a natural fit as CEO of the new Chicago Pacific Corporation.[39]

In the fall of 1984 Kapnick and the board wanted to purchase a major industrial firm and settled on Rhode Island–based Textron Corporation, a leading conglomerate with control of Gorham Silver and Bell Helicopters, among other investments. Textron was worth more than $2 billion, and Chicago Pacific offered to purchase the outstanding common stock for $43 per share, about one-third higher than the close of $27 per share (the total package was about $1.5 billion). The media reported that the offer could set off a bidding war for Textron; other firms interested in the company included General Motors and Penn Central Corporation. Yet Textron balked and said the offer was "unsolicited" and that the firm was not interested.[40] Kapnick said that "Textron was an ideal core by which to build a great industrial company." Chicago Pacific controlled only 1 percent of Textron's stock yet insisted it did not want a hostile takeover of the company.[41] A few days later,

Textron's board turned down the offer, believing the offer was not substantive enough and that Chicago Pacific did not have the means to acquire the company.⁴²

Thwarted by Textron, Kapnick in 1985 acquired Hoover Corporation, manufacturer of vacuum cleaners and other home appliances, for $700 million. It also acquired Rowenta A.G., a West German manufacturer of small appliances. These acquisitions, along with the continued rail asset disposition program and liquidation and sale of Rock Island properties (headed up by Richard Lane and Steve Crown, the grandson of Henry Crown), were the major activities of the company throughout the mid-1980s. With the purchase of major commercial appliance producers, Chicago Pacific's stock soared and the company's future seemed bright. The purchase of Hoover proved especially wise, as its operating income rose 20 percent in a year after its purchase and its corporate profits rose 32 percent by 1988.⁴³

Consumer products turned out to be frustrating investments, linked to high material costs and the whims of consumer demand. The industry had become intensely competitive, with fewer larger firms dominating production and sales. With mergers and fears of takeovers in the appliance-manufacturing sector, major companies, such as Maytag, looked to take over smaller makers. In 1986, Maytag took over Magic Chef, buying out yet another appliance brand. But Maytag eyed the Hoover Company, which had larger market share abroad than in the United States. Out of concern that Maytag might be taken over by a rival firm, CEO Daniel Krumm made a $1 billion bid for Hoover and Chicago Pacific Corporation in 1988.⁴⁴ After brief negotiations, Maytag finalized a deal to purchase Chicago Pacific and its appliance brands for $961 million. The Crown family controlled 15 percent of Maytag's stock after the sale, and other shareholders saw their investments in Chicago Pacific pay out handsomely. With that single purchase, the Rock Island Railroad, and its successor corporation, ceased to exist. With perhaps a little irony, yet with tremendous satisfaction, the Maytag Corporation's headquarters was in Newton, Iowa, on the east-west mainline of the former Chicago, Rock Island and Pacific Railroad Company. The Rock Island story could not have had a better ending.

Today, the Rock Island lives not only in memory but also as an operating railroad throughout most of the territory it once served. In many Midwestern states, one can still find traces of the Rock Island. Hundreds of depots bearing the distinctive Rock Island logo or the "bankruptcy blue" Rock logo stand throughout the Midwest. Many have been put to use as restaurants and new businesses; some continue as operating points or crew headquarters; many sit neglected and abandoned. Close to 5,000 miles of former Rock Island track is still in operation by other railroads. Many important segments of the former line, including the mainline from Chicago to Council Bluffs (still operated and owned by Metra, CSX Corporation, and the Iowa Interstate Railroad), the spine line from the Twin Cities to Kansas City, and the former Katy line from Herington to North Fort Worth, remain key operating segments to this day (now operated by the Union Pacific Railroad).

The Rock Island's core line, proposed in the reorganization plan devised by Gibbons in December 1980, remains one of the principal operating segments of the former Rock Island. The Iowa Interstate Railroad operates the line from Utica (using trackage rights over the CSX New Rock subdivision and Metra to reach the Chicago yard at Blue Island, Illinois) west to Council Bluffs. The Union Pacific operates the former Rock Island (and former C&NW) from St. Paul to Kansas City. The two railroads bypass and connect at Des Moines, the same proposed junction for the core railroad as proposed by Gibbons.

The Iowa Interstate Railroad is possibly the most beloved and successful of all former Rock Island properties, with its distinctive black, crimson, and yellow locomotives emblazoned with the former Rock Island herald on the front, drawing railfans and photographers trackside. The railroad embraces passenger specials, including the use of a Chinese-built Mikado steam engine, and there is talk of resuming passenger operations on the line with state-subsidized Amtrak service between Chicago and Iowa City. The current chairman of the railroad and president of Rail Development Corporation, Henry Posner III, told an audience in Cedar Rapids in 2012 that the Iowa Interstate "[was] in essence the unloved, unwanted, bastard stepchild of deregulation . . . but we are quite proud of that." Unlike the Rock Island Railroad, "We do not compete with the Union Pacific or BNSF for traffic between Omaha and Chicago; we survive on our local territory, which is Iowa and western Illinois. We have virtually no overhead business and, in fact, we are nothing more than a feeder railroad that connects to railroads east and west of us."[45]

What the Iowa Interstate Railroad did have along its property was plentiful corn, and the emergence of the ethanol boom in the late 1990s and into the first decade of the twenty-first century—what Fred Frailey referred to in an article on the railroad in *Trains* magazine as luck—helped the railroad attain a profitable balance sheet for the first time in 1999. Ethanol made up 25 percent of the railroad's carloads in 2011, and as long as demand for the fuel (and the federal subsidies to pay for it) remains strong, the Iowa Interstate will prosper. However, corn ethanol is a poor and inefficient substitute for regular gasoline, and it has led to the marked increase of corn prices, with detrimental impacts on the world's poorest populations who relied on cheap exports of corn for human consumption and animal feed. Even with hefty federal subsidies, the price of ethanol is not substantially less than gasoline.[46] The recent discovery of shale oil in the Bakken Oil Fields in North Dakota, and the technology available to extract oil from shale, may hurt the Iowa Interstate competitively if it relies too much on ethanol shipments as the basis for its revenue.[47]

But the railroad is scrappy and is trying to balance its shipments of commodities to handle downturns in any single commodity it ships. When former owner Maytag Corporation was purchased by Whirlpool in 2006, and the new company moved its production and corporate headquarters out of Newton, the railroad did not suffer. Instead it sought other business, continuing to develop shipments of grain, corn syrup, and other products produced by Archer Daniels Midland (ADM), which by the late 1990s was the largest shareholder in the Iowa Interstate. The railroad served ADM's huge processing plant at Cedar Rapids over trackage rights granted by the Cedar Rapids and Iowa City Railway (CRANDIC). Even after a two-and-a-half-year battle for stock control of the Iowa Interstate Railroad by Heartland successor Rail Development Corporation and ADM occurred, it did not impact traffic over the railroad, as ADM needed the Iowa Interstate to continue service of its facility.[48]

While the Iowa Interstate is profitable and well managed, its carloads reveal the true problem with the claim of the Trustee in 1980 that by the mid-1980s the core of the Rock Island would be hauling over 400,000 carloads per year. While carloads have grown substantially on the railroad from 1984 until the present day, the Iowa Interstate hauled only 120,000 carloads in 2011, a substantial number for a smaller regional railroad—but nowhere near the optimistic projections made by the Trustee in 1980. With growing demand for its production of corn, wheat, feed, ethanol, industrial products, and other resources in the communities it serves, Iowa Interstate remains a very important link in the former Rock Island properties, one that shippers rely on (as much as denying Union Pacific total monopoly over central Iowa shipping) and one that has pleased railfans, constituents in Iowa, and the business community it serves. It continues to fly the flag of the Rock Island and, perhaps, showcase what would have happened to the Rock if it had survived past 1980. There is even some talk of restoring passenger service between Chicago and Iowa City (and eventually on to Des Moines), but a financial crisis in the State of Illinois may make funding for the project scarce. Time will tell.

The Rock Island lives on. At harvest time it is not uncommon to find dozens of faded-blue Rock Island hopper cars at grain elevators throughout the Midwest, or to see them in passing freight trains. These were the same cars the Trustee purchased in 1977, which were later sold to the C&NW, and are still in use today. Metra, the commuter-rail operator for the RTA, calls its southwest suburban district the Rock Island District in tribute to its former owner. The Iowa Interstate Railroad and Iowa Northern Railroad have paid homage by painting locomotives in Rock Island color schemes. Daniel Sabin, president of the Iowa Northern, which operates former Rock Island grain branches in northern Iowa (between Cedar Rapids and Mason City, Iowa), has purchased two former Rock Island EMD E units (including the Rock's former bicentennial locomotive and the fabled E-6, the last such locomotive in active railroad service) and plans to restore them for service on special trains running on the Iowa Northern. These are just some of the ways the Rock Island lives, not only as memory but also in the truest sense of carrying on the legacy of John Dow Farrington and the high hopes he possessed for a railroad emerging from bankruptcy in 1948—a legacy of planned progress and of service and standards that once shaped modern railroading.

CONCLUSION

Why did the Rock Island collapse? For railfans, shippers, and former employees of the railroad, it is a question that has grown in importance in the years since 1980, especially as they see other railroads operating successfully on former Rock Island property. Many railfans have blamed specific individuals for the railroad's collapse. Among the culprits are Judge Frank McGarr, Henry Crown, John Ingram, and William Gibbons. Fred Frailey, a columnist for *Trains* magazine, wrote in 2011: "The fact that the railroad was dissolved by a bankruptcy judge but flourishes today under different owners, suggests [the Rock Island] wasn't redundant."[1] Henry Crown also has received plenty of invective for failing to invest more money into the railroad and for his interest in securing his money from it, sacrificing the continued operation of the railroad selfishly in favor of personal greed.[2] John Ingram and Gibbons have received a lot of blame as well, even though they fought hard to keep the railroad operating through the late 1970s.

The story of the railroad's collapse, as this book has shown, is much more complex. The blame rests not with any single individual, judge, or group of bondholders or stockholders. The demise and ultimate collapse of the Rock Island is part of a wider history of why the railroad industry generally, and this one railroad specifically, fell on hard times by the 1970s.

If one must assess blame for the collapse of the Rock Island, then the federal government deserves a lot of the responsibility for the Rock's demise—as well as for the weakness of the railroad industry from the end of World War II until the 1980s. Regulation was the major culprit. This is not to castigate the men and women who worked for the Interstate Commerce Commission and the jobs they performed during the era of regulation. Rather, it is to recognize that the regulation of railroads prevented innovation, hindered capital acquisition, and favored not only shippers but also other forms of transportation outside the scope of regulation (such as rural truckers). In post–World War II America, railroads were also hurt by taxation of property and real estate while their competitors were able to travel on government-subsidized highways and airports without the necessity of paying taxes to fund them (with the exception of gasoline taxes).

Specific government agencies hurt the Rock Island's efforts to improve its competitive posture. The ICC was one of the major obstacles, taking an astounding eleven years to decide the Union Pacific–Rock Island merger case. During the early 1970s, other government agencies, from the Department of Transportation to the newly created Federal Railroad Administration, also hindered Rock Island's efforts to rehabilitate its plant and equipment. After the Rock Island entered bankruptcy, federal agencies continued to refuse assistance to the Trustee while spending billions of dollars of taxpayer money on Conrail. After the railroad was ordered to be liquidated, Congress hindered the Rock Island's reorganization and liquidation by laws such as the Rock Island Transition Act, and by amendment to that law, designed to place labor protections on the estate and to allow the ICC a role in evaluating the railroad's property. Without a doubt, the federal government played the largest role in the collapse of the Rock Island.

The railroad industry itself, and rival railroads operating in the western territory, also contributed to the collapse of the Rock Island. Railroads could not reach an agreement on the Rock Island–UP merger in a manner that would have achieved a workable consensus for all parties. Their indifference and even hostility to do so forced the ICC and Nathan Klitenic to redraw the western railroad map—and still the rival railroads were unsatisfied with the results. The intervention by twelve railroads against the merger helped kill the Rock Island as a corporation and allowed the railroads that survived—especially its long rival, the Chicago and North Western Railway—to benefit by eventually picking off its lines. That was certainly the strategy followed by C&NW chairman Ben Heineman, who succeeded in his long guerrilla campaign against the merger of the two railroads. The C&NW survived and prospered until it was acquired by the Union Pacific itself in 1996. If one insists on blaming the Rock Island's collapse on one individual, that person should be Ben Heineman, not Henry Crown, John Ingram, William Gibbons, or Judge McGarr.

Organized labor must also receive part of the blame for the railroad industry's problems. Labor unions refused to negotiate new work-rule agreements that would have spared railroads massive increases in wages, allowed for increased productivity, and protected jobs. Labor received substantial wage increases during a time of high inflation, but the increased wages without concomitant changes in work rules threatened railroads' profitability. Unions did not believe the railroads were as poor as their executives claimed during this period, leading to a showdown that ultimately led to a weakening of organized labor on the railroads.

Fred Kroll of the Brotherhood of Railway and Airline Clerks was a young labor insurgent. His union's strike against the Norfolk and Western in 1978 brought him to national attention, but the strike failed and the N&W survived. His union's strike against the Rock Island in August 1979, joined by the United Transportation Union, was the death knell for the Rock Island, but also wound up costing his membership quite a bit as well. Why did BRAC and UTU strike the Rock Island? Labor had possessed tremendous clout with Congress and with Democratic presidents in the post–World War II era. Labor leaders gambled that, in the end, the Rock Island would be bailed out by government. Why wouldn't Congress provide the same bailout of the Rock Island as it had arranged for Conrail? By rolling the dice in an era of growing fiscal conservatism and stymied economic growth, rank-and-file workers suffered from the capriciousness of their leaders in organized labor. On the Rock Island, they were subsequently denied labor protection, and many lost their jobs within the railroad industry. The shift to deregulation and the changes in technology reduced railroad workforces even more.

Perhaps the biggest reason for the Rock Island's collapse are the changes in transportation and in the railroad industry: shifts in technology, demographics, communications, and government relations with business. The Rock Island's problems began as early as the recession of 1958, when Downing Jenks and the company's board of directors slashed maintenance of the railroad's property to save money. That determination was the beginning of the long decline of the railroad property. Demographics also played a crucial role in the demise of the Rock Island, as the territory it served relied heavily on agricultural commodities and served a declining population. It lacked major industries on most of its lines, and with the changing demographics and shift of population away from the Midwest the Rock Island could not have long survived. The demise of passenger trains, the growth of suburbs, and the improved highways and infrastructure of modern American cities—all of these changes (though outside the scope of the story of the Rock Island railroad itself) help explain the demise of the railroad industry during the twentieth century.

By arguing that these factors were more crucial than individuals in the demise of the Rock Island does not mean that individuals were blameless. Individual and management decisions, such as the refusal of the Rock Island board of directors to maintain the property after the start of merger proceedings with the UP, left the railroad vulnerable once that merger fell apart. If the board had instead invested in the property (and probably still combined with a major railroad), it may have averted bankruptcy. Yet, as has been shown here, there were ample reasons why the Rock Island could *not* invest heavily in maintenance: declining carloads, higher costs from labor and government regulation, passenger-train losses, depleted working capital, and the inability to speedily abandon branchlines and other money-losing lines and trains. All of these issues are tied into the failure of government to loosen its grip on the industry; when it finally did, it was too late for the Rock Island.

The years since the collapse of the Rock Island have seen a remarkable turnaround in the fortunes of the railroad industry. The partial deregulation of the industry with the passage of the Staggers Rail Act led to deceasing rates for shippers, with coal and grain shippers receiving tremendous rate decreases; the development of shipping contracts, which has allowed for the flourishing of unit trains and contracts between shipping companies (such as United Parcel Service) and railroads; and an improvement in railroad revenues per ton-mile. Railroads are once again attractive investments, and the industry is profitable and strong.

The collapse of the Penn Central Transportation Company and the creation of Conrail prodded government and railroads to find a way to keep the industry alive in the 1970s. But that method—a form of nationalization—failed miserably and was not attempted after both the Rock Island and the Milwaukee Road sought bankruptcy protection in federal court. Instead, politicians in the White House and Congress, seeing the lessons of nationalization with Conrail, sought a private-sector solution, which led to deregulation in 1980. This is not to argue that the Rock Island bankruptcy was necessary for deregulation, but it was a sufficient cause to help bring it about.

It was this private-sector solution to the railroad problem—wisely embraced by Jimmy Carter, Secretary of Transportation Brock Adams, and a Democratic Congress and promoted by the railroad industry trade group, the Association of American Railroads—that rejuvenated the industry. By speeding up mergers and abandonments, restricting the power of the Interstate Commerce Commission so that another Rock Island–Union Pacific merger imbroglio could not be repeated, and by finally embracing the rationalization of rail lines suggested in the Transportation Act of 1920, the industry produced leaner, wealthier railroads serving vital transportation corridors, making American freight railroading the envy of the world.

Not everything has been so rosy. The reduction in track and service to mainly rural towns and cities throughout America's heartland led to a continued reduction in population and service in states where railroads like the Rock Island operated. The Rock Island's Choctaw Route through Oklahoma and Arkansas was largely abandoned, for instance, negating a terrific opportunity for industrial development in this region. Abandonments of branchlines led to more trucks on the road as railroads looked toward profitable contracts with major shippers rather than smaller shippers in rural areas, typically leaving them to rely on trucks or shortline railroads. Service has often been compromised for profits as larger railroads no longer seem to care about smaller shippers in their pursuit of major contracts that they can now negotiate themselves. This situation has led shippers to seek new forms of regulation on railroads. Railroads today often seem to be mainline superhighways without off-ramps, the branches that acted as arteries for the rail network. Congress, sympathetic to the concerns of rural shippers and small businesses, one day may be willing to consider reregulating the railroads.

In the end, the Rock Island's collapse is an instructive tale about the weakening and revitalization of an important industry in American history. It also encapsulates the story of how government and business operate in the mixed economy, and how too much government intervention, in the case of stifling regulation, hindered private-sector railroads from innovations that could have alleviated many of their problems. While the Rock Island story, both in its bankruptcy and in its liquidation, seems so "old economy," in that it is a story lacking in the catalog of high finance we take for granted today—no junk bonds, collateralized debt obligations (CDOs), derivatives, or other complex financial instruments—it is instructive to remember that the firm that reemerged from the railroad's ashes was an investment firm, no longer involved in the transportation industry and no longer employing tens of thousands of workers.[3] Chicago Pacific Corporation, similar to the Penn Central Corporation, which emerged from the bankruptcy of that railroad, was a hugely profitable investment firm, better related to the new finance economy of junk bonds, CDOs, and derivatives on Wall Street than cabooses, passenger trains, and classification yards on Railroad Avenue. While the bankruptcy and corporate liquidation of the Rock Island proved beneficial for its shareholders and bondholders, it did not enrich the thousands of workers and dozens of rural communities that lost jobs and rail service as a result.

If viewed in a purely Schumpterian—and rather heartless—manner, this is the way the economic cookie crumbles. Businesses come and go, and there is little that can be done to prevent major shifts in economic systems or minor ones in corporate collapses or successes. This is the creative destruction on which the story of capitalism depends. The history of the Rock Island's collapse, therefore, remains an instructive lesson from a not-too-distant past with continued implications for the American economy's future. The failure of regulation in the railroad industry and the culture of too big to fail (and too small to succeed) that developed out of regulatory failure in the case of the Rock Island provide a crucial historical barometer for many of the economic problems facing the nation in contemporary times.

NOTES

Introduction

1. Michael J. de la Merced and Andrew Ross Sorkin, "Buffett Bets Big on Railroad's Future," *New York Times* (November 4, 2009), p. A1; Scott Patterson and Douglas A. Blackmon, "Buffet Bets Big on Railroad," *Wall Street Journal* (November 4, 2009), p. A1.

2. For a good summary of regulation in the twentieth century, see Mark H. Rose, Bruce E. Seely, and Paul F. Barrett, *The Best Transportation System in the World: Railroads, Trucks, Airlines, and American Public Policy in the Twentieth Century* (Philadelphia: University of Pennsylvania Press, 2010 [orig. pub. Columbus: Ohio State University Press, 2006]). See also Richard D. Stone, *The Interstate Commerce Commission and the Railroad Industry: A History of Regulatory Policy* (New York: Praeger, 1991), for an analysis of the ICC since 1976 and the impact of Staggers on the industry.

3. Under the law railroads were common carriers and had to continue operating until the ICC approved abandonment or embargo of a line.

4. Association of American Railroads, "The Staggers Act: Balanced Regulation That Works" (June 2009), p. 1. AAR data shows that "freight railroads re-invested some $440 billion back into their operations from 1980–2008."

5. Union Pacific Railroad, "Railroad Reregulation Update," 2006, copy in author's possession. For the 1970 figure, see *The American Railroad Industry: A Prospectus* (Washington, D.C., America's Sound Transportation Review Organization, 1970), p. 6 (known as the ASTRO Report), in Judith R. Hope Files (Domestic Council), Box 42 (Union Pacific), Gerald R. Ford Presidential Library, Ann Arbor, Michigan (hereafter Ford Presidential Papers).

6. For an excellent study of the impact of how this shedding of railroad mileage impacted communities, see Joseph P. Schwieterman, *When the Railroad Leaves Town: American Communities in the Age of Rail Line Abandonment, Volume 1: Eastern United States* and *Volume 2: Western United States* (Kirksville, Mo.: Truman State University Press, 2001 and 2004).

7. Michael W. Blaszak, "Free to Compete," *Trains* (October 2010): 25–33.

8. Fred W. Frailey, "Powder River Stories," *Trains* special issue: Coal (July 2010), pp. 41–49.

9. The Transportation Act of 1920 stipulated that the ICC undertake a rationalization project to bring about a reordering of the railroad system in the United States. See Rose, et al., *The Best Transportation System*, pp. 100, 101.

10. In 1979 there were fifty-eight Class I railroads defined by the ICC at the time (railroads with annual revenues above $50 million). Inflation has driven up the rev-

enue estimates; in 1939 there were 132 Class I railroads recognized by the ICC, with annual revenues of $1 million needed to qualify.

11. John P. Hoerr, *And the Wolf Finally Came: The Decline and Fall of the American Steel Industry* (Pittsburgh: Pittsburgh University Press, 1988); Jefferson Cowie, *Stayin' Alive: The 1970s and the Last Days of the Working Class* (New York: New Press, 2010).

12. Neil A. Hurl, *The Farm Debt Crisis of the 1980s* (Ames: Iowa State University Press, 1990); W. Carl Bliven, *Jimmy Carter's Economy: Policy in an Age of Limits* (Chapel Hill: University of North Carolina Press, 2001).

13. Brian Domitrovic, *Econoclasts: The Rebels Who Sparked the Supply-Side Revolution and Restored America's Prosperity* (Wilmington, Del.: ISI Books, 2009), p. 5.

14. Robert J. Samuelson, *The Great Inflation and Its Aftermath: The Past and Future of American Affluence* (New York: Random House, 2008); Robert M. Collins, *More: The Politics of Economic Growth in Postwar America* (New York: Oxford University Press, 2000); Robert Bartley, *The Seven Fat Years and How to Do It Again* (New York: Free Press, 1992); and Judith Stein, *Pivotal Decade: How the United States Traded Factories for Finance in the Seventies* (New Haven: Yale University Press, 2010).

15. See Kim Phillips-Fein, *Invisible Hands: The Businessman's Crusade Against the New Deal* (New York: W. W. Norton, 2010); Bethany Moreton, *To Serve God and Walmart: The Making of Christian Free Enterprise* (Cambridge: Harvard University Press, 2009); Shane Hamilton, *Trucking Country: The Road to America's Wal-Mart Economy* (Princeton: Princeton University Press, 2009); Stein, *Pivotal Decade*; Eduardo Canedo, "The Rise of the Deregulation Movement in Modern America, 1957–1980" (Ph.D. diss., Columbia University, 2009).

16. Philip J. Cooper, *The War Against Regulation: From Jimmy Carter to George W. Bush* (Lawrence: University Press of Kansas, 2009), 227. A counter to the idea of deregulation representing a war between competing political interests can be found in Marc Allen Eisner, *Regulatory Politics in Transition*, 2nd ed. (Baltimore: Johns Hopkins University Press, 2000). Eisner looks at the development of regulatory regimes throughout the twentieth century, focusing on how the New Deal–era regime developed and then collapsed, replaced by social regulatory regime (safety, health, environment) and how that regime has been challenged by a new globalization regulatory regime. In this context, the changes are products of political discussion, changes in analysis, new ideas entering the system, and the role of elite policymakers. It is not a war over regulation versus deregulation, but rather a process of historical change within the construct of state-centered policymaking.

Chapter 1. A Mighty Fine Line

1. William Edward Hayes, *Iron Road to Empire: The History of 100 Years of Progress and Achievements on the Rock Island Lines* (Omaha: Simmons-Boardman, 1953), 235–237. Hayes's book was a centennial history of the railroad written as a corporate history. Hayes was an employee in the Rock Island's publicity department at the time.

2. Lloyd E. Stagner, "In 4-8-4's, If Not in Finances, the Rock Island Excelled," *Trains* (March 1981), 22–30. On steam locomotives the number (4-8-4) refers to wheels on the axles, in this case two axles on the front, four in the middle, and two on the rear. The Rock Island owned eighty-five 4-8-4 locomotives by the time they were retired in 1954.

3. Trustee certificates are monies available from government to bankrupt railroads to purchase equipment and to operate a railroad in bankruptcy. The government becomes a lienholder on the property, and its loans have first claims in railroad reorganization. During the 1930s railroads secured loans and operating capital from the Reconstruction Finance Corporation (RFC), created under President Herbert Hoover in 1930.

4. An ad for the fair can be found in John Kelly, *Rock Island Railroad Photo Archive: Travel on the Rockets* (Hudson, Wis.: Iconographix, 2010), 85–87.

5. Hayes, *Iron Road to Empire*, 239–241. The Rockets were doing so well that they earned $16,654,673, for an average of $2.73 per mile. See *Trains* (May 1948): 4.

6. Hugh Hawkins, *Railwayman's Son: A Plains Family Memoir* (Lubbock: Texas Tech University Press, 2006), p. xix.

7. Hayes, *Iron Road to Empire*, 244–246.

8. Willard V. Anderson, "Rebirth of a Railroad," *Trains* (December 1947): 22–29.

9. Hayes, *Iron Road to Empire*, 235–237. See also Dan Butler, "John D. Farrington," in Keith L. Bryant Jr., ed., *Railroads in the Age of Regulation, 1900–1980: Encyclopedia of American Business History and Biography* (New York: Facts on File, 1988), pp. 140–142. See also, "Rock Island Has New Chief of Operations," *Chicago Daily Tribune* (May 1, 1936), p. 35.

10. "Bondholders Ask Trustee for Rock Island," *Chicago Daily Tribune* (October 25, 1933), p. 27.

11. James Stuart Olson, *Herbert Hoover and the Reconstruction Finance Corporation* (Ames: Iowa State University Press, 1977), remains the standard work on the RFC.

12. See John F. Stover, *American Railroads*, 2nd ed. (Chicago: University of Chicago Press, 1997), p. 200; Rose, et al., *The Best Transportation System*, pp. 56–63. An admiring biography of Eastman is Claude Moore Fuess, *Joseph B. Eastman: A Study in Public Service* (New York: Columbia University Press, 1952).

13. Bankruptcy Act of 1933, Section 77, 72nd Congress (H.R. 14359). See Lloyd K. Garrison, "Reorganization of Railroads Under the Bankruptcy Act," *University of Chicago Law Review* 1, no. 1 (May 1933): 71–81.

14. "Rock Island Plan Impractible, I.C.C. Declares in Ruling," *Chicago Daily Tribune*, December 11, 1935, p. 31.

15. Hayes, *Iron Road to Empire*, pp. 227–228.

16. "Rock Island Defeats RFC on Attorney," *Chicago Daily Tribune*, February 21, 1935, p. 23.

17. "Bars RFC Sale of Rock Island Loan Security," *Chicago Daily Tribune*, April 2, 1935, p. 25.

18. Hayes, *Iron Road to Empire*, pp. 225–229.

19. "RFC's Punishment of Rock Island May End, Jones Indicates," *Chicago Daily Tribune*, August 2, 1935, p. 29.

20. The Trustees met twice a year with the creditor interests to keep them informed

about the progress on the railroad. There, Trustees reported on progress the railroad was making on rebuilding and rehabilitating the property, including the impact of some New Deal programs on labor issues and pensions. For an example of the meetings, see Luncheon Meeting Minutes, Rock Island Trustees, October 6, 1937, Box 493, Chicago, Rock Island and Pacific Railroad Collection (hereafter CRIP), Western History Collections, University of Oklahoma.

21. "James Gorman, Rock Island Railroad's Head, Dies at 78," *Chicago Daily Tribune*, March 26, 1942, p. 28.

22. Hayes, *Iron Road to Empire*, pp. 247–251.

23. "Rock Island's Reorganizing Plan Approved," *Chicago Daily Tribune*, May 15, 1945, p. 21.

24. "Court Upholds Rock Island's Reorganizing," *Chicago Daily Tribune*, May 24, 1946, p. 33.

25. "Rock Island's Plan Returned to ICC by Igoe," *Chicago Daily Tribune*, June 29, 1946, p. 19.

26. Modification of Railroad Financial Structures, Hearings Before the Committee on Interstate Commerce, United States Senate, 79th Congress, S. 1253 (Washington, D.C.: GPO, 1946).

27. Hayes, *Iron Road to Empire*, 264–265. See Joseph Borkin, *Robert R. Young: The Populist of Wall Street* (New York: Harper and Row, 1969); and Herbert Harwood Jr., *Invisible Giants: The Van Sweringen Brothers of Cleveland* (Bloomington: Indiana University Press, 2003). The Alleghany Corporation was a holding company Young purchased after the deaths of the Van Sweringen brothers in 1932 and 1933, paying $3.5 million to control a variety of railroad interests, including the bankrupt Missouri Pacific, a valuable property.

28. Harry Truman, Memorandum of Disapproval, August 1946, White House Central Files, Official, Box 974 (OF 231 Bankruptcy 1), Folder 1, Harry Truman Presidential Library, Independence, Missouri.

29. "Offers Plan to Slash Debt on Rock Island," *Chicago Daily Tribune*, October 1, 1946, p. 29.

30. "Igoe Approves Colnon's Plan on Rock Island," *Chicago Daily Tribune*, November 23, 1946, p. 23.

31. "Appeals Heard in Rock Island Railroad Case," *Chicago Daily Tribune*, January 31, 1947, p. 27.

32. The best source on Robert Young is Borkin's *Robert Young*. Strangely, Borkin's biography makes no mention of the Rock Island purchases. His book is focused mainly on Young's proxy fight for control of the New York Central System, which Young initiated in 1951. His interest in the Rock Island was widely reported. "Young Boosts His Holdings in Rock Island," *Chicago Daily Tribune*, February 3, 1947, p. 31.

33. "Rock Island's Plan Ordered Put in Effect," *Chicago Daily Tribune*, February 22, 1947, p. 21.

34. "Delay Sought in Rock Island Reorganizing," *Chicago Daily Tribune*, May 3, 1947, p. 22.

35. "Judge Rips Lawyers in Rail Hearing," *Chicago Daily Tribune*, May 7, 1947, p. 39.

36. *Chicago Daily Tribune*, May 24, 1947, p. 19 (for the quotes). Hayes, *Iron*

Road to Empire, at p. 273, contains a similar narrative with a few changes in detail. According to Hayes, Bourne collected the $100 from attendees. There are some differences in quoted comments as well. I have chosen to use the quotes from the newspaper, which reflects the direct quotes from the day's events rather than Hayes's recounting (with no source listed).

37. "Appeals Court Studies Writ in Igoe Dispute," *Chicago Daily Tribune*, May 30, 1947, p. 24.

38. "Court Annuls Igoe's Plan on Rock Island," *Chicago Daily Tribune*, June 10, 1947, p. 43; Hayes, *Iron Road to Empire*, p. 276.

39. "Doubts Power to Act in Rock Island Case," *Chicago Daily Tribune*, June 12, 1947, p. 39.

40. "Igoe to Remain in Rock Island Railroad Case," *Chicago Daily Tribune*, June 21, 1947, p. 21.

41. Hayes, *Iron Road to Empire*, pp. 269–276.

42. Ibid., pp. 277–278.

43. "State of Texas Participates in Railroad Case," *Chicago Daily Tribune*, November 13, 1947, p. 41.

44. "Rail Ends 14 Years as Bankrupt," *Chicago Daily Tribune*, December 31, 1947, p. 17.

45. Hayes, *Iron Road to Empire*, pp. 278–280.

46. The Rock Island and Nickel Plate Railroad advertised a distribution center and other properties available in the Calumet Industrial District of Chicago on the South Side through the Calumet Industrial District Property Company. Pamphlet for the Calumet Industrial District (n.d.) (author's collection). The Rock Island board of directors authorized Farrington to purchase the property for no more than $2.5 million. Minutes of the Board of Directors, August 9, 1948, Box 60, CRIP.

47. Hayes, *Iron Road to Empire*, pp. 280–284. Highlights of the achievements can be found in *Rock Island Annual Report* (December 31, 1949), pp. 3–14 (author's collection).

48. In 1948 the Rock Island board approved the acquisition of twenty-eight diesel locomotives, new commuter cars, and an additional $8 million on improvements throughout the system. Minutes of Board of Directors, February 9, 1948, Box 60, CRIP.

49. Hayes, *Iron Road to Empire*, p. 281.

50. John Chi-Kit Wong, *Lords of the Rink: The Emergence of the National Hockey League, 1875–1936* (Toronto: University of Toronto Press, 2005); see also "Jim Norris, Wealthy and Rarely Quoted, Sports' Controversial, Versatile Figure," *Chicago Daily Tribune*, March 6, 1955, p. A3.

51. See Henry Mark Petrakis and David B. Weber, *Henry Crown: The Life and Times of the Colonel, Book One* (Chicago: Henry Crown Company, 1998), pp. 1–11.

52. Ibid., pp. 12–37.

53. Ibid., pp. 38–69.

54. Ibid., pp. 71–74, 95.

55. Ibid., pp. 103–117; Henry Mark Petrakis and David B. Weber, *Henry Crown: The Life and Times of the Colonel, Book Two* (Chicago: Henry Crown Company, 1998), p. 27.

56. Petrakis and Weber, *Henry Crown: Book Two*, pp. 27–29, 65. See "Midwest

Midas," *Time* (November 3, 1952). Crown continued to be a savvy investor, buying the Waldorf-Astoria, the Empire State Building, and defense contractor General Dynamics. He sold the Empire State Building in 1958 for a handsome profit and concentrated his empire on Material Services Corporation, General Dynamics, and railroads.

57. *Rock Island Annual Report*, December 31, 1948, p. 4.

58. *Rock Island Annual Report*, December 31, 1957, p. 7 (author's collection).

59. Testimony of Paul C. Major, Vice President—Finance, before the Interstate Commerce Commission, Finance Docket No. 23286, 1965, page 2, Box 135, CRIP.

60. Major Testimony, CRIP, pp. 4–5, 7.

61. Testimony of James Symes, President of The Pennsylvania Railroad Company to Surface Transportation Subcommittee of the Senate Interstate and Foreign Commerce Committee, January 17, 1958, p. 2, Box 23, Folder 2 (Transportation-2), Philip Areeda Papers, Dwight D. Eisenhower Presidential Library (hereafter DDE Library).

62. The figure of $500 million for the two railroads is from Rush Loving Jr., *The Men Who Loved Trains: The Story of Men Who Battled Greed to Save an Industry* (Bloomington: Indiana University Press, 2006), pp. 46–47; the Pennsylvania figure is from Symes testimony, p. 4.

63. Rose, et al., in *The Best Transportation System in the World*, pp. 97–100, provide a useful discussion of Eisenhower's goals.

64. Statement of Sinclair Weeks before the Subcommittee of Transportation and Communications, House Committee on Interstate and Foreign Commerce, April 21, 1956, Gerald D. Morgan Records, Box 28 (Transportation Policy—I), DDE Library, p. 5.

65. *Wall Street Journal* (April 19, 1955). See Rose, et al., *The Best Transportation System in the World*, pp. 100–102. The Weeks report had a greater impact on trucking, which began the twenty year effort to end government regulation of the trucking industry. Shane Hamilton, *Trucking Country: The Road to America's Wal-Mart Economy* (Princeton: Princeton University Press, 2008).

66. Hamilton, *Trucking Country*, p. 131.

67. Weeks statement, pp. 6–7.

68. Rose, et al., *The Best Transportation System in the World*, p. 122. See also H. Roger Grant, *North Western: A History of the Chicago and North Western Railway System* (DeKalb: Northern Illinois University Press, 1996), p. 195. For a story on early piggyback innovations, see John S. Gallagher Jr., "Even Highway Trailers Are Going by Rail," *Trains and Travel* (August 1952): 24–27.

69. Craig Miner, "Downing B. Jenks," in Keith L. Bryant Jr., ed., *Railroads in the Age of Regulation, 1900–1980: Encyclopedia of American Business History and Biography* (New York: Facts on File, 1988), pp. 235–239.

70. Ibid., p. 235; *Time* (December 26, 1955).

71. *Rock Island Annual Report 1957*, pp. 4–6.

72. *Rock Island Railroad Annual Report 1958* (copy in author's possession), p. 20. The railroad's ICC Annual Reports show the declining numbers when it came to maintenance of the property. The average number of ties replaced during the 1950s was around 550,000 per year. After the recession, the railroad had difficulty keeping up with that maintenance, averaging about 350,000 ties replaced throughout the 1960s. See ICC Annual Reports, Box 43, CRIP. I am indebted to John Rebensdorf,

former vice president of strategic planning with the Union Pacific Railroad, for pointing out the beginnings of maintenance neglect on the Rock Island. Rebensdorf worked for the Rock Island in the early 1960s.

73. Senate Subcommittee Hearings on the Deteriorating Railroad Situation, Association of American Railroads (January 1958), p. 4, DDE Library.

74. Letter from James Symes to Gabriel Hauge, January 11, 1958, and testimony before Senate Subcommittee, Box 23, Folder 2 (Transportation, 2), Philip Areeda Papers, DDE Library. In his prepared remarks Symes asked: "What is the real railroad problem? The trouble begins by Government—Federal, state and local—treating the railroad industry as if it were still the wealthy monopoly it was generations ago."

75. Senate Subcommittee Hearings on the Deteriorating Railroad Situation, DDE Library, pp. 22–23 (Jenks).

76. "What Railroads Urge to Keep from Going Broke," *U.S. News and World Report* (January 19, 1958), p. 111.

77. Richard Saunders Jr., *Merging Lines: American Railroads, 1900–1970* (DeKalb: Northern Illinois University Press, 2001), 122–124.

78. Report of the Transportation Study Group, March 15, 1958, White House Central Files, Official File, Box 810 (150-2), DDE Library.

79. *Fortune* (August 1960): 141.

80. Dan Cordtz, "The Fight for the Rock Island," *Fortune* (June 1966): 143.

81. Louis Dombrowski, "Two Rails to Consider Merging," *Chicago Daily Tribune*, November 10, 1959, p. D1.

82. Executive Committee Meeting, Rock Island Board of Directors, February 12, 1960, Box 63, CRIP.

83. Executive Committee Meeting, Minutes, Rock Island Board of Directors, October 10, 1960, p. 12, Box 63, CRIP.

84. Cordtz, "The Battle for the Rock Island," p. 200.

85. Craig Miner, *The Rebirth of the Missouri Pacific, 1956–1983* (College Station: Texas A&M University Press, 1983), pp. 48–49.

86. "Jenks of Rock Island in Line for Mopac Job," *Chicago Daily Tribune*, December 14, 1960, p. C7.

87. Letter from John Dow Farrington to RI Board of Directors, February 13, 1961, Board of Directors Meeting, March 13, 1961, Box 64, CRIP.

88. Farrington to CRIP Board, February 13, 1961, Box 64, CRIP. Grant, in *North Western*, p. 213, argues that "Heineman had discussed the possibilities of a Milwaukee Road, North Western and Rock Island consolidation. These railroads, encouraged by several life insurance companies with major bond holdings, agreed that it was an attractive concept."

89. "Milwaukee Road Eyeing Union with C&NW," *Chicago Daily Tribune*, February 10, 1961, p. C3.

90. "J. Farrington, Railroad Head, Is Dead at 70," *Chicago Daily Tribune*, October 14, 1961, p. C11.

Chapter 2. Merge or Die

1. Timeline of Merger, Box 120, CRIP.
2. Grant, *Northwestern*, pp. 183–184. Maury Klein, *Union Pacific, Volume 2: 1894–1969*, rpt. (Minneapolis: University of Minnesota Press, 2006 [1989]), p. 407.
3. Klein, *Union Pacific*, p. 517.
4. Timeline of Merger (no author), Box 120, CRIP.
5. Klein, *Union Pacific*, pp. 517–518.
6. Louis Dombrowski, "I.C. Weighs Merger with Two Other Rails," *Chicago Daily Tribune*, May 19, 1961, p. C9.
7. Klein, *Union Pacific*, pp. 518–519.
8. Ibid., pp. 519–520.
9. Report by Robert Ingersoll, Chairman of Rock Island board, Board of Directors Minutes, January 8, 1962, Box 64, CRIP.
10. *Rock Island Lines Annual Report* (1962): 5 (author's collection).
11. Don L. Hofsommer, *The Southern Pacific, 1901–1985* (College Station: Texas A&M University Press, 1986), p. 266. See also William Clark, "Rock Island, Southern Pacific Railroads Discussing Merger," *Chicago Daily Tribune*, June 19, 1962, p. B7.
12. Klein, *Union Pacific*, p. 520.
13. The Rock Island Executive and Finance Committees, headed by Ingersoll and Crown, respectively, asked New York Central president Alfred Perlman to become chairman of the Rock Island, but Perlman was busy with the merger between the NYC and Pennsylvania Railroad, so Ingersoll knew he would turn down the offer. See Ernest Fuller, "Ask Perlman to Take Helm at CRI&P," *Chicago Daily Tribune*, February 4, 1962, p. A9.
14. Descriptions of Johnson can be found in Dan Cordtz, "The Fight for the Rock Island," *Fortune* (June 1966): 200; and H. Roger Grant, *Visionary Railroader: Jervis Langdon Jr. and the Transportation Revolution* (Bloomington: Indiana University Press, 2008), p. 125.
15. For a flattering, Horatio Alger–like portrait of Johnson, see Robert Anderson, "In America: You Can Still Do It," *Chicago Daily Tribune*, March 4, 1962, p. C11.
16. For Lovett's quote on Crown, see Cordtz, "Fight for the Rock Island," p. 204.
17. "UP Entering Rock Island, SP Studies," *Chicago Daily Tribune*, September 19, 1962, p. C7.
18. Meeting dates in Timeline of Merger, Box 120, CRIP, p. 2.
19. Memorandum from Henry Crown to RI Board of Directors, Minutes of Executive Committee, February 11, 1963, Box 65, CRIP.
20. Telephone Transcript of Conversation between Henry Crown and Ellis Johnson, February 25, 26, 1963, Box 120, CRIP.
21. Grant, *Visionary Railroader*, p. 128.
22. Press Release, Rock Island Shareholders Meeting, May 13, 1963, Box 64.5, CRIP; Thomas Wolfsmith, "Rock Island Agrees to U.P. Merger," *Chicago Tribune*, May 14, 1963, p. C5.
23. Richard W. Barnsness, "Ben W. Heineman," in Keith L. Bryant, ed., *Railroads in the Age of Regulation, 1900–1980* (New York: Facts on File, 1988), pp. 193–195. The previous two paragraphs are based on the biography in this book.

24. Grant, *North Western*, 193–207.

25. Ibid., 209.

26. Letter from Ben Heineman to Roy Ingersoll, Henry Crown, and R. E. Johnson, June 24, 1963, Box 120, pp. 1–2, CRIP.

27. Letter from Heineman to Ingersoll, et al., pp. 2–3; see also Louis Dombrowski, "North Western Line Bids for Stock of Rock Island," *Chicago Tribune*, June 25, 1963, p. B5.

28. Brief Analysis of North Western Exchange Offer, June 26, 1963, Box 120, p. 8, CRIP.

29. "North Western Road to Ask ICC to Let It Seek Rock Island Stock," *Wall Street Journal* (July 5, 1963), p. 18.

30. Robert A. Lovett to Roy Ingersoll, Henry Crown, and R. E. Johnson, July 9, 1963, Box 124, p. 1–3, CRIP. Perhaps a more important point was revealed in a press release by the UP on July 26, 1963. Lovett stated: "If all Rock Island shareholders accepted the Northwestern offer of $5 in cash for each share of Rock Island, the cash required would be $15 million. As the Northwestern's application shows, on December 31, 1962, its working capital was only $7,109,907. This does not take into account long-term debt due within one year, which according to the year-end financial statement, amounted to $14,581,101." Union Pacific Press Release, July 26, 1963, Box 120, p. 2, CRIP.

31. Lovett to Ingersoll, et al., pp. 4–5, Box 124, CRIP.

32. Klein, *Union Pacific*, pp. 521–522.

33. Letter from R. E. Johnson to Ben Heineman, July 17, 1963, Box 123, pp. 1–2, and reply from Heineman, July 19, 1963, p. 1, Box 123, CRIP.

34. Letter from R. E. Johnson to Samuel H. Young, July 30, 1963, Box 123, CRIP; the nine, later reduced to eight, stockholders who formed the committee were first mentioned in the press on July 2, 1963. "Nine Rock Island Holders Eye Merger Plan," *Chicago Tribune*, July 2, 1963, p. C3. One of the nine stockholders claimed "I believe it is a flagrant violation to sell 95 percent of the shareholders down the river by accepting an offer of $29 a share from the Union Pacific railroad against an offer of $40 by the Chicago and North Western." The comment alleged that Rock Island directors owned only 5 percent of all stock in the company—the figure was much higher, around 37 percent.

35. Letter from Sidley, Austin, Burgess, and Smith to Eaton Adams, July 9, 1963, Box 120, CRIP.

36. *Union Pacific Railroad Company v. Chicago and North Western Railway Company*, No. 63 C 2051, U.S. District Court, Northern District of Illinois, February 18, 1964, 226 Supp. 400 (1964), pp. 2–3.

37. Louis Dombrowski, "Acts to Halt C&NW Move on Rock Island," *Chicago Tribune*, July 26, 1963, p. C7.

38. Louis Dombrowski, "SEC May Support Rock Island Group," *Chicago Tribune*, August 15, 1963, p. E7.

39. "Rock Island Assails Plan of CNW," *Chicago Tribune*, September 14, 1963, p. 5.

40. Louis Dombrowski, "Rock Island Opens Merger Proxy Drive," *Chicago Tribune*, October 2, 1963, p. C7.

41. Louis Dombrowski, "R.I., U.P. Officials Play Answer Please," *Chicago Tribune*, October 17, 1963, p. E5.

42. The estimate of one-third ownership by brokerage is from "Rail Proxy Fight Tempo Increases," *Spokane Daily Chronicle*, October 25, 1963, p. 14.

43. Louis Dombrowski, "Rail Analyst Casts Doubt on RI-UP Merger OK," *Chicago Tribune* October 19, 1963, p. B5.

44. Cordtz, "Fight for the Rock Island," p. 204.

45. "Warns of Alliance to Fight Rock Island-UP Merger," *Chicago Tribune*, October 31, 1963, p. D6.

46. Memo to R. E. Johnson, July 23, 1963, "Known Holdings of CRIP Stock as of June 30, 1963, re: Crown and Norris Families," Box 124, CRIP.

47. Memo from Martin Cassell, Law Department, November 25, 1963, Box 120, CRIP.

48. Cordtz, "Fight for the Rock Island," pp. 204, 209.

49. Louis Dombrowski, "Court Stays Rock Island Merger Vote," *Chicago Tribune*, November 15, 1963, p. C9.

50. Louis Dombrowski, "Rock Island Stockholders Meet Briefly, Adjourn Indefinitely," *Chicago Tribune*, November 16, 1963, p. B5.

51. *Chicago Tribune*, p. B5.

52. Louis Dombrowski, "Tells of UP Bids to Buy CRIP Shares," *Chicago Tribune*, November 30, 1963, p. C7.

53. *Union Pacific Railroad v. Chicago and North Western Railway*, February 18, 1964, p. 7.

54. Klein, *Union Pacific, Volume 2*, pp. 524–525.

55. Preceding paragraph is based on Memorandum from Theodore Desch to John W. Ingram, November 1974, Chronology of Important Events in the Rock Island-Union Pacific Merger, Box 123, Folder 8, pp. 6–8, CRIP.

56. "UP and Rock Island Directors OK New Plan for Stock Swap," *Chicago Tribune*, May 27, 1964, p. E5.

57. Louis Dombrowski, "C&NW Seen Nearly Out of RI Running," *Chicago Tribune*, May 28, 1964, p. C7.

58. Louis Dombrowski, "Heineman Eyes Victor's Role in Rock Island Tiff," *Chicago Tribune*, June 7, 1964, p. D1.

59. Memo from Theodore Desch to John Ingram, November 1974, Box 123, Folder 8, p. 10, CRIP.

60. Chicago and North Western Railway, "Analysis of the Proposed Northwestern-Rock Island Merger," n.d., Box 148, Rock Island Mergers, CRIP.

61. Klein, *Union Pacific*, pp. 526–527; Louis Dombrowski, "Rock Island Merger Approved," *Chicago Tribune*, January 11, 1965, p. 1.

62. Memorandum from Hunstall to R. E. Johnson, October 4, 1963, Box 150, pp. 1–4, CRIP.

63. *Rock Island Lines Annual Report* 1963, pp. 11–13.

64. Henry Crown, Rock Island Board of Directors Meeting, October 8, 1964, Box 66, CRIP.

65. Grant, *Visionary Railroader*, p. 129.

66. Grant's *Visionary Railroader* is the source for the previous four paragraphs. See also Louis Dombrowski, "Langdon to Get Chairman Post at Rock Island," *Chicago Tribune*, October 6, 1964, p. C7; and Louis Dombrowski, "Langdon New Rock Island Chief," *Chicago Tribune*, October 9, 1964, p. C9.

67. Memorandum from Martin Cassell Re: Basis for RI-UP Merger, May 13, 1964, Box 156, CRIP.
68. Louis Dombrowksi, "Four Rails to Fight Merger of UP and Rock Island," *Chicago Tribune*, December 18, 1964, p. C9.

Chapter 3. Bleak House

1. Letter from Dale Hardin to Everett Dirksen, September 24, 1968, Box 156 (RI-UP Merger, 1968), CRIP. The total number of pages of exhibits was estimated at more than 200,000 pages, with 258 days of testimony in the case. It proved the longest and largest case in the ICC's history.
2. The standard history of the ICC is Ari and Olive Hoogenboom, *A History of the ICC: From Panacea to Palliative* (New York: W. W. Norton, 1976). Gerald Berk, *Alternative Tracks: The Constitution of American Industrial Order, 1865–1917* (Baltimore: Johns Hopkins University Press, 1994), provides a sophisticated treatment of the limits to ICC's regulatory authority in a newly constructed corporate liberal order.
3. Albro Martin, *Enterprise Denied: Origins of the Decline of American Railroads, 1890–1917* (New York: Oxford University Press, 1971), p. 174.
4. Gabriel Kolko, *Railroads and Regulation, 1877–1916* (New York: Columbia University Press, 1965), pp. 7–31.
5. Richard White, *Railroaded: The Transcontinentals and the Making of Modern America* (New York: W. W. Norton, 2011), p. 355.
6. James W. Ely Jr., "Act to Regulate Commerce," *Encyclopedia of North American Railroads*, edited by William Middleton, George M. Smerk, and Roberta L. Diehl (Bloomington: Indiana University Press, 2007), pp. 921–922; Thomas K. McCraw, *Prophets of Regulation: Charles Francis Adams, Louis D. Brandeis, James M. Landis, Alfred E. Kahn* (Cambridge: Belknap Press of Harvard University Press, 1984), pp. 61–62.
7. Kolko, *Railroads and Regulation*, pp. 71–80, provides a useful discussion of self-regulation efforts by the railroads, as does White, *Railroaded*, pp. 359–365.
8. Sidney Fine, *Laissez-Faire and the General Welfare State* (Ann Arbor: University of Michigan Press, 1956), and Robert Green McCloskey, *American Conservatism in the Age of Enterprise, 1865–1910* (Cambridge: Harvard University Press, 1951), provide useful discussions of the intellectual and political construction of laissez-faire in the late nineteenth century.
9. Richard D. Stone, *The Interstate Commerce Commission and the Railroad Industry: A History of Regulatory Policy* (New York: Praeger, 1991), pp. 10–13.
10. George M. Smerk, "The Elkins Act, the Hepburn Act, and the Mann-Elkins Act," *Encyclopedia of American Railroads*, pp. 924–927.
11. Martin, *Enterprise Denied*, p. 355.
12. William R. Childs, *Trucking and the Public Interest: The Emergence of Federal Regulation, 1914–1940* (Knoxville: University of Tennessee Press, 1985), is a standard work on trucking regulation. Shane Hamilton, *Trucking Country: The Road to America's Wal-Mart Economy* (Princeton: Princeton University Press, 2008), is an excellent analysis of the development of wildcat trucking, which remained outside of government regulation.

13. John F. Stover, *American Railroads* (Chicago: University of Chicago Press, 1997), pp. 192–225; Rose, et al., *The Best Transportation System in the World*, pp. 97–133.

14. Hoogenboom, *History of the ICC*, pp. 145–151.

15. Rupert L. Murphy, "The Commission's Role in the Regulation of Transportation," Speech before the Tufted Textiles Manufacturers Association, February 13, 1957, no box number (Speeches and Writings), Jervis Langdon Papers, Accession 2068, Hagley Library and Museum, Wilmington, Delaware.

16. Speech by Paul Tierney at Biltmore Hotel, New York, October 15, 1964, Box 135 (RI-UP Merger, Part Five), CRIP.

17. Stone, *The Interstate Commerce Commission and the Railroad Industry*, pp. 20–22, contains a synopsis of the Transportation Act of 1920. The Great Depression interrupted the effort to rationalize the railroad system and to protect weak roads. See also H. Roger Grant, "Grouping America's Railroads: The Transportation Act of 1920," *Classic Trains* (Winter 2011): 30–37.

18. Tierney Speech, Box 135 (RI-UP Merger, Part Five), CRIP.

19. The best summary of the merger movement in modern times remains Saunders, *Merging Lines*.

20. The case was made by UP lawyers in "Background Memo on the Union Pacific-Rock Island Merger," November 30, 1966, Box 148, CRIP.

21. James R. MacDonald, "Milwaukee Road Assails Rock Island–UP Bid to Merge; Bitter Fight Before ICC Likely," *Wall Street Journal*, August 12, 1965, p. 4.

22. "Milwaukee Road Pleads Merger Halt," *Chicago Tribune*, August 12, 1965, p. E7.

23. James R. MacDonald, "Milwaukee Road Assails Rock Island-UP Bid to Merge," *Wall Street Journal*, August 12, 1965, p. 4.

24. Louis Dombrowski, "North Western Plans New Bid for Rock Island," *Chicago Tribune*, October 8, 1965, p. E7; and Louis Dombrowski, "Analysts Say C&NW's Offer is Grandstand Play, But Sound," *Chicago Tribune*, October 9, 1965, p. 9.

25. Louis Dombrowski, "Santa Fe Seeks Part of Rock Island," *Chicago Tribune*, October 27, 1965, p. E7; *Wall Street Journal*, October 27, 1965, p. 2.

26. Chicago and North Western Railroad, *The Proposed Rock Island Mergers: Which One is in the Public Interest?* Box 121, CNW Merger Proposal, CRIP.

27. Missouri Pacific Lines Brochure, "How the Union Pacific-Rock Island Merger and Related Proposals Affect You," Box 121 (File 9050 1965, Part III), CRIP; "MoPac Issues Booklet Opposing Rock Island, Union Pacific Merger," *Wall Street Journal*, September 24, 1965, p. 8.

28. Louis Dombrowski, "Doubts Grow about Merger of RI-UP," *Chicago Tribune*, December 10, 1965, p. E9. I could not find any source which revealed who the unnamed directors were.

29. Union Pacific and Rock Island Railroad Booklet, "How You Will Benefit from the Proposed Union Pacific-Rock Island Railroad Merger and the Sale of Rock Island's Southern Properties to the Southern Pacific," pp. 1–2, 8–9 (copy in author's collection).

30. Stephen Walt, *The Origins of Alliances* (Ithaca: Cornell University Press, 1990), shows how the attempt to bully rival nations does not lead to acquiescence on the part of threatened nations, but rather an attempt to build alliances against the aggres-

sor. The analogy fits well with the western railroads in opposition to the UP–Rock Island merger.

31. Rock Island Lines Annual Report, 1965, p. 3 (author's collection). Operating ratios are crucial barometers in the railroad industry to assess the health of a railroad. The higher the ratio is (based on a 100 percent), the higher the expenses and the greater the problem for costs and operations. The Rock Island through the 1950s averaged in the high 60s for its operating ratio, which was healthy, but it began to climb into the 70s and 80s by the end of the 1960s.

32. "G.W. Kelly Heads Operations; Succeeds O.W. Limestall," *The Rocket* (March-April 1965): 9. The Rocket was the Rock Island's employee magazine and was published until 1974.

33. Rock Island Lines Annual Report (1965), pp. 11–13.

34. Letter from Jervis Langdon Jr., to E. H. Bailey, April 23, 1965, Box 150, CRIP. In the mid-1960s there were no locomotive leasing companies from which railroads could lease locomotive power. Railroads had to finance equipment purchases or lease locomotive directly from the builder or pay other railroads for power during peak traffic times.

35. Jervis Langdon Jr., to Frank Barnett, May 19, 1965, Box 137, CRIP.

36. Paul Major, "Draft of Financial Testimony," May 18, 1965, Box 137, CRIP.

37. Major, "Draft of Financial Testimony," pp. 11–13.

38. Finance Docket 24182, Interstate Commerce Commission, Testimony of Jervis Langdon Jr., 1967, Box 9 (Rock Island), Jervis Langdon Papers, Hagley Library and Museum, Wilmington, Delaware.

39. Louis Dombrowski, "Justice Dept. Enters Scene of RI Scrap," *Chicago Tribune*, January 21, 1966, p. C9.

40. "CNW Bid for Rock Island Gets Boost," *Chicago Tribune*, March 8, 1966, p. C3 (for the ICC quote); "CNW Tells Offer for Rock Island Shares," *Chicago Tribune*, March 18, 1966, p. D9.

41. Louis Dombrowski, "Need Rock Island to Compete: UP," *Chicago Tribune*, March 13, 1966, p. C7.

42. Saunders, *Merging Lines*, pp. 338–339.

43. Louis Dombrowski, "Burlington Will Oppose RI Mergers," *Chicago Tribune*, April 30, 1966, p. B7.

44. Louis Dombrowski, "UP Denies Northern Refusal Discouraging," *Chicago Tribune*, May 7, 1966, p. D7.

45. Loving, *The Men Who Loved Trains*, pp. 12–16.

46. "A Case for the Penn-Central Merger," Pennsylvania Railroad and New York Central Railroad, 1963, Accession 1520, Box 1108 (PC Merger, 1962–1969), Reading Railroad Papers, Hagley Library and Museum.

47. Louis Dombrowski, "ICC Opens Hearing on UP-RI Merger," *Chicago Tribune*, May 5, 1966, p. F7; Dombrowski, "UP Claims Need of Western Outlet," *Chicago Tribune*, May 6, 1966, p. D9; Dombrowski, "Better Service Goal of Merger Plan: UP," *Chicago Tribune*, May 10, 1966, p. C7.

48. Louis Dombroski, "Better Service Goal of Merger Plan," ibid.

49. Louis Dombrowski, "First Bid for Rock Island Equaled 81 Millions: UP," *Chicago Tribune*, May 17, 1966, C7.

50. Louis Dombrowski, "UP Merger Savings Put at 27 Million," *Chicago Tribune*, May 21, 1966, p. C5; and "Cite Errors in UP-RI Data," May 26, 1966, p. E7.

51. H. Craig Miner, *The Rebirth of the Missouri Pacific, 1956–1983* (College Station: Texas A&M University Press, 1983), pp. 122–131.

52. Louis Dombrowski, "Milwaukee, C&NW File Bid for Merger," *Chicago Tribune*, June 7, 1966, p. C5; Saunders, *Merging Lines*, pp. 342–347.

53. Louis Dombrowski, "UP Official Confident of RI Merger," *Chicago Tribune*, June 17, 1966, p. E9.

54. Louis Dombrowski, "UP May Ask Compromise with CNW," *Chicago Tribune*, June 30, 1966, p. E9; "North Western Road Opposes Consolidation of Rail Merger Cases," *Wall Street Journal*, July 22, 1966, p. 12.

55. Saunders, *Merging Lines*, pp. 343–344.

56. Klein, *Union Pacific*, 530.

57. Testimony of Jervis Langdon Jr., before the ICC (Finance Docket No. 23286), August 1966, Accession 2068, Box 9 (Rock Island), p. 7, Langdon Papers.

58. Langdon Testimony, p. 7.

59. Shane Hamilton, *Trucking Country: The Road to America's Wal Mart Economy* (Princeton: Princeton University Press, 2008), documents this development in great detail.

60. Langdon Testimony, p. 14.

61. Ibid., p. 16.

62. "Rock Island Sees 5-Year Outlay Need of 87 Million," *Chicago Tribune*, August 18, 1966, p. G7.

63. "Rock Island Bases Future on U.P. Merger," *Chicago Tribune*, August 20, 1966, p. F6.

64. UP Railroad, "Background Memo," Box 148, CRIP.

65. William J. Dixon, "Notes of First Meeting of Rock Island Witnesses," April 27, 1966, Box 148, CRIP.

66. "S.P. Makes Plea to Own Rock Island's South Lines," *Chicago Tribune*, October 6, 1966, p. D12.

67. Don L. Hofsommer, *The Southern Pacific, 1901–1985* (College Station: Texas A&M University Press, 1986), pp. 266–268.

68. An overview of Heineman's concerns can be found in H. Roger Grant, *North Western: A History of the Chicago and North Western Railway System* (DeKalb: Northern Illinois University Press, 1996), pp. 212–214.

69. Testimony of Ben W. Heineman before the ICC (Finance Dockets 22688 et al.), November 1966, p. 15, Accession 2068, Box 9 (Rock Island), Langdon Papers. In marginalia in Heineman's dockets, Langdon wrote comments. On the matter cited above, Langdon wrote "savings absorbed by rising costs."

70. Heineman Testimony, p. 18, Langdon Papers.

71. Ibid., p. 26.

72. Ibid., pp. 32–33.

73. Ibid., pp. 43–44 (italics added).

74. Klein, *Union Pacific*, 531.

75. Rock Island Lines, Annual Report, 1967, p. 4 (copy in author's collection).

76. Rock Island Railroad brochure, "You Are Witnessing the Birth of a Market," Accession 2068, Box 9 (Rock Island), Langdon Papers.

77. Rock Island Lines, 1966 Annual Report, p. 14 (in author's collection).
78. Copy of *Official Guide* passenger train schedules, at http://www.streamliner-schedules.com/concourse/track9/goldstate196803.html (accessed June 20, 2011).
79. "Golden State Train Makes Last Run," *Chicago Tribune*, February 20, 1968, p. C6.
80. Rock Island Lines, Annual Report, 1966, p. 5 (in author's collection).
81. Rock Island Lines, Annual Report, 1966, p. 6 (in author's collection).

Chapter 4. The Waiting Is the Hardest Part

1. Max Weber, *Economy and Society*, edited by Guenther Roth and Claus Wittich (Berkeley: University of California Press, 1978), pp. 956–998.
2. Alfred DuPont Chandler, *The Visible Hand: The Managerial Revolution in American Business* (Cambridge: Harvard University Press, 1977), p. 1.
3. See Alfred DuPont Chandler, *The Railroads: The Nation's First Big Business* (New York: Harcourt, Brace and World, 1965). Berk, *Alternative Tracks*.
4. For summaries of the challenge to establishment corporate liberalism among such constituent groups, see David Frum, *How We Got Here: The 70's, the Decade That Brought You Modern Life—for Better or for Worse* (New York: Basic Books, 2003); Jefferson Cowie, *Stayin' Alive: The 1970s and the Last Days of the Working Class* (New York: New Press, 2010); the classic statement of antiorganization is Robert C. Townsend, *Up the Organization* (New York: Fawcett ed., 1983). Townsend was president of Avis Car Rental and an advocate of moving away from corporate organizational models.
5. Richard Saunders Jr., *Main Lines: Rebirth of North American Railroads, 1970–2002* (DeKalb: Northern Illinois University Press, 2003), pp. 5–12, contains a good summary of the railroad problem.
6. Speech by Jervis Langdon Jr., at College Station, Texas, March 28, 1968, Accession 2068, no box number (Speeches and Writings), p. 8, Langdon Papers.
7. Maury Klein, *Union Pacific: The Reconfiguration of a Railroad, 1969–2004* (New York: Oxford University Press, 2011), pp. 22–24; Saunders, *Merging Lines*, pp. 294–296.
8. Hoogenboom, *History of the ICC*, p. 170. Morgan was writing in response to Samuel Huntington, "The Marasmus of the ICC: The Commission, the Railroads, and the Public Interest," *Yale Law Review* 61, no. 4 (April 1952): 467–509, in which Huntington stated that the ICC had favored railroads as opposed to other transportation modes and argued for the commission's abolition with its functions moved into the Commerce Department, a proposal put forth by a commission led by former President Herbert Hoover in 1953.
9. John Robert Meyer, *The Economics of Competition in the Transportation Industries* (Cambridge: Harvard University Press, 1959), 1–18.
10. "Nathan Klitenic's Game Plan," *Forbes* (October 18, 1972): 33.
11. "Katy Seeks Rock Island Merger Role," *Chicago Tribune*, May 25, 1967, p. G7.
12. Kenneth Ross, "Rail Merger Savings Put at 29 Million," *Chicago Tribune*, February 7, 1967, p. C5. At the end of April 1967 the ICC approved C&NW control of the Chicago Great Western.

13. Testimony of Jervis Langdon Jr. before the ICC (FD 24182) Applications of CNW and Milwaukee Road, p. 17, Accession 2068, Box 9 (Rock Island), Langdon Papers.

14. Kenneth Ross, "ICC Refuses to Tie Two Rail Mergers," *Chicago Tribune*, June 1, 1967, p. F13.

15. "Rock Island Chairman Urges New U.S. Agency Help in Merger Snarl," *Wall Street Journal*, February 3, 1967, p. 12.

16. "I.C.C. Head Scores Roads in Western Rail Picture," *Wall Street Journal*, April 18, 1967, p. 7.

17. Testimony of Ben W. Heineman on Rebuttal before the ICC, Sept. 1967, pp. 1–3, 7.

18. Ibid., p. 18.

19. Ibid., p. 14.

20. "U.P.–Rock Island Merger Would Hurt—Heineman," *Chicago Tribune*, September 29, 1967, p. C7.

21. "I.C., G.M.&O. Executives Agree on Merger Terms," *Chicago Tribune*, October 3, 1967, p. C7.

22. Kenneth Ross, "Alternate Merger Plan Seen for U.P.," *Chicago Tribune*, October 4, 1967, p. E9.

23. Maury Klein, *Union Pacific, Volume 2: 1894–1969* (Minneapolis: University of Minnesota Press, 2006), p. 530.

24. Ibid., p. 527.

25. Letter from Jervis Langdon to Ben Biaggini, December 15, 1967, Box 153, CRIP Papers. Langdon was writing to Biaggini to influence his thinking as he was due to have a conference on the Rock Island with Frank Barnett without Rock Island officials present.

26. Testimony of Ben W. Heineman, In Opposition to Applications of Union Pacific Railroad Company, Chicago, Rock Island and Pacific Railroad Company, and Southern Pacific Railroad Company, Before the ICC, p. 4, Accession 2068, Box 9 (Rock Island), Langdon Papers.

27. Ibid., p. 19.

28. "MoPac Swings Backing to C&NW in Battle For Rock Island Road," *Wall Street Journal*, February 5, 1968, p. 12.

29. Letter from Jervis Langdon to Frank Barnett, May 29, 1968, p. 2, Box 156 (UP-RI Merger, 1968), CRIP.

30. Ibid., p. 3.

31. "U.P. Offers Loss Rebate to C.&N.W.," *Chicago Tribune*, May 10, 1968, p. C11.

32. Klein, *Union Pacific, Volume 2*, p. 531; Grant, *North Western*, pp. 214–215; Grant, *Visionary Railroader*, pp. 158–160.

33. "Battle to Gain Control of Rock Island Road at a Milestone Today," *Wall Street Journal*, August 21, 1968, p. 7; Kenneth Ross, "Decision on RI by ICC Expected in 1 to 1 ½ Years," *Chicago Tribune*, September 10, 1968, p. C5.

34. Testimony of Jervis Langdon Jr. before Interstate Commerce Commission, FD 25103 (GM&O/IC merger), Box 122 (GM&O, Part One), p. 9, CRIP.

35. Maury Klein, *Union Pacific: Regeneration* (New York: Oxford University Press, 2011), p. 37.

36. Ibid., p. 37.
37. Ibid., pp. 37–45.
38. Grant, *NorthWestern*, pp. 214–215.
39. Ibid., p. 215.
40. "Justice Dept. Backs U.P. Bid for Rock Island," *Chicago Tribune*, January 28, 1969, p. B5.
41. Kenneth Ross, "C&NW Seeks Power to Prove Who Controls IC," *Chicago Tribune*, January 30, 1969, p. D9.
42. "North Western Bids ICC Reopen Hearings in Rock Island Case," *Wall Street Journal*, September 29, 1969, p. 24; "ICC to Again Review A Rock Island Merger With the Union Pacific," *WSJ*, November 6, 1969, p. 6; "ICC, on C&NW Plea, Reopens Rock Island Merger Plan Hearing," *WSJ*, February 20, 1970, p. 28.
43. "ICC Reopens Rock Island Merger Case," *Chicago Tribune*, February 20, 1970, p. C9.
44. Grant, *North Western*, pp. 215–218.
45. Saunders, *Merging Lines*, pp. 345–347.
46. Motion to Strike North Western's Affirmative Case to Control Rock Island, March 9, 1970 before ICC (FD 23285, et al.,) Box 143 (Merger, General—UP), pp.1–3, CRIP; Kenneth Ross, "Rock Island Asks ICC to Halt CNW Bid," *Chicago Tribune*, March 10, 1970, p. C7; "Rock Island Asks ICC to Erase Control Bid by North Western," *Wall Street Journal*, March 10, 1970, p. 7.
47. Rock Island Motion, p. 7.
48. North Western's Response to Rock Island's Motion to Strike its Affirmative Case before the ICC (FD 22688, et al.), March 26, 1970, Box 130, p. 9, CRIP.
49. Grant, *Langdon*, pp. 144–145.
50. Letter from Jervis Langdon to George Stafford, February 13, 1970, Box 143 (Merger-General), CRIP.
51. "Joining UP, RI Is Recommended," *Chicago Tribune*, July 9, 1970, p. D9; Kenneth Ross, "RI Puzzle Far From Solved," *Chicago Tribune*, July 10, 1970, p. C9 (for the quotes). "ICC Aide Advises Rock Island Merge Into Union Pacific," *Wall Street Journal*, July 9, 1970, p. 3; "Rock Island Road Hopes ICC Aide's Suggestions Will Help Solve Dispute," *Wall Street Journal*, July 10, 1970, p. 10.
52. "Judge Appoints Four to Run the Penn Central," *Chicago Tribune*, July 23, 1970, p. D7; Kenneth Ross, "Langdon Respected Throughout Rail Industry," *Chicago Tribune*, July 23, 1970, p. D7.
53. George Gunset, "Name 3 to Top Rock Island Posts," *Chicago Tribune*, September 15, 1970, p. C7.
54. Grant, *Langdon*, pp. 81–84.
55. Interview with Theodore Desch, Naperville, Illinois, August 4, 2010.
56. "Rock Island Puts '71 Loss at $26.3 Million," *Chicago Tribune*, September 3, 1970, p. C3.
57. Rock Island Lines Annual Report 1970, pp. 4–11 (author's collection).
58. Finance Docket 22688, et al., CNW Control of CRIP, Report and Order Recommended by Nathan Klitenic, Hearing Examiner, Volume I, Interstate Commerce Commission Papers, Record Group 134, Box 3962 (Klitenic Report), National Archives and Records Administration (NARA) (Archives II), Suitland, Maryland (ICC Papers).

59. Saunders, *Merging Lines*, p. 348.
60. "Western Railroad Mergers," January 1969 in Box 59 (Mergers), Daniel O'Neal Papers, Hoover Institution on War, Revolution, and Peace, Stanford, California (hereafter O'Neal Papers).
61. Rock Island Lines Annual Report, 1971, pp. 4–5 (copy in author's collection).

Chapter 5. Too Big to Fail

1. "Railroads Plead for Help," *Business Week* (May 10, 1958), p. 31.
2. Ibid., p. 32.
3. Loving, *The Men Who Loved Trains*, pp. 25–35.
4. Robert Sobel, *The Fallen Colossus* (New York: Weywright and Talley, 1977), explores the two corporate cultures and the merger between the two lines. See also Loving, *The Men Who Loved Trains*.
5. See The Penn-Central Merger Information Committee, "Key Facts about the Proposed Merger of the Pennsylvania and New York Central Railroads," 1962 in Accession 1520, Box 1108 (PC Merger, 1962–1967), Reading Railroad Company Papers, Hagley Library, Wilmington, Delaware.
6. Rose, et al., *The Best Transportation System in the World*, p. 128.
7. Loving, *The Men Who Loved Trains*, pp. 45–47.
8. H. Roger Grant, *Erie Lackawanna: Death of an American Railroad, 1938–1992* (Stanford: Stanford University Press, 1994), pp. 152–154.
9. Saunders, *Merging Lines*, pp. 375–376.
10. Grant, *Erie Lackawanna*, pp. 158–177.
11. Penn Central 1967 Annual Report, pp. 2, 36–37 in Accession 1807, Box 1650 (Annual Reports), Penn Central Transportation Company Papers, Hagley Library, Wilmington, Delaware (hereafter Penn Central Papers).
12. Staff Report of the Committee on Banking and Currency, House of Representatives, 92nd Cong., 1st Sess., *The Penn Central Failure and the Role of Financial Institutions* (New York: Arno Press, 1972), pp. 25–27. Bevan denied this was a factor in the railroad's collapse. See Salsbury, *No Way to Run a Railroad: The Untold Story of the Penn Central Crisis* (New York: McGraw Hill, 1982), pp. 196–197.
13. Testimony of Stuart Saunders before House Committee on Foreign and Interstate Commerce, July 21, 1970, Accession 1096-001, Box 122, Folder 1 (ERSA), Brock Adams Papers, University of Washington Special Collections, Seattle, Washington (hereafter Adams Papers).
14. The Penn Central collapse has been well chronicled. The first book written on the Penn Central was Joseph R. Daughen and Peter Binzen, *The Wreck of the Penn Central* (New York: Little, Brown and Company, 1971), which was published before the full magnitude of the bankruptcy was known and contributed to the general interpretation that the railroad was ruined by its attempts to diversify its holdings by purchasing other companies. Such an analysis coincided with congressional investigations into the Penn Central bankruptcy, released in 1971, that claimed the railroad's failure was owed to diversification and corruption on the part of management.
15. The books critical of Bevan's role in the Penn Central collapse include Robert Sobel, *The Fallen Colossus* (New York: Weybright and Talley, 1977), Daughen and

Binzen, *The Wreck of the Penn Central*; and Loving, *The Men Who Loved Trains*. See also Staff Report of the Securities and Exchange Commission to the Special Subcommittee on Investigations, *The Financial Collapse of the Penn Central* (Washington: GPO, 1972). For a defense of Bevan, using personal diaries unavailable to earlier scholars, see Stephen Salsbury, *No Way to Run a Railroad*.

16. For a general history of railroads, see John Stover, *American Railroads* (Chicago: University of Chicago Press, 1997); for expansion to the West, see David Howard Bain, *Empire Express: Building the First Transcontinental Railroad* (New York: Penguin, 2000); Stephen Ambrose, *Nothing Like It in the World: The Men Who Built the First Transcontinental Railroad, 1863–1869* (New York: Simon and Schuster, 2001); Walter R. Borneman, *Rival Rails: The Race to Build America's Greatest Transcontinental Railroad* (New York: Random House, 2010); and Richard White, *Railroaded: The Transcontinentals and the Making of Modern America* (New York: Norton, 2011). For railroad technology, see Steven W. Usselman, *Regulating Railroad Innovation: Business, Technology, and Politics in America, 1840–1920* (New York: Cambridge University Press, 2002); John K. Brown, *The Baldwin Locomotive Works: A Study in Industrial Practice, 1831–1915* (Baltimore: Johns Hopkins University Press, 2001); and Mark Aldrich, *Death Rode the Rails: American Railroad Accidents and Safety, 1828–1965* (Baltimore: Johns Hopkins University Press, 2009). For labor, see Paul Michael Taillon, *Good, Reliable, White Men: The Railroad Brotherhoods, 1877–1917* (Urbana: University of Illinois Press, 2009); and Beth Tompkins Bates, *Pullman Porters and the Rise of Black Protest Politics in America, 1925–1945* (Chapel Hill: University of North Carolina Press, 2000).

17. Stephen Fried, *Appetite for America: Fred Harvey and the Business of Civilizing the West* (New York: Bantam, 2011).

18. For the Lockheed loan, see "Why a Government Guaranteed Loan for Lockheed," May 27, 1972, and Letter, J. G. McCurdy to Brock Adams, June 23, 1971, in Accession 1096-001, Box 98, Folder 14 (Lockheed Loan, 1971), Brock Adams Papers. Lockheed was loaned the money to develop a new commercial airliner as its sources of credit in the private sector, and the cancellation of a Defense Department contract for a new transport plane, contributed to the company's financial problems.

19. See "History of U.S. Government Bailouts," at http://www.propublica.org/special/government-bailouts (accessed July 25, 2011).

20. Loving, *The Men Who Loved Trains*, pp. 81–82.

21. Andrew Ross Sorkin, *Too Big to Fail* (New York: Viking, 2009), provides the best overview of the financial crisis and government's response to it. Henry Paulson, *On the Brink: Inside the Race to Prevent the Collapse of the Global Financial System* (New York: Harcourt Brace, 2010), provides a first-person account, as does Neil Barofsky of his role as the inspector general in charge of TARP funds. See Neil Barofsky, *Bailout: An Inside Account of How Washington Abandoned Main Street while Rescuing Wall Street* (New York: Free Press, 2012). Barofsky was a Democrat appointed by George W. Bush as inspector general and served until 2010 in that role at the Treasury Department.

22. Critics of too big to fail charged that the deregulation of financial markets and the repeal in 1999 of the Glass-Steagall Act, a statute to separate the functions of commercial and investment banks, helped cause the 2008 financial crisis. The rise of systemic risk, shrugged off by Federal Reserve Chairman Alan Greenspan at the time

of the passage of the Gramm–Leach–Bliley Act, which repealed Glass-Steagall, became the norm as the nation faced one financial crisis after another following repeal of the law. The merger of banks into bigger and more powerful institutions pursuing new investment strategies, such as collateralized debt obligations (CDOs) and credit default swaps, placed depositors and ultimately the taxpayers at risk as the house of cards surrounding the housing bubble collapsed in 2007. See John Cassidy, *How Markets Fail: The Logic of Economic Calamities* (New York: Farrar, Straus and Giroux, 2009), pp. 229–231. The federal government's role in the manufacture of the housing bubble, particularly the role of Fannie Mae, is explored in Gretchen Morgenson and Joshua Rosner, *Reckless Endangerment: How Outsized Ambition, Greed, and Corruption Led to Economic Armageddon* (New York: Times Books, 2011).

23. ASTRO, "The American Railroad Industry: A Prospectus," June 30, 1970, Judith R. Hope Files (Domestic Council), Box 42 (Union Pacific), Gerald R. Ford Presidential Library, Ann Arbor, Michigan. The use of the term ASTRO was a reflection of the space age and how railroads were still vital to such an age. AAR even employed astronaut Wally Schiara as a television and radio voice for the industry. See David P. Morgan, "The Bad Old Summertime," *Trains* (October 1970): 3.

24. Ibid., p. 8.

25. Ibid., p. 10.

26. Ibid., pp. 20–29.

27. Ibid., p. 32.

28. The subject of government officials discussing regulation of transportation was broached as as early as June 1970. See Memorandum from John Volpe, Secretary of Transportation, to John Erlichman, June 12, 1970, White House Central Files, Box 2 (RG 25, DOT, 6/1/70–7/31/70), Richard M. Nixon Presidential Papers, National Archives and Record Administration, II, Suitland, Maryland.

29. Fred W. Frailey, *The Twilight of the Great Trains* (Milwaukee: Kalmbach Books, 1998), p. 9.

30. Memorandum from John Volpe to John Erlichman, "Railpax," February 18, 1970, Box 6 (TN—Railroads, 4/3/70), White House Central Files, Nixon Presidential Papers.

31. Part of the problem lay in how to determine losses for passenger service. According to an ICC determination of fully allocated costs, part of the passenger losses could include the president's salary, maintenance of way employees and other railroad personnel who did not *directly* work on passenger trains, and a number of other costs associated with the railroad and not passenger service in general. On that basis, passenger trains lost $421 million in 1967. On the basis of direct costs, which included losses attributed to passenger service alone, by which most railroads figured their ledgers, the figure was closer to $200 million—still substantial, but half that of the older measurement, which the ICC had even moved away from in 1967. Frailey, *Twilight of the Great Trains*, 6.

32. Memo from John Volpe to the President, no date (March 1970), Box 6 (TN—April 1970), WHCF, Nixon Papers.

33. Memorandum to the President from John Erlichman, March 2, 1970, Box 1 (FG 25 DOT, 1/1/70–3/31/70), Nixon Presidential Papers.

34. Memorandum to the President from John Erlichman, March 4, 1970, Box 1 (FG 25 DOT, 1/1/70–3/31/70), Nixon Presidential Papers. Erlichman was dubious of

all aid to railroads, preferring to see the railroads solve their own problems. Don Phillips, "Richard M. Nixon: Rail Romantic," *Trains* (November 1971): 50.

35. Don Phillips, "The Road to Rescue," *Classic Trains* 12, no. 2 (Summer 2011): 23–31.

36. Memorandum from George Shultz to the President, October 29, 1970, Memorandum from Volpe to the President, October 29, 1970, Memorandum for Ken Cole from William Timmons, October 29, 1970, White House Central Files, Box 6 (TN, Railroads, 11/1/70–11/30/70), Nixon Papers.

37. Memorandum from Peter Flanigan to John Erlichman, October 27, 1970, White House Central Files, Box 6 (TN—Railroads, 11/7/70–12/31/70), Nixon Papers.

38. Phillips, "The Road to Rescue," p. 31.

39. Ibid.

40. Aside from the Rock Island, the Georgia Railroad, the Southern Railway, the Reading, the Denver and Rio Grande Western, and the Chicago, South Shore and South Bend did not join Amtrak. The Southern, Rock Island, and Rio Grande operated independent passenger trains through the 1970s, with the Rock ending service in 1978, the Southern joining Amtrak in 1980, and the Rio Grande joining in 1983.

41. Kenneth Ross, "Passenger Train Service Saved for Peoria and Rock Island," *Chicago Tribune* (April 2, 1971), p. B15.

42. Rose, et al., *The Best Transportation System in the World*, pp. 152–153.

43. Memorandum for John Erlichman from John Volpe, June 12, 1970, White House Central Files, Box 2 (FG 25 DOT, 6/1/70–7/31/70), Nixon Presidential Papers. Flanigan replied that DOT should be involved in the discussion.

44. Memorandum on Financial Condition of Penn Central Transportation Company, May 22, 1970, Federal Reserve Subject File, Box B88 (Penn Central, 5/1970–6/1970), Arthur Burns Papers, Gerald R. Ford Presidential Library, Ann Arbor, Michigan (hereafter Burns Papers).

45. Remarks of Wright Patman (D–Tex.) on the floor of the House, July 22, 1970, with quotations from New York Federal Reserve report, attached, on Penn Central, Box B88 (Penn Central, June 16, 1970–July 1970), Burns Papers.

46. Memorandum for the President from Paul McCracken and Memorandum from George Shultz to the President, July 7, 1970, White House Central Files, Box 6 (TN—Railroads, 5/1/70–11/5/70), Nixon Papers.

47. David P. Morgan, "Great Expectations Department," *Trains* (November 1970): 3.

48. "News from the Penn Central," November 23, 1970, Accession 1807, Box 1651 (Press Releases, 7/1970–12/1970), Penn Central Papers.

49. Peter Rickershauser, "Jersey Central Had a Great Fall," *Trains* (March 1972): pp. 20–28, provides an excellent analysis of the problems of the Central of New Jersey.

50. Memorandum for the File by Loken, November 11, 1970, Inter-Agency Meeting on Railroad Problems, November 10, 1970, White House Central Files, Box 6 (TN—Railroads, 4/1/71–7/29/71), Nixon Presidential Papers. The Philadelphia Federal Reserve Bank studied the PC's financial problems. On the issue of private credit, the bank concluded that "the magnitude of the PC's current indebtedness is a negative factor in the financial community's response to requests for credit since reorganization. A large group of commercial banks is owed $617 million, $442 million of which

is unsecured. In addition, subsidiary companies for the PC Transportation Company are indebted to banks for more than $113 million, of which $74 million is unsecured. . . . The company is indebted for $1.917 billion, excluding non-bank current liabilities. In light of this huge volume of debt, it is understandable that the financial community is reluctant to make further commitments" (pp. 4–5).

51. Penn Central Transportation Company News Release, December 15, 1970, Accession 1807, Box 1651 (Press Releases, 7/1970–12/1970), Penn Central Papers.

52. "Impact of an Interruption in Penn Central Services: Conclusions," Box B88 (Penn Central, 11/23/1970–2/1971), Burns Papers.

53. Statement by Paul Volcker before the Senate Committee on Commerce, November 24, 1970, Box B88 (Penn Central, 11/24/1970), Burns Papers.

54. Testimony of John Volpe before Senate Commerce Committee, November 24, 1970, Box B88 (Penn Central, 11/24/1970), Burns Papers.

55. Rose, et al., *The Best Transportation System in the World*, pp. 157–160.

56. Sobel, *The Fallen Colossus*, p. 322.

57. Grant, *Visionary Railroader*, p. 180.

58. Al Chesser, "Position of the UTU in the Penn Central Fiasco," Accession 1096–001, Box 9, Folder 31 (Railroads, 1971–1972), Brock Adams Papers.

59. John W. Ingram, Speech at the Comstock Club, San Francisco, p. 4, September 13, 1973, Accession 1807, Box 1652 (NE Rail Crisis), Penn Central Papers.

60. Todd E. Fandell, "Railroads Aim to Trim Losses by Abandoning Some Freight Service," *Wall Street Journal* (September 30. 1970): 1.

61. Grant, *Erie Lackawanna*, pp. 175–176.

62. Penn Central, Erie Lackawanna, Reading Railway System, and Lehigh Valley Railroad Press Release, August 2, 1972, Accession 1807, Box 1651 (Press Releases, 1/1973–6/1973), Penn Central Papers.

63. Grant, *Erie Lackawanna*, p. 182.

64. Penn Central Press Releases, January 2, 1973, January 9, 1973, February 1, 1973, and February 6, 1973, in Accession 1807, Box 1651 (Press Releases, 1/1973–6/1973), Penn Central Papers.

65. Penn Central Transportation Company, Debtor, 1972 Annual Report, Accession 1807, Box 1650 (Annual Reports), Penn Central Papers.

66. Saunders, *Main Lines*, pp. 87–88.

67. Penn Central Transportation Co. News, Accession 1807, Box 1651 (Press Releases, 1/1973–6/1973), Penn Central Papers.

68. Saunders, *Main Lines*, p. 88.

69. Ibid., pp. 88–89.

70. William McDonald of the Union Pacific wrote Adams a warm letter thanking him for "his leadership in the field of transportation legislation." "We are, all of us in the rail industry as well as members of railway labor, rail transportation users, and the states and communities throughout the northeast region, irrevocably in your debt." Letter from McDonald to Adams, Accession 1096–001, Box 87, Folder 36 (Sponsored Bills, NE Transportation Act, 1973), Adams Papers.

71. See a summary of testimony on the bill before the Senate Commerce Committee in Memorandum from W. A. Lashley, November 19, 1973, Accession 1807, Box 1652 (3R Act), Penn Central Papers. Senator Vance Hartke opposed the bill but eventually voted for it after there was no further chance for his ConFac proposal to be enacted.

72. John F. Stover, *American Railroads*, 2nd ed. (Chicago: University of Chicago Press, 1997), p. 238.

Chapter 6. Bankruptcy Blue(s)

1. "Rock Island, Union Pacific Merger Approved: Certain Conditions are Imposed," Press Release, Interstate Commerce Commission, November 8, 1974, O'Neal Papers, Box 62 (Rock Island Railroad).
2. Memorandum from Tad (unidentified staff member) to Commissioner Daniel O'Neal, December 7, 1973, Box 62 (Rock Island, 11/12, 1975), O'Neal Papers. The "Godfather" approach first was mentioned by Commissioner Willard Deason in "A Skeleton Proposal for Deciding the Rock Island Case," November 1973, in ibid. After outlining the conditions for the railroads to accept in the approval of a UP-RI merger, Deason wrote, "Let's make offers which they can't refuse."
3. Memoraundum to George Stafford from Commissioner MacFarland, December 7, 1973, Box 62 (Rock Island, 11–12, 1975), O'Neal Papers.
4. Memorandum from O'Neal to Chairman Stafford, December 14, 1973, Box 62 (Rock Island, 11–12/75), O'Neal Papers.
5. Ibid., 3.
6. Memorandum from Commissioner Jesse Tuggle, December 18, 1973, Box 62 (Rock Island, 11/12–1975), O'Neal Papers.
7. E. Houston Harsha Memo to File, March 12, 1973, Meeting with UP on March 7, 1973, Box 20, Folder 8, CRIP, pp. 1–2.
8. Ibid., pp. 3–6.
9. Executive Committee Meeting Minutes, June 18, 1973, Box 71, CRIP.
10. Memorandum of Union Pacific–Rock Island Meeting, June 26, 1973, by Ted Desch, Box 17, Folder 3, CRIP.
11. Rock Island Board Meeting Minutes, July 16, 1973, Box 71, CRIP.
12. Rock Island Lines Press Release, July 17, 1973, Box 71, CRIP.
13. Maury Klein, *Union Pacific: The Reconfiguration—America's Greatest Railroad from 1969 to the Present* (New York: Oxford University Press, 2011), p. 97.
14. Memo from E. Houston Harsha to File, August 3, 1973, Box 132, CRIP. For the appointment to the board, see Rock Island Lines Annual Report, 1973, p. 6 (copy in author's possession).
15. Memo from Desch to Claude Brineger, August 30, 1973, Box 17, Folder 3, CRIP.
16. Discussion about whether to hire a Washington representative for the company was held at a June 19, 1974, board meeting. Executive Committee Meeting Minutes, June 19, 1974, Box 72, CRIP.
17. Letter from John W. Ingram to Robert Michel, November 14, 1973, Box 17, Folder 3, CRIP.
18. Rock Island Board Meeting Minutes, November 19, 1973, Box 72, CRIP.
19. Rock Island Loan Application, Box 72, CRIP; Cash position of railroad from Rock Island Railroad Annual Report, 1973, p. 14 (copy in author's possession).
20. Robert M. Collins, *More: The Politics of Economic Growth in Postwar America* (New York: Oxford University Press, 2000).

21. Allen Matusow, *Nixon's Economy: Booms, Busts, Dollars, and Votes* (Lawrence: University Press of Kansas, 1998), pp. 214–222.

22. Ibid., pp. 285–286.

23. Ibid., pp. 300–301.

24. "Fuel Crisis," *The Rocket* (November/December 1973): 8–9. *The Rocket* was the railroad's employee magazine.

25. Data on carloads from Rock Island Annual Report, 1973, p. 7, and Annual Report, 1974, p. 2 (copies in author's possession).

26. "Claims Shutdown of Iowa Rail Lines Can Be Avoided," *Des Moines Register* (January 28, 1974).

27. "Subsidy for Rock Island?" *Des Moines Register* (August 10, 1973).

28. Contract between Rock Island, Iowa DOT, and the Audubon-Atlantic Branch Line Improvement Association, Executive Files, Box 1, Folder 1 (Subject, Abandonments, Audubon, Iowa Branch), CRIP. FRA Class II standards equaled freight train speeds of up to 25 miles per hour.

29. Board Meeting Minutes, May 1972, Box 71, CRIP.

30. Board Meeting Minutes, February 12, 1973, Box 71, CRIP.

31. Memorandum to File from E. Houston Harsha, March 27, 1974, Meeting with DOT officials on February 27, 1974, Box 122, CRIP.

32. Application by Rock Island for Loan from USRA pursuant to Section 211 of the Regional Rail Reorganization Act of 1973, March 1974, Box 72 (Loan Application 1974), CRIP.

33. Ibid., p. 15.

34. Letter from Theodore Desch to Frank Barnett, September 3, 1974, and letter from Barnett to Desch, September 10, 1974, Box 125 (UP–RI), CRIP. The exchange offer between the UP and RI, agreed to in 1963, had expired on its own in August 1974. All that remained was whether the UP would be willing to renegotiate terms with the railroad.

35. Letter from Frank Barnett to Theodore Desch, September 25, 1974, and Rock Island press release, Box 125, CRIP.

36. Rock Island Board of Director Meeting Minutes, October 10, 1974, Box 72 (Board Mtg. 10/10/74), CRIP. Henry Crown was not in attendance due to illness. "Troubled Rock Island Shaking Up Top Officers," *Chicago Tribune* (October 15, 1974), p. C9.

37. Memorandum to File from E. Houston Harsha, April 24, 1974, Box 122, CRIP.

38. Memorandum from E. Houston Harsha to File, April 24, 1974, Box 122, CRIP.

39. Ibid., p. 6.

40. Robert K. Bedingfield, "Ingram Being Suggested to Head the Rock Island," *New York Times*, April 27, 1974, p. 39.

41. Memorandum from E. Houston Harsha to File, May 1, 1974, re: Meeting in New York, April 29, 1974, Box 122, CRIP.

42. Ibid., p. 6 (for Arias), and pp. 1–2 (for meeting with UP officials).

43. "An Interview with John W. Ingram," by John W. Barriger IV (February 7, 2004), Palm Harbor, Florida. Railroad Executive Oral History Program, John W. Barriger III National Railroad Library, Saint Louis Mercantile Library, University of Missouri–St. Louis.

44. Memorandum From John Barriger to John W. Ingram, April 2, 1974, Box 58

(Corporate Records, CRIP), John W. Barriger III, Papers, John W. Barriger III National Railroad Library, Saint Louis Mercantile Library, University of Missouri–St. Louis.

45. Linn H. Westcott, "Today's Monon," *Trains* (March 1951): 16–22.

46. John W. Barriger III, *Super-Railroads for a Dynamic American Economy* (Omaha: Simmons-Boardman, 1956).

47. George W. Hilton, "John W. Barriger III," in *Railroads in the Age of Regulation, 1900–1980*, edited by Keith L. Bryant (New York: Facts on File, 1988).

48. "An Interview with John W. Ingram," by John W. Barriger IV. The *Panama Limited* was one of the IC's marquee passenger trains.

49. Ibid.

50. Rock Island Annual Report, 1974, end page (in author's collection).

51. Paul D. Schneider, "In the Violet Hour," *Trains* (March 1983): 22–30.

52. "The Old Rock Island News Bulletin," February 22, 1975, in Rock Island collection, Iowa Department of Transportation Collection, Ames, Iowa.

53. Theodore Desch, "UP-RI Merger Chronology," Box 20 (Folder 8), CRIP.

54. John W. Ingram to Rock Island Employees, November 14, 1974, Box 120 (Stockholders), CRIP.

55. Letter from E. Houston Harsha to John Ingram, November 15, 1974, Box 20 Folder 9, CRIP.

56. "Rock Island Gets U.S. Rail Loan," *Chicago Tribune*, February 5, 1975, p. C11.

57. "Rock Island Maps Plan for survival," *Chicago Tribune*, March 1, 1975, p. 9; Lee Strobel, "Rock Island Line Running Out of Gas," *Chicago Tribune* March 2, 1975, p. 5.

58. Richard Hatfield and Melinda Voss, "Iowa Impact If Railroad Quits," *Des Moines Tribune*, February 28, 1975, p. 1.

59. David Gilbert, "RTA Eyes Buying Own Rolling Stock," *Chicago Tribune*, March 2, 1975, p. 38; Lee Strobel, "Rock Island to Seek Pay Cuts," *Chicago Tribune* March 3, 1975, p. 6.

60. David Gilbert, "Coal Pilferer, 83, Aids Rock Island," *Chicago Tribune*, March 8, 1975, p. F3.

61. James Coates, "Rock Island Fights for Life," *Chicago Tribune*, March 4, 1975, p. 1.

62. David Gilbert, "Rock Island Threatened by ICC Attorney," *Chicago Tribune*, March 5, 1975, p. A1.

63. For the Pearson bill, see U.S. Senate Committee on Commerce, Surface Transportation Subcommittee Hearings, "The Financial Condition of the Rock Island Railroad," March 10, 1975, 94th Cong., 1st Sess. (Washington, D.C.: GPO, 1975), pp. 3–4. For Eyster testimony, see "Statement of Rodney F. Eyster, General Counsel, Department of Transportation, before the Senate Commerce Committee Regarding the Chicago, Rock Island and Pacific Railroad, Monday, March 10, 1975," in Judith Hope Files (Domestic Policy Council), Box 40 (Rock Island Railroad), Gerald R. Ford Presidential Library, Ann Arbor, Michigan.

64. Testimony of John W. Ingram, President, Chicago, Rock Island and Pacific Railroad Company, before the Senate Commerce Committee, March 10, 1975, pp. 21–22, Box 4 (Bankruptcy Proceedings), CRIP.

65. Ibid., p. 19.

66. Statement of Senator John Culver, "Rock Island Financial Condition," Senate Commerce Committee Hearings, March 10, 1975, p. 8, CRIP.

67. Statement of Rep. Glenn English, "Rock Island Financial Condition," pp. 9–10.

68. Testimony of Ingram, "Rock Island Financial Condition," p. 21.

69. Testimony of Edward Jordan, USRA, "Rock Island Financial Condition," p. 111.

70. Testimony of Larry Provo, C&NW Chairman, "Rock Island Financial Condition," pp. 129–130.

71. Ibid., p. 131.

72. Ibid., p. 143.

73. Martin Cassell, Rock Island Statement in Regard to Exercise of Section 1(16)(b), March 4, 1975, Box 4 (Bankruptcy Proceedings), CRIP. The date of Cassell's memo is due to an ICC meeting between principals in Midwestern railroading to discuss directed service. That meeting occurred on March 3; Provo made his argument about liquidating the Rock Island at that meeting and reiterated it at the Senate hearings on March 10.

74. Memo from Patricia A. Strunk to Mike Duval, March 13, 1975, Box 40 (Rock Island Railroad), Judith Hope Files (Domestic Council), Ford Presidential Papers.

75. James Coates and David Satter, "Rock Island Loan Denied," *Chicago Tribune* (March 15, 1975), p. B1.

76. Meeting of Board of Directors, March 17, 1975, Box 73 (March 17, 1975), CRIP. At this time, Norman Nachman, an expert in bankruptcy law, was hired to present the bankruptcy to the federal district court. Two days later, Ingram sent a $25,000 check to the Chicago firm Jenner & Block to retain the firm as its counsel in the bankruptcy hearings. The check was returned in May 1975 after Jenner & Block decided to represent Henry Crown in his intervention against the Rock Island reorganization proceedings. See Letter from Ingram to Jenner & Block, March 19, 1975, Box 4, Folder 4 (Bankruptcy Proceedings), CRIP.

77. Handwritten Notes by James Cannon of Phone Call to Henry Crown, March 18, 1975, Box 31 (Rock Island Railroad), James Cannon Files (Domestic Council), Ford Presidential Papers.

78. Transcript of Proceedings, In the Matter of Chicago, Rock Island and Pacific Railroad Company, Debtor No. 75 B 2697, March 17, 1975, Box 4 (Bankruptcy Proceedings), p. 2., CRIP. David Gilbert, "Bankruptcy Petition Filed by Rock Island," *Chicago Tribune*, March 18, 1975, p. 1.

79. Transcript of Proceedings, March 17, 1975, pp. 5–6.

80. Ibid., p. 9.

Chapter 7. Stayin' Alive

1. "The Little Engine That Did!" Rock Island Railroad, 1976 (in author's collection). I am grateful to my son Balin for reminding me of this fairy tale and for pulling it out of a box of train material in my basement.

2. "Five Railroads Seek Parts of Rock Island," *Chicago Tribune* (March 19, 1975): 5. The railroads, including the Union Pacific, Chicago and North Western,

Illinois Central Gulf, Milwaukee Road, and Burlington Northern, petitioned the ICC to allow them to operate over Rock Island lines "for an indefinite period."

3. "Ford to City: Drop Dead," *New York Daily News*, October 30, 1975, p. 1.

4. Laura Kalman, *Right Star Rising: A New Politics, 1974–1980* (New York: Norton, 2010), p. 63. Ford eventually provided federal aid to New York.

5. "Judge Grants 12-day Reprieve to Rock Island," *Chicago Tribune*, March 22, 1975, p. N1.

6. Text of bill is in Meeting with Senators, April 16, 1975, James Cannon Files (Domestic Council), Box 31 (Rock Island Railroad), Ford Presidential Papers.

7. Letter from William Gibbons to Representative Tom Steed (R–Okla.), April 7, 1975, Box 13, Folder 1, Tom Steed Collection, Carl Albert Congressional Research and Studies Center, University of Oklahoma.

8. Testimony of John W. Ingram Before the Transportation Subcommittee of the Senate Commerce Committee, May 1, 1975, Box 15, Folder 1, Tom Steed Collection, Albert Center. Ingram and Gibbons consistently made the case to Washington officials that "the Rock Island does not seek a federal 'bail out.' We have consistently sought to borrow, not beg. . . . Whether the Rock Island retains ownership or whether service is assumed by another carrier, the government will be fully compensated for its investment in a better, more efficient railroad system for the nation." Letter from Gibbons and Ingram, May 20, 1975, Box 13, Folder 1, Steed Collection, Albert Center.

9. Transcript of Proceedings, U.S. District Court, Northern District of Illinois, Eastern Division, In the Matter of Chicago, Rock Island and Pacific Railroad Company (No. 75 B 2697), March 28, 1975, pp. 30–32 (hereafter Transcript of Proceedings), from the author's collection.

10. For the list of Rock Island candidates, which did not include Gibbons's name, see "Candidates or Rock Island Trustee," Box 4, Folder 4, CRIP.

11. Transcript of Proceedings, March 29, 1975, p. 27.

12. The ship's history can be found in the Naval Historical Center, Department of the Navy, *Dictionary of American Fighting Ships* (Washington, D.C.), online, at http://www.history.navy.mil/danfs/h8/howard_f_clark.htm (accessed February 6, 2012).

13. "Former Federal Judge Frank McGarr Dies," *Chicago Tribune*, January 10, 2012, at http://articles.chicagotribune.com/2012-01-10/news/ct-met-mcgarr-obit-20120110_1_chief-judge-federal-bench-environmental-case (accessed July 20, 2012).

14. Gibbons background is from "Trustee's Evidence," In the Matter of CRIP, No. 75 B 2697, Box 167, CRIP.

15. "Nicholas G. Manos, 1922–2010," *Chicago Tribune* October 21, 2010, at http://articles.chicagotribune.com/2010-10-21/features/ct-met-manos-obit-1022-2010 1021_1_nuremberg-trials-reorganization-plan-bankruptcy-attorney (accessed June 24, 2011).

16. Transcript of Proceedings, No. 75 B 2697, April 2, 1975, p. 3.

17. Ibid., p. 6.

18. John W. Ingram to Howard Butcher, March 25, 1975, Box 4, Folder 4 (Bankruptcy Proceedings, 1975), CRIP.

19. Transcript of Proceedings, April 15, 1975, No. 75 B 2697, pp. 3, 4.

20. Ibid., p. 10. At the same hearing Continental Bank of Illinois entered the pro-

ceedings as an intervenor in the case. Continental held $52 million of Rock Island debentures, both as mortgage bonds and as equipment trusts and leases.

21. Letter from Gibbons to Reed, May 5, 1975, reply from Reed to Gibbons, May 15, 1975, and reply from Gibbons to Reed, May 19, 1975, in Box 4, Folder 2 (ATSF Sales of Lines and Negotiations), CRIP.

22. "Rock Island Lines Fires 200 Office Staff," *Chicago Tribune*, April 23, 1975, p. B1. The railroad had 10,000 employees, the majority of them in labor unions. Gibbons warned that if business did not improve soon some of the unionized employees would be laid off. Within a year of the bankruptcy, the railroad had slashed 2,000 jobs.

23. "R.I. Deficit in Quarter Doubles," *Chicago Tribune*, May 20, 1975, p. C7.

24. Letter, with attachments, from E. M. Hodges to John W. Ingram, June 11, 1975, Box 3, Folder 1, CRIP.

25. Transcript of Proceedings, In the Matter of Chicago, Rock Island and Pacific, No. 75 B 2697, July 30, 1975, pp. 2, 5.

26. Petrakis and Weber, *Henry Crown, Book Two*, p. 170.

27. Letter from Donald W. Bennett, Chief Counsel, FRA, August 15, 1975, Box 62 (Rock Island, Nov.–Dec. 1975), Daniel O'Neal Papers, Hoover Institution, Stanford University.

28. Gibbons to Bennett, with attachments, September 9, 1975, ibid.

29. Questions and Answers for William Coleman, re: Trustees certificates, summer 1975, Box 13, Folder 1, Steed Collection, Albert Center.

30. Ibid., p. 7.

31. Transcript of Proceedings, In the Matter of CRIP, No. 75 B 2697, September 10, 1975, p. 3.

32. Ibid., p. 40.

33. In the Matter of CRIP, No. 75 B 2697, Report and Testimony of Richard J. Barber, p. 3, Box I-394 (Law), Folder 3 (Richard Barber Report and Correspondence), Collection B-6, Milwaukee Road Papers, John W. Barriger III National Railroad Library, Saint Louis Mercantile Library, University of Missouri–St. Louis. Biographical information on Barber can be found on pp. B-1–B-4.

34. Barber Report, ibid., pp. 4–5.

35. Barber Report, ibid., p. 13.

36. Barber Report, ibid., pp. 21–23.

37. Barber Report, ibid., p. 54.

38. *Chicago Tribune* (September 18, 1975): A1.

39. Transcript of Proceedings, In the Matter of CRIP, No. 75 B 2697, September 23, 1975, p. 2 (Nachman quote) and pp. 4–5 (Mullin quote).

40. Memorandum from Tad to Daniel O'Neal, November 17, 1975, Box 62 (Rock Island, 11/12, 1975), O'Neal Papers.

41. Memorandum from Fritz Kahn, General Counsel, ICC to Commissioner Virginia Mae Brown, November 6, 1975, pp. 2, 6, Box 62 (Rock Island, 11/12, 1975), O'Neal Papers.

42. Memo from Tad [no last name] to O'Neal, p. 7, Box 62, O'Neal Papers.

43. Transcript of Proceedings, Ocober 28, 1975, In the Matter of CRIP, No. 75 B 2697, p. 4.

44. Ibid., pp. 13–15. The cash on hand was a consequence of deferring payments of interest and taxes while in bankruptcy.

45. Ibid., p. 19.

46. Leonard Wiener, "Court OKs 300 Cars for Rock Island Line," *Chicago Tribune*, November 4, 1975, p. C7.

47. *Chicago Tribune*, January 17, 1976, p. J7.

48. Richard Phillips, "Crown Wants Outsider to Figure R.I. Repair Bill," *Chicago Tribune*, February 27, 1976, p. C7.

49. "Judge Denies Plea to Bar Rock Island Renewal," *Chicago Tribune*, May 28, 1976, p. C9.

50. "Rock Island Cuts Loss in 2d Quarter, Posts June Profit," *Chicago Tribune*, August 5, 1976, p. C9.

51. David Young, "RTA Votes $1.7 Million to Aid Rock Island Line," *Chicago Tribune*, June 26, 1976, p. I7.

52. Press Release from Rock Island Trustee, n.d. (July 1976), Box 22, Folder 9 (Executive Files, RTA Authority), CRIP.

53. David Young, "RTA Studies Purchase of Rock Island," *Chicago Tribune*, August 11, 1976, p. 3.

54. David Young, "Rock Island Line Far From Finished," *Chicago Tribune*, August 15, 1976, p. A11.

55. David Young, "RTA Weighs Rock Island Alternatives," *Chicago Tribune*, August 16, 1976, p. E7. The Union Station connection at Englewood was never built, and a rebuilt LaSalle Street Station still serves Rock Island District commuters on Metra, which is the railroad arm of the RTA.

56. Stanley Ziemba, "RTA Offers Rock Island $7 Million Commuter Aid," *Chicago Tribune*, September 8, 1976, p. 1.

57. "Take the Cash and Run the Trains," *Chicago Tribune*, September 12, 1976, p. A4.

58. Transcript of Proceedings, No. 75 B 2693, June 7, 1976, pp. 3–5.

59. Ibid., pp. 15–16.

60. Ibid., pp. 9–10.

61. Transcript of Proceedings, In the Matter of the Rock Island Railroad, No. 75 B 2697, June 24, 1976, p. 9.

62. Press Release, 1977, Box 24, Folder 1 (Executive Files), Southern Pacific RR, CRIP.

63. Memo from Newton Swain to Ingram and Gibbons, November 24, 1976, Box 24, Folder 4 (Executive Files, Subject, SP Sale of Tucumcari Line, 1974–1976), CRIP.

Chapter 8. The Omen

1. For skiffle's impact on British rock guitarists, see Eric Clapton, *Clapton: The Autobiography* (New York: Broadway Books, 2007); Keith Richards, *Life* (New York: Little, Brown and Company, 2010); and Pete Townshend, *Who I Am: A Memoir* (New York: Harper, 2012). For Jimmy Page and skiffle, including footage of Lonnie Donegan, see *It Might Get Loud*, directed by Davis Guggenheim (Thomas Tull Productions, 2008).

2. *Source Code*, Summit Entertainment (2011).

3. *Rock Island Trail*, Republic Pictures (1950). The movie was discussed at a June 13, 1949, executive committee meeting. John Dow Farrington told the board that Republic Pictures had approached him about making the motion picture. It would cost the Rock Island about $25,000 to transport the crew and actors from Los Angeles to MacAlester, Oklahoma, where the movie was filmed. Farrington also spoke about how the film would provide "excellent publicity for our railroad at a very small out-of-pocket cost." It was overwhelmingly approved by the board. Box 60, Folder (Board Meeting Minutes, 6/13/49), CRIP.

4. *Damien: Omen II*, 20th Century Fox (1978). Unfortunately, I could not find any source regarding negotiations with the director and the Trustee regarding the payment to the Rock Island for use of its property.

5. *Chicago Tribune*, November 10, 1976, p. C9.

6. Transcript of Proceedings, In the Matter of CRIP, No. 75 B 2637, December 28, 1976, pp. 1–8.

7. Ibid., p. 9.

8. Ibid., pp. 14–17.

9. Biography of William Jenner by Ronald Rotunda, Bert Jenner Endowed Chair of Law, University of Illinois College of Law. Courtesy of Daniel Murray, Senior Partner, Jenner & Block.

10. Biography of Jenner, ibid., p. 2.

11. "Albert E. Jenner, Jr.: In Memoriam," remarks of Peter Hay, Dean of Illinois College of Law, *University of Illinois Law Review* vol. 198 (1988): 818.

12. For Crown's relationship with Jenner, see Henry Mark Petrakis and David B. Weber, *Henry Crown*, Book One, p. 76, and Book Two, pp. 119–120, 176. Interview with Daniel Murray, August 7, 2009.

13. Transcript of Proceedings, December 28, 1976, pp. 27–31.

14. Ibid., p. 37.

15. Ibid., pp. 44–45.

16. Ibid., pp. 49–51.

17. Memo of Telephone Conversation with Ben Biaggini and William Gibbons, December 8, 1976, Box 23, Folder 7, CRIP.

18. Ibid., p. 2.

19. Memo from Newton Swain to Ingram and Gibbons, November 24, 1976, Box 23, Folder 4 (Executive Files, Subject, SP purchase of Tucumcari Line), CRIP.

20. Transcript of Phone Conversation between William Gibbons, John Ingram, and Ben Biaggini, January 7, 1977, Box 24, Folder 3, CRIP. Ben Biaggini later told a different story about the negotiations with Gibbons. "In a mood of keeping the discussions alive, I invited Gibbons to Palm Springs. We talked a little. We played a little golf. Finally, he and I were on the golf course between the ninth and tenth holes and I stopped the cart about halfway between and I said, 'C'mon Bill, what will you take for part of the railroad up through Tucumcari to KC and over to St. Louis, including. . . . ' I think I asked for the whole Memphis line. And so he thought for a moment and said, 'My people tell me that the least number I can take is 47 million dollars [sic],' and I said, 'we have a deal.'" Interview with Ben Biaggini by John W. Barriger IV, January 22, 2003, pp. 23–24, Railroad Executive Oral History Program, John W. Barriger III National Railroad Library, Saint Louis Mercantile Library, University of Missouri–St. Louis.

21. "Rock Island Asks 180-day Delay to Study Track Sale," *Chicago Tribune*, January 7, 1977, p. C7.

22. Letter from Gibbons to Henry Crown, April 21, 1978, Box 9, Folder 3 (Executive Files, Subject, Executive Dept., William Gibbons Correspondence, 1978), CRIP.

23. Letter from Gibbons to John Ingram, May 26, 1976, Box 7, Folder 10 (DRGW Purchase of Line), CRIP.

24. Letter from Gibbons to S.R. Freeman, March 21, 1977, Box 7, Folder 10 (Executive Files, Subject, General, DRGW), CRIP.

25. Letter from Newton Swain to Gibbons, April 7, 1978, Box 7, Folder 11 (Executive Files, Subject, Sale of Rock Island to DRGW), CRIP.

26. Draft: Trustee's Report to Court on Track, December 27, 1978, Box 4, Folder 10, CRIP.

27. Ibid., pp. 15–16.

28. "Iowa Rail Assistance Program" Box 238, Folder 9 (DOT, 1982), Governor Robert Ray Papers, State of Iowa Historical Society, Des Moines (hereafter Ray Papers).

29. "Iowa's Statement on Project Independence," September 11, 1974, Box 38, Folder 1 (1974), Department and Subject Files, Vermeer, Energy Policy Council, Ray Papers; see Iowa Rail Assistance Program, in ibid., for the branch lines.

30. Don L. Hofsommer, *Steel Rails to Hawkeyeland: Iowa's Railroad Experience* (Bloomington: Indiana University Press, 2005), pp. 228–232, discusses the efforts to rehabilitate branch lines in Iowa.

31. Minutes of the Board of the Iowa Energy Policy Council, September 3 and 4, 1974, Box 38, Folder 3, Ray Papers.

32. Energy Policy Council Railroad Report, August 1974, Box 173, Folder 5 (Energy Policy Council), Vermeer, Ray Papers, pp. 14–15. The route is now a paved nature trail.

33. Dan Piller, "Trip Dramatizes Rock Island Woes," *Des Moines Register*, May 18, 1975, pp. 1, 7–10.

34. A picture of Gibbons receiving the check can be found in "Working for the Railroad," *Des Moines Register* (October 24, 1975). For the traffic on the branch, see Memo from Richard Lane, December 5, 1977, Box 1, Executive Files (Abandonment), Folder 1, CRIP.

35. Letter from Gibbons and Ingram to Ray and Iowa Legislature, March 5, 1976, Box 1, Folder 5 (Abandonments, General, 1975–1976), CRIP.

36. "Rock Island's Revival," *Des Moines Register*, September 6, 1977, Rock Island Clippings Collection, Iowa Department of Transportation Library, Ames, Iowa (hereafter IDOT Library).

37. Larry Provo to John Millhone, March 31, 1975, Box 173, Folder 7, Vermeer (Energy Policy Council, 1975), Ray Papers.

38. Dan Piller, "Railway Chief's Blunt Talk wins Few Friends in Iowa," *Des Moines Register*, March 15, 1976, IDOT Library. Other railroad executives, such as Alan Boyd, president of Illinois Central Gulf, praised the Railway Assistance Fund, expressing to Governor Ray "my admiration and appreciation at the foresight you and the legislature have shown . . . in coming to grips with the problems of transportation and energy." Letter from Alan Boyd to Ray, March 19, 1975, Box 38, Folder 1 (Vermeer, Energy Policy Council), Ray Papers.

39. Paul D. Schneider, "In The Violet Hour," *Trains* (March 1983): 24.

40. Dr. Paul Banner, an executive vice president with the Rock Island from 1975 to 1980, was told by an official with the FRA that "we're going to force you to the wall and get you to stop running." He also said that on his visit to Washington to speak with FRA officials he witnessed some graffiti in the men's room, saying, "The Rock Island is here today, flush twice." Interview with Paul Banner, June 11, 2012. The FRA had been administered by John Ingram, the Rock's president, and Ingram was universally disliked within the agency, according to several sources.

41. Anthony Haswell, "My Ride on the Rock," *Trains* (March 1983): 37–46.

42. "Trustee's Petition for Authority to Discontinue Intercity Passenger Train Service," September 2, 1976, Proceedings in U.S. District Court No. 75 B 2697, page 2. Box 4576 (FD 28532—1977), ICC Papers, RG 134, NARA, Suitland, Maryland.

43. Haswell, "My Ride on the Rock," 44.

44. "Trustee's Petition," page 3.

45. "Memorandum Opinion and Order on Trustee's Petition for Authority to Discontinue Intercity Passenger Train Service," September 8, 1976, No. 75 B 2697, pp. 9–10, Box 4576 (FD 28532–1977), RG 134, ICC Papers.

46. *Last Ride of the Rocket?* A production of WHBF Television, 1977. Video in possession of author.

47. Edward J. Brunner and Stu Eidson, "Tales from the Peoria Rocket," *Trains* (December 1981): 45–49.

48. Brief of City of Chicago, February 2, 1977, Before the Illinois Commerce Commission Docket No. 76–0405, pp. 6–8. Chicago's attorney also argued that this willful neglect extended to passenger equipment, making the amazing argument that "although slow order speeds have been imposed on its tracks, Rock Island's intercity trains do not afford its passengers with a smooth ride" (p. 7).

49. Brief on Behalf of John W. McGinness, Illinois Legislative Director of United Transportation Union, February 15, 1977, Before the Illinois Commerce Commission, Docket 76–0405, pp. 1–12. Box 4576 (FD 28532–1977), RG 134, ICC Papers (emphasis added).

50. Official Transcript of Testimony before the Interstate Commerce Commission, February 1, 1978, Box 4576 (FD 28532–1977), RG 134, ICC Papers.

51. Testimony of John W. McGinness before the Interstate Commerce Commission, February 1978, Box 4576 (FD 28532–1977), RG 134, ICC Papers, pp. 6–8.

52. Letter from E. M. McIntosh, Executive Secretary, RLEA to Robert Oswald, ICC, August 30, 1977; Brief of Illinois State Legislative Board Brotherhood of Locomotive Engineers, March 21, 1978, both in Box 4576 (FD 28532–1977), RG 134, ICC Papers.

53. Amtrak would create a daily Chicago to Peoria run, the *Prairie Marksman*, using the Illinois Central Gulf to Chenoa, Illinois, and then the Toledo, Peoria, and Western to East Peoria, Illinois. It began service in August 1980 and ended in October 1981, after averaging only sixty-five daily passengers on its run. Subsidized by the State of Illinois, Amtrak lost $120,000 per month on the route. "Amtrak Cut," *Southeast Missourian*, September 1, 1981, at http://news.google.com/newspapers?id=-NEfAAAAIBAJ&sjid=5tgEAAAAIBAJ&pg=5460,253719&dq=prairie-marksman&hl=en (accessed May 27, 2012).

54. Initial Decision, ICC FD 28532, Box 4576 (FD 28532–1977), RG 134, ICC

Papers. The *Chicago Tribune* reported that "daily ridership on the Peoria Rocket, which was 91 in 1974, dwindled to 16 last year. Daily ridership on the Rock Island Rocket declined from 143 in 1974 to 26 last year." David Young, "Railroad to end runs to Peoria and Rock Island," *Chicago Tribune*, May 10, 1978, p. 3.

55. Brunner and Eidson, "Tales from the Peoria Rocket," p. 47.

56. Tom Skilling, "Chicago's Severe Winter Trifecta of the Late 1970s," *Chicago Tribune*, December 27, 2009, at http://articles.chicagotribune.com/2009-12-27/news/0911280248_1_winters-frank-wachowski-weather-updates (accessed July 31, 2012).

57. *Trains* (May 1977): 13–17, contains images of the railroads combating winter weather.

58. Trustee's News Bulletin, February 24, 1978, Press Clippings, Box 79 (78 and 79 Review and Outlook), CRIP.

59. Manager's Newsletter, Volume 3, Number 1, March 18, 1977, p. 1. Box 13, Folder 1, Tom Steed Collection, Carl Albert Center for Congressional Records and Studies, University of Oklahoma.

60. Trustee's Evidence, In the Matter of CRIP, No. 75 B 2697, Box 167, p. 3, CRIP.

61. Manager's Newsletter, pp. 2, 3, Box 13, Folder 1, Tom Steed Collection.

62. Ibid., pp. 3–4.

63. Draft, Traffic for 1978, January 23, 1979, Box 4, Folder 10, CRIP.

64. Transcript of Proceedings, In the Matter of CRIP, No. 75 B 2697, December 14, 1977, pp. 4–5.

65. Ibid., pp. 8–9.

66. Ibid., p. 18.

67. Ibid., pp. 19–20.

68. Ibid., pp. 28–29.

69. Ibid., pp. 37–38.

Chapter 9. Walking Dead Men

1. Jim Scribbins, *The Milwaukee Road, 1928–1985* (Forest Park, Ill.: Heimburger House Publishing, 2001).

2. For a good overview of the bankruptcy, see Saunders, *Main Lines*, pp. 160–168.

3. The *Wall Street Journal* reported on May 9, 1978, that the railroads had to end the track-sharing arrangement due to the Federal Railroad Administration placing onerous terms on a $50 million loan to repair the track. So the 14-month arrangement between the two railroads ended with the resumption of service over their separate, yet parallel, track.

4. Stephen M. Aug, "Joint Operation of Midwestern Lines Urged," *Washington Star*, January 4, 1978, n.p. Press Clippings, Boxes 78 and 79–Review and Outlook, CRIP.

5. Farm Rail went nowhere; see David Morgan in *Trains* (April 1978): 9–10 (because "it was regarded as a delaying tactic by those who wished the Rock would dry up and go away"). The Katy and the KCS were also surprised to be included, pinning their hopes on acquiring lines of the bankrupt railroads, with the KCS even eyeing an extension into Chicago.

6. Albert R. Karr, "Midwest Roads Fall Deeper Into Trouble; Federal Planners Map a Possible Shakeup," *Wall Street Journal*, January 12, 1978, p. 34.

7. Memorandum for the President from Brock Adams, December 2, 1977, p. 2, Box 64 (12/14/77(1)), Staff Offices, Office of Staff Secretary—Handwriting Files, Jimmy Carter Presidential Library, Atlanta, Georgia (hereafter Carter Papers).

8. Ibid., p. 3.

9. Ibid., pp. 4–5.

10. Memo for the President from Brock Adams, January 13, 1978, Box TN-3 (1/20/77–1/20/81), White House Central Files (WHCF)—Executive, Carter Papers. In an additional memo to the president from Stu Eizenstat, Carter's young domestic policy adviser, Eizenstat reminded the president of Adams's upcoming conference in Chicago: "Congressional hearings will be held this session to explore these and other railroad matters. Some members have expressed their intention to introduce bills to provide subsidies to the bankrupt Milwaukee Railroad and other Midwestern systems. Secretary Adams' statement will signal the Administration's intention to oppose quick-fix, government bailout legislation. I recommend that you support the approach which Secretary Adams has outlined."

11. Ibid., pp. 2–3.

12. Karr, "Midwest Roads Fall Deeper Into Trouble," *Wall Street Journal*, January 12, 1978, p. 34.

13. "Rock Island Trustee Blasts Adams's Statement on Road," *Wall Street Journal*, January 13, 1978, p. 26. Gibbons had strong support from the State of Kansas. The state attorney general, Curt Schneider, sent Adams a letter taking issue with the comment he made in the paper. "The Rock Island is not a 'walking,' but a 'running' line, for in Kansas the past three years while in reorganization it has RUN.... The fact that the Rock Island has survived the past three years without your help is plain proof that it is viable." Letter from Curt Schneider to Brock Adams, January 18, 1978, Box 110, Folder 6 (Railroads), Keith Sebelius Papers, Kansas State Historical Society, Topeka.

14. *Des Moines Register*, January 19, 1978, n.p., Rock Island Clippings File, IDOT Library.

15. Draft Comments of Brock Adams, January 9, 1978, pp. 4, 4A, Box TN-3 (1/20/77–1/20/81), WHCF—Executive, Carter Papers.

16. Ibid., pp. 7–8.

17. *Des Moines Register*, January 19, 1978, IDOT Library. Wolfe would make the argument throughout the spring, in rather Social Darwinist terms: "If weaker railroads are liquidated, it would make others stronger." Wolfe also argued that the Rock's Farm Rail concept "is a self preservation plan" that would require revolutionary changes in work rules. "Unions will never agree to it unless you line them up and shoot them." Dale Kueter, "Urges Liquidation of Rock Island, Milwaukee," *Cedar Rapids Gazette*, April 6, 1978, Press Clippings, Box 79, CRIP. Wolfe wasn't alone in his denigration of the two bankrupts. ATSF's John Reed stated: "the blunt truth is that the Midwest could get along without either the Rock or the Milwaukee Road." *Trains* (April 1978): 4.

18. United States Railway Association, Final System Plan, July 26, 1976, pp. 2–4, Box 1652 (USRA-FSP), Accession 1807, Penn Central Papers.

19. "Penn Central Company's Position on the Final System Plan of the United

States Railway Association," September 15, 1975, pp. 1, 3, Box 1653 (Penn Central Co.), Accession 1807, Penn Central Papers.

20. Penn Central Transportation Company News, September 16, 1975, Box 1651 (Press Releases, July–December 1975), Penn Central Papers. See also, "Statement of the Penn Central's Trustees on the USRA's Final System Plan," September 16, 1975, No Box (Penn Central), Accession 2068, Jervis Langdon Papers, Hagley Museum and Library, Wilmington, Delaware. This was a 25-page question-and-answer form, documenting the main opposition to the FSP and the conveyance of the assets of the Penn Central. A special court was created to hear arguments about the valuation of Penn Central assets, a process that continued into the 1980s.

21. Congressman Robert Michel News, November 7, 1975, Box 1652 (Final System Plan), Accession 1807, Penn Central Papers.

22. Saunders, *Main Lines*, pp. 108–111, provides a good summary of the 4R Act. The act also spun off the Northeast Corridor (the old Pennsylvania Railroad line between Washington, D.C., to Boston) to Amtrak.

23. Jervis Langdon, "Review of Rail Operations During and After the Penn Central Bankruptcy," March 7, 1982, pp. 52–53, No Box Number (Penn Central), Accession 2068, Langdon Papers.

24. Loving, *The Men Who Loved Trains*, p. 208.

25. Langdon, "Review of Rail Operations," pp. 54–56. A February 15, 1978, Five Year business plan showed how Conrail would need an additional $1.8 billion in federal funding. Accession 1096-016, Box 174, Folder 5 (Railroad Settlement Policy Commission), Adams Papers.

26. Letter from John Ingram to Brock Adams, February 9, 1978, Box 11, Folder 1 (Executive Files, Subject, FRA-General), CRIP.

27. "End Game for the Rock Island?" *Business Week* (March 20, 1978).

28. "Southern Pacific and Rock Island Reach an Accord," *Wall Street Journal*, April 7, 1978, p. 5, announced the deal; "Reprieve for the Rock," *Des Moines Register*, April 13, 1978, n.p., IDOT Library.

29. "Rock Island Trustee To Sign Aid Papers," *Journal of Commerce* (September 21, 1978), Press Clippings, Box 79, CRIP. I could not find the letter referenced in the Brock Adams papers.

30. "Work a Month, Rest a Month—for $30,000!," *Des Moines Register*, June 16, 1978. Press Clippings, ibid., CRIP.

31. Tim Jarrell, "Rock Island, Unions Reach Shuttle Train Agreement," *Dallas Times Herald*, July 8, 1978. Press Clippings, ibid., CRIP.

32. Ray Potter, "Railroad Line 'Doing the Unheard of'" *Colorado Springs Gazette-Telegraph*, November 29, 1978. Press Clippings, ibid., CRIP.

33. For the advertisements, see Press Clippings, Box 79 (78 and 79 Review and Outlook), CRIP.

34. David Young, "Rock Island Had Worst Accident Rate," *Chicago Tribune*, January 9, 1979, p. C6.

35. David Young, "C&NW to Get $90 Million for Track Work," *Chicago Tribune*, August 9, 1978, p. D3.

36. David Young, "It Looks Like a Rail Merger, But It's Not," *Chicago Tribune*, August 21, 1978, p. E10.

37. Notes on Meeting and Telegram from Gibbons to Wolfe and reply, July 14,

1978 (meeting) and July 18, 1978 (telegrams), Box 7, Folder 5, CRIP.

38. David Young, "Once Bankrupt MoPac one of Strongest Rails," *Chicago Tribune*, September 5, 1978, p. C7.

39. Transcript of Proceedings, September 18, 1978, In the Matter of Chicago, Rock Island and Pacific Company, No. 75 B 2697, pp. 3–26 (Manos report).

40. Ibid., p. 31.

41. Ibid., p. 56 (for the quote), pp. 25–56 for the response of Jenner.

42. Ibid., pp. 59–60.

43. Ibid., pp. 71–72.

44. Ibid., pp. 81–86.

45. Ibid., p. 92.

46. Ibid., pp. 95–106.

47. Ibid., pp. 111–113.

48. Report of the Trustee, Rock Island Review and Outlook, 1978, Box 79 (Executive Files), pages 1.0 and 1.1, CRIP.

49. Stanley Changnon Jr., David Changnon, and Phyllis Stone, *Illinois Third Consecutive Severe Winter: 1978–1979*, Illinois State Water Survey 94 (Urbana, Il. 1980), p. 1, at http://www.isws.illinois.edu/pubdoc/RI/ISWSRI-94.pdf (accessed July 6, 2012).

50. "Brutal Winter of 1978–1979," National Weather Service Forecast Office, Quad Cities/Moline, Ill., at http://www.crh.noaa.gov/dvn/?n=01011979_brutalwinter (accessed July 12, 2012).

51. Trustee's Report, 1978 and First Four Months 1979, June 18, 1979, Box 4 (Bankruptcy 1979), pp. 41–42, Chicago, Rock Island and Pacific Railroad Papers.

52. Verified Statement of Thomas Schmidt, RI Chief Engineer, May 1979, Before the ICC, Rock Island Abandonment of Entire System, p. 13, April 22, 1980, Collection B-6, Milwaukee Road Papers (Miscellaneous S-1119) (AB-46 (sub 22), John W. Barriger III National Railway Library, Saint Louis Mercantile Library, University of Missouri–St. Louis.

53. Transcript of Proceedings, In the Matter of Chicago, Rock Island and Pacific, No. 75 B 2697, March 13, 1979, pp. 2–6. The escrow account was worth $7.25 million.

54. Transcript of Proceedings, In the Matter of Chicago, Rock Island and Pacific, No. 75 B 2697, March 14, 1979. Getzendanner was representing Continental Bank as part of the Milwaukee Road bankruptcy as well, and provisions had been made for that carrier to borrow funds against an escrow account earlier that month.

55. Robert Bombaugh, attorney for Henry Crown, raised these questions; see Transcript of Proceedings, in the Matter of Chicago, Rock Island and Pacific, No. 75 B 2697, p. 14.

56. W. Carl Bliven, *Jimmy Carter's Economy: Policy in an Age of Limits* (Chapel Hill: University of North Carolina Press, 2002), pp. 93–94.

57. Data on CPI in Robert J. Samuelson, *The Great Inflation and Its Aftermath: The Past and Future of American Affluence* (New York: Random House, 2008), pp. 262–263.

58. Ibid., pp. 47–63; Robert M. Collins, *More: The Politics of Economic Growth in America* (New York: Oxford University Press, 2002). Collins labeled the new economics strategy "growth liberalism."

59. Robert M. Collins, "Growth Liberalism: Great Societies at Home and Grand

Designs Abroad," in David Farber, ed., *The Sixties: From Memory to History* (Chapel Hill: University of North Carolina Press, 1992).

60. Samuelson, *The Great Inflation and Its Aftermath*, pp. 63–74, addresses these issues and calls the price controls a failed policy.

61. Allan Matusow, *Nixon's Economy: Booms, Busts, Dollars, and Votes* (Lawrence: University Press of Kansas, 1998), is a superb examination of the debates over the decision to leave Bretton Woods. See also Arthur F. Burns and Robert Ferrell, eds., *Inside the Nixon Administration: The Secret Diary of Arthur F. Burns, 1969–1974* (Lawrence: University Press of Kansas, 2010).

62. Bliven, *Jimmy Carter's Economy*.

63. Shane Hamilton, *Trucking Country: The Road to America's Walmart Economy* (Princeton: Princeton University Press, 2008), pp. 1–2, documents the story of Rusell Parkhurst, editor of *Overdrive*, a magazine of independent trucking, who blamed the shutdown not on gas prices but on the regulations imperiling the free-market economy and contributing to the enslavement of independent truckers to a system that sustained union truckers at the expense of "wildcat" or "cowboy" truck drivers. Brock Adams was provided updates on the truckers' strike on June 29, 1979: "The truck strike remains very serious. Recent incidents in the truck strike include trucks snarling traffic on expressways in New York and Chicago. . . . Shooting incidents were confirmed in Arkansas, Maryland, Missouri, and Delaware, and reported in Michigan, Illinois and Minnesota." Memo from Jack Watson to Adams, June 29, 1979, Accession 1096–016, Box 147, Folder 19 (WH Memos), Adams Papers.

64. Memorandum, June 26, 1979, Personal and Confidential, "General Summary of Diesel Fuel Situation," Box 58 (Energy Meetings), O'Neal Papers.

65. Ibid.

66. Statement of William H. Dempsey, President of AAR, before the Transportation and Commerce Subcommittee of the House Interstate and Foreign Commerce Committee, April 24, 1979, p. 8, Box 3, Folder 10 (AAR Deregulation), CRIP.

67. Michael E. Levine, "Revisionism Revised? Airline Deregulation and the Public Interest," *Law and Contemporary Problems* 44, no. 1 (Winter 1981): 180.

68. George J. Stigler, "The Theory of Economic Regulation," *Bell Journal of Economics and Management Science* 2, no. 1 (1971): 3–21, remains the classic paper. Stigler wrote, "Regulation may be actively sought by an industry, or it may be thrust upon it. A central thesis of this paper is that, as a rule, regulation is acquired by the industry and is designed and operated primarily for its benefit" (p. 3). A huge literature both within economics and policy studies on the deregulation movement exists on the deregulation/regulation controversy. In recent years, with the collapse of the financial sector in 2008, most analysts have called for a return to regulation of certain key sectors of the economy, especially Wall Street. For a survey of the critical view of deregulation see Phillip J. Cooper, *The War Against Regulation: From Jimmy Carter to George W. Bush* (Lawrence: University Press of Kansas, 2009). For a critical historical perspective, relating deregulation to the development of conservatism in American politics, see Eduardo Canedo, "The Rise of the Deregulation Movement in Modern America, 1957–1980" (Ph.D. diss., Columbia University, 2008).

69. The best study of Alfred Kahn is Thomas K. McCraw, *Prophets of Regulation*. Kahn helped develop the idea of peak and offpeak prices for electric utilities, a common development in the utility industry since that time. Kahn was great for witty

quotations. When told by Frank Borman of Eastern Airlines at a hearing about the different planes owned by the airline, Kahn replied, "I really don't know one plane from another. To me, they're all marginal costs with wings" (p. 224).

70. Martha Derthick and Paul Quick, *The Politics of Deregulation* (Washington, D.C.: Brookings Institution, 1985), remains the classic account of the deregulation of airlines, trucking, and telephones. See also Rose, et al., *The Best Transportation System in the World*, pp. 186–195.

Chapter 10. The Rock Is Dead

1. Ingram told David Young of the *Chicago Tribune* after he was fired that during the BRAC strike on the Rock Island the railroad was "winning the strike" before the government took it over and made a deal with the unions. Ingram stated that "we had moved more grain out of Iowa in the week immediately preceding the DSO than any week in the history of the railroad." David Young, "Ex-Rock Island Chief Hints Takeover," *Chicago Tribune*, January 2, 1980, p. E7. Ingram expressed his view that the strike on the Rock Island was the coup de grâce for the railroad. See "An Interview with John Ingram by John W. Barriger IV," February 7, 2004, Railway Executives Oral History Program, John W. Barriger III National Railroad Library. Ingram did take a dim view of labor unions. His executive vice president on the Rock Island, John Mitros, who was in charge of personnel, had an antagonistic attitude toward labor. Interview with Paul Banner, June 17, 2012.

2. See Seth H. Bramson, *Speedway to Sunshine: The Story of the Florida East Coast Railway* (Buffalo, N.Y.: Boston Mills Press, 2010), pp. 149–153; and David P. Morgan, "Where Did the Railroad Go That Once Went to Sea?" *Trains* (February 1975): 22–28.

3. Saunders, *Main Lines*, pp. 134–135.

4. For the view of the 1970s as the major period of transition in labor-management relations, see Cowie, *Stayin' Alive*; Stein, *Pivotal Decade*; and Nelson Lichtenstein, *State of the Union: A Century of American Labor* (Princeton: Princeton University Press, 2002). None of these works deal with railroads or railroad unions.

5. Cowie, *Stayin' Alive*, p. 135; for McGarr and unions, see Transcript of Proceedings, pp. 29–30, n.d. (1978), In the Matter of Chicago, Rock Island and Pacific Railroad, No. 75 B 2697. McGarr stated: "I must confess that in the past I have looked for cooperation from unions in terms of work rules in the instance of insolvent railroads. . . . I would suspect that someday the unions have got to recognize that one reason why these railroads are insolvent are the unreasonable work rules—and while their self-preservation instincts are very obvious and understandable, they don't seem to have bent or yielded enough, in terms of cooperation with railroads."

6. Robert E. Bedingfield, *The Norfolk and Western Strike of 1978* (Norfolk, Va.: The Norfolk and Western Railway Company, 1979), documents the strike from a company perspective.

7. Ibid., p. 136.

8. "Court Acts in Rail Strike," *Chicago Tribune*, September 27, 1978, p. 1.

9. "The Week the Trains Stopped," *Time* (October 9, 1978): 62–63. DOT was

debating what to do about the national strike from the start, with Brock Adams eventually recommending to President Carter that an emergency board be established. The cost to railroads was outlined in a memo on September 29, 1978, with updates on what railroads were being picketed by BRAC. Memorandum for the President from Brock Adams, September 29, 1978, Accession 1096–016, Box 147, Folder 10 (White House Memos), Adams Papers.

10. Report of the Trustee, Rock Island Review and Outlook, 1978, pp. 1.0, 1.1, Box 79 (Executive Files), CRIP.

11. Ibid., p. 37.

12. "Rock Island Railroad Strike OKd by Clerks," *Chicago Tribune*, April 3, 1979, p. B1.

13. Summaries of the issues and the dates of mediation can be found in Report to the President by Emergency Board No. 191, National Mediation Board, October 22, 1979, Staff Offices, Office of Staff Secretary—Handwriting Files, Box 153 (10/22/79 [1]), WHCF, Jimmy Carter Presidential Library, Atlanta.

14. Transcript of Proceedings, In the Matter of Chicago, Rock Island and Pacific, No. 75 B 2697, May 22, 1979, pp. 1–9.

15. Ibid., pp. 18–19, 23.

16. Transcript of Proceedings, May 23, 1979, In the Matter of the Chicago, Rock Island and Pacific Railroad, No. 75 B 2697, p. 6.

17. Ibid., p. 7. The NW book became a bible for planning strike operations should they be necessary, and the Rock Island managers had every confidence they could duplicate the feat of the NW managers in breaking the strike on their railroad.

18. Ibid., p. 36.

19. Dave Schneidman, "Workers Call Off Strike of Rock Island Trains in 11th-hour Agreement," *Chicago Tribune*, May 24, 1979, p. B13.

20. "Rock Island Rail Strike Delayed," *Chicago Tribune*, August 18, 1979, p. B6.

21. James Strong, "Rock Island Faces No-Warning Strike," *Chicago Tribune*, August 25, 1979, p. B2.

22. For McGarr interview, see James Strong, "Judge Tells Why He Let Rail Clerks Go on Strike," *Chicago Tribune*, August 29, 1979, p. 1. For the $14 million figure, see Report to the President by Emergency Board, No. 191, p. 9. The emergency board reports stated: "Rock Island estimated that the total cost of retroactivity would approximate $14 million," which referred to paying all union workers on the railroad retroactive wages.

23. Strong, "Rock Island Faces No-warning Strike," *Chicago Tribune*, August 25, 1979, p. B2. He had said similar things in the NW strike, telling a Roanoke, Virginia, radio station that the railroad was "totally regressive" and that their proposal to settle "would take us 30 years backwards in the industry." See Bedingfield, *The Norfolk Western Strike*, p. 55. John Ingram said later, "The union had a president who . . . really didn't care much about what happened to the railroad industry. I remember calling him up for some reason and finally got referred to a number that was owned by a nightclub in New York. . . . When I finally got to talk to him, he told me in no uncertain terms that he didn't give a damn what happened to the Rock Island. As far as he was concerned it could go up a rope or something like that and that's basically what happened." Interview with John Ingram, John Barriger National Railroad Library. Sadly, Kroll died from leukemia in 1981 at age forty-five.

24. George de Lama, "Union Sets Rock Island Strike for 6 A.M. Today," *Chicago Tribune*, August 28, 1979, p. 3.

25. One document shows the attitude of one union member in Kansas testifying about restoring service to the Rock Island after the DSO had expired in April 1980. It points to a few misunderstandings concerning the Rock Island bankruptcy and the power of the court. "It is now clear that Federal Judge Frank McGarr and the ICC were set on the demise of the Rock Island, irrespective of the adverse affects on our already inadequate transportation system" (p. 2). Prepared Statement of Jack A. McGlothin, Kansas State Legislative Board, UTU, April 7, 1980, Topeka, Box 131 (Miscellaneous Railroad Legislation), Bryan Whitehead Papers, Spencer Research Library, University of Kansas.

26. David Young, "Rock Island Intends Limited Operations," *Chicago Tribune*, September 2, 1979, p. W1; for news on the parts train, see David Young, "Rock Island Loses GM Parts Business," *Chicago Tribune*, September 6, 1979, p. C7.

27. Crown Interveners Motion to Liquidate, September 12, 1979, Box I-356 (Law) (Sept, 1979—RI Reorganization), Collection B-6, Milwaukee Road Papers, John W. Barriger III National Railroad Library, Saint Louis Mercantile Library, University of Missouri–St. Louis.

28. Jay Branegan, "Rock Island Closing Plea by Creditor," *Chicago Tribune*, September 12, 1979, p. C3.

29. David Young, "3,000 Mile Cut in Track Studied by Rock Island," *Chicago Tribune*, August 29, 1979, p. C3. The meeting was occurring, according to Young, so the Rock Island could qualify for $30 million in funding from the Emergency Rail Services Act. The FRA had proposed that both the Rock Island and the Milwaukee Road pare down their mileages.

30. Transcript of Proceedings, September 10, 1979, In the Matter of the Chicago, Rock Island and Pacific Railroad Company, No. 75 B 2697, pp. 4, 5. Amazingly, given the financial problems faced by the Rock Island, on May 11, 1979, Gibbons had contacted the Milwaukee Road bankruptcy trustee, Stanley Hillman, about purchasing "certain lines of the Milwaukee system," including significant track segments in Iowa and South Dakota. Letter from Gibbons to Stanley E.G. Hillman, May 11, 1979, Box 7, Folder 3 (Executive Files, Subject), CRIP.

31. Transcript, ibid., pp. 11–13.

32. Transcript of Proceedings, September 18, 1979, In the Matter of Chicago, Rock Island and Pacific Railroad, No. 75 B 2697, pp. 5–6.

33. Ibid., p. 12.

34. Ibid., p. 17.

35. Ibid., pp. 30–31. At the same hearing Manos argued a motion to allow the Trustee to purchase 35 EMD GP-38-2 locomotives for delivery in November. Manos argued that the estate would benefit from the new power, which could be employed on a reorganized system or go back to the lessee—with no encumbrance on the estate—should a liquidation occur.

36. Memorandum from Stu Eizenstat to the President, September 14, 1979, Box TN-4 (1/1/79–9/30/79), WHCF, Executive, Carter Presidential Library. Goldschmidt was a 39-year-old mayor of Portland, Oregon, and was elevated to the role as secretary of DOT in August 1979, following a month interim management by W. Graham

Claytor. See "DOT News," Accession 1096–016, Box 167, Folder 10 (Clippings), Adams Papers. Goldschmidt would later serve as governor of Oregon.

37. Press Announcement by the President Concerning the Rock Island Railroad, September 20, 1979, Staff Offices, DPS—Eizenstat, Box 272 (RI Rail Programs), WHCF, Carter Library. It is clear that Carter did not want to make the statement and had to be prompted to do so by Eizenstat, who reminded him the morning of September 19, "I believe that you should personally appear on TV, however briefly, in this matter. Conversations with affected Congressmen and Senators have convinced me that this is *the* issue at this time in the Midwest." Carter wrote "OK" on the side of the memo. Memo from Eizenstat to Carter, September 19, 1979, ibid.

38. Statement of Secretary of Transportation Neil Goldschmidt on the Rock Island Situation, September 20, 1979, ibid.

39. The closed door meeting in McGarr's chambers was revealed in David M. Elsner, "Troubled Railroad May Need Takeover," *Chicago Tribune*, September 19, 1979, p. C3.

40. "The Rock and a Hard Place," *Chicago Tribune*, September 25, 1979, p. A2.

41. Transcript of Proceedings, September 21, 1979, In the Matter of the Chicago, Rock Island and Pacific Railroad, No. 75 B 2697, pp. 21–25.

42. Ibid., pp. 31–35.

43. Ibid., pp. 36–43.

44. Ibid., pp. 44–50.

45. Ibid., pp. 71–73.

46. Ibid., pp. 74–75.

47. Ibid., p. 81.

48. Ibid., p. 99.

49. Ibid., pp. 109–111. The FRA analyzed the Rock Island's presentation and "concluded that the projected results [were] (1) unrealistic; (2) unresponsive to the company's service obligations; and (3) ignore the cash obligations of the company." They doubted the projected carloads expressed by Ingram, stating that "through September 21, the Rock Island had handled 5,665 cars or 265 per day on a reduced car basis, so that handling an average of 926 cars per month would be required for the remainder of the month to achieve that goal." Analysis of Rock Island Projections, p. 10, Box 33, Folder 5, CRIP.

50. Press Briefing by Vice President Mondale and Chairman of the ICC Dan O'Neal, September 26, 1979, pp. 1–3, Box 272 (RI Railroad), Staff Office Files, DPS—Eizenstat, Subject, WHCF, Carter Library.

51. Ibid., p. 7.

52. "Is This Rescue Necessary?" *Chicago Tribune*, September 28, 1979, p. E2.

53. David M. Elsner, "Rock Island Freight Lines Will Roll on Friday: ICC," *Chicago Tribune*, October 4, 1979, p. B1. Ingram claimed in his interview with John Barriger IV that he was not fired but left the railroad at that time, yet he admitted he received unemployment insurance, which assumes he was let go. Ingram retired from railroading at that point. He died in 2008.

54. Trustee's Answer to Creditors' Motion and Statement of Trustee's Preliminary Planning for Debtor's Estate, October 9, 1979, Box 4 (Bankruptcy 1979), CRIP.

55. Transcript of Proceedings, October 10, 1979, In the Matter of Chicago, Rock Island and Pacific Railroad, No. 75 B 2697, pp. 5–21 (Manos), 21–32 (Jenner).

56. Letter from Neil Goldschmidt to Judge Frank McGarr, October 5, 1979, Box 31, Folder 21, CRIP. The letter was harsh, including comments that "the delay by the Trustee in developing a feasible plan of action to cope with the railroad's problems is inexcusable." He accused Gibbons of "draining all cash from the estate in a futile effort to maintain uneconomic operations" (p. 2) and argued that "we have no reason to believe that the Rock Island contains any financially self-sustaining railroad core" (p. 2), prejudging the Trustee's efforts to find one.

57. Ibid., pp. 39–50.

58. Ibid., pp. 58–62.

59. Ibid., pp. 81–94.

60. Ibid., p. 118.

61. David Young, "Service 'Normal' on Rock Island—at Taxpayer Cost," *Chicago Tribune*, November 12, 1979, p. D10.

62. Summary of Hearing Officer's Reports on Rock Island Directed Service, October 1979, Box 61 (Hearing Officer's Reports), O'Neal Papers.

63. Ibid., pp. 2–3.

64. Ibid., p. 6.

65. Ibid., p. 8.

66. Memorandum for John Stapleton from John Barnum November 14, 1979, Box 32, Folder 21, CRIP.

67. Memorandum from L. Katz to William Gibbons, re: Open Special Conference on Rock Island Directed Service by the ICC, November 19, 1979, and Letter from Neil Goldschmidt to Daniel O'Neal, November 19, 1979, Box 31, Folder 21, CRIP. For Manos's comment on the "garbled meeting," see Transcript of Proceedings, November 26, 1979, In the Matter of Chicago, Rock Island and Pacific Railroad, No. 75 B 2697, pp. 7–8. Goldschmidt included a list of railroads that had expressed interest in segments of the Rock Island, including the SP's agreement to purchase the Tucumcari–St. Louis lines. The DRGW was listed as a interested party in the Kansas City–Denver lines, the Santa Fe in the Choctaw Route from Memphis to Tucumcari, and the C&NW, Burlington Northern, and Kansas City Southern along major segments of the Rock in Iowa and Illinois. Of all the major western railroads, the Rock's former merger partner, the Union Pacific, failed to express interest in any of the Rock Island's major line segments, expressing interest only in a few branches in Nebraska, Kansas, and Colorado.

68. Transcript of Proceedings, November 1, 1979, In the Matter of the Chicago, Rock Island and Pacific Railroad, No. 75 B 2697, p. 23.

69. Memorandum for the President from Neil Goldschmidt, December 5, 1979, Box TN-4, WHCF, Carter Library. Stu Eizenstat recommended that Carter have Goldschmidt appoint a special representative so that "this difficult problem does not come too close to your desk." I could not ascertain through any source whether a representative was appointed by Goldschmidt. Kennedy had mistakenly referred to the Rock Island as the "Wabash Railroad," which had been leased by the NW in 1964.

70. Plan of Reorganization for the Chicago, Rock Island and Pacific Railroad Company, December 28, 1979, Box 5, Folder 4, CRIP.

71. Ibid., pp. 7–13.

72. Transcript of Proceedings, January 23, 1980, In the Matter of the Chicago, Rock Island and Pacific Railroad, No. 75 B 2697, pp. 11–15.
73. Ibid., pp. 19–22.
74. Ibid., pp. 22–27.
75. Ibid., pp. 27–28.
76. Ibid., p. 31.
77. Transcript of Proceedings, January 25, 1980, In the Matter of the Chicago, Rock Island and Pacific Railroad Company, No. 75 B 2697, pp. 15–37 (Murray).
78. Ibid., pp. 38–55.
79. Ibid., pp. 93–94.
80. Ibid., pp. 95–97.
81. Ibid., pp. 97–98.

Chapter 11. Too Late the Hero

1. As a 17-year-old sentimentalist, the author did wax poetically on the decline of the railroads in a column titled "A Requiem for the Railroads" that was printed in the *Chicago Tribune* (November 6, 1982), p. W8.
2. Baron Alfred Tennyson, *The Works of Alfred Lord Tennyson, Volume 3* (New York: Macmillan, 1896), p. 56. The stanza is taken from a long-form poem, "The Princess: A Medley." The portion from the quote is known as "Tears, Idle Tears." I was reminded of the poem as it was used in a Quad Cities TV program that aired in 1978 (on the end of the Rocket era in the Quad Cities). Paul Meincke, a longtime Chicago reporter for ABC affiliate WLS-TV, was the host of this program.
3. March 31, 1980, has been established by journalists, railfans, and historians as the last day of Rock Island service. This is partially true, as it is the final day a Rock Island train was run in revenue service using Rock Island crews. However, the date of directed service operations, October 5, 1979, effectively transferred the Rock Island into the management and operation of the KCT, with financial assistance coming from the federal government. While Rock Island crews operated the trains, the corporation had no control over finances, operations, or any other aspect of the railroad after October 5, 1979.
4. Letter from V. E. Coe, President, Kansas City Terminal, to Joel Burns, Director, ICC, February 7, 1980, Box 33, Folder 2, CRIP. The instructions for winding down operations were quite detailed. Regarding the security of locomotives, about 400 locomotives were to be stored, drained of coolant, batteries stored and secured, switches and circuits in "off" position, test cocks opened, exhaust stacks covered, handbrake set, with fire extinguishers, cab seats, radios, and fuses removed and stored. The operation was very efficient and capably handled by the KCT.
5. Federal Railroad Administration, Office of Federal Assistance, February 4, 1980, "Midwest Railroad Restructuring," Box 35, Folder 4, CRIP, pp. 2–3. The creditor attorneys and the Trustee disputed the numbers, as there had been no contact between interested railroads and the Rock Island. See Transcript of Proceedings, February 28, 1980, In the Matter of the Chicago, Rock Island and Pacific Railroad, No. 75 B 2697, pp. 11–12.

6. Letter from Frank McGarr to Thomas Railsback, January 28, 1980, Box 4, Folder 11, CRIP.

7. Milwaukee Railroad Restructuring Act, U.S. 96–101, November 4, 1979, 93-STAT 737 (45 U.S.C. 901 et seq.).

8. Letter from Neil Goldschmidt to Darius Gaskins Jr., February 14, 1980, Box 33, Folder 2, CRIP.

9. Transcript of Proceedings, February 19, 1980, In The Matter of Chicago, Rock Island and Pacific Railroad, No. 75 B 2697, p. 19.

10. Ibid., pp. 20–24.

11. Transcript of Proceedings, March 19, 1980, In the Matter of the Chicago, Rock Island and Pacific Railroad, No. 75 B 2697, p. 14.

12. Ibid., p. 27.

13. The RTA ran the commuter operations beginning on March 24. The Southern Pacific took over the Tucumcari line, while the Burlington Northern, Chicago and North Western, Denver and Rio Grande Western, Missouri Pacific, Frisco, and Milwaukee Road were among the other Class I carriers operating on the Rock Island.

14. Transcript of Proceedings, April 1, 1980, In the Matter of the Chicago, Rock Island and Pacific Railroad, No. 75 B 2697, pp. 21–25.

15. Ibid., pp. 11–13.

16. Motion to Confirm the Discontinuance of Railroad Operations, April 11, 1980, Box 4, Folder 11, CRIP. Judge McGarr allowed the ICC 40 days to respond to the motion, recognizing the severity of the Rock Island's situation. Henry Rush argued that in the Milwaukee Road case the ICC had been given 120 days; but given the liquidation order on January 25, Judge McGarr believed the ICC had enough information on which to act.

17. Transcript of Proceedings, April 14, 1980, In the Matter of Chicago, Rock Island and Pacific Railroad, No. 75 B 2697, pp. 22–24.

18. Ibid., p. 64.

19. "Business Briefs," *Chicago Tribune*, May 10, 1980, p. S3. The Trustee was in negotiations with the Chicago Board of Options Exchange to sell LaSalle Street Station, which would have also necessitated the RTA's building a new train station if trains could not be moved to Union Station in Chicago.

20. "Rock Island Offer Is Called Too Low," *Chicago Tribune*, May 20, 1980, p. B1.

21. Memorandum for the President, May 29, 1980, Rock Island Transition Act, Box 64 (Carter—RI Corr. Legislation), White House Staff Offices collection, Jimmy Carter Presidential Library.

22. Letter from Albert Jenner to Lloyd Cutler, May 29, 1980, Box 110 (Rock Island Railroad, 10/79–5/80), Staff Offices collection, Carter Library.

23. Transcript of Proceedings, June 2, 1980, In the Matter of Chicago, Rock Island and Pacific Railroad, No. 75 B 2697, pp. 6–7.

24. Ibid., pp. 13–25.

25. Kansas Railroad Working Group, Report to Governor John Carlin, March 19, 1980, Box 131 (Railroad Legislation), Bryan Whitehead Papers, Spencer Research Library, University of Kansas.

26. Ibid., pp. 37–48 (Murray); quotes are at pp. 33, 37.

27. Ibid., p. 62.

28. Ibid., p. 68. The ICC did make a provision for a two-year DSO for the Chicago commuter properties to continue to be operated by the RTA. This was confirmed in the order of abandonment.

29. Transcript of Proceedings, June 9, 1980, In the Matter of the Chicago, Rock Island and Pacific Railroad, No 75 B 2697, p. 8.

30. Ibid., p. 27.

31. Ibid., pp. 27–28. Murray also quoted Fred Kroll in a *Traffic World* story from April 1980 saying that BRAC might strike Rock track being operated by other carriers if the labor issues between the Rock and BRAC were not settled promptly. Murray hypothesized that this could have led Congress to act on the bill.

32. Ibid., pp. 62–79 (Clarke).

33. Ibid., p. 76.

34. Ibid., pp. 76–77.

35. *Railway Labor Executives' Association v. Gibbons,* 448 U.S. 1301 (July 2, 1980).

36. For a summary of the Supreme Court's opinion and the options for government, see Memorandum from Myles Link to Stu Eizenstat, July 1, 1980, and July 17, 1980, Box 236 (Subject File—Midwest Railroads), Staff Offices, Director of Policy—Eizenstat, WHCF, Carter Presidential Library.

37. Transcript of Proceedings, June 29, 1980, In the Matter of the Chicago, Rock Island and Pacific Railroad, No. 75 B 2697, p. 6.

38. Ibid., pp. 15–28 (Clarke).

39. Ibid., pp. 30–31.

40. Ibid., p. 68.

41. David M. Cawthorne, "Rock Labor Ruling Stands," *Journal of Commerce* (July 2, 1980), n.p., Rock Island Clipping File (in author's possession).

42. Trustee's Report of Liquidation for Period Ending August 31, 1980, Box 4, Folder 11, CRIP.

43. Ibid., p. 4.

44. Ibid., p. 5.

45. Message to the Congress of the United States from Jimmy Carter, March 23, 1979, Box TN-4 (1/1/79–9/30/79), pp. 2–3, WHCF, Executive, Carter Library.

46. Ibid., pp. 3–4.

47. Memoradum to Rick Hutcheson, Staff Secretary, White House from Brock Adams, January 5, 1979, Box 168 (Surface Transportation Deregulation, 1/6/79–3/15/79), White House Staff Offices, Congressional Liaison—Francis, Staff Offices collection, Carter Presidential Library.

48. Memorandum for the President from Stu Eizenstat and Bill Johnston, Jan. 1979, Box 76, Budget Task Force File (Railroad Deregulation and Commission, 2/23–24/1979), Congressional Liaison—Moore, WHCF, Carter Presidential Library.

49. Memorandum for the President from John P. White, February 23, 1979, Box 76, Budget Task Force (Railroad Deregulation and Budget, 3/23/79), Staff Office—Congressional Liaison—Moore, Staff Offices collection, Carter Presidential Library.

50. Memorandum from Rush Loving to John White, et al., December 4, 1979, Box 247, Subject File (Railroads, 12/4/79–4/24/80), Congressional Liaison—Thomson, Staff Offices collection, Carter Presidential Library.

51. Memorandum for Stu Eizenstat from Steve Simmons, March 19, 1980, Box

265 (Rail Deregulation), DPS—Eizenstat, White House Staff Offices, Carter Presidential Library.

52. Letter from Russell Long to Colleagues, with *Business Week* attachment, March 25, 1980, ibid.

53. Memorandum from Steve Simmons to Stu Eizenstat, April 7, 1980, Box 265 (Railroad Deregulation), DPS—Eisenstat, White House Staff Offices, Carter Presidential Library.

54. Memo from Bill Squadron, et al., to Stu Eizenstat, May 6, 1980, ibid. Staggers was a supporter of Amtrak and used his clout to get West Virginia a train (nicknamed "Harley's Hornet" and the "Staggers Special"), which ran between Washington, D.C., and Parkersburg, West Virginia. Called the *West Virginian*, the Amtrak train ran daily for two years before its discontinuance in 1973.

55. Memo from Bill Squadron, et al., to Stu Eizenstat, May 5, 1980, ibid.; and Memo from Steve Simmons to Stu Eizenstat, May 12, 1980, re: Eckhardt Amendment, ibid.

56. The administration and DOT were considering proposals to provide $532 million in loan guarantees for the Chicago and North Western Railway to construct a line to the Powder River basin in order to allow competition with the Burlington Northern Railroad for the coal hauled to utilities. See Memorandum for the President from Brock Adams, September 1, 1978, Accession 1096–014, Box 144, Folder 10 (Cabinet Meeting, 9/18/78), Adams Papers.

57. Memo for the President from Stu Eizenstat and Steve Symmons, July 21, 1980, Box TN-4 (6/1/80–1/20/81), Deregulation and Staggers, WHCF, Carter Presidential Library.

58. Summary of the main points of the bill in Memo from Stu Eizenstat, et al., to the President, October 11, 1980, ibid.

59. Transcript of Proceedings, October 7, 1980, In the Matter of Chicago, Rock Island and Pacific Railroad, No. 75 B 2697, pp. 6–18.

60. Ibid., pp. 31–32.

61. Richard J. Lane, "First Person: Liquidating the Rock: How Much is a Railroad Worth," *Railroad History* 181 (Autumn 1999): 103–112, provides a useful narrative of Lane's role in the liquidation.

62. Memorandum of Meeting with Arkansas and Oklahoma Representatives, October 21, 1980, Box 131, Folder (A-OK/Farmrail), pp. 1–4, Rock Island Technical Society Papers, Western History Collections, University of Oklahoma (hereafter RITS Papers). What is interesting about Gibbons's assertion of the value of the Memphis–Little Rock segment is that the line was never sold and was abandoned. The bridge over the Arkansas River in Little Rock still stands as the approach to the William Jefferson Clinton Presidential Library, which occupies the site of the old Little Rock passenger depot. The old passenger station is the home of the Clinton Center.

63. Memorandum of Meeting between Gibbons and A-OK Group, June 1, 1981, Box 131, (A-OK/FarmRail), RITS Papers.

64. Trustee's Progress Report of Liquidation for Period Ending June 30, 1981, Box 5, Folder 1, CRIP.

65. Letter from Judge McGarr to Robert Dole, August 26, 1981, Box 5, Folder 1, CRIP.

66. Letter to Governor John Carlin, August 27, 1981, ibid.

67. Henry Tatum, "Rock Island Tracks Offered for Sale to City," *Dallas Morning News,* October 8, 1981, n.p. Dallas officials were not at all hesitant about the price for the line, which ended at Dealey Plaza in downtown Dallas and went to Fort Worth on the southern boundary of Dallas–Fort Worth International Airport. Fort Worth officials called the price "unreasonable" and said Dallas officials were too optimistic about affording the price. Carl Freund, "Rock Island Price 'Unreasonable,'" *Dallas Morning News,* October 9, 1981, p. 20. The line was eventually purchased for $34 million in 1983 but did not begin operations until 1996 with service provided by Trinity Rail Express. See Matt Van Hatten, "Trinity Rail Express," *Trains.com* (July 2, 2006), at http://trn.trains.com/en/sitecore/content/Home/Railroad%20Reference/Passenger%20Trains/2006/07/Trinity%20Railway%20Express.aspx (accessed August 11, 2012).

68. Letter from William Gibbons to George Nigh, October 12, 1981, Box 5, Folder 1, CRIP.

69. Ibid., p. 2.

70. Remarks by William Gibbons, Oklahoma City Governor's Conference, March 4, 1982, Box 38, Folder 2, p. 6, CRIP.

71. Ibid., p. 6.

Chapter 12. Long Live the Rock

1. The oral argument in this case can be heard at http://www.oyez.org/cases/1980-1989/1981/1981_80_415 (accessed August 17, 2012).

2. Ibid. Exchange between Stillman and Judge Stevens is between 36:00 and 38:00 minutes.

3. *Railway Labor Executives' Association v. Gibbons,* 55 U.S. 457 (102 S. Ct. 1169, 71 L. Ed., 2d 335). This was the first time the Supreme Court had ever decided a case based on the constitution's uniform standard of bankruptcy clause.

4. Testimony of William Gibbons, Hearings Before the Senate Committee on Commerce, Science, and Transportation, December 6, 1981, Milwaukee Railroad and Rock Island Railroad Amendments Act, S. 1879 (Washington, D.C.: GPO, 1981), pp. 45–46.

5. Ibid., pp. 52–53.

6. Transcript of Proceedings, February 1, 1982, In the Matter of Chicago, Rock Island and Pacific Railroad, No. 75 B 2697. In 1984, the Chessie purchased the line for $20 million.

7. Transcript of Proceedings, June 2, 1982, In the Matter of Chicago, Rock Island and Pacific Railroad, No. 75 B 2697.

8. Transcript of Proceedings, May 6, 1982, In the Matter of Chicago, Rock Island and Pacific Railroad, No 75 B 2697, pp. 3–5, 9.

9. Transcript of Proceedings, October 13, 1982, In the Matter of Chicago, Rock Island and Pacific Railroad, No. 75 B 2697.

10. Trustee of the Property of Chicago, Rock Island and Pacific Railroad Company and Subsidiaries, Financial Statements December 31, 1981 and 1980, Price Waterhouse, May 12, 1982, Box 30, Folder 6, CRIP.

11. Ibid., Financial Statements, December 31, 1982 and 1981, Box 31, Folder 1, CRIP.

12. The Rock Island settled with major leasing companies, including U.S. Lease Financing (paid $4 million out of $5.9 million owed), with $550,000 to Connecticut Bank for leases on jumbo hopper cars; $250,000 to Trailer Train; $9 million (out of $16 million owed) to Evans Railcar for 2,150 car leases; and $6 million to Greyhound Car Leasing. The Rock Island estate had negotiated with North American Car Company to reassign Rock Island leases to the C&NW in 1981, which led to the C&NW acquiring leases on 4,800 newer jumbo-hopper and other freight cars. See Box 30, Folder 4 (CRIP Liquidation—Accounting—Early Payment Program) and Box 34 (North American Car), CRIP.

13. Letters from Ingram and Mitros to Gibbons, Box 32, Folder 21 (Staff), CRIP.

14. Transcript of Proceedings, January 19, 1983, In the Matter of Chicago, Rock Island and Pacific Railroad, No. 75 B 2697, pp. 15–19.

15. Ibid., pp. 24–25.

16. Transcript of Proceedings, January 19, 1983, pp. 25–26.

17. Ibid., pp. 30–31.

18. Ibid., pp. 37–38. On February 8, 1983, the ICC reported that it would have no opinion on the reorganization but would still be involved to approve or disapprove of line sales.

19. 1983 Plan of Reorganization for Chicago, Rock Island and Pacific Railroad Company, Debtor, January 19, 1983, Box 5, Folder 5 (Reorganization Plan), p. 2, CRIP.

20. Ibid., pp. 12–15.

21. "Rock Island Road Files Plan to Pay All Claims, Interest," *Wall Street Journal*, January 20, 1983, p. 33.

22. Planning Division, Minnesota Department of Transportation, *The Minnesota North/South Rail Corridor: A Study of the Alternatives for a Mainline Route and Local Service Needs* (June 1981), Iowa Department of Transportation Library, Ames.

23. Don L. Hofsommer, *Steel Trails of Hawkeyeland: Iowa's Railroad Experience* (Bloomington: Indiana University Press, 2005), p. 254.

24. Memorandum of Meeting with Soo Line, January 25, 1983, Box 132 (Iowa Railroad—II), Rock Island Technical Society Papers, University of Oklahoma Western History Collections.

25. Larry Fruhling, "Soo Line Offers to Buy Rock Trackage in Iowa," *Des Moines Register,* September 15, 1982. Rock Island Clippings Collection, IDOT Library.

26. Transcript of Proceedings, March 15, 1983, In the Matter of Chicago, Rock Island and Pacific Railroad, No. 75 B 2697, pp. 5–6.

27. C&NW Press Release, August 3, 1983, IDOT Library.

28. Transcript of Proceedings, June 29, 1983, In the Matter of Chicago, Rock Island and Pacific Railroad, No. 75 B 2697, pp. 12–13.

29. Ibid., p. 76.

30. Ibid., p. 67.

31. See 1983 First Amended Plan of Reorganization for Chicago, Rock Island and Pacific Railroad Company, Debtor, August 3, 1983, Box 5, Folder 7, pp. 1–2, CRIP.

32. Direct Testimony of Trustee William M. Gibbons in Support of 1983 First Amended Plan of Reorganization, September 27, 1983, Box 5, Folder 3, pp. 6–7, CRIP.

33. Memorandum Opinion and Order, November 28, 1983, Box 6, Folder 7, p. 9, CRIP. There were some problems in terms of money owed in taxes to the IRS (about $2.5 million) and other federal government agencies (about $1.6 million), which were settled by attorneys in early 1984.

34. Carol Jouzatis, "Rock Island to Emerge as a Second Penn Central," *Chicago Tribune*, January 8, 1984, p. F1.

35. For debates over the Iowa Railroad and discussion with TRAIN officials, see Memorandum of Meeting with TRAIN and Iowa Railroad, June 8, 1983, Box 132 (Iowa Railroad, Part II), RITS Papers. For the difficulties of starting up the operation, see William Petroski, "Fledging Heartland Rail Sets Out to Prove Its Critics Wrong," *Des Moines Register*, November 4, 1984, pp. 1F, 4F. For the current successes on the railroad, see Fred Frailey, "The Iowa Interstate Story," *Trains* (June 2011).

36. Carol Jouzaitis, "Rock Island Nearing End of Bankruptcy," *Chicago Tribune*, April 19, 1984, p. B5 (on end of bankruptcy); Bill Barnhart, "Chicago Pacific Picks Chief," *Chicago Tribune*, April 21, 1984, p. A7 (for Kapnick).

37. Carol Jouzaitis, "Court Approves Rock Island's Reorganization," *Chicago Tribune*, April 20, 1984, p. B1.

38. Transcript of Proceedings, May 22, 1984, In the Matter of Chicago, Rock Island and Pacific Railroad, No. 75 B 2697.

39. Biographical information from "Harvey Kapnick, 77, Former Chairman at Arthur Anderson," *New York Times*, August 20, 2002, http://www.nytimes.com/2002/08/20/business/harvey-kapnick-77-former-chairman-at-arthur-andersen.html (accessed September 21, 2012); Fern Schumer Chapman, "Harvey Kapnick's Incredible Club Hug," *Fortune* (December 10, 1984): 162; and Susan Squires, Cynthia Smith, Lorna McDougall, and William Yeack, *Inside Arthur Anderson: Shifting Values, Unexpected Consequences* (New York: Financial Times Press, 2003), pp. 62–65.

40. Charles Storch and Herb Greenberg, "Textron Rejects Chicago Pacific Bid," *Chicago Tribune*, October 25, 1984, p. C1.

41. "Textron May Be Sitting Duck," *Business Week* (November 5, 1984): 33.

42. Charles Storch, "Chicago Pacific Hints Textron Fight Not Over," *Chicago Tribune*, November 1, 1984, p. C2.

43. Nancy J. Perry, "A Happy Homemaker," *Fortune* (March 14, 1988): 149.

44. Brian Bremner, "Can Maytag Clean Up the World?" *Business Week* (January 30, 1989): 86–87.

45. Henry Posner III, "'Not Quite Normal'—The Story Behind the Iowa Interstate Story," speech before the 2012 National Railway Historical Society Convention, Cedar Rapids, Iowa, June 22, 2012, at http://www.iaisrr.com/sites/iaisrr.com/files/speech_Cedar_Rapids_NRHS_062212_print.pdf (accessed October 25, 2012).

46. "The Ethanol Election Delay," *Wall Street Journal*, October 30, 2012, p. 22. The United States commits 40 percent of its corn crop to ethanol in spite of massive increases in food prices, which harm impoverished people around the world who rely on American grain exports.

47. Fred W. Frailey, "The Iowa Interstate Story," pp. 30–38.

48. Ibid., pp. 35–36.

Conclusion

1. Fred W. Frailey, "Behold the Life After Death of the Rock Island Lines," *Trains* (February 2011): 14–15. Frailey wrote this column after traveling on an Iowa Interstate train that makes one daily round-trip between Chicago and Council Bluffs; by comparison, the Rock Island, even as late as 1979, had plentiful traffic and dozens of trains per day. While there was room for a railroad to take over the traffic that remained, the argument is strained when one compares the carloads hauled by the Iowa Interstate even with the bankrupt Rock Island.

2. Rob Kitchen, "The Fall of the Rock Island," at http://www.american-rails.com/support-files/fall_of_the_rock_island_railroad.pdf (accessed August 21, 2012). To be fair, Kitchen also blames Judge McGarr and Fred Kroll of BRAC for the railroad's demise.

3. The author is indebted to Edward Brunner, who worked for the Rock Island in the 1970s, for reminding him of this salient fact. For an illuminating take on how nineteenth-century insurance and railroad companies used the type of modern financial debt instruments that helped engender the 2008 economic collapse, see Scott Reynolds Nelson, *A Nation of Deadbeats: An Uncommon History of America's Financial Disasters* (New York: Alfred A. Knopf, 2012).

BIBLIOGRAPHY

Manuscript Collections

Dwight Eisenhower Presidential Library, Abilene, Kansas
  —Philip Areeda Papers
  —Sinclair Weeks Papers
  —White House Central Files, Ann Whitman File
Gerald Ford Presidential Library, Ann Arbor, Michigan
  —Arthur Burns Papers
  —Federal Reserve Board Papers
  —White House Central Files
Hagley Library and Museum, Wilmington, Delaware
  —Jervis Langdon, Jr. Papers
  —Penn Central Transportation Company Papers
  —Reading Railroad Papers
Harry S Truman Presidential Library, Independence, Missouri
Hoover Institution on War, Revolution and Peace, Stanford University
  —Daniel O'Neal Papers
Iowa Department of Transportation Library, Ames, Iowa
  —Rock Island Collection
Jimmy Carter Presidential Library, Atlanta, Georgia
  —Jimmy Carter Handwriting File
  —Stu Eizenstat Papers
  —White House Central Files
John Barriger III National Railroad Library, St. Louis Mercantile Library, St. Louis, Missouri
  —John Barriger III Papers
  —Milwaukee Road Papers
  —Railroad Executive Oral History Collection
National Archives, Suitland, Maryland
  —Interstate Commerce Commission Papers
  —Richard M. Nixon Presidential Papers
Newberry Library, Chicago, Illinois
  —Chicago, Burlington and Quincy Railroad Papers
  —Illinois Central Railroad Papers
Spencer Research Library, University of Kansas, Lawrence, Kansas
  —Bryan Whitehead Papers
State Historical Society of Iowa, Des Moines, Iowa
  —Robert Ray Papers

State Historical Society of Kansas, Topeka, Kansas
  —Keith Sebelius Papers
University of Oklahoma, Carl Albert Center, Norman, Oklahoma
  —Carl Albert Papers
  —David Boren Papers
  —Glenn English Papers
  —Tom Steed Papers
University of Oklahoma, Western History Collections, Norman, Oklahoma
  —Chicago, Rock Island and Pacific Railroad Collection
  —Rock Island Technical Society Papers (Richard Lane)
University of Washington Special Collections, Seattle, Washington
  —Brock Adams Papers, Congressional and Department of Transportation

Author's Collection

Rock Island Annual Reports, 1948–1975
Transcript of Proceedings, In the Matter of Chicago, Rock Island and Pacific Railroad, In the Federal District Court, Northern Illinois District, Eastern Division, No. 75 B 2697—1975–1984
  —The entire transcript can be found in National Archives, Great Lakes Branch, Chicago, Illinois.

Newspapers/Magazines

Business Week
Chicago
Chicago Daily Tribune
Chicago Tribune
Classic Trains
Des Moines Register
Forbes
Fortune
Journal of Commerce
New York Times
Railroad History
Railway Age
Remember the Rock
Time
Trains
U.S. News & World Report
Wall Street Journal
Washington Post
Washington Star

Bibliography

Interviews

Theodore Desch, Naperville, Illinois (August 2010)
Paul Banner, phone interview (June 2012)

Government Documents

Bankruptcy Act of 1933, Section 77, 72nd Congress (H.R. 14359)
Modification of Railroad Financial Structures, Hearings Before the Committee on Interstate Commerce, United States Senate, 79th Congress, S. 1253 (Washington, D.C.: GPO, 1946)
Railway Labor Executives' Association v. Gibbons, 455 U.S. 457 (102 S. Ct. 1169, 71 L.Ed., 2d 335)
Staff Report of the Committee on Banking and Currency, House of Representatives, 92 Congress, First Session, *The Penn Central Failure and the Role of Financial Institutions* (New York: Arno Press, 1972)
Union Pacific Railroad Company v. Chicago and North Western Railway Company, No. 63 C 2051, US District Court, Northern District of Illinois, February 18, 1964, 226 Supp. 400 (1964)
U.S. Senate Committee on Commerce, Surface Transportation Subcommittee Hearings, "The Financial Condition of the Rock Island Railroad," March 10, 1975, 94th Congress, 1st session (Washington, D.C.: GPO, 1975)

Books/Articles

Aldrich, Mark. *Death Rode the Rails: American Railroad Accidents and Safety, 1828–1965*. Baltimore, MD: Johns Hopkins University Press, 2009.
Ambrose, Stephen. *Nothing Like It in the World: The Men Who Built the First Transcontinental Railroad, 1863–1869*. New York: Simon and Schuster, 2001.
Bain, David Howard. *Empire Express: Building the First Transcontinental Railroad*. New York: Penguin Books, 2000.
Barofsky, Neil. *Bailout: An Inside Account of How Washington Abandoned Main Street and Bailed Out Wall Street*. New York: Free Press, 2012.
Barriger, III, John W. *Super-Railroads for a Dynamic American Economy*. Omaha, NE: Simmons-Boardman, 1956.
Bartley, Robert. *The Seven Fat Years and How to Do It Again*. New York: Free Press, 1992.
Bates, Beth Tompkins. *Pullman Workers and the Rise of Black Protest Politics in America, 1925–1945*. Chapel Hill: University of North Carolina Press, 2000.
Bedingfield, Robert E. *The Norfolk and Western Strike of 1978*. Norfolk, VA: The Norfolk and Western Railroad Company, 1978.
Berk, Gerald. *Alternative Tracks: The Constitution of American Industrial Order, 1865–1917*. Baltimore, MD: Johns Hopkins University Press, 1994.
Bliven, Jr., Carl W. *Jimmy Carter's Economy: Policy in an Age of Limits*. Chapel Hill: University of North Carolina Press, 2001.

Borkin, Joseph. *Robert R. Young: The Populist of Wall Street*. New York: Harper and Row, 1954.

Borneman, Walter R. *Rival Rails: The Race to Build America's Greatest Transcontinental Railroad*. New York: Random House, 2011.

Bramson, Seth H. *Speedway to Sunshine: The Story of the Florida East Coast Railway*. Buffalo, N.Y.: Boston Mills Press, 2010.

Brown, John K. *The Baldwin Locomotive Works: A Study in Industrial Practice, 1831–1915*. Baltimore, MD: Johns Hopkins University Press, 2001.

Bryant, Jr., Keith L., ed. *Railroads in the Age of Regulation, 1900–1980: Encyclopedia of American Business History and Biography*. New York: Facts on File, 1988.

Burns, Arthur, and Robert Ferrell, ed. *Inside the Nixon Administration: The Secret Diary of Arthur F. Burns, 1969–1974*. Lawrence: University Press of Kansas, 2010.

Canedo, Eduard. "The Rise of the Deregulation Movement in Modern America, 1957–1980." Ph.D. dissertation, Columbia University, 2009.

Cassidy, John. *How Markets Fail: The Logic of Economic Calamities*. New York: Farrar, Straus and Giroux, 2010.

Chandler, Alfred DuPont. *The Railroads: The Nation's First Big Business*. New York: Harcourt, Brace and World, 1965.

———. *The Visible Hand: The Managerial Revolution in American Business*. Cambridge, MA: Harvard University Press, 1977.

Childs, William R. *Trucking and the Public Interest: The Emergence of Federal Regulation, 1914–1940*. Knoxville: University of Tennessee Press, 1985.

Clapton, Eric. *Clapton: The Autobiography*. New York: Broadway Books, 2007.

Collins, Robert M. *More: The Politics of Economic Growth in the Postwar Era*. New York: Oxford University Press, 2000.

Cooper, Phillip J. *The War Against Regulation: From Jimmy Carter to George W. Bush*. Lawrence: University Press of Kansas, 2009.

Cowie, Jefferson. *Stayin' Alive: The 1970's and the Last Days of the Working Class*. New York: The New Press, 2010.

Daughen, Joseph R., and Peter Binzen, *The Wreck of the Penn Central*. New York: Little, Brown, 1971.

Derthick, Martha, and Paul Quinn. *The Politics of Deregulation*. Washington, D.C.: The Brookings Institution, 1985.

Domitrovic, Brian. *Econoclasts: The Rebels Who Sparked the Supply-Side Revolution and Restored America's Prosperity*. Wilmington, DE: ISI Books, 2009.

Eisner, Marc Allen. *Regulatory Politics in Transition*, 2nd ed. Baltimore, MD: Johns Hopkins University Press, 2000.

Fine, Sidney. *Laissez-Faire and the General Welfare State*. Ann Arbor: University of Michigan Press, 1956.

Frailey, Fred W. *The Twilight of the Great Trains*. Milwaukee, WI: Kalmbach Books, 1998.

Fried, Stephen. *Appetite for America: Fred Harvey and the Business of Civilizing the West*. New York: Bantam, 2011.

Fuess, Claude Moore. *Joseph B. Eastman: A Study in Public Service*. New York: Columbia University Press, 1952.

Garrison, Lloyd K. "Reorganization of Railroads Under the Bankruptcy Act." *University of Chicago Law Review* 1, no. 1 (May 1933): 71–81.

Grant, H. Roger. *Erie Lackawanna: Death of an American Railroad, 1938–1992.* Stanford, CA: Stanford University Press, 1994.

———. *North Western: A History of the Chicago and North Western Railway System.* DeKalb: Northern Illinois University Press, 1996.

———. *Visionary Railroader: Jervis Langdon, Jr., and the Transportation Revolution.* Bloomington: Indiana University Press, 2009.

Hamilton, Shane. *Trucking Country: The Road to America's Walmart Economy.* Princeton, N.J.: Princeton University Press, 2009.

Harwood, Jr., Herbert. *Invisible Giants: The Van Sweringen Brothers of Cleveland.* Bloomington: Indiana University Press, 2006.

Hawkins, Hugh. *Railwayman's Son: A Plains Family Memoir.* Lubbock: Texas Tech University Press, 2006.

Hayes, William Edward. *Iron Road to Empire: The History of 100 Years of Progress and Achievements on the Rock Island Lines.* Omaha, NE: Simmons-Boardman, 1953.

Hoerr, John P., *And the Wolf Finally Came: The Decline and Fall of the American Steel Industry.* Pittsburgh, PA: Pittsburgh University Press, 1998.

Hofsommer, Don L. *The Southern Pacific, 1901–1985.* College Station: Texas A&M University Press, 1986.

———. *Steel Trails to Hawkeyeland: Iowa's Railroad Experience.* Bloomington: Indiana University Press, 2005.

Hoogenboom, Ari and Olive. *A History of the ICC: From Panacea to Palliative.* New York: W. W. Norton, 1976.

Huntington, Samuel. "The Marasmus of the ICC: The Commission, the Railroads and the Public Interest." *Yale Law Review* 61, no. 4 (April 1952): 467–509.

Hurl, Neil A. *The Farm Debt Crisis of the 1980s.* Ames: Iowa State University Press, 1990.

Kalman, Laura. *Right Star Rising: A New Politics, 1974–1980.* New York: W. W. Norton, 2010.

Kelly, John. *Rock Island Railroad Photo Archive: Travel on the Rockets.* Hudson, WI: Iconographix, 2010.

Klein, Maury. *Union Pacific, Volume 2: 1894–1969.* Minneapolis: University of Minnesota Press, 2006.

———. *Union Pacific: The Reconfiguration of a Railroad, 1969–2004.* New York: Oxford University Press, 2011.

Kolko, Gabriel. *Railroads and Regulation, 1877–1916.* New York: Columbia University Press, 1965.

Lane, Richard J. "Liquidating the Rock: How Much is a Railroad Worth?" *Railroad History* 181 (Autumn 1999): 103–112.

Lichtenstein, Nelson. *State of the Union: A Century of American Labor.* Princeton, N.J.: Princeton University Press, 2002.

Loving, Jr., Rush. *The Men Who Loved Trains: The Story of Men Who Battled Greed to Save an Industry.* Bloomington: Indiana University Press, 2006.

Martin, Albro. *Enterprise Denied: Origins of the Decline of American Railroads, 1890–1917.* New York: Oxford University Press, 1971.

Matusow, Allen. *Nixon's Economy: Booms, Busts, Dollars, and Votes.* Lawrence: University Press of Kansas, 1998.

McCloskey, Robert Green. *American Conservatism in the Age of Enterprise, 1865–1910.* Cambridge, MA: Harvard University Press, 1951.
McCraw, Thomas K. *Prophets of Regulation: Charles Francis Adams, Louis M. Brandeis, James Landis, and Alfred E. Kahn.* Cambridge, MA: Harvard University Press, 1984.
Meyer, John Robert. *The Economics of Competition in the Transportation Industries.* Cambridge, MA: Harvard University Press, 1959.
Middleton, William, George M. Smerk, and Roberta L. Diehl, eds. *Encyclopedia of North American Railroads.* Bloomington: Indiana University Press, 2007.
Miner, Craig. *The Rebirth of the Missouri Pacific Railroad, 1956–1983.* College Station: Texas A&M University Press, 1983.
Moreton, Bethany. *To Serve God and Walmart: The Making of Christian Free Enterprise.* Cambridge, MA: Harvard University Press, 2009.
Morgenson, Gretchen, and Jonathon Rosner. *Reckless Endangerment: How Outsized Ambition, Greed, and Corruption Led to Economic Armageddon.* New York: Times Book, 2011.
Nelson, Scott Reynolds. *A Nation of Deadbeats: An Uncommon History of Financial Crisis.* New York: Alfred A. Knopf, 2012.
Olson, James Stuart. *Herbert Hoover and the Reconstruction Finance Corporation.* Ames: Iowa State University Press, 1977.
Paulson, Henry. *On the Brink: Inside the Race to Prevent the Collapse of the Global Financial System.* New York: Harcourt Brace, 2010.
Petrakis, Henry Mark, and David B. Weber. *Henry Crown: The Life and Times of the Colonel, Book One and Book Two.* Chicago, IL: Henry Crown Company, 1998.
Phillips-Fein, Kim. *Invisible Hands: The Businessman's Crusade Against the New Deal.* New York: W. W. Norton, 2010.
Richards, Keith. *Life.* New York: Little, Brown and Company, 2011.
Rose, Mark H., Bruce E. Seely, and Paul F. Barrett. *The Best Transportation System in the World: Railroads, Trucks, Airlines, and American Public Policy in the Twentieth Century.* Columbus: Ohio State University Press, 2006.
Salsbury, Stephen. *No Way to Run a Railroad: The Untold Story of the Penn Central Crisis.* New York: McGraw Hill, 1982.
Samuelson, Robert J. *The Great Inflation and Its Aftermath: The Past and Future of American Affluence.* New York: Random House, 2008.
Saunders, Richard M. *Main Lines: The Rebirth of American Railroads, 1970–2000.* DeKalb: Northern Illinois University Press, 2003.
———. *Merging Lines: American Railroads, 1900–1970.* DeKalb: Northern Illinois University Press, 2001.
Schweiterman, Joseph P. *When the Railroad Leaves Town: American Communities in the Age of Rail Line Abandonment, Volume One (Eastern United States).* Kirksville, MO: Truman State University Press, 2001.
———. *When the Railroad Leaves Town: American Communities in the Age of Rail Line Abandonment, Volume Two (Western United States).* Kirksville, MO: Truman State University Press, 2004.
Scribbins, Jim. *The Milwaukee Road, 1928–1985.* Forest Park, IL: Heimburger House Publishing, 2001.

Sobel, Robert. *The Fallen Colossus*. New York: Weywright and Talley, 1977.
Sorkin, Andrew Ross. *Too Big to Fail*. New York: Viking Press, 2009.
Stein, Judith. *Pivotal Decade: How the United States Traded Factories for Finance in the 1970s*. New Haven, CT: Yale University Press, 2009.
Stone, Richard D. *The Interstate Commerce Commission and the Railroad Industry: A History of Regulatory Policy*. New York: Prager, 1991.
Stover, John F. *American Railroads*, 2nd ed. Chicago: University of Chicago Press, 1997.
Taillon, Paul Michael. *Good Reliable White Men: The Railroad Brotherhoods, 1877–1917*. Urbana: University of Illinois Press, 2009.
Tennyson, Baron Alfred. *The Works of Alfred Lord Tennyson, Volume 3*. New York: Macmillan, 1896.
Townshend, Pete. *Who I Am: A Memoir*. New York: Harper, 2012.
Townshend, Robert C. *Up the Organization*. New York: Fawcett, 1983.
Usselman, Steven W. *Regulating Railroad Innovation: Business, Technology, and Politics in America, 1840–1900*. New York: Cambridge University Press, 2002.
Walt, Stephen. *The Origins of Alliances*. Ithaca, N.Y.: Cornell University Press, 1992.
Weber, Max. *Economy and Society*. Guenter Roth and Claus Wittich, eds. Berkeley: University of California Press, 1978.
White, Richard. *Railroaded: The Transcontinentals and the Making of Modern America*. New York: W. W. Norton, 2011.
Wong, John Chi-Kit. *Lords of the Rink: The Emergence of the National Hockey League, 1875–1936*. Toronto, Canada: University of Toronto Press, 2005.

INDEX

AAR. *See* Association of American Railroads
Abex, 93
Adair, IA, 250
Adams, Brock, 120 (photo), 199, 201, 223 (photo), 233
   background of, 203
   Conrail and, 205, 206
   railroad problems and, 119, 199, 202, 205, 209, 210, 267, 300
Adams, Eaton, 40, 47, 53 (photo), 75
A.G. Becker, 290
agriculture industry
   economy and, 3–4
   railroads and, 13, 31–32, 34, 74, 231, 281, 299
Ailes, Stephen, 119
Airline Deregulation Act (1978), 222
airline industry, 28, 33, 66, 70, 92, 105, 148, 222
Akron, OH, 206
Albus, Paul, 69, 73, 85, 912
Alexandria, LA, 271
Alleghany Corporation, 20–21
Amarillo, TX, 125, 142, 183
"American Railroad Industry, The" (ASTRO) 107–109
American Truckers Association, 30
America's Sound Transportation Review Organization, 107–108
Amoco, 221
Amtrak, 116, 190, 221, 293
   creation of, 6, 109–112, 164
   in Northeast Corridor, 207, 259
   Rock Island and, 112, 134, 194–195
Anderson, Hugo, 27
Ann Arbor Railroad, 3
Arab (OPEC) oil embargo, 4, 132, 220
Archer Daniels Midland, 294
Arias, Salvo, 136, 137, 138

Arkansas, railroad routes in, 231, 265, 271, 300
Arkansas-Oklahoma Railroad (A-OK), 271, 272
Armourdale Yard, 24
Armour Institute, 175
Army Military Railroad Service, 98
Arthur Anderson, 5, 106, 290
Association of American Railroads, 107, 119, 130, 210, 241, 300
Association of Southeastern Railroads, 55
ASTRO (America's Sound Transportation Review Organization), 107–108
Astro Report, 107–109
Atchison, Topeka and Santa Fe Railway (ATSF; Santa Fe), 43, 56, 105, 190
   Rock Island–UP merger and, 64–65, 69, 71, 72–73, 76, 85, 89, 97, 125, 127, 142, 148, 159, 182, 183, 288
   Southern Pacific and, 39, 94
Atlantic, IA, 133
ATSF. *See* Atchison, Topeka, and Santa Fe Railway
Audubon, IA, 133
Audubon–Atlantic Branchline Improvement Association, 133, 188
Ayers, Thomas, 289
Ayers, William, 289

Bailey, Edd, 38, 64, 69, 71–72, 73–74
bailouts by government, 105–106, 107, 109, 114, 136, 146, 153–154, 203, 204, 206, 291, 299
Bakken Oil Fields, 294
Baldwin Locomotive Company, 105
Baltimore and Ohio Railroad (B&O), 27, 55–56, 71, 98, 102, 206
Bancroft, Jean Gordon, 55
B&O Railroad. *See* Baltimore and Ohio Railroad

Banker's Trust Company, 288
bankruptcies, 3. *See also under individual railroads*
Bankruptcy Act of 1933, 258
    Section 77 of, 16–17, 18, 101, 130, 150, 163, 181, 230, 240, 248, 256, 288
Banner, Paul, 142
Bannister, Scott, 236, 241
Barber, Richard J., 164–165, 167, 198
barge industry, 28, 31–32, 33, 61, 66, 74, 92, 105, 108, 132, 144, 183, 197
Barnett, Frank, 38, 40, 67, 79, 90, 92, 135–136
    plan for Penn Central of, 119
    on RI–UP merger, 41–42, 50, 51, 69, 70, 73, 88, 89, 91, 127–128, 135–136, 138
    as Union Pacific Corp. CEO, 92
Barnum, John, 135, 137
Barriger, John W., III, 85–86, 136–139
Bartlett, Dewey, 154, 156 (photo)
Bauer, William, 179
Beckley, Thomas, 285–286
Bedingfield, Robert, 137, 138
Beecher, Henry, 54
Bell Helicopters, 291
Bellrose Silica, 242
Bentsen, Lloyd, 269
Berkshire Hathaway Corporation, 1
Bevan, David, 103
B.F. Goodrich, 95
Biaggini, Ben, 40, 51, 75, 88, 89, 173
    purchase of Rock Island lines and, 182–184
Big John hopper-car case, 84–85, 140
Bilandic, Michael, 217
Blanchette, Robert, 107
Bleak House (Dickens), 59
Blue Island, IL, 266, 280, 289, 290 (photo)
BNSF, 1, 293
Bolos, Hercules, 171
Bombaugh, Robert, 161, 167, 180, 197
Bordes, John, 150
BorgWarner, 22, 25
Boston, MA, railroad routes to, 111, 207
Boston and Maine Railroad, 103, 139
Bourne, Edward, 20, 21–22

Bouse, Jerry, 169
BRAC. *See* Brotherhood of Railway and Airline Clerks
Bretey, Pierre, 49–49, 50
Bretton Woods, 220
Brinegar, Claude, 129
Broadley, John, 214, 235–236, 237, 240–241, 246–247, 248, 256, 264, 270
Brosnan, William, 84, 140
Brotherhood of Locomotive Engineers, 194, 210–211
Brotherhood of Railway and Airline Clerks (BRAC), 229, 239, 244, 298
    strike against Rock Island by, 8, 223, 226–227, 229–231, 235, 238, 298–299
Brown, Edward, 14 (photo), 22, 25
Brown, Mark, 22, 25
Brown Brothers Harriman & Co., 51, 94
Buffalo, NY, railroad routes to, 103, 196
Buffett, Warren, 1
Bureau Junction, IL, 266, 280, 289
Burlington Northern Railroad, 34, 62, 63, 70, 133, 179, 190, 198, 201, 269, 281
Burlington Northern Santa Fe Railway (BNSF), 1, 293
Burnett, John, 132
Business Week, 161, 209, 219, 268
Butterworth Tours, 171
Byrne, Jane, 217

Cabinet Committee on Economic Policy, 112
Cabot, Bruce, 176
Calumet, OK, 272
Canada Life Company, 283
Canadian National Railroad, 144
Canadian Pacific Railway, 22, 144
Canaryville, 179
C&NW. *See* Chicago and North Western Railway
C&O Railroad, 55, 102, 206
Cannon, Howard, 268–269
Cannon, James, 150, 156 (photo), 208 (photo)
Carlisle, IA, 187
Carnegie Institute of Technology, 98

Carter, Jimmy, 212, 223 (photo), 233, 260
   deregulation and, 1, 5, 8, 109, 222, 253, 265–269, 300
   economy and, 4, 132, 218–221, 225
   railroad problem and, 202–203, 204, 206
   Rock Island strike and, 226, 229, 230, 231, 232, 234–235, 238–239, 244, 259
Cascade Mountains, 201
Cash, Johnny, 175
Cassell, Martin, 49, 56, 148
Caterpillar Tractor, 25
CEA, 111, 112, 219, 267
Cedar Rapids, IA, 212, 217, 293, 295
Cedar Rapids and Iowa City Railroad (CRANDIC), 294
Central National Chicago Corporation, 290
Central Railroad of New Jersey, 3, 103, 114
Cestaro, Peter, 129
CGW Railway, 42, 52, 63, 69, 73, 86, 88
Chamberlain, Neville, 66
Chandler, Alfred, 83
Chemung Coal Company, 55
Chesapeake & Ohio Railroad (C&O), 55, 102, 206
Chesser, Al, 117, 203
Chessie System, 206–207, 265, 280, 289
Chicago, IL
   commuter service in, 96, 112, 130, 133–135, 143, 151, 168–171, 172–173 (photos), 175, 190, 192, 193, 195, 226, 229, 230, 241, 259
   natives of, with ties to railroad, 25–27, 42–43, 46, 98, 155–157, 179
   1978 Midwestern railroad crisis meeting in, 204–205
   railroad routes through, 14, 15, 30, 56, 69, 88, 103, 129, 184, 186, 191, 201–202, 212, 239, 245, 289, 293
   Rock Island board members from, 25
   Rock Island property in, 24
   Union Pacific and, 37–38, 40, 49–52, 62–63, 71, 90, 129, 246
   Union Station, 170
   weather-related problems in, 195–196, 217
Chicago, Burlington and Quincy Railroad (CBQ), 13, 14, 72, 80
   merger plan with GN and NP, 34, 38, 56, 62
   on Rock Island–UP merger plan, 70
Chicago, Indianapolis and Louisville Railroad (Monon), 43, 139
Chicago, Milwaukee, St. Paul and Pacific Railroad (Milwaukee Road), 24, 69, 71, 78, 125, 181, 189, 197, 225, 231
   bankruptcy and, 3, 107, 201–202, 204, 206, 209, 216, 255, 300
   federal assistance to, 120–121, 209, 243
   financial losses of, 217
   merger plan of, with CN&W Railway, 43, 50, 52, 63, 73, 86, 87–88, 91, 94, 95, 201–202
   merger plan of, with Rock Island, 34–35, 37, 201–202
   on Rock Island–UP merger plan, 56, 64
   sale of, 280–281
   State of Iowa assistance to, 133
   Union Pacific and, 38
   See also Milwaukee Road Restructuring Act
Chicago, Rock Island and Pacific Railroad, (Rock Island Railroad; The Rock)
   accidents and, 211
   administrative claims of, 281–282, 283
   agricultural dependency of, 79, 132–134, 178
   bankruptcy (1909), 250
   bankruptcy (1933), 13, 15–17, 18
   bankruptcy (1975), 3, 6–7, 8, 150–151, 154–155, 157–159, 161–66, 209, 250, 259–260, 277
   board of directors (*see* Chicago, Rock Island and Pacific Railroad board of directors)
   BRAC strike and, 8, 226–227, 229–232, 235–239, 243, 244, 299
   branch lines of, 132–134, 142, 143–144, 183, 186–187, 188–189

Chicago, Rock Island and Pacific
    Railroad, *continued*
  C&NW Railway takeover attempt of,
    44–51, 63, 64–65, 76–79, 100
  cash shortages of, 6, 67–68, 108, 134,
    144–147, 218, 223, 231–233,
    235–238
  Chicago commuter service of, 96, 134,
    143–144, 157, 168–170, 172
    (photo), 173 photo), 190, 192,
    226, 230–231, 241
  court-supervised reorganization plan
    of, 178, 213, 214, 216, 231, 232,
    239–240, 241, 245–247, 278–291
  DRGW Railroad offer on lines of,
    162, 166–167, 178, 182–183,
    184–185, 212–213, 215, 231, 235
  federal government and, 28, 107,
    120–121, 129–130, 144, 189–190,
    204, 209, 213–214, 281, 297–298
  in films, 175–177
  FRA loan and, 181, 209, 210, 212–213
  ICC directed service and, 216, 223,
    238, 240, 243
  ICC hearings testimony of, 74–76
  Kansas lines of, 34, 68, 183–184, 242,
    260, 273, 279, 280, 282
  labor unions and, 29, 31, 210–211,
    216, 236–237, 260–265, 277–278,
    298–299
  legacy of, 292–295, 301
  liquidation (*see* Chicago, Rock Island
    and Pacific Railroad liquidation)
  locomotives of, 13, 164, 167, 170,
    265, 295
  maintenance conditions of, 32, 80–81,
    91–92, 125, 130, 164–165, 178,
    213–214, 241
  management of, 30–31, 127–128,
    299–300
  merger attempt of, with Milwaukee
    Road, 34–36, 43, 44
  merger plan of, with Union Pacific (*see*
    Chicago, Rock Island and Pacific
    Railroad–Union Pacific Railroad
    merger plan)
  merger prospects of, 34
  operating losses of, 66, 96, 185,
    213–214
  operating problems of, 31–32, 53–54,
    66–67, 74, 79, 91–92, 130, 135,
    164–165, 181, 196–197, 236–237,
    241
  paint scheme and logo update of, 140,
    142, 153
  passenger service of, 6, 14–15, 24, 79,
    80, 96, 109, 112, 133–134,
    168–169, 171–172, 190–195, 299
  in popular culture, 175
  rebuilding of, 24–25, 128–129, 135,
    185
  reorganization of (1930s–1940s),
    15–23
  reorganization of (1960s), 92–93
  reorganization of (1960s), 92
  reorganization efforts of (1970s), 6–7,
    156–157, 159, 161–163, 166–167,
    177, 181–182, 213–216, 231–232,
    259, 278
  revenue and income of, 25, 39, 69, 74,
    98–99, 130, 216, 240, 282,
    287–288
  RTA and, 134, 143–144, 157,
    168–170, 227–228, 232, 241,
    257–259
  sale of assets by, 265, 271–272,
    280–281, 284–285
  sale of lines to Southern Pacific and,
    166–167, 178, 182–184, 209, 215,
    235, 258, 265
  State of Illinois subsidies of, 112,
    171–172, 190–191
  taxes and, 28–29
  track conditions of, 185–186,
    187–188, 211–212, 217
  Union Pacific relations with, 127–128
  unit grain trains of, 84, 132, 142, 178,
    230–231
  USRA loan and, 135, 146, 147–149,
    154
  valuation of, 161
  weather-related losses and, 195–196,
    216–217
  See also under Chicago and North
    Western Railway
Chicago, Rock Island and Pacific Railroad
    board of directors
  on Amtrak, 134

on bankruptcy, 150
on C&NW Railway takeover offer, 44–46, 51, 78–79
members of, 14 (photo), 21, 25, 30–31, 39, 40, 97, 129, 137
on mergers, 34, 35, 37, 39
Rock Island finances and, 25, 93, 128, 130–131, 133, 229, 299
on Rock Island leadership, 54, 56, 97, 136
on Union Pacific merger plan, 51–52, 56, 91, 136, 299
Chicago, Rock Island and Pacific Railroad liquidation
bankruptcy trustees on, 6–7
Crown and, 7, 139, 150, 162, 163–164, 198, 216
courts on, 7, 8, 223, 237, 247–249, 255–257, 277–278, 283–284, 287
Gibbons (Trustee) on, 162, 163–164, 239–240, 246, 248, 254, 256, 261, 272–273, 277–280, 284–285, 287–288
ICC and, 240–241, 283–284
labor union and, 255–256, 259, 277–278
support for, 147–148, 205–206, 216, 232, 248
U.S. government on, 214, 240–241, 254, 256, 259–260
Chicago, Rock Island and Pacific merger plan with Union Pacific
ATSF intervention over, 64–65, 69, 71, 72–73, 76, 85, 89, 97, 125, 127, 142, 148, 159, 182, 183, 288
Barnett on, 41–42, 50, 51, 69, 70, 73, 88, 89, 91, 127–128, 135–136, 138
C&NW Railway intervention over, 43, 64–65, 69, 71–72, 76–79, 85, 87, 90, 147–148, 298
CBQ Railroad intervention over, 70
Crown on, 40–42, 48–49, 52, 97, 127–128
DRGW Railroad on, 64
Farrington on, 37–38, 40–41
Heineman on, 69, 76, 77 (photo), 78, 79, 94, 298
ICC and, 56, 59, 62–64, 67, 69, 81, 91, 94–95, 121, 125, 127,
142–143, 145, 166–167, 173, 298, 300
ICC report on, 85, 99–100, 121, 125, 126–127, 142
Jervis on, 59, 64, 70, 79
Milwaukee Road intervention on, 64
MoPac Railroad intervention on, 64, 65, 71, 72–73, 90
negotiations over, 37–43
Rock Island board on, 51–52, 56, 91, 136, 299
Southern Pacific Railroad testimony on, 75–76
U.S. Justice Department approval of, 94
Chicago and Eastern Illinois Railroad, 17, 31, 73, 165, 212
Chicago and North Western Railway (C&NW), 185, 230, 237, 246, 295
commuter operations and, 43, 76, 144, 259
financial problems of, 43, 95, 147
government assistance and, 211–212
Heineman and, 34, 42–43, 298
line abandonment and, 189
liquidation of Rock Island and, 205–206
merger attempt with Chicago Great Western and, 52
merger attempt with Milwaukee Road and, 35, 36, 43, 52, 64, 73, 86, 87–88, 94, 95, 96, 202
merger attempt with Rock Island, 35–36
Minneapolis & St. Louis acquisition by, 43
purchase of Rock Island lines and, 272, 281, 285–287
Rock Island takeover bid by, 44–51, 63, 64–65, 76–79, 100
on Rock Island–UP merger plan, 43, 64–65, 69, 71–72, 76–79, 85, 87, 90, 147–148, 298
routes of, 30, 43, 265, 269
sale to employees of, 7, 95
Union Pacific and, 37–38, 43–44, 129, 293, 298
weather-related losses of, 217

Chicago Great Western Railway (CGW),
    42, 52, 63, 69, 73, 86, 88
Chicago Pacific Corporation, 7, 289–292,
    301
Chicago Railroad Fair, 14
Chicago Tribune, 21, 49, 52, 69, 73, 75,
    150, 154, 169–170, 184, 212, 229,
    235, 239, 288, 290
Chillicothe, IL, 190
Choctaw Route, 231, 271, 272, 300
Chrysler Corporation, 3, 105, 264
Clarke, Michael, 260, 262, 264, 270,
    277–278, 287
Clinton, IA, 43, 211, 212
Cole, Ken, 111
Coleman, William, 156 (photo), 163,
    208 (photo)
Colin, Justin, 129
Colin & Hochstein, 129
Collins, Robert, 131
Colnon, Aaron, 19, 20–21, 22, 23, 24
Colorado
    coal properties of Rock Island in, 288
    See also Denver, CO
Commerce Department, U.S., 33, 317n8
Commonwealth Edison, 289
commuter trains, 116, 133–135, 151,
    171, 172–173, 175, 193, 195, 241,
    259
    Rock Island and, 96, 112, 130, 134,
        143–144, 157, 168–170, 189, 190,
        192, 226, 229, 230, 241
ConFac (Consolidated Facilities), 119,
    209
Congress, U.S., 30, 109, 118, 129, 154,
    198, 204, 225, 255, 259, 262, 263,
    270, 277, 278–279, 298, 299, 300,
    301
    passenger trains and, 109–110
    Penn Central bankruptcy and,
        104–105, 106, 114
Conkling, Roscoe, 54
Connecticut commuter operations, 116
Conrail (Consolidated Rail Corporation),
    153, 204, 205, 225, 230, 244, 255,
    270, 300
    companies joined into, 3
    cost of, 120, 207, 208–209, 298
    creation of, 109, 120, 206–209

    problems of, 6, 8, 196, 208–209,
        221–222, 267
    Rock Island line connections with,
        170, 196
    subsidization of, 189
Consumer Price Index (CPI), 131, 219
Continental Bank of Illinois, 105, 291
    Rock Island bankruptcy and, 165,
        198, 214, 216, 218, 288
Cook, William, 127–128
Cooper, Philip, 5
Corcoran, Howard, 168
Cotton Belt, 258, 265
Council Bluffs, IA, 88, 184, 185, 212,
    245, 246, 289, 290, 293
Council of Economic Advisors (CEA),
    111, 112, 219, 267
Court of Appeals for Seventh Circuit,
    U.S., 19, 21, 22, 24, 179, 262–263,
    265, 277
Coverdale and Colpitts, 35, 40, 44, 48
CPI (Consumer Price Index), 131, 219
Craft, Joseph, 4
CRANDIC, 294
Cross, Paul, 192, 194–195
Crown, Arie, 26
Crown, Henry, 7, 41 (photo), 78, 168,
    182, 215, 231, 284, 289, 292, 297,
    298
    Background, 25–28
    on C&NW takeover bid, 49, 51–52,
        78
    federal financing of railroads and,
        197–198
    Jenner and, 179–180
    Rock Island bankruptcy case and, 139,
        150, 161, 162, 163–164, 165, 174,
        177, 209, 288
    as Rock Island board member, 25, 35,
        150
    on Rock Island leadership, 54, 56
    Rock Island liquidation and, 8, 150,
        161–162, 163–164, 177, 198, 216
    on a Rock Island–Milwaukee Road
        merger, 34–35, 36
    as Rock Island stockholder, 7, 25, 27,
        49, 150, 161
    on a Rock Island–Southern Pacific
        merger, 39–40

on a Rock Island–Union Pacific merger, 40–42, 48–49, 52, 97, 127–128
on sale of Rock Island to Southern Pacific, 184
Crown, Ida, 26
Crown, Irving, 26
Crown, Lester, 289
Crown, Sol, 26
Crown, Steve, 292
CSX Corporation, 293
Culver, IA, 280
Culver, John, 146
Cutler, Lloyd, 259

Daily Illini, 179
Dakota, Minnesota and Eastern Railway, 2
Dallas, TX, 34, 86, 186 (photo), 211, 273, 284
Damien: Omen II (film), 176–177
Darby, Harry, 14 (photo), 25, 136–137
D'Arcy, John, 127–128
Darmstadter, Henry, 86
Davenport, IA, 280
Defense Production Act, 113
Delaware and Hudson Railroad, 207
Democratic Party, 109–110
De Nova, 119
Denver, CO, 34, 80, 94, 125, 142, 167, 184, 185, 211, 212
Denver and Rio Grande Western Railroad (DRGW), 56, 73–74, 94, 125, 142
offer to buy Rock Island line, 162, 166–167, 178, 182–183, 184–185, 212–213, 215, 231, 235
on Rock Island–UP merger, 64
Denver Post, 211
Department of Defense, U.S., 113
Department of Justice, U.S., 68, 102, 112, 114, 157, 267, 272, 286
on Rock Island reorganization/liquidation, 214, 218, 234, 235, 237, 240, 256, 262
on Rock Island–UP merger, 94
Department of Labor, U.S., 112, 267
Department of Transportation, U.S., 33, 86, 87, 203, 267
passenger service and, 109–110, 111–112, 259

Penn Central and, 114, 115
on railroad mergers, 99–100
Rock Island Railroad and, 135, 145, 154, 164, 167, 196, 205, 232, 243, 256, 261–262, 263, 298
Dereco, 103, 117
deregulation, 5, 22
crash of 2008 and, 106–107
railroad industry and, 2, 5–6, 8, 9, 29, 84, 85, 94, 112, 113–114, 116, 204, 208, 221–222, 265–266, 300
Des Moines, IA, 34, 160, 187, 288, 294
Des Moines Register, 133, 143, 188, 189, 210, 232
Desch, Theodore, 97, 127, 138, 139
background of, 98
passenger service and, 112, 133–134
resignation from Rock Island of, 136
Rock Island's problems and, 129–130, 135
Dickens, Charles, 59
Dirksen, Everett, 59
District Court for the Northern District of Illinois, Eastern Division (U.S.), 6, 15, 150
District of Columbia. *See* Washington, D.C.
Dixon, William J., 97, 98, 127, 136, 138, 139
Dodge City, KS, 183
Dole, Robert, 272
Dombrowski, Louis, 69
Donegan, Lonnie, 175
DOT. *See* Department of Transportation, U.S.
Dows, IA, 189
DRGW. *See* Denver and Rio Grande Western Railroad
Durham, Edward M. "Ned", Jr., 18

Eastman, Joseph, 16
Eckhardt, Bob, 269
Economics of Regulation (Kahn), 222
economy, U.S., 275
energy and, 131–132, 220–221
inflation and, 4–5, 8, 28, 31, 131–132
in 1970s, 2–3, 4–5, 8, 177
supply-side economics and, 4–5
Eisenhower, Dwight, 28, 29, 32, 87

Eisenhower Tunnel, 98
Eizenstat, Stu, 223 (photo), 233–234
Electro-Motive Corporation, 13–14
Electro-Motive Division (EMD), 13–14, 105, 167, 170, 176, 295
Elk City, OK, 272
Elmira, NY, 54
El Reno, OK, 67, 186, 271, 272
EMD E-8 locomotives, 192, 195 (photo)
Emergency Labor Board, 114
Emergency Loan Guarantee Act, 105
Emergency Rail Facilities Restoration Act, 118
Emergency Rail Services Act, 162, 254
energy crisis, 131–133, 143–144, 220–221
Energy Policy Council, 132–133, 187
Englewood (Chicago), 170
English, Glenn, 146
Enron Corporation, 106
Equitable Life Insurance Company, 35–36
Erie Lackawanna, 3, 71, 103, 117–118, 206, 207
Erlichman, John, 110, 112
E-6 locomotive, 170, 295
Estherville, IA, 188
Evans, Dale, 176
Evans, Evan, 18, 23
Executive Jet Aviation, 103
Eyster, Rodney, 145

Fannie Mae, 119
Farm Rail, 202
Farrington, John Dow, 13, 14 (photo), 30, 31
 background of, 15
 death of, 36, 40
 merger with Milwaukee Road and, 35–36
 merger with Union Pacific and, 37–38, 40–41
 planned progress reforms of, 15, 24–25, 295
 Rock Island reorganization and, 14–15, 18–19, 240–241
Fay, Gordon, 271
FEC Railway, 225–226
Federal Communications Commission, 289

Federal Deposit Insurance Corporation, 291
Federal Railroad Administration (FRA), 164, 205, 231, 237, 243, 258, 270, 271
 Barriger and, 136, 138–139
 contribution to Rock Island's downfall of, 212, 213–214, 298
 funding for C&NW Railway and, 211, 212
 funding for OKT Railroad and, 273
 funding for Rock Island and, 130, 197, 198, 209, 212, 216, 218, 232, 234–235, 288
 Ingram and, 117, 135, 136, 137, 140
 railroad bankruptcies and, 134
 on Rock Island accidents, 211
 Rock Island liquidation and, 210, 240, 254, 282
 Rock Island loan application and, 135, 179, 181
 sale of Rock Island lines and, 274–275
 track standards of, 133, 188, 217
 on trustee certificates for Rock Island, 162, 165, 210
 "Western Railroad Mergers" report of, 99
Federal Reserve Board, 105, 113, 115, 219
 and Great Inflation, 4, 5, 220, 244, 281
Fifth Amendment (U.S. Constitution), 277–278
Final System Plan (FSP), 120, 134, 206–207, 208
First National Bank of Chicago, 22, 25, 26–27, 165, 197, 198, 214, 216, 288, 291
Fisher, Milton, 256
Flanigan, Peter, 111, 112, 116
Fleming, Joseph, 15, 19
Florida East Coast Railway (FEC), 225–226
Florio, James, 269–270
Forbes magazine, 83, 85, 184
Ford, Bacon & Davis, 161, 279
Ford, Gerald, 6, 8, 109, 153–154, 156 (photo), 178, 208 (photo)
 economy and, 132, 220

Index

railroad bankruptcies and, 134–135, 206, 221
    Rock Island and, 150
Ford Motor Company, 3, 264, 278
Fort Dearborn Mortgage Company, 19
Fortune magazine, 34, 35
Fort Worth, TX, 273, 284
Fort Worth and Denver Railroad, 13, 15
4R Act. *See* Railroad Revitalization and Regulatory Reform Act
FRA. *See* Federal Railroad Administration
Frailey, Fred, 109, 293–294, 297
Freeman, Sam, 184–185
Fremont, NE, 43, 129, 211
Friedman, Milton, 4, 219
Friendly, Henry, 237
Frisco. *See* St. Louis–San Francisco Railroad
Frost, Robert, 84
Fruitland, IA, 281
FSP. *See* Final System Plan
Fullam, John P., 101, 118

Galbraith, John Kenneth, 83
Galveston, TX, 67, 79, 231, 272, 273
General Dynamics Corporation, 179
General Motors, 3, 32, 105, 230, 278, 291
General Theory of Employment, Interest and Money, The (Keynes), 219
Gerdes, John, 21
Getzendanner, Susan, 214, 218
GG-1 locomotives, 102
Gibbons, William, 153, 160 (photo), 165, 173, 188, 196, 205, 212, 218, 233, 234, 235, 236, 239, 257, 283, 297, 298
    appointment of, as bankruptcy Trustee, 6, 155, 157
    background of, 156–157
    BRAC strike and, 231–232
    commuter service and, 169, 170, 228–229, 258–259
    labor unions and, 226–227, 277
    liquidation of Rock Island and, 162, 239–240, 246, 248, 254, 261, 271–274, 277–280, 284–285, 287–289
    negotiations of, to sell lines, 182–184,
258–259, 265, 271, 273–274, 279–281, 282, 285–287, 289
    on passenger service, 190–191, 193, 195
    Rock Island reorganization and, 159, 161, 162, 177–178, 204, 215–216, 217, 231, 243–244, 245–247, 291, 293
    salary of, 194, 216
    trustees certificates and, 161, 162–163, 210
Glenn, Otis, 18
Glore Forgan, 40, 41, 48
Golden State Limited, 14, 39, 75, 80, 87, 109
Golden State Route, 15, 39, 40, 167
Goldschmidt, Neil, 233–234, 240, 243, 244–245, 255, 259
Goodland, KS, 132
Gorham Silver, 291
Gorman, James, 15, 18–19
Gould, Jay, 1
Grant, H. Roger, 54
Grant, Lee, 176
Grant, Ulysses, 54
Gray, Lorna, 175
Great Depression, 4, 13, 16, 26, 42, 98, 220, 250
Great Northern Railway, 15, 30, 38
    merger of, with CB&Q Railroad and NP Railway, 34, 56, 62
"Great Recession" (2008–2010), 6
Great Society, 131, 220
Great Southwest, 103
Green Bay, WI, 30
Gulf, Mobile & Ohio Railroad, 88, 94
Gulf of Mexico ports, 32, 34, 79–80, 84, 89, 132, 142, 143, 183
Gyllenhaal, Jake, 175

Hagerty, Harry, 22
Harahan Bridge, 271
Harder, Lewis, 129, 136
Hardin, Daniel, 59
Harriman, E. H., 114
Harriman, E. R. (Roland), 40, 92
Harris Bank and Trust Company, 22, 25
Harsha, E. Houston, 75, 127, 129, 136–138, 142, 150

Hartke, Vance, 119, 146
Harvey, Fred, 105
Harvey House restaurants, 105
Haswell, Anthony, 190
Hayden, Stone, 48, 50
Heartland Rail Corporation, 287, 289, 294
Heineman, Ben, 34, 36, 49, 52, 73, 93, 94, 148, 212
 background of, 42–43
 improvements to Chicago North Western by, 43
 Milwaukee Road proposed merger and, 35, 36, 43, 64, 73, 86, 87–88, 90, 94, 95, 96, 202
 on Rock Island–UP merger plan, 69, 76, 77 (photo), 78, 79, 94, 298
 takeover bid of Rock Island and, 44–52, 64–65, 69–72, 88
 testimony of, before ICC, 76–78, 87–88, 90
Heller, Walter, 219
Henry Crown Company, 290
Hepburn Act (1906), 60, 85
Herington, KS, 183, 184, 272, 273, 280, 282, 293
Hewitt, H. K,. 157
Hill, Donald, 246
Hill, James J., 15
Hilton, Conrad, 27
Hoboken, NJ, 103
Hodson, Leslie, 51
Hoffman, Julius, 49–50
Holden, William, 176
Hoover, Herbert, 16
Hoover Corporation, 7, 292
Hopkins, Sutter, Mulroy, Davis & Cromartie, 228
Horton, Herbert L., 14 (photo)
House Committee on Un-American Activities (HUAC), 179
House of Representatives, U.S., 111, 268–270
 Budget Committee of, 203
 Interstate and Foreign Commerce Committee of, 203
 northeast railroad bankruptcies and, 114–115
Houston, TX, 34, 67, 79, 80, 132, 186

Hurricane Agnes, 103, 117–118
Huttig, William, 155

IBM, 99
ICC. *See* Interstate Commerce Commission
Igoe, Michael, 18, 19, 20–24, 47
Illinois
 charter of Rock Island in, 249
 Rock Island lines in, 34
 State subsidy to passenger trains, 112, 133–134, 190–191, 294–295
 weather-related problems in, 217
Illinois Central Gulf Railroad, 3, 88, 155, 197, 202
Illinois Central Industries, 93, 94
Illinois Central Railroad, 38, 88, 94, 140, 142, 290
Illinois Commerce Commission, 169, 172–173, 191, 192
Illinois Department of Transportation (Illinois DOT), 171
Illinois Supreme Court, 170
Indianola, IA, 187
Ingersoll, Robert, 39, 40, 42
Ingersoll, Roy, 22, 25
Ingersoll Steel and Disc Company, 22
Ingram, John W., 141 (photo), 184, 283, 297, 298
 background of, 139–140
 controversy in hiring of, 136–139
 Farm Rail and, 202
 as FRA administrator, 117, 130, 135, 136
 labor unions and, 210, 225–226, 231, 236–237
 as Rock Island president, 134, 136, 140, 142, 143, 144, 154, 157, 158, 188, 191, 209, 210–211, 236–237, 238, 239
 sale of lines to Southern Pacific and, 173, 183
 Senate testimony of, 125, 145–146
International Mining Corporation, 129
Interstate Commerce Act, 238
Interstate Commerce Commission (ICC), 24, 140, 154, 165, 171, 210, 211, 234, 249, 279, 297, 300
 bankruptcies and, 16–17

Bureau of Economics and Statistics, 85
C&NW control application and, 63
controversy over Midwest railroad
    problems and, 126–127
deregulation and, 1–2, 30, 222, 267,
    268–269
directed-service order (DSO) and, 145,
    190, 238–239, 240–243, 254, 256,
    257, 261, 280
history of, 59–61
on labor negotiations, 262, 264
mergers and, 38, 42, 56, 62, 70, 73
Office of General Counsel, 166–167
Office of Proceedings, 166
Penn Central bankruptcy and, 115, 116
Penn Central merger and, 87, 102, 104
railroad industry and, 83–85
rates and, 29–30, 31, 33, 60, 84–85,
    98–99, 221
Rock Island (RI)
    liquidation/bankruptcy and,
    240–241, 246, 261, 283–284
RI 1943 reorganization plans and, 19,
    20, 21
on RI problems, 144, 158, 180
RI reorganization plan and, 284–285
RI–UP merger and, 56, 59, 62–64, 67,
    69, 81, 91, 94–95, 121, 125, 127,
    142–143, 145, 166–167, 173, 298,
    300
RI–UP merger hearings and, 6, 7,
    63–64, 69–80, 91
sale of RI lines and, 184, 230,
    286–287
track abandonment and, 96, 117
truckers' strike and, 221
Interstate Highway system, 28, 98, 101
Iowa
    Amtrak in, 190
    C&NW Railway in, 43, 129, 189,
        211–212, 285, 286
    Heartland Rail Corporation in, 287,
        289
    Milwaukee Road in, 201, 280
    Rock Island and, 34, 79, 80, 84, 142,
        143–144, 163, 231, 239, 245, 248,
        260
    Rock Island–State of Iowa partnership
        in, 132–133, 186–187, 189, 236

weather-related problems in, 217
Iowa City, IA, 293
Iowa Department of Transportation (Iowa
    DOT), 133, 187, 214, 236, 240,
    241
Iowa Falls, IA, 188
Iowa General Assembly, 186–187
Iowa Interstate Railroad, 289,
    290 (photo), 293, 294–295
Iowa Northern Railroad, 295
Iowa Rail Assistance Program, 186–187
Iowa Rail Finance Authority, 289
Iowa Railroad, 289
Isham, Lincoln & Beale, 198

James, Jesse, 250
Jenkins, George, 290
Jenks, Cyrus, 30
Jenks, Downing Bland, 30, 33, 37, 138,
    299
    background, 31
    as president of Missouri Pacific, 65,
        90, 212
    as president of Rock Island, 31–32, 36
    Rock Island merger with Milwaukee
        Road and, 35–36
Jenner, Albert, 163–164, 181–182, 210,
    212–213, 214, 231–232, 236, 237,
    259–260, 284
    background of, 179–180 (photo)
Jenner & Block, 8, 161, 164, 168, 177,
    179, 180, 233, 248, 278
J. Langdon and Company, 54
John Deere & Company, 22, 25
Johnson, Lyndon, 87, 102, 179, 203, 220
Johnson, R. Ellis, 40, 41–42, 46–47, 48,
    49, 53 (photo), 54, 56
Johnson, William, 94
Joliet, IL, 143, 169, 192, 247 (photo),
    280
Jones, Jesse, 17–18
Jordan, Edward, 146, 147
Judy, Paul, 290

Kahn, Richard, 222
Kansas
    Katy Railroad in, 265
    railroad taxes owed to State of, 17,
        288

Kansas, *continued*
  Rock Island (RI) assets in, 288
  RI grain transportation and, 79, 80, 84
  RI lines in, 34, 68, 183–184, 242, 260, 273, 279, 280, 282
Kansas City, KS, 24, 67
Kansas City, MO, 34
  railroad routes to, 15, 39, 40, 42, 76, 80, 88, 94, 147, 173, 182–185, 202, 212, 232, 243, 245, 265, 272, 285, 286, 293
  Rock Island board member from, 25
  Rock Island facilities in, 24
Kansas City Board of Trade, 242
Kansas City Southern Railroad, 126, 202
Kansas City Terminal Railroad, 223, 254
  as Rock Island directed service operator, 238, 239, 240–241, 243, 257
Kansas Railroad Working Group, 260
Kapnick, Harvey, 290, 291
Karnes, William, 155
Kassebaum, Nancy, 259, 279, 280, 284
Kelly, G. W., 66–67, 74, 75
Kenefick, John, 93, 127–128, 129, 138, 183, 212
Kennedy, Edward, 222, 244
Kennedy, John F., 50, 179, 203, 219
Kerner, Otto, 20
Keynes, John Maynard, 219
Keynsian economics, 4, 131, 219–220
Kiewit, Peter, 97, 98, 127
Kingfisher, OK, 274 (photo)
Kirkland, Ellis, Hodson, Chaffetz & Masters (Kirkland & Ellis), 51, 75, 127, 150
Klein, Carter, 180
Klemme Corporation, 189
Klitenic, Nathan, 83, 85, 97, 99, 184, 298
  report on Rock Island–UP merger by, 99–100, 121, 125, 126–127, 142
Knapton, Christopher, 142, 212
Korean War, 28, 113
Kramer, John, 91
Kroll, Fred, 226, 229–230, 231–232, 235, 238, 298–299
Krumm, Daniel, 292

labor unions
  Rock Island and, 29, 31, 210–211, 216, 236–237, 260–265, 277–278, 298–299
  Gibbons and, 226–227, 277
  ICC and, 262, 264
  Ingram and, 210, 225–226, 231, 236–237
  McGarr and, 226, 228, 229, 260, 262–263, 264–265, 287
  Penn Central and, 102, 114, 117, 118
  See also Railway Labor Executives' Association (RLEA)
Lackawanna Railroad, 54
Laffer, Arthur, 4
Lane, Richard, 133, 187, 188, 271–272, 292
Langdon, Jervis, Jr., 37, 55 (photo), 59, 96, 170
  background of, 54–56 (photo)
  C&NW Railway–Milwaukee Road merger and, 64, 86
  as chairman of Rock Island Railroad, 54, 56, 57, 66, 96, 97, 138–139
  negotiations with other railroads in merger case, 89–90
  as Penn Central Trustee, 97, 116, 118–119, 208–209
  on railroad industry, 78, 84, 86, 89, 90
  retirement from Rock Island of, 97
  Rock Island's problems and, 66–67, 68, 79, 80, 92, 96–97
  Rock Island–UP merger and, 46, 57, 59, 64, 67, 69, 70, 73, 78, 79, 81, 86, 89, 91, 95, 96
  testimony of, before ICC, 68, 74–75, 87, 95
LaSalle Street Station, 134, 170, 172, 173 (photo), 176, 192, 195, 265, 266 (photo)
Last Ride of the Rocket?, 191
Ledbetter, William Huddie ("Leadbelly"), 8, 175
Lehigh and Hudson River Railroad, 3
Lehigh Valley Railroad, 3, 55, 103
Leighton, Leon, 71, 72
Limon, CO, 80
Lincoln, Abraham, 176, 249
"Little Engine That Did, The," 153

"Little Joes," 201
Little Rock, AR, 34, 67, 210, 271
Lockheed Corporation, 105
Lomax, John, 175
Long, Russell, 268, 269
Long Island Railroad, 140
Loomis, Reed, 176
Los Angeles, CA, 39, 56, 80
Louisiana, Rock Island lines in, 231, 271
Louisville, KY, 201
Lovett, Robert, 38, 39, 40, 45–46, 51, 69, 71, 73, 92, 129
Loving, Rush, 209, 268
Lowden, Frank, 15, 18, 19

MacAnally, J. R., 38, 72
MacDougall, Gordon, 193
Madigan, Edward, 269–270
Magic Chef, 292
Major, J. Paul (judge), 20
Major, Paul (VP of finance), 28–29, 67–68, 74
Mann–Elkins Act (1910), 60
Manos, George, 157
Manos, Nicholas, 160 (photo), 162, 196, 236, 243, 254, 272, 277, 288
  background, 157
  on commuter and passenger service, 168–169, 171, 172, 227
  on conflict of interest by Rock Island (RI) intervenors, 163, 198, 199, 215
  4R Act and, 178–179, 197
  on leasing RI cars, 167–168
  liquidation of RI and, 164, 244, 256, 257, 258–259, 260, 262, 264, 271, 281–282, 283–284, 286
  on progress of RI reorganization, 177–178, 180, 181, 212–213, 215
  on RI cash flow, 167, 218, 232, 233, 235
  RI reorganization plan and, 178, 216, 231–232, 240–241, 245–250, 242, 244
  on Rock Island Transition Act, 279, 280, 284
  on rumors of RI demise, 158–159, 163–164
  salary of, 193, 194
  status updates of, 182, 197, 290–291
Mara, Adele, 176
MARC-EL, 207
Marsh, E. S., 65, 72
Marsh, Jeremiah, 227
Martin, Albro, 61
Mason City, IA, 295
Material Service Corporation, 25, 26, 27, 289
Maxwell, Gregory, 118
Mayer, Frederick M., 14 (photo)
Maytag Corporation, 7, 8, 289, 292, 294
McClellan, John, 154
McCracken, Paul, 113
McDonald, William, 119, 127, 139
McGarr, Frank, 158 (photo), 235, 290
  appointment of Rock Island (RI) bankruptcy Trustee by, 6, 150, 151, 155, 216
  background, 155–156
  Chicago Pacific Corporation board and, 289
  demise of RI and, 225, 297, 298
  federal assistance to RI and, 198–199, 234, 255
  on intervenors in RI bankruptcy, 161–162, 198
  labor issues and, 226, 228, 229, 260, 262–263, 264–265, 287
  order to abandon RI operations and, 261
  on passenger and commuter service, 171–172, 191, 228–229
  postponement of RI shutdown and, 157–158, 159, 209–210, 215, 218
  Regional Transportation Authority (RTA) and, 228–229, 241
  RI bankruptcy petition and, 150, 151
  on RI cash flow, 233, 237, 238
  RI liquidation and, 7, 8, 164, 223, 232, 239, 253, 254–258, 272–273, 280–281, 286, 287
  on RI–MoPac Railroad merger petition, 166
  on RI rebuilding plans, 167–168, 170, 181–182, 212, 215
  on RI reorganization plan, 241, 244, 248–249, 253, 282, 283, 284, 288

McGarr, Frank, *continued*
  Rock Island Transition Act and, 263, 271, 272, 277, 278
  Rock Island Transition and Employee Assistance Act (RITA) and, 263–265, 270–271
McGinness, John, 193–194
McGovern, William, 71–72
McKinney, Robert, 14 (photo)
Meincke, Paul, 191
Memphis, TN, 85, 125, 142, 186, 271
Menk, Louis, 56, 70
Mesa, AZ, 271
Metra, 175, 290 (photo), 293, 295
Metroliners, 102
Metropolitan Life Insurance Company, 22, 35, 290
Michel, Robert, 130, 195, 207–208
Midas Brakes, 93
Mid States Port Authority, 280
Midwestern railroads, problems of, 78, 204–205, 206
Midwest Governors' Conference, 273–274
Milhone, John, 187
Milwaukee Road. *See* Chicago, Milwaukee, St. Paul and Pacific Railroad
Milwaukee Road Restructuring Act (MRRA), 255, 258, 277, 279
Miner, Craig, 35, 73
Minneapolis, MN, 34, 239, 265
Minneapolis and St. Louis Railway, 34, 43
Minnesota, Milwaukee Road in, 201
Minow, Newton, 289
Minton, Sherman, 20
Mississippi River, 28, 32, 132, 142, 144, 176, 202, 249, 271
Mississippi River Corporation, 72
Missouri–Kansas–Texas Railroad Company (Katy), 3, 197, 202
  mergers and, 85–86, 125
  Rock Island lines and, 265, 272, 273, 274 (photo), 282, 293
  Santa Fe Railroad and, 139, 142
Missouri Pacific Railroad (MoPac), 17, 20, 35, 37, 165, 166, 212, 265
  on Rock Island–UP merger plan, 64, 65, 71, 72–73, 90

Missouri River, 37, 63
Mitros, John, 142, 143, 148, 150, 283
Mobile, AL, 88
Mokena, IL, 172 (photo)
Mondale, Walter, 238
Monopoly board game, 175
MoPac. *See* Missouri Pacific Railroad
Moore, Frank, 223 (photo)
Moore, William H., 114, 118
Morgan, Charles, 85
Morgan, David P., 114
Moritz, Terry, 198, 214, 248
Morris, IL, 195 (photo), 242
Morrow, Kirby, 176
Moses, Gibbons, Abramson & Fox, 155
Motor Carrier Act (1935), 61
MRRA, 255, 258, 277, 279
Mullin, Patrick, 166
Mundell, Robert, 4
Murdock, David, 289–290
Murphy, Robert, 61
Murray, Daniel, 180, 233, 248, 256, 260–261, 262, 277–278, 279 (photo)
Muscatine, IA, 280

NAACP Legal Defense Fund, 179
Nachman, Munitz & Sweig, 150
Nachman, Norman, 150–151, 155, 161, 165, 214–215
National Association for Railroad Passengers, 190
National Commission of the Causes and Prevention of Violence, 179
National Grange, 60
National Hockey League, 25
National Mediation Board, 227
National Passenger Railroad Corporation. *See* Amtrak
National Transportation Safety Board, 108
National United States Loyalty Review Board, 179
Navy, U.S., 27, 156, 157
Nebraska, C&NW Railway in, 43, 129, 211
Neumiller, E. L., 14 (photo), 25
Nevada, IA, 189
Newark, NJ, 114

Index 375

New Deal, 5, 16, 222, 253
New Jersey, commuter line in, 114
New Orleans, LA, 88, 142
Newton, IA, 292, 294
New York (state)
   State support for commuter operations in, 116
   hurricane damage in, 117
New York, New Haven and Hartford Railroad (New Haven), 70, 71, 103, 116
New York Central System, 21, 27, 29, 33, 34, 55, 92
   financial problems of, 101–102
   merger with Pennsylvania Railroad and, 33–34, 36, 62, 70–71, 101
New York City, 153
   meetings in, 35, 38, 40, 51, 127, 129, 137
   railroad investors from, 129
   railroad routes to, 70, 71, 103, 116
   Rock Island assets in, 288
   Union Pacific Railroad in, 92
New York Daily News, 153, 154
New York Metropolitan Transit Agency, 116
New York Times, 1, 137, 138
Nickel Plate Railroad, 102
Nigh, George, 273
Nitze, Paul, 21
Nixon, Richard M. (Nixon administration), 4, 8, 106, 109, 112, 129
   economy and, 131–132, 220
   passenger trains and, 110
   Penn Central and, 113, 114–115, 118–119
   railroad industry and, 116, 134–135, 206
Norfolk and Western Railway, 34, 102, 103
   and BRAC strike, 226, 228–229, 231, 298–299
Norris, Bruce, 25, 40, 42, 49, 127–128
Norris, James, 22, 25, 27
Norris Grain Company, 22, 25, 155
North Dakota oil field, 294
Northeast Corridor, 102, 111, 190, 207, 259

Northern Pacific Railroad, 34, 38, 56, 62
North Fort Worth, TX, 280, 282, 293
Northwest Industries, 91, 93, 95
NW-2 4901 locomotive, 176

Oakes, James J., 36
Obama, Barack, 1
Office of Management and Budget (OMB), 111, 112, 234, 267, 268
Ogilvie, Richard, 133
Oklahoma
   Katy Railroad in, 265
   Rock Island (RI) assets in, 288
   RI grain transportation and, 79, 80, 84
   RI lines in, 34, 272, 279, 300
Oklahoma, Kansas, Texas Railroad (OKT), 273, 274 (photo), 280, 282
Oklahoma City, OK, 242, 272, 273–274
Omaha, NE, 37, 38, 43, 69, 89, 92, 125, 142, 167, 230, 239, 245
Omaha Union Station, 98
O'Malley, Patrick, 169
OMB. *See* Office of Management and Budget
Omen, The (film), 176
O'Neal, Daniel, 126–127, 205, 221, 231, 234, 238
OPEC (Arab) oil embargo 4, 132, 220
Ottumwa, IA, 281

Pacific Holdings, 289
passenger service, 33
   deficits of, 29
   McGarr on, 191, 228–229
   Rocket trains and, 6, 14, 80, 96, 109, 112, 133, 175, 190, 191, 195
   of Rock Island, 6, 14–15, 24, 79, 80, 96, 109, 112, 133–134, 168–169, 171–172, 190–195, 299
   State of Illinois subsidies for, 112, 133–134, 190–191, 294–295
   Union Pacific and, 38
   U.S. Congress, 109–110
   U.S. Department of Transportation and, 109–110, 111–112, 259
Patman, Wright, 113
Pearson, James, 144–145, 154, 156 (photo)

Pearson, Joe, 192
Peat Marwick Mitchell, 218, 240, 241, 246, 248
Peck, Gregory, 176
Penn Central Corporation, 265, 291, 301
Penn Central Transportation Company (PC; Penn Central Railroad), 87, 92, 93, 97, 107, 129, 143, 205, 209, 226, 237, 239, 288
    bailout of, 105–106, 149, 163
    bankruptcy of, 94, 101, 103, 106, 112, 114–115, 301
    causes of failure of, 101, 104–105
    commuter operations of, 116
    Conrail and, 3, 207, 209
    creation of, 62, 70–71, 101
    diversification and, 103–104
    federal government on failure of, 104, 106, 112–113, 115–116, 300
    financial irregularities and, 104–105, 106
    financial problems of, 101–104, 113, 116–117, 118
    labor unions and, 102, 114, 117, 118
    New Haven Railroad and, 70, 103
    reorganization plan of, 118–119
    Trustees of, 114, 115, 118
Pennsylvania
    hurricane in, 117
    State lease agreement with Penn Central, 116
Pennsylvania Company, 104
Pennsylvania Railroad, 29, 32, 34, 43, 139, 226
    financial problems of, 101–102
    merger with New York Central of, 33–34, 36, 62, 70–71, 101
Peoria, IL, 43, 171, 191, 195, 245, 289
Peoria Rocket, 96, 112, 133, 175, 190–195
Pepsi-Cola Company, 93
Percy, Charles, 143
Perlman, Alfred (Al), 70–71, 92–93, 101–102, 103, 129
Philadelphia, PA, 118
Phillips, Don, 111
Phillipsburg, KS, 242
Pioneer Zephyr, 14
Pitarsky, Milton, 150

Pittsburgh, PA, 98, 118
Posner, Henry, III, 293
Posner, Richard, 222
Pottstown, PA, 55
Powder River, WY, 269, 281
Presidential Advisory Commission on Transport Policy and Organization, 29–30
President's Emergency Board, 243
Price Waterhouse, 282
Prouty, Jim, 111
Provo, Larry, 50, 76, 95, 97, 129, 147–148, 149 (photo), 189
Pryor, Nicholas, 176
Puget Sound, 201
Pullman cars, 80
Pullman Company, 105
Pullman Railroad, 24
Putnam, IL, 192

Quad Cities, 190, 217
Quad Cities Rocket, 112, 133, 170, 190–195
Quinn, William, 35, 64, 73, 95

Rail Development Corporation, 293, 294
Railpax, 109–110, 111
railroad industry, 1–2, 297, 299
    accidents and, 211
    decline of, 9, 60–61, 94, 104–105, 203–204
    deregulation and, 2, 5–6, 8, 9, 29, 84, 85, 94, 112, 113–114, 116, 204, 208, 221–222, 265–266, 300
    diversification in, 92–94, 103–104
    federal government and, 28, 32–33, 57, 112–113, 202
    government bailouts and, 105–106, 107, 109, 114, 136, 146, 153–154, 203, 204, 206, 291, 299
    ICC and, 83–85
    inflation and, 104, 131, 203, 220–222, 244, 298
    innovation in, 30, 105
    nationalization concerns and, 84, 108, 140, 202, 221–222, 300
    piggyback and TOFC operations and, 30
    private investment and, 28–29

problems of, after deregulation, 300–301
profitability of, 1–2, 28, 84, 177
regulation of, 60–62, 108–109, 140, 297, 301
taxes and, 28, 33
track abandonment and, 2, 116–117, 167, 300
weather-related losses and, 117–118, 195–196, 216–217
Railroad Retirement Board, 263
Railroad Revitalization and Regulatory Reform Act (4R Act), 178–179, 197, 204, 205, 208, 221, 240, 254
Railroad Temporary Operating Authority Act, 145
Railsback, Thomas, 254–255
Railway Labor Act, 226, 227, 232, 234
Railway Labor Executives' Association (RLEA), 194, 255–256, 260, 261, 262, 270, 281, 287, 288
Railway Labor Executives' Association v. Gibbons, 277–278, 279 (photo)
Ray, Robert, 132–133, 188
Reading Corporation, 93
Reading Railroad, 3, 103, 206
Reagan, Ronald, 5, 260, 266, 280
recessions, 32, 275
of 1973–1974, 131–132
Reconstruction Finance Corporation (RFC), 15, 16, 17–18, 106, 139
Reed, Chauncey, 24
Reed, Clyde, 24
Reed, John, 159, 161, 182, 183
Reed bill, 21, 23–24
Regional Rail Reorganization Act (3R Act), 109, 129, 130–131, 134–135, 145, 164, 203, 206, 207
description of, 119–120
Regional Transportation Authority (RTA), 172 (photo), 173 (photo)
creation of, 134–135, 143
efforts to keep Rock Island (RI) commuter lines open, 157, 227–228, 239
purchase of RI commuter lines by, 150, 151, 178, 192, 193, 232, 257, 258–259, 280
RI subsidies from, 157, 168–170

Rehnquist, William, 278
RFC. *See* Reconstruction Finance Corporation
RLEA. *See* Railway Labor Executives' Association
Rock, The, 7. *See also* Chicago, Rock Island and Pacific Railroad
Rocket trains, 6, 14, 80, 96, 109, 112, 133, 175, 190, 191, 195
Rock Island, IL, 191
Rock Island. *See* Chicago, Rock Island and Pacific Railroad
Rock Island and LaSalle Railroad Company, 249
Rock Island District (Metra), 175, 290 (photo), 293, 295
"Rock Island Line," 8, 175
Rock Island Motor Transit, 30
Rock Island Railroad Transition and Northeast Corridor Improvement Act, 259–260, 262, 263, 270, 271, 272, 274, 277–278, 298
Rock Island Trail (film), 175–176
Rock Island Western, 184
Rocky Mountain News, 211
Rocky Mountain Rocket, 14, 80, 109
Rodman, IA, 188
Rogers, Roy, 175–176
Roland, IA, 189
Roosevelt, Franklin D., 13, 16, 18
Root, Elihu, Jr., 15–16
ROUTE ROCK, 211
Rowenta A.G., 292
RTA. *See* Regional Transportation Authority
Rush, Henri, 240–241, 248, 256, 262, 264, 270, 286–287
Russell, Donald, 39, 40, 75

Sabin, Daniel, 295
Salina, KS, 184
Samson of the Cimarron bridge, 15
Samuelson, Robert, 219
Santa Fe Industries, 93
Santa Fe Railway. *See* Atchison, Topeka and Santa Fe Railway
Santa Rosa, NM, 15, 39, 173, 182, 183
Saunders, Richard, 95, 99, 226
Saunders, Stuart, 101, 102, 103, 104, 114

Schmidt, Thomas, 217
Schneiderman, Michael, 228
Schultze, Charles, 219, 223 (photo)
Schumann, Mary, 223 (photo)
Schumpeter, Joseph, 9, 301
Scott, Hugh, 111
Scranton, PA, 114
Seaboard Air Line Railroad, 27
Section 77. *See under* Bankruptcy Act of 1933
Securities and Exchange Commission (SEC), 47
Senate, U.S.
    Appropriations Committee, 154, 243
    Bill 917 (1975), 144–145, 154–155
    Commerce Committee, 110, 115, 145, 268
    Subcommittee on Surface Transportation, 32
Shoup, Richard, 119, 120 (photo)
Shoup–Adams Bill, 119, 203
Shultz, George, 111, 118–119
Sidley, Austin, Burgess & Smith, 46–47
Sidley & Austin, 289
Signore, Danny, 191
Silvis, IL, 24, 212, 265
Small Business Administration, 183
Smathers, George M., 32, 107
Smith, Adam, 83
Snoqualmie Pass, 201
Sol R. Crown Company, 26
Soo Line Railroad, 95, 285–287
Source Code (film), 175
South Dakota, rail lines in, 43, 201
Southern Pacific Corporation, 93
Southern Pacific Railroad, 15, 66, 88, 90, 94, 168
    merger hearings, 65
    merger negotiations with Rock Island and, 39, 40–42, 51, 89
    sale of Rock Island lines to, 51, 52, 72, 75, 97, 125, 162, 166–167, 178, 182–184, 209, 215, 235, 258, 265
    testimony on Rock Island–UP merger plan, 75–76
    Union Pacific and, 39–40, 142
Southern Railway, 84, 114, 140, 207
Soviet grain deal, 177, 187
Soviet Union, 4, 98, 132, 201

Special Board of Inquiry, 227
Spokane, Portland and Seattle Railroad, 30
Springfield, IL, 88
Stafford, George, 96–97, 125, 127, 144
Staggers, Harley, 269
Staggers Rail Act, 1, 6, 8, 253, 265–266, 278, 300
    debates over, 266–270
Stalin, Joseph, 201
Stamler, Jeremiah, 179
Standard and Poor's, 37
State Department, U.S., 42
St. Charles, IL, 169
Stearns, Neele, 290
Stevens, John Paul, 263, 270, 277–278
Stigler, George, 222
Stillman, Elinor, 277–278
St. Lawrence Seaway, 28
St. Louis, MO, 38, 39, 76, 85, 173, 182, 183, 184, 231, 265
St. Louis–San Francisco Railroad (Frisco), 17, 27, 56, 126, 197–198
Stoddard, A. E., 37, 38, 39–40, 48
Strombeck, George, 192
Strong, Constance, 176
Stuart, Jackson, 290
Stuttgart, AR, 271
Sullivan, Lawrence, 205
Sullivan, Thomas, 180, 210, 213–214, 234
Sunbelt Line, 271–272
Supreme Court, U.S., 18, 21, 24, 60, 84, 179, 263, 264, 265, 274, 277–278, 280, 281
Surface Transportation Board, 2
Sutton, Reginald, 72, 87
Swain, Newton, 173–174, 183
Swiren, Max, 42
Symes, James, 32, 71, 102

Tacoma, WA, 201
Taft, William Howard, 15
TARP (Troubled Assets Relief Fund), 105, 106
Teamsters International Union, 116
Temple-Barker & Sloan, 198
Tennyson, Alfred Lord, 253
Texaco Oil Company, 143

Texas, 288, 291
  Dallas, 34, 86, 186 (photo), 211, 273, 284
  Rock Island (RI) assets in, 288, 291
  RI grain transportation and, 80
  RI lines in, 34, 231, 260, 272
  State of, as intervenor in RI reorganization, 24
Texas and Pacific Railroad, 165, 212
Textron Corporation, 291–292
Thompson, James, 192
Thompson, William, 26
Thorn, Damien, 176–188
Thorn, Mark, 176
Thorn, Richard, 176–177
Thorn, Robert, 176
3R Act. *See* Regional Rail Reorganization Act
Tierney, Paul, 62
Time, 13
Timmons, William, 111
TOFC (trailer on a flat car), 30
Toledo, Peoria and Western Railway (TP&W), 43
Topeka, KS, 15, 144, 182, 183, 184
Touhy, Walter, 102
Trailer Train Corporation, 144
Trailways Bus Company, 190
Trains (magazine), 114, 189, 293, 297
Trans-Iranian Railroad, 98
Transportation Act
  of 1920, 56, 60–61, 62, 300
  of 1940, 61
  of 1958, 108
Transportation Association of America, 86
Trenton, MO, 173
Troubled Assets Relief Program (TARP), 105, 106
trucking industry, 28, 29, 61
  deregulation and, 116, 222
  independent strike and, 221
Truman, Harry S., 20, 24, 179
Tucker, Forrest, 175
Tucker, William, 87
Tucker Act, 207, 270
Tucumcari, NM, 80, 94, 142, 183, 231, 235, 265
Tuggle, Kenneth, 126–127

Twentieth Century Railroad Club, 192
Twin Cities, 80, 286, 293. *See also* Minneapolis, MN; St. Paul, MN
Twin Star Rocket, 80, 109

Union Pacific Corporation, 92, 93, 94–95
Union Pacific Railroad, 2, 49, 107, 114, 153, 168, 183, 184, 212, 246, 281, 282, 293, 294
  board of directors of, 38
  C&NW takeover of Rock Island and, 45–46, 51–52, 56–57
  financial health of, 90, 92–93, 179
  ICC and, 59, 69, 71–74, 85–88, 94–95
  passenger trains and, 38
  relations with Rock Island of, 67, 88, 89–90, 91–92, 127–128
  Southern Pacific and, 39–40
  See also Chicago, Rock Island and Pacific merger plan with Union Pacific
United States Railway Administration (USRA), 119–120, 134–135, 139, 143, 206, 207, 209
  Rock Island loan and, 135, 143, 146–147, 148, 150, 154, 196
United Transportation Union (UTU), 117, 193–194, 203, 229, 244
  strike against Rock Island and, 223, 227, 235, 238, 299
Utica, IL, 242, 293
UTU. *See* United Transportation Union

Van Nostrand, Martin, 133
Varlan Company, 265
Velsicol Chemical Corporation, 93
Vietnam War, 118, 119, 131, 203, 220
Virginian (coal hauler), 34
Volcker, Paul, 4, 115, 244
Volpe, John, 109, 110, 111, 112, 115

Wabash Railroad, 102, 244
Wabash Railroad v. Illinois, 60
Wall Street, 106, 301
Wall Street Journal, 45, 64, 184, 204, 206
War Production Board, 19
Warren, Richard, 176–177
Warren Commission, 179
Warren County, IA, 187

Washington, D.C., 32, 111, 144, 149, 164, 168, 190, 199, 207, 243, 244
Washington, IA, 280
Washington Post, 4, 111
Washington Star, 202
Watergate, 118, 132
Watson, Jack, 223
Wayne, John, 175
Weber, Max, 83
Weeks, Sinclair (Weeks Report), 29–30
Weicker, Lowell, 111
Weiner, Morton, 136, 155
Western Maryland Railroad, 206
"Western Railroad Mergers," 99
Westinghouse Corporation, 105
Wheeler, Burton, 19, 20–21, 23
Whirlpool Corporation, 294
White, John, 267–268
White, Richard, 60

Whitman Corporation, 93
Wichita Northwestern Railway, 17
Wilkerson, James, 15, 18
Wiman, Charles Deere, 22, 25, 27
Wisconsin lines, 86
Witherspoon v. Illinois, 179
Wolfe, James, 205–206, 212
World War I, 60
World War II, locomotive production and, 201
Wyer, Dick, 38–39
Wyer, William, 38, 50, 72

Young, David, 169
Young, Robert, 20, 21, 24, 27, 101
Young, Samuel, 46–47
Young Committee, 47, 49
Youngstown Sheet and Tube Company, 3
Ypsilanti, MI, 291

www.ingramcontent.com/pod-product-compliance
Lightning Source LLC
Chambersburg PA
CBHW070232240426
43673CB00044B/1761